This P
t

The Diversity of Meaning

The
Diversity of Meaning

L. JONATHAN COHEN

FELLOW OF THE QUEEN'S COLLEGE, OXFORD

LONDON
Methuen & Co Ltd
36 ESSEX STREET · WC2

First published in 1962
© 1962 *by L. Jonathan Cohen*
Printed in Great Britain by
Western Printing Services Ltd, Bristol
Catalogue No. 2/2533/10

To G.M.C.

Contents

V Meanings Conceived as what are Understood in an Act of Communication

VI Meaning and the *a Priori*

VII Meaning and the Law of Extensionality

VIII Meanings Conceived as Topics for Formal-logical Investigation

IX Meaning and Vagueness

X The Concept of Meaning in the Problem of Natural Necessity

CONTENTS

Preface

Chapters I, II, III and V of this book formed the substance of my lectures at Oxford during Hilary and Trinity terms, 1958. §§26, 27 and 30 incorporate some material from articles I have already published in *The Journal of Symbolic Logic*, vols. xxii (1957), pp. 225 ff., and *Philosophical Studies*, vol. xii (1961), pp. 72 ff., and from another article, 'A Formalisation of Referentially Opaque Contexts,' which is shortly to be published in *The Journal of Symbolic Logic*. I am grateful to the editors and officers of these journals for permission to reprint.

I am also indebted to my College for a period of sabbatical leave in Michaelmas term, 1960, in which I was able to complete the book.

Prof. G. Ryle, Prof. W. Kneale, Mr J. O. Urmson and Mr P. L. Heath very kindly read the whole or part of the book in typescript, and I have profited a great deal from their helpful comments and criticisms. Over a long period I have also gained much from discussions of most of the issues raised in the book with other friends, colleagues or pupils, too numerous to mention here.

L.J.C.

I

An Eighteenth-century Innovation
in the Concept of Meaning

§1. Can meanings change?

Philosophers have said much, especially during the past half-century, about the different kinds of meaning that different kinds of words have and about the different kinds of ways in which words are used. Their arguments have often relied on such distinctions as those between customary and indirect meaning, logical words and object words, informative and emotive idioms, dispositional and occurrent predicates, or performatory and non-performatory verb-uses. Yet they have said little about the variety of ways in which it is useful to think about ordinary word-meanings. They have distinguished between kinds of meaning rather than between concepts of meaning. Certainly they have differentiated meaning from reference, or literal meaning from verbal associations, or the meaning of words from the meaning of clouds or of life, or the meaning of a man's words, in the sense of what his utterance would normally convey, from the man's meaning, in the sense of what he intends his utterance to convey. But in their general theories about the meaning of words philosophers have tended to treat the concept of linguistic meaning as essentially homogeneous. Meanings, they have said, are subsistent entities, or the causes and effects of speech, as if there is some single, nuclear pattern of discourse about meaning that constitutes the only proper subject-matter for philosophers analysing the concept of linguistic meaning. No relational theory of meaning will do, they have said, or any adequate theory must be a contextual one, as if there is just one philosophical problem of meaning, not many.

The main destructive purpose of what follows is to show that this has been a mistake, and one of mark. The constructive purpose is to draw some, but by no means all, of the distinctions that need to be drawn in the field, to expose certain relations of dependence and independence between the various concepts of meaning that emerge, and to show how confusion between those concepts can hamper important intellectual interests both inside and outside philosophy. Thus the book aims not so much to describe how people of various kinds do actually think about meanings, but to evaluate what is gained or lost by their so thinking, and to do this not speculatively or from the standpoint of some special interest but within the perspective of an inter-disciplinary survey in which some measure of regard is paid to the literature of the various disciplines concerned.

One question at least should have a simple answer if meaning is essentially a homogeneous concept. Yet the answer turns out to be far from simple, and to ask the question is to cut a path into the heart of the whole problem. Can meanings change? Have they periods of growth and periods of decay, like habits of dress or house-building? Or are they as fixed beyond recall as the ratio one natural number bears to another? Have they histories to be traced or just single, once-and-for-all accounts to be drawn up? Have they dates and durations, or is time irrelevant to them? Are we to think of them temporally or timelessly?

Perhaps the most tempting answer to this question is to echo some remarks of Frege's. 'The same words,' Frege writes, 'on account of the variability of language with time, take on another sense, express another thought.' Meanings do change, but just in the sense that words change their meanings. Words are continuous through change of meaning, but meanings themselves have no core of continuity relative to which they may undergo a peripheral change. Not even the utterance of the same words 'this tree is covered with green leaves' on different occasions presents us with an example of a thought or meaning that changes, since a different thought is expressed on each occasion. The words 'this tree is covered with green leaves' are insufficient to express any thought at all except in association with their circumstances of utterance. In Frege's view all thought, all meaning, whether it be the thought expressed by Pythagoras' theorem or the thought that the tree in his garden is, at the time he writes, covered with green leaves, is equally 'timeless, eternal, unchangeable'.[1] Thus justice seems to be done both to the lexicographer's interests and to the logician's. On the one hand it is recognized that dictionaries can chronicle the succession of meanings a word may have in the long history of a language. On the

[1] 'The Thought: a Logical Inquiry', tr. A. M. and M. Quinton, *Mind*, lxv (1956), pp. 309 f.

other hand formal logic is provided with a distinctively timeless sub-ject-matter, where the truth-value of a thought and its consistency or inconsistency with other thoughts are equally invariant.

Yet here as elsewhere (compare §24 below) Frege has too concen-trated a vision for him to be a reliable guide in the general problem of meaning. Anyone who answered the question 'Can meanings change?' along such lines, even if he held that to treat meanings as timeless is not necessarily to treat them, like Frege, as subsistent entities, would be erring or oversimplifying in at least four crucial respects. There is both less change and more change than Frege allows for. In a still important use of 'meaning' and of 'word' it is true to say that no word of any utterance ever changes its meaning. In a use of 'meaning' that was im-portant till the eighteenth century, and sometimes still occurs, it is true to say that no word in any language ever changes its meaning. In the use of 'meaning' that is of principal importance to modern lexico-graphers the meaning of an English sentence is no more timeless than the purpose for which an Englishman marries. In a use of 'meaning', 'thought', or 'concept' that is important to modern historians mean-ings, thoughts or concepts themselves can have a core of continuity through change. To establish these four theses against the Fregean position is a first step in exposing just how multiform is the concept of meaning.

§2. Meanings as unchangeable properties

A speech has a date and duration, not so its meaning. When a speech is over nothing can change what it meant. What has been said cannot be unsaid, though later remarks may contradict it. Even the ambiguities in this evening's speech must remain such for ever, though tomorrow's press conference may clarify the speaker's intentions. Though the speech may be differently translated in different countries or at different periods, no one could judge the correctness of each new translation unless he assumed the meaning of the original speech to remain the same. Though expositions of what has been said can change, they can always be criticized, and the question whether a given exposition is loose or close, fair or biased, accurate or inaccurate, would not arise unless the meaning itself were invariant under exposition. People often make up their minds that some statement in a speech is false, some inference invalid, some promise unworthy or some exhortation ignoble. But they would never be justified in doing this if the speech's meaning could change, and it is often of no slight importance to come to a final decision on such matters. A people might be forced by its government to transform its language. But if the government claimed to be legislating retrospectively so as to change the meaning of last year's election addresses its opponents would be entitled to object that it was enforcing an incorrect exposition of those speeches rather than changing their meaning.

If the meaning of a speech is as undatable and unlocatable, as timeless and unchanging, as the ratio of one natural number to another, so too are the meanings of its thousand-odd words or its hundred-odd sentences. 'Word', 'sentence', 'clause', etc., turn out to have two uses that differ from one another not only in their criteria for what is to be reckoned as a countable unit, but also in their relation to time and change. Not only is the first sentence of this book thirty-four words long, though only twenty-six English words occur in it. In addition, its meaning is in principle unchangeable, unlike that of the English sentence it instantiates. The thirty-four words that compose it have a history in space and time, in so far as their initial writing down and subsequent printing or publication are datable events. But they cannot have now one meaning, now another, like the English words they instantiate.

It would be a mistake to suppose that the difference between these two uses of 'word', 'sentence', 'clause', etc., is covered by C. S. Peirce's terminology of 'types' and 'tokens'. Peirce's aim[1] was to distinguish between the sense of 'word' in which one might say of a particular man that he has a vocabulary of five thousand words or of English that it has more words than Latin, and the sense in which one might say of a particular piece of paper that five words have been written on it, or of a particular room on a particular afternoon that only five words were spoken in it. The words of a language are certainly types in Peirce's sense. But the words of a speech are not what he called tokens. If a speech is written down or its tape-recording played over, the number of tokens produced is doubled, while the number of words remains precisely the same. Conversely, if two men proclaim the same slogan 'Disarmament' by shouldering together a single banner on which this slogan is inscribed, there is only one token (until they are

[1] *Coll. Papers*, ed. C. Hartshorne and P. Weiss (1931), 4.537.

4

photographed) but two one-word proclamations. The words of a book, speech, letter, conversation or statute should not be confused with the tokens composing its original utterance or with the tokens composing one of its copies or recitals, any more than with the English or French words occurring in it.

Suppose therefore we call the first of these three things *utterance-words*, and the last *language-words*, leaving the sense of quotation-marks to be determined by their context. Any two tokens are the same utterance-word or utterance-sentence if they are, are intended to be, and would normally be taken as being copies, recordings, recitals, etc., of the same token, or if one is such a copy of the other. Then what has been established is that utterance-words have meanings that are time-less and unchanging in the very strong sense of being unalterable properties of the utterance-words to which they belong.

Can language-words have meanings that are timeless and unchanging in anything like the same sense? Until about two centuries ago almost no one would have ascribed them meanings in any very different sense. The uses of words changed then as they do now. But whatever their interest in language people almost always talked about meanings in much the same timeless kind of way as they still talk about the ratio of two to four. Metaphor was recognized, but only as a figure of speech, not as a process by which eventually the non-metaphorical use of a word may be extended. If a usage was metaphorical on one occasion, it must also be so on any other occasion. The meaning of a word was thought of as far too integral a property of that word, far too intimately linked with the word itself, whether by nature or by convention, for the word ever to lose one meaning or acquire another. Even when this notion of an intimate linkage between word and meaning did not support a superstitious belief in the magical power of words, it normally blocked the way to the historical study of semantic change. Similarly the signifi-cance of a sentence's grammatical construction was assumed to be as timeless and unchanging as a statement's logical form, with which it was often in part confused. Occasionally an author might stipulate a special sense for his own purposes or argue what the true meaning of a word was. But the basic meanings of every word and construction in the language, whether properly acknowledged or not, were assumed to be invariable.

It was not that all features of a language were assumed eternally the same. The origin of language was a notorious problem as early as the date of Plato's *Cratylus*. Ancient writers also often distinguished between forms or inflections that had once been popular and those that were now so. Sometimes, like Phrynichus, they made the proviso that the classical forms were more correct.[1] Sometimes, like Horace, they accepted current usage as arbiter.[2] Bacon went so far as to remark that the pronunciation of words is continually changing.[3] All scholars recognized that new words, along with their meanings, might come into use, or old ones, along with theirs, drop out. But words were rarely, if ever, thought of as having one meaning at an earlier period and another at a later. A seventeenth-century nominalist like Hobbes was in no way ahead of Plato here. Adam, says Hobbes, and others added new words to the language given by God, and after the destruction of Babel 'the diversity of tongues that now is' proceeded by degrees from the survivors and their descendants, 'and in tract of time grew everywhere more copious'.[4] Though he noticed the gradual addition of new words, he ignored the gradual extension of old ones, separately or in combination, to new uses. Yet it is in the latter as well as, if not more than, in the former that the power and richness of a language is evident.

From Timothy Bright's *Characterie* of 1588 onwards many thinkers even proposed the construction of new written languages and their use for certain purposes in place of either Latin or the local vernacular. But they took for granted that such languages when in general use would retain all the grammatical and lexicographical features originally given them by their inventors. Only on this assumption could it make sense for Descartes, Dalgarno, Wilkins, Leibniz and others to propose a language that would combine the essentials of an international auxiliary with those of a systematically precise scientific terminology.[5] New

---

[1] *Ecloge*, preface.

[2] *De Arte Poetica*, ll. 47–72.

[3] *De Augmentis Scientiarum*, VI, i (*Philosophical Works*, ed. J. M. Robertson, 1905, pp. 525 f.).

[4] *Leviathan*, I, iv (Everyman edition, 1914, pp. 12 f.).

[5] Descartes, letter to Mersenne of 20th November 1629, *Œuvres*, ed. C. Adam and P. Tannery (1897), vol. i, pp. 76 ff.; J. Wilkins, *Essay towards a Real Character and a Philosophical Language* (1668); G. Dalgarno, *Ars Signorum* (1661); Leibniz, *Opuscules et Fragments Inédits*, ed. L. Couturat (1903), pp. 27 f. Cf . J. R. Firth, *Papers in Linguistics* (1957), pp. 103 ff.; L. J. Cohen, 'On the Project of a

words might need to be added to such a language as human knowledge grew. But there could not be divergent directions of semantic change, one prompted by the needs of everyday life and the other by those of theoretical knowledge, because there would not be any semantic change at all. Just as at that period an acceptable scientific theory was not thought open to revision or recall, so too the meanings of words in a satisfactory new language were not thought open to change.

The kind of event that would nowadays be called a change of meaning did not by any means go unnoticed. It was known under another name. It was called a deviation from, or a reversion to, the true meaning. When a Renaissance humanist, like Lorenzo Valla,[1] preferred the Latin of Cicero and Quintilian to that of Boethius and the Schoolmen, and tried to show in detail what such a preference implied, he did not conceive of his task as a reversal of the change by which the classical language had been transformed into the medieval one. For him Latin itself had not changed at all, but only the correctness with which it was written or spoken. As he conceived it, his task was not to reform Latin but to revive it. Later, when a standardized vernacular was taking the place of Latin as a literary medium, seventeenth-century French grammarians, like Vaugelas, normally treated provincial and plebeian usages as corruptions of the 'pure French' spoken by most people at court. The sovereign usage determining the laws of French was 'la façon de parler de la plus saine partie de la Cour, conformément à la façon d'écrire de la plus saine partie des Auteurs du temps'. Vaugelas admitted that over a generation a minute change in 'good' or 'pure' French might occur. But he conceived of linguistic change primarily as the appearance of new words or combinations of words and the disappearance of old ones, not as a combination of this with a process of transformation in the meanings of continuously existing words.[2] On such a view there could be no history of a given word's meaning, but only a chronicle of the word's popularity. Vaugelas's contemporaries disagreed with him on many points of grammatical or lexicographical

Universal Character', *Mind*, lxiii (1954), pp. 49 ff.; R. W. V. Elliot, 'Isaac Newton's "Of an Universall Language"', *Mod. Lang. Review*, lii (1957), pp. 1 ff.

[1] Cf. *de Linguae Latinae Elegantia* I, xiii; I, xvi; and *passim*, esp. the preface (ed. of 1577, pp. 52, 58, etc.).

[2] *Remarques sur la Langue Françoise*, ed. of 1738, vol. I, pp. 18 ff., 68 ff., and *passim*.

detail. Two critics, la Mothe le Vayer and Scipion Dupleix, also objected in general that Vaugelas's rules were too strict and tended to impoverish the language. Dupleix refused to accept the speech of court ladies as a standard, and la Mothe le Vayer held it a fault in Vaugelas that he took court speech at all as a criterion of good usage. But none of Vaugelas's contemporaries seem to have had anything more than he to say about change of meaning.[1]

The prevailing attitude is neatly summed up in Hobbes's political philosophy. In what he called 'the state of nature' controversies might arise about the meanings of words like 'right' and 'wrong', or 'pound' and 'quart', and it was for the sovereign, set up by the social contract, to settle such a dispute. When the sovereign does so, Hobbes does not think of him as changing the sense of a word, but as determining its proper sense.[2] A normative approach to the study of meaning excluded a historical one. Similarly from the time of Panini in ancient India the task of a grammarian had remained the same. It was still to give rules, not to describe, narrate or explain. Even if his analysis of a language was as subtle and comprehensive as Panini's, it was constructed in terms of a system of permanent or quasi-permanent rules[3] which blocked all interest in the temporal dimension of language-study.

Apparent exceptions to these generalizations are hard to find and, when found, seem not to be downright counter-examples, though it would perhaps be rash to claim that no such counter-examples exist at all. Thucydides remarked how in the bitterness of civil strife the Corcyreans and others changed the meanings of certain Greek words as they thought fit. Reckless daring came to be described as loyal courage and prudent delay as disguised cowardice.[4] But if Thucydides had thought alterations of meaning from period to period, or culture to culture, a commonplace he would not have chosen this way of high-lighting the enormities of Greek civil strife. For his point to be a telling one he must have relied on his readers' sharing the assumption that changes of meaning were utterly abnormal. In any case the changes he

---

[1] Cf. *Commentaires sur les Remarques de Vaugelas*, ed. J. Streicher (1936), pp. 971, 977, 987, 990, etc.; and F. Brunot, *Histoire de la Langue Française* (1909), vol. III, pp. 24 ff.

[2] *Elements of Law*, ed. F. Tönnies (1928), II, 10, 8.

[3] Cf. O. Böhtlingk's ed. (1887), pp. 20, 337, etc.

[4] *History of the Peloponnesian War*, III, lxxxii, 4.

remarked on consisted in the adaptation of familiar words to the needs and passions of the moment. They were not long-term changes in the Greek language that a good dictionary would nowadays record. John Locke recognized, in a sense, that the meanings of words may sometimes be altered. But for him the phrase 'altering of a signification' does not refer to a change in English or some other language. It refers just to some special use of a word that a particular individual may decide to make, and Locke advises this to be done warily, sparingly, and only after due stipulation, since 'men think it a boldness'. Locke admits the possibility that such a special usage may one day pass into common parlance, but shows no awareness that new usages which have not been deliberately coined as technical terms are constantly developing within most languages.[1] Occasionally Vaugelas speaks about the disappearance of a word in one of its senses. But even this is not quite the same as recognizing that it may change its sense.[2]

A second thesis against the Fregean position is thus reasonably well established. The meanings of language-words, at least until the eighteenth century, were normally regarded as unchangeable properties of them. One must take account of this if one wishes to appraise Aristotle's theory of definition, Spinoza's analysis of scientific knowledge, or any other piece of classical philosophy that hinges partly on a theory of meaning, without doing a great injustice to its author. But the same charity should not extend to modern theories of meaning or to philosophies that rely on them.

§3. Meanings as changeable properties

The late eighteenth century was the first period to treat words' meanings as raw material for historians as well as for normative grammarians and language-planners. To prepare the way for the new point of view some bold spirit had to cry down the pretensions of normative grammar and lexicography. No one did this with better irony than J. G. Hamann when in 1760 he remarked of the French Academy – the principal function of which, according to Article 24 of its statutes, was to determine the 'rules' of the French language – that 'in as large a city as Paris are foregathered *annually* without expense, *forty* learned men

[1] *An Essay Concerning Human Understanding*, III, vi, 51.
[2] E.g. *Remarques*, ed. of 1738, I, p. 62.

who know infallibly what is pure and decent in their mother-tongue
and what is necessary for the monopoly of this second-hand trade'.
Hamann insisted that 'the purity of a language diminishes its riches, a
too strict correctness diminishes its strength and manhood', and that 'a
mind which thinks at its own expense will always interfere with the language'.[1] The way was now clear for J. G. Herder's explicit acceptance
of meaning-change as a normal phenomenon in human history. In 1770
he wrote that on occasions, in the development of a language, 'one
word was lost to a person, another retained, another was diverted from
the main point by a secondary view; sometimes, with the revolution of
ages, the sense of the original idea became changed'.[2] If one compares
this with Hobbes's account of the origin of language it is most notice-
able that what Herder has added is the conception of meaning-change.

Like many intellectual innovations the new way of thinking about
meanings did not at its outset always appear in an unalloyed form.

Samuel Johnson, in the preface to his *Dictionary* published in 1755,
had recognized that 'in every word of extensive use it was requisite to
mark the progress of its meaning and show by what gradations of inter-
mediate sense it has passed from its primitive to its remote and accidental signification'. He noted also that 'as by the cultivation of various
sciences a language is amplified, it will be more furnished with words
deflected from their original sense. . . . The tropes of poetry will make
hourly encroachments, and the metaphorical will become the current
sense.' But he retained enough of the old normative approach to language to prevent him from paying equal respect to all changes of meaning. The writers of the century prior to the Restoration were those
whose works he took as 'the wells of English undefiled, as the pure
sources of genuine diction'. Where earlier or later usage differed from
this classical model it was almost always to be disregarded as an im-
perfection.

Lord Monboddo, in a volume first published in 1776, noted that
what he called radical words often changed their meanings. 'There is
nothing, either in nature or in the grammatical art, that determines the
proper signification of a radical word. It is fixed by use alone; and, as
that is variable in all living languages, it frequently happens that words
change their signification.' But he thought derivative, inflected and

[1] *Schriften*, ed. F. Roth (1821), vol. II, pp. 151 f. and 130 f.
[2] *Über den Ursprung der Sprache*, Eng. tr. of 1827, p. 100; cf. also pp. 59 ff.

compounded words 'have what may be truly called a proper and natural signification, being such as is ascertained by grammatical rules. . . . When such words lose this signification, and denote something else, it is an abuse and corruption of language.'[1] For radical words Monboddo was a modern, descriptive lexicographer, for others an old-fashioned, normative one, though even here he conceded that we had to submit to any abuse that was firmly established by custom.

Many thinkers, like Condorcet in 1793,[2] did not clearly distinguish the fact of semantic change from the value they attributed to it. But their faith in human progress was not merely a reversal of the Renaissance humanists' tendency to see in contemporary Latin usage a decline from the perfections of antiquity. They did not aim to replace the old doctrine that all present differences from classical usage were a falling away by a new doctrine that all past differences from present usage were a falling short. They held instead that it was language itself which changed, rather than the degree of human fidelity to its rules. They sought histories of linguistic development, not chronicles of elegance and solecism. And wherever 'enlightened' contempt, like Condorcet's, for the primitive and medieval gave way under the advocacy of Herder and his followers to an attempt to understand each period, people or culture in its own circumstances, interest in the value of linguistic change soon disappeared into a scholarly preoccupation with the pattern of its detail, and in particular into the immense labours of those who then began to study the history of the Indo-European, Finno-Ugrian and other language families. When Sir William Jones suggested in 1786 that Latin, Greek, Persian and the Germanic languages were all probably derived from a common parent, he sowed a seed in ground that had already been fertilized by Herder's historical-mindedness. It is true that philologists did not begin to study meaning-change systematically until more than half a century after they had reached a comparable stage in morphological enquiry.[3] But at any rate the new conception of a word's meaning as something that may be in a continual

[1] *Of the Origin and Progress of Language*, II, iv, 3.
[2] *Sketch for a Historical Picture of the Progress of the Human Mind*, tr. J. Barraclough (1955), pp. 22, 37, 166.
[3] Cf. Sir W. Jones, 'Third Anniversary Discourse of the Asiatic Society' in *Works* (1799), vol. I, p. 26; and S. Ullmann, *The Principles of Semantics* (1951), p. 1.

state of transformation soon spread to philosophers whose main interests were not in the field of language. In 1810 the moral philosopher Dugald Stewart was discussing historical changes in the meaning of words with an obvious recognition of their importance,[1] and a little later J. S. Mill was doing the same and at somewhat greater length in his *System of Logic*.[2]

All that remained was for Saussure and others to emphasize that an exclusive interest in linguistic history is too one-sided a reaction against the old muddling-up of normative and descriptive linguistics. Descriptive studies are also needed to abstract and record the pivotal stages in a continuum of change. Synchronistic and diachronistic enquiries – studies of a single period and studies through several periods, respectively – can and should complement each other.[3] Differences in a word's meaning from place to place are as interesting as those from period to period. But this is not to reintroduce a timeless mode of discourse about meanings in a language. Though dialect surveys and other synchronistic studies do not narrate changes, they nevertheless resemble statements about habits of dress or house-building more than they resemble statements about the ratios between natural numbers. They describe no timeless features of a language, but only what was true of it between certain dates.

In the past two generations, also under Saussure's powerful advocacy,[4] the programme of treating speech rather than literature as the primary material for linguistic study, and phonemes rather than letters as its primary units, has doubly reinforced the nineteenth-century tendency to exclude normative discussion from academic linguistics. First, since the norms of good style, though not irrelevant to speech, have most often been invoked in the criticism of literature, it is easier to separate the science of language from the criticism of style if linguists are supposed to study the spoken word rather than the written one. Secondly, even outside literature written utterances tend to be more standardized in language than do spoken ones: we thus take advantage of their relative permanence and achieve communication over much

---

[1] *Philosophical Essays* (1810), pp. 222 ff.

[2] IV, iv, 6; and IV, v.

[3] *Cours de Linguistique Générale*, ed. C. Bally and A. Sechehaye (1916), pp. 119 f., etc.

[4] Ibid., pp. 47 ff.

wider stretches of space and time. Those who concentrate their interest on speech are therefore less likely to be preoccupied with the problem of norms and more open-minded in discerning variation. No doubt the reaction here too, as in the case of the historical movement, has been somewhat excessive. But when linguists return, as some of them are now doing,[1] to the study of written language they are interested in facts not rules, in how people do write, not in how they ought to write.

The meaning of a language-word, therefore, to a modern lexicographer or grammarian is a changeable property. That is why he can discuss, as Herder's predecessors could not, how a decline in the relative importance of pastoral wealth extended the meaning of the Latin word 'pecunia', or how the use of the rosary gradually changed that of the English word 'bede' or 'bead'.[2] Whereas the causal liaisons of semantic change were beyond the conceptual reach of those who treated meanings as unchangeable properties, they are now a familiar topic of research – because it is generally accepted that a word may remain the same while changing its meaning. If a word itself changes, its continuity through change is now normally thought to consist in similarities of form alone rather than in those conjoined with identity of meaning. When a linguist explains the meaning of the modern French word 'épices' as having evolved out of the medieval druggists' use of 'species' to refer to the four kinds of ingredients in which they traded (saffron, cloves, cinnamon, and nutmeg),[3] he is explaining a later meaning of a word in terms of an earlier meaning of the same word, even though the form of the word has changed, and his explanation presupposes that morphological similarities are sufficient to establish verbal continuity. If verbal continuity required semantic identity as well, every explanation of this kind would either break down altogether or be weakened into a tautology.

Finally, if a linguist thus conceives a word to vary its meaning, rather than a meaning to vary its word, he is not thereby committed to thinking of each meaning in itself as something eternal and out of time, in the Fregean manner. He is like a historian of dress who thinks of men

---

[1] E.g. A. McIntosh, 'The Analysis of Written Middle English', *Trans. Philological Soc.* (1956), pp. 26 ff.

[2] M. Bréal, *Semantics*, tr. H. Cust (1900), p. 116, and L. Bloomfield, *Language* (1935), p. 440.

[3] M. Bréal, op. cit., p. 109.

as varying their clothes, rather than clothes their men, and does not therefore have to suppose that clothes or fashions are timeless. Whatever is needed for other kinds of concern with the meanings of language-words, whatever the timelessness of utterance-words' meanings, the lexicographer's concept of meaning can safely be a temporal one. For him the meanings a word has at different times are as much historical phenomena as the various forms it takes. The thoughts it expresses are items in the flux of history, not eternities in a timeless realm of formal logic.

§4. Meanings as changing continuants

But though a grammarian or lexicographer does not need to think of a meaning as something timeless, and would not naturally do so, the main pattern of his work, considered in isolation from other disciplines, would nevertheless remain undamaged if he in fact thought of them in the Fregean manner. Dialect surveys, historical researches and other empirical enquiries would merely need to be interpreted as showing which words expressed which timeless thoughts at what times and places. The element of timelessness would be unnecessary and incongruous, not radically detrimental. But this is not true for the modern historian of ideas. He has much to lose if he cannot take meanings to have dates, durations and changing forms.

To see this one must first distinguish between what it is convenient to call the verbal and the conceptual planes of discourse about meaning. Though an apparatus of technical terms here is perhaps ugly, and certainly not indispensable, it will serve to bring into relief a serious error in the Fregean position.

On the verbal plane statements about specific meanings cannot be translated throughout into another language or paraphrased in their own: quoted words and sentences must be left in their original form. When someone tells me 'The German word "Katze" means a cat' and I pass on this information to a Frenchman in his own language, my translation would turn a true statement into a false one if I put 'chat' for 'Katze' as well as for 'cat'. Though a non-specific statement like 'The meanings of all common English words are to be found in *The Pocket Oxford Dictionary*' can be translated as a whole, such a statement is normally to be reckoned at the verbal level if a specific discussion of the meanings referred to cannot be so translated.

14

On the conceptual plane almost all statements about meanings, specific and non-specific alike, can at least in principle be translated as a whole from one language to another. Discussions about the meaning of 'western civilization' in modern political parlance, or about the meaning of 'mass' in seventeenth-century physics, can be rendered throughout into any language sufficiently rich to contain methods of expressing the concepts concerned. The quotation-marks around these words do not bar us from translating them. Certain other statements also belong to the conceptual plane even though a straightforward application of the translatability criterion would place them on the verbal one. When a word-use has been more or less confined to the speakers of one particular language a historian of ideas can conveniently refer to it by some such locution as 'the meaning of "religio" in ancient Latin culture'. The quoted word cannot here be translated. But if it can, at least in principle, be paraphrased by other words in the same language without being considered to alter the sense of the statement – if the word-meaning concerned is as much that of the word's synonyms, if any, as of the word itself – the statement belongs to the conceptual plane.

This distinction applies to discourse about the meanings of speeches, books, conversations, statutes, etc., as well as to that about meanings in languages, and thus, in the light of the distinction drawn in §2 between a language-word and an utterance-word, two further senses of words like 'word', 'phrase', 'sentence', etc., are generated. Corresponding to the notion of a language-word or language-sentence, as when a lexicographer is concerned with the meaning of the German word 'Katze', we also have the notion of a *culture-word* or *culture-sentence*, as when a historian of ideas is concerned with the meaning of the word 'mass' in seventeenth-century physics. Quoted culture-words are translatable: quoted language-words, which exemplify them, are not. Corresponding to the notion of an utterance-word or utterance-sentence, as when a translator of Newton's *Principia* is concerned to render the meaning of each sentence in turn from Latin into English, we also have the notion of a *saying-word* or *saying-sentence*, as when an editor of Newton's great work is concerned to elucidate the implications of his opening sentence. Quoted saying-sentences are translatable: quoted utterance-sentences, which exemplify them, are not. The number of saying-words, saying-sentences, etc., in a speech or book is indeterminate, unlike the number of utterance-words, utterance-sentences, etc. A three-word phrase in French may have a one-word translation in English, and a five-sentence remark in English may have a one-sentence translation in Japanese. The language we are using generally determines whether we talk here, on the conceptual plane, about a word or about a phrase, a sentence or a passage. In short, two tokens are the same saying-word or saying-sentence if either they are the same utterance-word or utterance-sentence, respectively, or if they are, are intended to be, and would normally be taken as being translations or paraphrases of the same token, or if one is such a translation or paraphrase of the other.

The meanings of saying-sentences are to be reckoned as timeless as those of utterance-sentences, for reasons already given: their truth-values and logical implications are absolutely unchanging. But the meanings of culture-words turn out to be temporal and changeable in a stronger sense than those of language-words. To see this one must first observe that for most purposes there is no important difference between historians' statements about concepts or ideas and statements about the meanings of words that belong to the conceptual rather than the verbal plane. Some interesting psychological research has been done on the ways in which many people often think in terms of mental images rather than of words,[1] and here it would obviously be dangerous to substitute statements about the meanings of words for statements about concepts. Even historians of ideas sometimes want to trace the concept of time through such non-linguistic expressions of it as the painting of an old man with a scythe, or to discover the manifestation of Romantic ideas in the vogue of the English garden which spread so rapidly in France and Germany after 1730.[2] But in most cases one can interchange conceptual statements about word-meanings with the corresponding statements about concepts, since it is by means of language that people give the most articulate and intelligible expression to the concepts with which they think. To analyse the concept of time is to analyse, on the conceptual plane, the meaning of the word 'time'.

---

[1] Cf. *Handbook of Experimental Psychology*, ed. S. S. Stevens (1951), pp. 732 f., and R. S. Woodworth and H. Schlosberg, *Experimental Psychology* (1954), pp. 815 f.

[2] E. Panofsky, *Studies in Iconology* (1939), pp. 69 ff., and A. O. Lovejoy, *The Great Chain of Being* (1936), p. 15.

The history of the idea of time, strictly conceived, is the history of the meaning of the culture-word 'time'.

It was no doubt because of this interchangeability that the period in which changes of language-words' meanings were first accepted as commonplace was also the period in which the history of ideas first became a subject of serious enquiry. In 1764 the Swiss historian Isaac Iselin was discussing the 'better development' of certain concepts, like those of order, justice and morality; and, even before Herder, Jacob Wegelin, who migrated from Switzerland to Berlin in 1765, advocated studying the ways in which the nature and development of ideas affect the course of human history.[1] The late eighteenth century was a period of innovation on both planes of discourse about meaning.

Not that before then every feature of people's thoughts had been assumed eternally the same. Diodorus, Ockham, Buridan and other logicians commonly supposed that what was true at one time might be false at another. For them, unlike Frege, there was a proposition 'This tree is covered with green leaves' that changed its truth-value with the time of year at which it was uttered. But they did not take it to change its meaning.[2]

Scholars had also long taken for granted that not every community and every age operated with precisely the same stock of concepts or word-uses. Differences of religion or culture within a mileu of commercial or military intercommunication sufficed to make this evident to most observant writers of the ancient and early modern world. Lucretius complained that the poverty of his native language made it difficult for him to discuss certain matters that had long been familiar topics of Greek philosophical writing,[3] and Locke remarked how difficulties of translation from one language to another indicate that certain complex ideas exist in some countries and not in others.[4] The belief that important ideas had disappeared from circulation and were now being rediscovered was itself a causal factor in the ferment of the Renaissance.[5]

[1] Cf. I. Iselin, *Geschichte der Menschheit*, 1768 ed., vol. II, p. 31, and H. Bock, 'Jacob Wegelin als Geschichtstheoretiker', *Leipziger Studien*, ix, 4 (1902).

[2] Cf. B. Mates, 'Diodorean Implication', *Philosophical Review*, lviii (1949), pp. 234 ff., and E. A. Moody, *Truth and Consequence in Medieval Logic* (1953), pp. 53 ff.

[3] *De Rerum Natura*, I, 136–9.

[4] *Essay*, III, v, 8.

[5] H. Weisinger, 'The Renaissance Theory of the Reaction against the Middle Ages as a Cause of the Renaissance', *Speculum*, xx (1945), pp. 461 ff., esp. p. 463.

It was not unnatural to suggest, like James Harris in 1751, that nations like individuals have their peculiar ideas and the wisest nations have the most and best ideas.[1] For Locke it was not even paradoxical to talk about someone's having altogether new notions which require the coining of new words or phrases to express them.[2] But in all, or almost all, such cases prior to the closing decades of the eighteenth century the incidence of a concept's employment was what was thought to change, and not also a concept itself, just as on the verbal plane grammarians like Vaugelas noted the presence or absence of a word in the usage of different generations but not also the transformation of a word's meaning over the whole period.

Unless one is careful to notice this one might easily overlook the principle of method that marks off a genuine historian of ideas from a mere chronicler of their popularity. Only when historians concern themselves with changes in the role or content of a concept as well as in its incidence can they guard against a tendency to distort their account of the human past in certain characteristic ways. To say that Newton invented the modern concept of mass would be grossly unfair to Galileo, Huyghens and others. But, if a historian may speak of changes in an idea's content, he can say that Newton achieved a crucial new development in the concept of mass by defining it in terms of density and volume rather than in terms of weight.[3]

The danger to be surmounted here – a blind eye to the possibility of change in the topic of one's narrative – occurs also in other fields, such as biography or the history of political institutions. Tacitus was notoriously unfair to Tiberius in conceiving of his character as something so substantial and unchanging that the emergence of vices in later life had to be taken as evidence of hypocrisy in earlier years.[4] Similarly many sixteenth-century Englishmen, struggling against the executive power of Tudor monarchs, were guilty of wishful thinking in their search for historical precedents. They supposed that Parliament had always existed as an institution with precisely the same customarily

---

[1] *Hermes, or a Philosophical Enquiry concerning Universal Grammar*, 1794 ed., pp. 407 f.

[2] *Essay*, III, vi, 51.

[3] Cf. E. A. Burtt, *Metaphysical Foundations of Modern Science* (1932), pp. 238 ff.

[4] *Annals*, ed. H. Furneaux (1884), i, p. 135.

granted rights and privileges as they now alleged it to have.[1] But the point is particularly important if a historian's subject-matter is not just a single concept but a whole movement of ideas, like the fifteenth-century Renaissance or the rise of modern science in the sixteenth and seventeenth centuries. It was not merely ignorance that for so long distorted accounts of these movements, but also a certain conceptual blindness. A chronicler of the popularity of ideas cannot explain such movements in any other way than by supposing either that certain foreigners, perhaps refugees from the sack of Constantinople, have introduced new ideas, or that certain forgotten principles, like the mathematicism of Plato's *Timaeus*, have now been rediscovered, or that certain altogether new notions, like that of experimental enquiry, have now been born. As a result he overemphasizes discontinuities and may miss important factors in the stream of events. He may be tempted to exaggerate out of all proportion the innovating influence of the Byzantine refugees.[2] He may too easily ignore what was contributed to the mathematization of science by medieval influences like Roger Bacon's stress on the need for a strictly mathematical treatment of optics, or what was contributed to the empiricism of science by the practical co-operation of improvement-minded artisans and the long experimental tradition of the Padua medical school.[3]

That is why Ernst Cassirer and many other historians of ideas have held that 'whenever . . . we make any comparison between the Middle Ages and the Renaissance it is never enough to single out particular ideas or concepts. What we want to know is not the particular idea as such, but the importance it possesses, and the strength with which it is acting in the whole structure.' Changes in the content of a concept necessarily involve changes in its relations to other concepts, so that no single concept's history can be studied in isolation. 'The historian of ideas is not asking primarily what the *substance* is of particular ideas. He is asking what their function is.'[4] 'What is new about the Renaissance is

---

[1] Cf. J. E. Neale, *Elisabeth I and her Parliaments 1559–1581* (1953), pp. 17 ff., 100, 188 ff., etc.

[2] Cf. R. G. Collingwood, *The Idea of History* (1946), p. 80.

[3] E. Cassirer, 'Some remarks on the question of the originality of the Renaissance', *J. Hist. Ideas*, iv (1943), p. 51; E. Zilsel, 'The Genesis of the Concept of Scientific Progress', *J. Hist. Id.*, vi (1945), pp. 325 ff.; J. H. Randall, 'The Development of Scientific Method in the School of Padua', *J. Hist. Id.*, i (1940), pp. 177 ff.

[4] E. Cassirer, op. cit., p. 55.

not so much the ideas themselves, but the ways in which they were recombined into new intellectual constructions.'[1] For example, 'the concept of the human individual was no innovation of the Renaissance', but 'that the portrayal of a particular man *as* a particular man – with all his peculiarities, accidents and idiosyncrasies – could have theoretical interest, was recognized by no philosophy before the Renaissance': previously the portrayal of men gave rise to types or 'characters' – like the *Characters* of Theophrastus.[2] Or what was importantly new about Galileo's mode of scientific thought was neither his recourse to experiments, nor his preoccupation with quantitative variations rather than qualitative differences, nor his rejection of Aristotelian mechanics, nor his interest in acceleration, nor yet his systematic use of ideally simplified concepts, in which Euclid at least had anticipated him, but rather the way in which he combined all five to produce the prototype of a modern scientific theory.

A modern historian of ideas must therefore be something more than a mere chronicler of their popularity. In studying their 'nature, genesis, development, diffusion, interplay and effects'[3] he must treat them as continuants with changeable contents. He must narrate 'the general development of the concept . . . of genius', describe the post-medieval 're-evaluation' of 'the concept of friendship', or trace a recurrent instability in the European idea of God to an original incoherence in Plato's theology.[4] Nor are any concepts exempt from this kind of treatment. At first sight the uses of certain kinds of words, such as personal pronouns and logical connectives, might seem to show insufficient change over several millennia to deserve treatment as a topic of conceptual study by historians. But that would be to ignore the changing conception of autobiography,[5] the varying importance attached by logicians at different periods to truth-functional conditionals, or the

---

[1] H. Weisinger, 'Ideas of History during the Renaissance', *J. Hist. Id.*, vi (1945), p. 435.

[2] E. Cassirer, op. cit., p. 54.

[3] A. O. Lovejoy, 'Reflections on the History of Ideas', *J. Hist. Id.*, i (1940), p. 8.

[4] H. Dieckman, 'Diderot's Conception of Genius', *J. Hist. Id.*, ii (1941), pp. 151 ff.; B. N. Nelson, *The Idea of Usury* (1949), pp. 141 ff.; A. O. Lovejoy, *The Great Chain of Being, passim*.

[5] Cf. G. Misch, *History of Autobiography in Antiquity* (1950), pp. 3 ff.

way in which ideas of 'I' and 'if' change even within a single generation of children as they grow to maturity.[1]

When meanings are thus taken as the topic of diachronistic narrative, or of the synchronistic surveys that complement such narrative, it is meanings that vary their language-words rather than language-words their meanings. The development of a concept may be followed through different words in the same language, like 'Christendom' and 'western civilization'.[2] Or it may be followed through different languages that coexist or succeed one another within the same culture. In a work on primitivism and related ideas in antiquity A. O. Lovejoy and G. Boas list sixty-six 'meanings of "nature"' and their list is not intended as a substitute for a dictionary article. 'The development of meanings of *physis*, *natura* and the derivatives of the latter in modern European languages, is treated as a single semasiological process, of which the greater part belongs to the history of the Greek word.'[3] All that is essential for discourse about culture-words is that one should be able to get cross-bearings on them, as it were. There must be one way of identifying the meaning talked about and another way of talking about it – one bearing to locate the concept and another to ascribe it a certain content at a certain time or place. Because we have such cross-bearings on the concept of friendship, for instance, we can see it as a development from the ancient and medieval idea, preserving the factors of association, mutual benevolence and independence of kinship, while replacing those of exclusiveness and aristocratic solidarity by a warmly felt companionship of interests.[4]

Hence a culture-word, like the 'nature' studied by Lovejoy and Boas, is individuated by meaning, not by form. It need have no morphological unity or continuity from one place or period to another, and its meaning is discussed on the conceptual plane, whereas a language-word is identified by its form and its meaning is normally discussed on the verbal plane. Frege made it seem at least plausible to suppose that all thoughts or meanings were timeless because he failed to notice the sense of 'meaning' which is vital for the history of ideas. He took all

---

[1] Cf. J. Piaget, *The Language and Thought of the Child*, tr. M. Gabain (1932).

[2] F. Le Van Baumer, 'The Conception of Christendom in Renaissance England', *J. Hist. Id.*, vi (1945), pp. 131 ff.

[3] *Primitivism and Related Ideas in Antiquity* (1935), pp. 447 ff.

[4] B. N. Nelson, *The Idea of Usury*, pp. 149 ff.

B

discourse about meanings to be concerned with the meanings of language-words, and none with those of culture-words. He would no doubt have agreed in principle with G. E. Moore's dictum that 'to define a concept is the same thing as to give an analysis of it',[1] which makes it impossible for a historian to give different analyses of a concept in respect of different periods. In his own legitimate concern for the timeless domain of formal logic, and his desire to defend it against confusion with the temporal domain of psychology, he overlooked the equally legitimate need of historians to treat thoughts and meanings – the meanings of culture-words – as temporal continuants with changeable states or contents.

It is no use objecting that Frege was right here to ignore culture-words because language-words are more basic. In what respect are they more basic? Perhaps the use of 'word' in the former sense was developed earlier in human history and is still acquired earlier by each individual in his own lifetime. But temporal priorities of this kind are an unreliable guide to intellectual importance. Perhaps the notion of a culture-word is reducible by definition, since it might be defined as a family of inter-translatable language-words. But a language-word might equally well be defined as a uniform example of a culture-word. Perhaps the concept of a culture-word is an even more abstract one than the concept of a language-word. But the level of abstraction at which a science operates is at least one criterion of fundamentality, rather than the reverse. Moreover, from any point of view from which the meaning of a culture-word is a temporal continuant, one must in consistency regard the meanings of the language-words that exemplify it as temporal phenomena. So far as Frege was wrong in omitting to take account of culture-words, he was also wrong in thinking the meanings of language-words to be out of time.

The opposite error to Frege's has also been made. Friedrich Engels explicitly held all thought and meaning to be temporal, and none timeless. Though it was concerned with topics like contradiction, validity and truth, which seem to have no concern with time, the dialectical logic that he envisaged was nevertheless to have the temporal quality of historical discourse.[2] It is hardly surprising that dialectical logic, thus

[1] 'A Reply to my Critics', *The Philosophy of G. E. Moore*, ed. P. A. Schilpp (1942), p. 665.
[2] *Dialectics of Nature*, tr. C. Dutt (1940), pp. 153 f., 161, 206, 224, 237 ff. Cf.

conceived, has made little or no progress since Engels's day, as compared with formal logic's most notable century of advance. Nor is it surprising that recent attempts by Russian logicians to reconcile Engels's theory with some measure of respect for formal logic have encountered great difficulties and led to as yet unresolved controversy within the Soviet Union.[1] If thought is not caught up in the flux of history what room is there for dialectical logic? But if all thought is caught up in the flux of history, how can there be laws determining unchangeable features of valid thinking? And if no such laws exist what room is there for formal logic? These difficulties are part of the philosophical price paid for converting Hegel's dialectic of spirit into a Marxist dialectic of matter. Hegel could distinguish the eternal logical relations within the Absolute Idea from their historical manifestations in the development of human thought. For Marx and Engels there was only the historical play of material forces and the equally historical manifestation of these in human minds.

The philosophy of meaning has to steer a course between these two extremes of oversimplification, between Engels's obsession with time and Frege's with timelessness, and to achieve that feat of navigation without steering into the fogs engendered by a dialectic of spirit or a doctrine of subsistent entities. It will be one object of the following chapters so to avoid jettisoning the vital interests either of temporal or of timeless semantics.

also 'Ludwig Feuerbach and the Outcome of Classical German Philosophy' in *Karl Marx, Selected Works*, ed. C. P. Dutt (1942), vol. I, pp. 424 ff. and 451 ff.

[1] Cf. A. Philipov, *Logic and Dialectic in the Soviet Union* (1952), pp. 45 ff. and 78 f., and O. Wetter, *Dialectical Materialism*, tr. P. L. Heath (1958), pp. 523 ff.

II

Meanings Conceived as what Words have in a Language or Culture

---

§5. *De facto* and *de jure* theories of meaning

The notorious obscurity of the word 'meaning', and of its equally slippery synonyms, like 'sense' and 'significance', have in the past two generations provoked almost every active philosophical thinker to seek some resolution of the concept into clearer and sharper outlines. Though it would be excessively tedious and unprofitable to examine each such thesis in detail, it is useful to sketch out, with their main variations, two cardinal types of theory to one or other of which most views in current favour will readily be granted to belong. Roughly, one type, to be called *de facto*, holds that most statements about meanings are, or should be construed as, statements about occurrences, states, situations or habits of certain sorts and their observable or introspectible relations to one another. The other type, to be called *de jure*, holds instead that most statements about meanings are or should be construed as statements about rules of certain kinds and the extent to which they have been broken or obeyed. For *de facto* theories a language is a pattern of events, for *de jure* ones a system of rules. The former suppose correct accounts of a word's meaning to state something that happens whether it ought to or not: the latter, something that may or ought to happen whether it does so or not.

Perhaps the commonest form of *de facto* theory is that in which the meaning of a word or sentence is equated with events that are somehow causally related to its utterance. The dominant object of philosophers holding such a theory has generally been to assimilate statements about meaning to those in certain of the natural sciences, and so to remove any temptation to suppose that they must be concerned with something very special and mysterious, like Descartes's mental ideas or Meinong's subsistent entities. The meaning of a word for its hearer is held to be a causal property of a vocal sound, acquired fundamentally through the mechanism of conditioned reflexes. To say that a car-driver understands the meaning of the exclamation 'Red light!' is to say that he responds to the phrase as he responds to the actual sight of a red light. Meaning for the typical speaker is the state of mind or the situation which ordinarily causes him to speak thus, such as a sensation of redness or the flashing of a red light in his field of view. Some words or phrases, however, he normally utters as a result of some experience, which they are said to 'express', rather than as a response to events, which they might have been said to 'indicate'. The word 'or' is generally used, we are perhaps told, only when the speaker experiences a sense of hesitation, a conflict between two or more motor impulses, and the word 'not' when certain impulses exist but are inhibited. Sentences combine in one way or another the causal properties of the words occurring in them. They are said to be meaningful within a given community if they possess the causal property of arousing certain mental attitudes in their hearers, such as belief, doubt or rejection, and to be equivalent to one another if normally uttered in precisely the same circumstances. At their simplest, as in 'I am hot', they make true statements about observable facts if and only if the belief they express is caused by what they indicate.

This is only a bare selective outline of a kind of theory that has been elaborated by Bertrand Russell, Charles Morris, and others, in great complexity of detail so as to cope with the many varieties of human utterance.[1] What is relevant here is not the particular way in which such theories try to get round some difficulties they encounter about lies, predictions or formal logic, but rather their insistence that somehow all statements about meaning are to be construed in causal terms. They are therefore sometimes attacked by subscribers to another form of *de facto* theory, like Karl Popper,[2] on the ground that they ignore the specifically human element in the subject-matter of discourse about meaning. These critics point out that even the direction of a barometer-pointer may be said to reflect other events than merely the movement of its own pulley: it may be said to register, accurately or inaccurately, the

---

[1] B. Russell, *Enquiry into Meaning and Truth* (1940), pp. 170 ff.; C. W. Morris, *Signs, Language and Behaviour* (1946). Cf. C. K. Ogden and I. A. Richards, *The Meaning of Meaning* (10th ed., 1949), *passim*.

[2] 'Language and the Body-Mind problem', *Proceedings of the XIth International Congress of Philosophy* (1953), vol. VII, pp. 101 ff.

atmospheric pressure on an attached column of mercury, to signal changes in the weather, and to evoke appropriate responses in those who read it. Nevertheless, they object, the barometer would not itself be said to issue a description or forecast of the weather that could be assigned a truth-value, nor to advance an argument that could be appraised as valid or invalid. Only the person who consults the barometer is said to do this. Accordingly, the objection runs, we should not construe all statements about meaning in purely causal terms. So far as a man's use of language is symptomatic of his own feelings, as in exclamations of pain, or evocative of others', as in war-cries, the causal theory applies. But when his utterances are descriptive and reasoned, as well as symptomatic and evocative, the causal theory is inadequate and we must take into account his intentions or purposes. He does not merely behave as if his utterances were intentional, in the way that a barometer might do which indicated the weather incorrectly whenever it was tapped roughly: he actually does intend to speak about the weather or support his prediction of it. Statements about the meaning of a description or argument are thus statements about the purposes of an utterance, not just about its causes and effects. The causal theory lends itself too easily to a behaviourist philosophy of mind.

Modern *de jure* theorists have found their starting-point in comparing statements about meaning to the norms and laws of formal logic rather than to the causal hypotheses of natural science. Some, like Alonzo Church, tell us that a 'natural language', such as English, does not differ in principle from a 'formalized' one. A calculus can be specified which when appropriately interpreted is indistinguishable in any important respect from English.[1] The calculus is interpreted as a formalized language when rules are given assigning meanings to its well-formed formulas. Criteria of theoremhood in the calculus then come to determine what is necessarily true in English. All rigorously accurate discourse about meaning is thus held to be concerned with the content of certain rules and with obedience or disobedience to them, whether they be the rules that constitute a calculus or the rules that interpret one. The difference of the formalized language from the natural language 'lies not in any matter of principle but in the degree of completeness that has been attained in the laying down of explicit syntactical and

[1] 'Contributions to the Analysis and Synthesis of Knowledge', *Proceedings of the American Academy of Arts and Sciences*, lxxx (1951), pp. 100 ff.

semantical rules and the extent to which vagueness and uncertainties have been removed from the meanings'.

This formal kind of *de jure* theory is strongly attacked by supporters of a more informal one. An ordinary language, they tell us, is neither a calculus nor an interpretation of one. Few or none of its meanings have the single, uniform meanings which such a view suggests. Even simple conjunctions, such as 'and' or 'if', have a wealth and variety of legitimate use that should deter anyone from identifying them with the connectives of the propositional calculus. Unlike the symbols of a calculus, the words of a natural language differ in meaning or in reference according to the context or the tone of voice in which they are uttered. Sentences of invariant meaning are what figure as premises and conclusions of proofs in a formalized language, but it is statements – not sentences, but assertions of them – that are the premises and conclusions of arguments in ordinary speech. Nor would these *de jure* theorists be satisfied by a more carefully developed version of the formal theory, which held that a formalized language could be constructed that has a meaningful symbol to correspond to every word-use, not merely to every word, and a meaningful formula to correspond to every statement, not merely to every sentence. They have a radical objection against any attempt whatever to equate a natural language with a formalized one. Such an attempt, they say, necessarily assumes that we use language meaningfully only when we make statements that can be assigned a truth-value. But we can do an infinite variety of other jobs with language besides making statements. We can ask, thank, greet, curse, promise or pray, as well as state. Hence discourse about meaning must often go beyond the limited range of subject-matter to which the theory of formalized languages seems to be confined.

The rules of language are therefore conceived of much more loosely. They are compared with the rules of games or dances, or with precepts for the use of tools, rather than with laws of logic, and considered too heterogeneous to be formulated in anything but a very piecemeal fashion. The use of a word is given when its verbal and non-verbal contexts of correct utterance are given, so that its meaning comes to depend on certain relations of combinability with other words and of appropriateness to circumstances. (It is unfortunate that a few leading advocates of the theory, which talks so much about these relations, have chosen the term 'relational' to describe some other theories of meaning, such as Carnap's, to which they particularly object.)[1] Of course, emphasis is often placed more on the concept of use than on that of rule. To talk about the uses of words rather than about their meanings directs attention to their variety of function and removes the dangerous temptation to confuse meaning with naming or saying with stating. Occasionally the concept of rule is so little stressed that the rules of language are regarded merely as regularities, and this view then collapses into a *de facto* theory – the meaning of a word is found in the verbal and non-verbal circumstances of its use. But for certain purposes at least it is still thought important to maintain a *de jure* theory, however varied and flexible are the rules in question. If all statements that are true independently of experience have their truth rooted in language, their truth must be determined by principles of meaning that cannot be experiential facts and must therefore be regarded as rules of language controlling what is sayable and the validity of inferences from what is said. Philosophers refusing to believe in the existence of synthetic *a priori* truths have often claimed, like Wittgenstein in 1933, that ' "The colours green and blue can't be in the same place simultaneously" . . . is a grammatical rule and states a logical impossibility.'[2] In this informal sense of 'logical' the view is still widely held that, as Gilbert Ryle puts it, 'to know what an expression means involves knowing what can (logically) be said with it and what cannot (logically) be said with it. It involves knowing a set of bans, fiats and obligations, or, in a word, it is to know the rules of the employment of that expression.'[3] 'It is . . . trivially obvious', we are told, 'that a language has rules, rules governing the use of words, the construction of sentences, and so on. . . . The notion of a language without rules can . . . be said to be a contradiction in terms.'[4]

Those who hold these various theories of meaning mostly believe

[1] E.g. G. Ryle, review of R. Carnap's *Meaning and Necessity*, *Philosophy*, xxiv (1949), p. 76, and J. L. Evans, 'On Meaning and Verification', *Mind*, lxii (1953), pp. 4 ff.

[2] *The Blue and Brown Books*, ed. R. Rhees (1958), p. 56. Cf. *Philosophical Investigations* (1953), p. 80.

[3] 'The Theory of Meaning', *British Philosophy in Mid-century*, ed. C. A. Mace (1957), p. 254. Cf. also R. Rhees, 'Can there be a private language ', *Proc. Arist. Soc.*, Supp. Vol. xxviii (1954), pp. 77 ff.

[4] H. Hervey, 'The Private Language Problem', *Philosophical Quarterly*, vii (1957), p. 63. Cf. W. Kneale, *Probability and Induction* (1949), pp. 34 ff.

that their own particular theory, whether it be a *de jure* or a *de facto* one, accounts equally well for meanings in a language, meanings of utterances, and any other such ways in which the word 'meaning' is used. It will be argued in this and the following four chapters, however, that outside certain special contexts temporal semantics demands a *de facto* theory and excludes a *de jure* one, while timeless semantics excludes a *de facto* theory and demands a *de jure* one, though not nowadays a *de jure* theory of either kind so far described. A rules-of-use theory turns out to apply only in certain technical and educational contexts, and in connection with the older, pre-Herder way of conceiving meanings; and some important contexts emerge in which to ask for the meaning of a word is not to ask in any way at all for its use – neither for a rule of use nor for a regularity of use. The present chapter contributes to this thesis by arguing that from the temporal point of view of a lexicographer, grammarian or historian of ideas there are no rules of word-use whatever, but meanings are to be conceived as facts of certain kinds.

§6. The implications of changeability

Few philosophers would think it worth while to discuss the concept of a material particle without any regard for the ways in which physical scientists have sought to use that concept. Physicists presumably use it more often, more carefully and more knowledgeably than anyone else, and it is therefore their use of it which must be the starting-point for any reflective investigation of the concept. But though lexicographers, grammarians and historians of ideas presumably use the concept of meaning at least as often, carefully and knowledgeably as anyone else, modern philosophers propounding a theory of meaning have rarely paid any explicit attention to their use of it. W. V. Quine is perhaps the only exception among philosophers of first rank.[1] One would need to search very hard in the published works of Frege, Russell, Moore, Schlick, Wittgenstein, Carnap and Ryle for any display of knowledgeable interest in the methodology of linguistics, despite their frequent concern with problems about meaning. No doubt the explanation of this neglect is in some cases that the striking development of formal logic in the past century has made puzzles in or about logic the major

[1] From a *Logical Point of View* (1953), ch. iii; *Word and Object* (1960), ch. i, ii and iii.

starting-point of interest in the problem of meaning, and in other cases philosophers have come to the problem through traditional epistemology and its concern for the criteria of empirical truth, the legitimacy of metaphysics, and the possibility of communication with other minds. These intellectual preoccupations have generally prevented them from seeing the problem of meaning as at least in part a problem in the philosophy of linguistics, much as the problem of matter is at least in part a problem in the philosophy of physics. But when any general theory of meaning is to be proposed, as most philosophers have wanted, one can hardly afford to neglect altogether the innumerable expert operations with the concept of meaning in which lexicographers, grammarians and historians of ideas engage. It may be that these operations are not always quite the same as those with which logicians or epistemologists are concerned. But the similarities and differences will at least need pointing out.

If there were an agreed theory of meaning among linguists, the philosopher's task here would probably be very easy. But as in all fields of intellectual study that are active and alive, the experts disagree as much as philosophers in their reflective accounts of the concepts with which they operate. Some tell us that speech is a triangular relation, others a quadrilateral one.[1] Some treat language as 'an endeavour to represent materially what is essentially immaterial', others as just that whole mode of vocal reaction to physiologically detectable stimuli which is the common habit of a human community.[2] Hence if we wish for uniform guidance at all, we must attend to their statements with these concepts rather than to their statements about them and not so much to the actual terms in which the statements are cast as to what is gained or lost for the subject by so casting them.

It has already been shown what would be lost for linguistics and the history of ideas if meanings were conceived from their point of view to be timeless and unchanging rather than temporal and mutable. So a *de jure* theory of meaning that seeks to represent this temporal point of view must claim not merely that talk about meanings should be construed as talk about rules of word-use but also that all such rules are

---

[1] E.g. C. K. Ogden and I. A. Richards, *The Meaning of Meaning*, p. 10, and A. H. Gardiner, *The Theory of Speech and Language* (1932), p. 62.

[2] E.g. L. H. Gray, *The Foundations of Language* (1939), p. 15, and L. Bloomfield, *Language* (1935), pp. 23 ff.

MEANING IN A LANGUAGE

changeable, like the rules of children's games or English law, rather than unchanging, as the laws of logic and arithmetic are sometimes supposed to be by those who seek to improve their knowledge of them. Yet if an activity is thought to be governed by rules, any change in it is *prima facie* evidence that a rule has been broken, unless a new rule authorizing the new operation has been explicitly set up or the new operation has already become sufficiently widespread for one to claim with reason that a new rule has become implicit in practice. This must be as true of word-use as of children's games or English law. If a *de jure* theory is right for temporal semantics we should certainly expect lexicographers or historians to hesitate about how to classify the first occurrence of an old word in a new use for which no explicit stipulation has been made. We should expect them to ponder at least a moment whether they should regard it as constituting a breach of an old rule or obedience to a new one, just as do other historians of rules. What will legal historians say of the current tendency for a constituency party to try and control how its member speaks and votes in the House of Commons: that it breaks an old customary rule of the constitution or that it starts a new one? There is a history of English crime, successful and unsuccessful, as well as of English law. Both before and after the famous feat of the Rugby schoolboy who is now taken by common repute to have originated the game of rugger, many other players have handled the ball at soccer, and most of them would still be thought, even by rugger enthusiasts, to have deserved penalization for so doing.

This issue does not, however, arise within the standard forms of temporal semantics. The Oxford *New English Dictionary* takes the first use, about 1400, of the word 'bead' in which it apparently refers to 'a small perforated body . . . used as an ornament' simply to mark the beginning of a new stage in the evolution of that word's meaning. If a historian is tracing the way in which the concept of Christendom developed into the concept of western civilization, he would record the earliest known uses in this sense of the French word 'civilisation' and of the corresponding English one, in 1766 and 1772, respectively, as landmarks in that development. Since it never occurs to them to treat such uses as breaking an old rule, there is no reason to suppose either that they treat them as following a new one. To treat them thus would be to try to combine a normative with a historical view of language,

31

and to risk old prejudices rising again to block the path of dialect-studies. The only safe way is simply to describe linguistic phenomena as they occur, with due regard to their frequency and distribution. *De jure* theories of temporal semantics therefore ascribe to that mode of discourse a pattern of conception which is quite alien to it. As soon as one contrasts the lexicographer's concept of semantic change with the way in which people conceive of changes in a game like football, one can see how, at least in respect of its *de jure* character, the Wittgensteinian analogy between a language and a game or system of games is just as misleading as the analogy favoured by many formal logicians between a language and an interpreted calculus. Not that the word 'rule' never occurs in connection with word-use in the professional writings of modern descriptive and historical linguists. It does in fact occur occasionally, even today.[1] But the term is generally otiose or misleading in such contexts – a mere synonym for 'regularity' or 'uniformity'. Whatever the actual words they use, modern lexicographers and grammarians have long since learned to profit by conducting their researches and promulgating their conclusions in a way that would be barred to them if they still took the old rules-of-use model seriously.

Perhaps *de jure* theorists will object that a historian or lexicographer must hesitate at least as to whether a new word-use is a genuine instance of meaning-change, or merely some uneducated person's malapropism. 'Moreover,' they might continue, 'a malapropism is certainly regarded as a mistake in speech; if it is a mistake it is presumably a breach of some rule; and what rule can this be but a rule of word-use? What are grammatical solecisms but breaches of the rules of grammar?'

It may well be of interest to learn whether the first occurrence of a word in a new meaning or new construction resulted from the speaker's lack of education, from a deliberately thought-out plan to change the language, or from some other cause. But the genuineness of a meaning-change for a historian, lexicographer or grammarian is entirely a matter of whether it in fact occurred, not of why it occurred, so long as its occurrence was not wholly accidental as in the case of a slip of the tongue. Snobs and stylists may condemn a new usage as slang, jargon, vulgar, affected or provincial. But nowadays it is nevertheless taken to deserve a paragraph of its own in an appropriately comprehensive

[1] E.g. T. Johannison, 'On the *Be* and *Have* Constructions with Mutative Verbs', *Studia Linguistica*, xii (1958), p. 108.

dictionary. No doubt a single isolated malapropism would never be recorded as a meaning-change in the dictionary of a living language; but no more would a deliberately contrived innovation that only occurred once. A word-use must be known to have achieved some measure of currency before it is taken to be worth recording, unless the texts or surveys affording evidence of usage are, as in the case of a dead language, considerably more scanty than lexicographers would prefer. Otherwise anyone could fill the next edition of the Oxford *New English Dictionary* with as many of his own creations as he liked.

When we do describe someone as showing in his speech a mistake about the meaning of a word in a language there are at least five different things we might be saying without committing ourselves to any theory that the philologist or historian conceives meanings as rules of word-use.

First, the mistake alleged might be an error of understanding. The speaker might have made a mistake about a language-word's meaning in paraphrasing or translating someone else's utterance, or he might have shown by the inferences he has drawn from the utterance that he does not understand some concept in it. But this kind of blunder is not an error in initiating utterance. If it constitutes a breach of any general rules at all, such rules cannot be the rules of word-use that some philosophers imply to be the object of linguistic researches – rules permitting or forbidding us to use this word in one situation or context and that word in another. They must instead be rules for paraphrasing the word in its own language or for translating it into another or for arguing from a statement in which the concept occurs. To know the meaning of a word in this sense is to know how to paraphrase or translate it or argue about the truth of statements in which it occurs, not to know how to use it. People often have the former knowledge without the latter.

Secondly, the mistake might be a lapse in linguistic taste or conceptual wisdom, and in §12 I shall discuss in some detail the conception of meaning appropriate to modern treatises on good style or on worthwhile ways of thinking. Here it will suffice to point out how Fowler's *Modern English Usage* and the *Concise Oxford Dictionary* were written with obviously different aims in view, even though they had an author in common. The evaluative approach is as pervasive and characteristic in the former as it is rare and superfluous in the latter, which is based on a larger work that declares itself on its title-page to be constructed 'on historical principles'. A modern lexicographer's task, as he himself conceives it, is to record all usages in his field of study and to suspend judgement on their stylistic merits or demerits. Hence to admit that stylistic mistakes occur is not to commit oneself to a *de jure* theory of lexicographical semantics.

Thirdly, the mistake might be a breach of some legal principle, or of some explicit undertaking or agreement, that in certain contexts certain words should be used in certain ways only. But an international convention for talk-down procedures at airfields, or the rule Newton imposed on himself for using the term 'mass' is not a rule of English, French or Latin. It may have a considerable effect on the meanings of certain words that lexicographers record for a given period of those languages, and in appropriate contexts questions about meaning may be directly concerned to elicit the content of such a rule. But to suppose therefore that all, or nearly all, meanings are constituted by rules of word-use would be to argue invalidly from a very small part to a very large whole. One danger of distinguishing between 'natural' and 'conventional' words, as philosophers sometimes do[1] – between words like 'cuckoo' and words like 'eagle', respectively – is that it can encourage belief in the existence of a very wide implicit linguistic convention alongside such partial, explicit conventions. We may well wonder what sense it makes to think of a convention as having been arranged without any of these so-called conventional words' being used at all in the course of arranging it. But in any case, when the distinction made is instead between onomatopoeic words and non-onomatopoeic ones – between one kind of means to an end and another – a conventionalist theory of language is rendered as pointless as utilitarianism rendered social contract theories of democracy.

Fourthly, the mistake alleged might be an error about the means to a desired end. Anyone who tried to irrigate his garden with sea-water might well be said to have made such a silly mistake, and if Mrs Malaprop wanted to communicate her esteem for an arrangement of epithets she might similarly be said to have made a silly mistake about the means of communication if she spoke of a nice derangement of epitaphs. But to criticize an action as being the product of factual ignorance or carelessness about the means to a desired end is not the same as criticizing it

[1] E.g. L. S. Stebbing, *A Modern Introduction to Logic* (7th ed., 1950), pp. 11 ff.

for the breach of a rule. Similarly, if a man is unable to speak the same language as his neighbours do, what constrains him to try is not so much a feeling of social pressure to conform to rules, as in some etiquette of speech or action, but rather the need to communicate successfully. It is not so much that the neighbours will resent his eccentricity, as footballers resent an offside kick, but rather that he will fail to achieve his own purposes.

Finally, if the person said to have committed a 'mistake' were a child, an ill-educated adult or a foreigner, he might be accused of breaking certain rules of word-use. From any factual statement about the means to a certain end a rule can be derived that instructs those desirous of this end how to obtain it, and from a general statement about the function of a word in achieving the purposes of human communication we can derive a simple rule for using that word, breach of which could be termed a mistake. Similarly, schematic and over-simplified instructions about grammar can usefully be given by a language-teacher to his pupils during the elementary stages of their education. 'Every English sentence', a teacher may say, 'must have both a subject and a predicate', and every pupil would then be faulted who broke this rule in his daily essay. Yet nobody is held to speak a country's language like an adult native unless he has got beyond the stock idioms and rigid syntax of the schoolroom and phrase-book. An important part of what people call 'getting the feel of' a language is acquiring the ability to adapt it intelligibly to their constantly changing needs and circumstances instead of merely to the paradigm problems of educational exercises and examinations. It is more like driving an all-purpose jeep than a saloon that has to stay on the roads, more like coming on to a board of directors than like learning the routine job of an employee, more like the creative art of architecture than like the standardized technique of bricklaying. The good chess-player makes the most of the opportunities allowed him by the rules of chess: the native speakers of a language do not operate within any such fixed framework. If by laying down further rules a teacher could anticipate all the adaptations his pupils would later need to make, these would at least in part be rules for the future development of the language. But not even the French Academy has ever been in a position to legislate effectively along these lines; and if the rules were not so much pieces of legislation as of advice based on predictions of future development, the teacher would have to predict every new idiom or metaphor with which orators, poets, scientists, inventors, journalists, advertisement copy-writers, and even bus conductors are going to enrich the language during the pupil's lifetime, since each individual innovation opens up further horizons of linguistic expansion. And he can hardly be able to predict the whole future of a language without being able to predict the whole future of the community that speaks it. Hence the rules of word-use that language-teachers find it useful to enunciate are far too schematic and oversimplified to constitute a living language, as certain rules constitute the eightsome reel or the game of chess. They cannot embrace the potentiality of creative development that from an adult's point of view is as much a part of his native language at any one moment as its established usages. Knowing how to speak a language is neither to be identified with, nor does it necessarily include, knowing how to speak in accordance with certain permissive and prescriptive rules. Not that bilingual facility makes a man a good lexicographer any more than political skill qualifies him for appointment to a chair of political science. Knowing how, when and where to use a word is not the same as knowing what its use is. But if the rules-of-use theory does not even fit the sense in which most educated Englishmen might be said to know the meanings of about twenty thousand words, it certainly does not fit the sense in which the Oxford *New English Dictionary* tells us the meanings of about half a million. Lexicographers have abandoned normative semantics just because it does not jibe with the reality of living languages – with the phenomena of linguistic development in time.

It helps confusion here that the normative and descriptive senses of the word 'grammar', and associated words like 'sentence', 'word', 'inflection', etc., are still insufficiently distinguished. A teacher wishes not merely to teach a boy to write Latin, but to write good Latin. Hence what he refers to by phrases like 'the rules of Latin grammar' turn out on closer examination to be the rules a schoolboy must obey if he is to ape the written style of Cicero or some other author lionized by Renaissance humanists, most of which rules were probably broken innumerable times in unrecorded Roman conversations of the same period. These other usages would deserve just as much attention in a grammatical account of classical Latin that was not intended only for schoolboys and did not share with the older grammarians like Valla and

Vaugelas their confusion of normative and descriptive linguistics. Similarly, in one sense the phrase 'grammatical English' means in England the same as 'standard English' – the English of B.B.C. announcers and the London *Times*. But from a descriptive or historical point of view every dialect, Cockney no less than standard English, has its own grammar even if this grammar is not taught in elementary schools. Many *de jure* theorists seem to have carried with them from their schooldays an exclusively normative conception of grammar. 'Grammar', they tell us, 'does not allow "Tom, Dick, Harry" as a sentence.'[1] Yet in the sense of 'sentence' that many academic grammarians find convenient[2] this is a sentence, since in some circumstances, such as in checking over a list, it can stand alone as an utterance.

A *de jure* theorist might protest that the rules of word-use and sentence-construction of which he speaks are rules to be broken or bent, wherever there is a point in doing so, rather than rigidly obeyed. But in effect that is just to admit that the *de jure* theory of meanings in a language is only to be taken seriously in the schoolroom and not outside it. Perhaps many more people still speak of meanings as rules of word-use in this sense, than as anything else. If so, it is because there are more schoolboys than philologists, more people interested in learning languages than in learning about them. But it can hardly be considered an overriding merit in the rules-of-use theory that it fits best the discourse of those who are least expert in their knowledge of language. Even if the concept of meaning creates a problem in the philosophy of education, it creates a no less important one in the philosophy of linguistics, which no *de jure* theory can solve.

§7. Meanings in a language

One way of seeing what kind of a theory does apply to the concept of meaning in linguistics is to imagine in turn several increasingly complex modes of vocal behaviour in a community, until something is reached that philologists would accept as a language. In carrying out such a thought-experiment each state of affairs is to be considered as a putative model of the subject-matter for philological discussion of word-use, not as a putative model of word-use. The interest is not in

[1] P. F. Strawson, *Introduction to Logical Theory* (1952), p. 225.
[2] O. Jespersen, *The Philosophy of Grammar* (1924), p. 307.

one out of many ways of using words, but in one out of many ways of discussing word-use.

Imagine first a community whose members' repertoire of distinguishable vocal sound-patterns was sufficiently extensive for them to utter instances of each such sound-pattern only when they were in a particular kind of mental state, as evidenced by their non-vocal behaviour, or in a particular kind of situation. Then an outsider at least would have reasons for conceiving each pattern of utterance to indicate something. But he would have no reason for conceiving it to indicate anything to any member of the community unless we also suppose those within earshot of an utterance to tend to react similarly to similar sound-patterns, though these reactions may require further conditions to set them off, as when a man is warned to walk carefully if there is ice. Even if we do suppose this, the community's sound-patterns could still only be called meaningful in the same sense as the warning-cries of birds or the groans of a sick man that make us feel sympathy for his sufferings or the laughter of children that makes us cheerful. The difference between language and groans or laughter such as these is the measure of the inadequacy of a purely causal theory of meaning, i.e. a theory that pays no regard to the purposes of utterance.

Nevertheless a causal theory may be quite adequate for some non-philological concerns with meaning. In particular, it is all that is required by a psychologist investigating the processes of language-learning in early infancy. Such an experimenter wants to know two main things. What makes the infant begin to produce an appropriate response to human speech, and what makes it begin to mouth words appropriate to a given situation? He might well put these two questions in the form: what makes an infant begin to apprehend the meaning of speech, and what makes it begin to vocalize meaningfully? But since the only evidence for the infant's apprehension of meaning is appropriateness of response, the meaning of a vocal sound for its hearer can conveniently be conceived by the experimenter as its causal property of generating such-or-such responses. Similarly, since the only evidence for the meaningfulness of the infant's vocalization is the appropriateness of this sound to its circumstances, the meaning of a vocal sound for its speaker can conveniently be conceived as a causal property of these circumstances, viz. their power to generate the utterance. In either case to call the infant's behaviour appropriate is merely to say that it accords with a certain causal generalization defining the meaning to be learned. Psychologists themselves must settle how far such a generalization describes a conditioned reflex, a reinforced echo, or some other process. But some kind of causal theory is clearly all that is needed by them, or by those interested in the closely connected problem of how to begin teaching a language to deaf and dumb children. Nor is this fact, like the existence of conditioned reflexes, a psychological discovery. It is merely a consequence of the way in which the problem is most conveniently conceived.

Unfortunately a few psychologists and philosophers have not been content with this. They have assumed that the phenomenon of speech can only be conceived in one way, and that a terminology suited to the semantics of experiments in early language-learning must also be suited to all other kinds of discourse about meaning. But the meanings of infant-talk, so conceived, are for the most part too jejune and imprecise to interest linguists. Nor does a dictionary or phrase-book list two meanings for every entry, one a meaning for the speaker and the other a meaning for the hearer. Indeed in adult life, if a speaker does not believe what he says, or a hearer what he hears, the speech is not thereby deprived of its meaning either for the speaker or for the hearer. Hence the most obvious fault with the situations so far considered is the absence of any assumed desire on the vocalist's side for those reactions to the sound-patterns uttered that he believes to be normal in his community. He cannot be said to be giving orders, conveying information, communicating gratitude, or seeking to achieve any other purpose in his utterances, because he has not been ascribed any beliefs about their effects. The nearest that adult speakers ever seem to approach his mode of utterance is in involuntary exclamations. Imagine therefore that normally when anyone gives tongue in our imaginary community he is not only in a characteristic situation or state of mind, as already postulated, but also has correct beliefs about a hearer's normal reaction to the particular sound-pattern he is producing and desires that reaction more than anything else he believes the utterance to effect independently of it, though each utterance is still completely self-contained and has no regular effect on the hearer's reaction to preceding and following utterances. There is then good reason to say that he is vociferating in order to give instructions, convey information, etc., and to conceive the meaning of each sound-pattern as the normal purpose for which it is uttered. Moreover the normal purpose of a particular sound-pattern's utterance in the community cannot normally fail to be achieved by the utterance, unless a man normally expects others to react differently to its utterance from the way in which he himself reacts. Hence one can speak indifferently of the normal purposes for which the sound-pattern is uttered, or of the purposes normally achieved by its utterance.

Since one must thus distinguish between the conditions under which a causal, and the conditions under which a purposive, theory is applicable, the 'symbolic-emotive' dichotomy once popular in discussions about the problem of meaning[1] was not altogether without its point. It was as useful for distinguishing different kinds of discourse about meaning as it was misleading if taken to distinguish the different kinds of meaning a single utterance could have. The dichotomy is valid if taken to point to the different concepts of meaning required for the consideration of purposive utterance, on the one hand, and non-purposive utterance, on the other. It is invalid if taken not as a classification of semantic statements, but rather as itself a semantic statement of a very sweeping character, drawing attention to what it alleges to be the two main kinds of word-use. For sentences are not only uttered in order to convey information and express or evoke feelings, but also in order to seek information, procure obedience, communicate gratitude, convey greetings, and to achieve a wide variety of other purposes. Supporters of the dichotomy generally required to have it interpreted in this latter, invalid sense in order that it should have the philosophical punch they sought from it, as in the so-called 'emotive' theory of moral judgements. Yet they needed to have it interpreted in the other sense if the dichotomy itself were to be defensible, and in that sense one would not be able to ascribe an emotive element to any kind of utterance without implying that its presence there was involuntary or unintentional. Exclamations of moral horror, such as sometimes are still raised by atrocity stories, could be ascribed emotive meaning, but not the prosy ethics of newspaper editorials.

More specifically, if moral judgements could be shown to attribute neither natural nor non-natural properties, it only followed that they must be emotive if all meaning must be either symbolic or emotive.

[1] E.g. C. K. Ogden and I. A. Richards, *The Meaning of Meaning*, pp. 123 ff., and R. Robinson, H. J. Paton and R. C. Cross, 'The Emotive Theory of Ethics', *Proc. Arist. Soc.*, Supp Vol., xxii (1948), pp. 79 ff.

But no dichotomy is necessarily exhaustive unless its terms are mutually contradictory, and 'symbolic' and 'emotive' are mutually contradictory in a relevant sense only if interpreted as equivalent to 'purposed' and 'non-purposed', respectively. Hence, since at least some moralizing sentences, if not most of them, are obviously the normal vehicles of important purposes rather than of involuntary exclamation, the emotive theory of moral judgement was in fact faced with a dilemma which neither its supporters nor its critics always appreciated. If the symbolic-emotive dichotomy was accepted in the higher-level sense in which it was a true statement about semantics, it could not clinch the main argument that moral judgements were characteristically emotive, while in the lower-level sense in which it could clinch this, it was itself merely a piece of unacceptably oversimplified semantics. Unfortunately the confusion between these two senses, which enabled the theory to become a topic of serious discussion, was made easier by a loose ambiguity in the term 'emotive', by a convenient shift, when helpful, from 'symbolic' to 'descriptive' or 'cognitive' as the other term in the dichotomy, and by an echo of the old tripartite division of mental faculties into emotion, conation and cognition.

Returning now to our series of models for the subject-matter of philological discourse we can see that the system to which a purely purposive theory of meaning would apply need not be devoid of philological interest. An investigator might classify its different sound-patterns as uttering reports, predictions, commands, questions, exclamations, and so on. Conceivably, it might even have different sounds to execute the normal purposes with which a man might say, 'It will rain shortly', 'I believe it will rain shortly', and 'I want you to think I believe it will rain shortly'. But it could not articulate any form of reasoning, any definition of one concept in terms of others, or any assertion that a particular sound-pattern is meaningful or meaningless in the same system or another. Any such explicit tracing of connections between the significance of one sound-pattern and the significance of another would be excluded by the fact that each utterance is still completely self-contained and the order of sound-patterns uttered by a person corresponds merely with the order in which he aims to achieve his several purposes therewith. To talk about meanings or truth-values a man would need certain sound-patterns that are supplementary of their context, so as to be able to make statements like 'The sound-pattern just uttered is to be understood self-referentially and is the topic of the sound-pattern I shall utter next.' Suppose now that the system included some sounds which would thus help to indicate the purposes for which certain other sounds preceding or following them in an utterance were being used. A purely purposive theory would no longer fit the meaning of all sound-patterns. But it would still fit all stock strings of sound-patterns, much as in discussions of linguistic meaning it fits all stock strings of sentences besides fitting all completely self-contained stock sentences such as are commonly listed in phrase-books.

In this system everything could be said that can be said in a language. Yet there is still a very good reason why such a mode of communication should not itself be called a 'language' in the same sense as English or Chinese are so called. Investigators of it would need to compile a dictionary, but not a grammar. Only a few sound-patterns would need to be treated as supplementary of their contexts, whereas every language-word must be so treated. Every word can occur as a component of an utterance of which the meaning as a whole depends as much on the order in which the component words occur as on what, if anything, these words would signify if uttered in isolation from one another. 'The dog bit the cat' does not mean the same as 'The cat bit the dog'. Linguistics cannot do without such distinctions as those between paratactic and syntactic constructions, between isolating, agglutinative, polysynthetic and inflecting languages, between those with semantically important pitch-schemes and those without, between words like 'run' and lexical units like 'running', or between morphemes that can conveniently be called 'words', regarded as the components of 'sentences', and listed in dictionaries, and morphemes that are better catalogued in tables of inflections.

The root of the matter is presumably practical economy. If a mode of communication has to introduce a new element into its repertoire of significant sound-patterns each time a language-speaker would merely utter a new combination of familiar morphemes, it requires a degree of intellectual and muscular effort out of all proportion to its utility. Not only would it often be extremely difficult to introduce the new sound-pattern into the community's repertoire. Not only would the point of making a remark disappear long before it could be understood. But an educated individual might have to face the task of learning to vocalize a number of sound-patterns equal, say, to the number of non-equivalent statements, commands, promises, etc., containing some four dozen words or less that can be constructed from the five-thousand odd words of commonest use in mid-twentieth-century English. If a race of creatures using such a mode of communication were ever found any-where in the universe one would not expect much trouble in persuading them to use a language instead, once they had grasped the essential features in which it differed from their own mode of communication. Certainly some languages have inconveniently complicated grammati-cal structures. But the schoolboy who longs for a language without any grammar at all does not appreciate how much more difficult he would find it to learn.

In short a purely causal or a purely purposive theory of meaning fits statements about the meaning of stock sentences, or stock strings of sentences, that normally constitute self-contained utterances, and it also fits statements about the meanings of other self-contained sentences if it be construed as claiming that these statements concern what would be the normal causes, effects or purposes of uttering such sentences, were utterance of them more common. It is true that the purposes, or causes and effects, of uttering such sentences as 'Stop!', 'Fire!', or 'Where is the nearest hotel?' are for the most part conveyed to foreigners by mentioning words or sentences in their own language that are normally uttered alone with the same purpose or with the same causes and effects. Conversational phrase-books generally appear as a list of linguistic equations, without any explicit use of the word 'purpose' or 'cause' in asserting these equations. But whenever such exact equivalences are not to be found the statements then made about the meanings of solitary words and sentences are cast in a form that makes apparent the underlying conception in terms of purpose or cause. Such-and-such a formula, we may be told by students of some culture remote from our own, is used to placate the rain deity, or such-and-such a shout occurs at the culmination of a war-dance. Even the meaning of the English sentence 'Upon my soul!' is more accurately conveyed by saying that it is a mild expletive, than by attempting to find equivalents in English or some other language.

But neither a purely causal nor a purely purposive theory fits any statement about the meaning of an individual word that is not exclu-sively concerned with the word's meaning when uttered in isolation. In particular neither theory applies to the equivalences asserted where possible by lexicographers. Instead the meaning of a word or common phrase as dictionaries conceive it is the part it plays in achieving the normal purposes of the serial arrays of words in which it occurs. Its meaning is the function or functions it performs in the utterances of those who speak the language to which it belongs.

This is apparent not only from the comparison of language with the various model systems of communication already examined, but also from the ways in which one needs to individuate purposes, causes and effects in discourse about words and sentences. The sentence 'Come here!' has one characteristic or primary purpose, not two. It is normally uttered to get the addressee to come to the speaker. Its utterance may have other, secondary purposes, such as to facilitate further communication with the person addressed. But when such a multiplicity of purposes is apparent this multiplicity is a contingent feature of the speaker's state of mind and is not conceived to depend on the number of words he uses. The further purposes are ends that can be described independently of the meaning of the utterance inasmuch as one can know the meaning of the utterance, through one's knowledge of the language, without knowing these further purposes, while to know the characteristic purpose of the utterance it is quite sufficient to know its meaning. Similarly a man who exclaims 'God bless my soul!' is taken to have been astonished once, not four times, nor is a hearer's awareness of this astonishment taken to imply that the exclamation has had a characteristic set of four distinguishable effects. Hence we should not conceive discourse about the meaning of a word to be concerned with the normal purposes, causes or effects of its use. When used in conjunction with other words, the word does not constitute in itself the means to some characteristic purpose of speech but only one factor among others contributory to such a purpose. Even when the word is used by itself in a one-word sentence this is generally still true, since to constitute one kind of sentence rather than another – a command, perhaps, rather than a question – it probably needs to be pronounced with a particular tone of voice or speech-rhythm or written with a particular style of punctuation.

People do sometimes talk about 'the normal purposes for which the English word "nice"', say, 'is used'. But this is generally just a loose way of talking about the normal purposes *with* which it is used, such as to convey praise of whatever the context shows to be under consideration, and then the communication purposed is accomplished by the whole remark, not just by one word in it. When someone says 'That is a nicely planned garden' he would not be construed therefrom as having said one word of praise and five of something else: to echo his praise is to echo the whole remark, not just one word in it. The meaning of any one word is its function in a whole sentence.

Such a function is most conveniently described by mentioning a word or phrase in another language, or another word or phrase in the same language, that performs more or less the same function, and a lexicographer needs great ingenuity and perceptiveness to choose words or phrases that will enable him to achieve an appropriate combination of brevity and precision in doing this. But the similarity of such a procedure to the listing of equivalences for 'Stop!', 'Fire!', 'Help!' and other solitary word-uses should not be taken to imply that the meaning is being conceived in the same way. That the underlying conception is now different becomes clear in two ways. First, most dictionaries need to state the kind of syntactical function or functions that each word performs. The Oxford *New English Dictionary* reports, in the case of each word it lists, whether it is a noun, verb, adjective or one of the other traditionally distinguished parts of speech. No such grammatical information is required from a conversational phrase-book's list of solitary word-uses because each of these is already a complete sentence in itself. Secondly, even when a language, like classical Chinese,[1] is such that it is not altogether obvious whether any forms can usefully be classified according to regular syntactical functions, the *de facto* functional character of lexicographical discourse often emerges clearly when the lexicographer finds it insufficient to list partially equivalent speech-forms in the same or another language. The meaning in question may then be indicated by the mention of stock sentences, or the quotation of actual remarks, in which the form occurs, together with equivalent whole sentences in the same or another language if necessary. The word's or morpheme's meaning is not shown by the description of ends that its use achieves or of occasions that evoke its exclamation, as a purely purposive or purely causal theory would suggest, but by indicating what it contributes to the meaning of those whole utterances

[1] Cf. J. R. Ware, 'Grammar, Chinese', *Studies and Essays in the History of Science and Learning offered in Homage to George Sarton*, ed. M. F. Ashley Montagu (1944), pp. 49 ff.

in which it occurs. Even descriptive definitions like ' "Duck-bill" denotes a furred mammal which has a duck-like bill and feet and lays eggs' force one to a functional theory of lexicographical semantics. If a word is said to denote something it can normally occur in various sentences along with other words that say different things about what it denotes. If it could only be uttered by itself, as in 'Duck-bill!', one might say that it signified the presence of a furred mammal with duck-like bill, but there would be no point in saying that it denoted such a mammal.

When pointed out, the difference between the semantics of individual words and the semantics of one-word sentences may seem obvious. Yet it is easy to neglect, and its neglect easily leads philosophers far astray. Perhaps the most potent temptation to neglect it lies in the feeling that when we first teach a child to speak, we are teaching it words like 'car' or 'drink'. But what in fact we are teaching it are one-word sentences with meanings like 'There's a car' or 'Give me a drink'. It is only much later, when the child has built up a considerable repertoire of somewhat longer stock sentences and begins to be able to construct new sentences on its own, that we have ground for saying that it has learned some words. If a philosopher makes the mistake of supposing that a child learns words from the start, it becomes natural for him to take this initial process of instruction as a paradigm for all teaching of word-meanings. The meaning of a word thus becomes fixed in his thought as something that must be pointed out for one to learn it, and he is always on the look-out for objective correlates to set against the expressions he finds in everyday use. A gate is opened for the confusions and over-simplifications so well exposed by Wittgenstein in his *Philosophical Investigations*. Similarly some psychologists have encouraged an over-simplified causal theory of meaning by concentrating their attention on the processes by which an infant first learns to utter and understand one-word sentences while neglecting the processes of analysis and synthesis by which it learns to construe the many-worded sentences of others and to compose its own.[1] But to avoid these confusions one does not need a *de jure* theory of meaning. It is quite sufficient, and more correct, to emphasize that the meaning of a word in a language should be conceived as the function or functions it performs, as a matter of fact, in the

[1] Cf. N. Chomsky's review of B. F. Skinner, *Verbal Behaviour* (1957), in *Language*, xxxv (1959), pp. 26 ff.

sentences of that language. The one-word sentences of the nursery, with their indicatable correlates, are a primitive stage of speech that is surmounted when and only when the child learns to compose his own sentences and to let words perform a wide variety of functions in these sentences.

To say that sentences themselves never have functions, however, would be like saying, as Ryle has done,[1] that though we can ask whether a person knows how to use a certain word, we cannot ask whether he knows how to use a certain sentence; and this is only partially true. If 'know how to use' means 'know how to operate as one component factor along with others in achieving a human purpose' it is clear that a man may be ascribed knowledge how to use not only a word but also a sentence, when the sentence is a spell, slogan, equation or some other formula that has come to play a determinate part in a particular form of human activity, or a stock sentence like 'Here is the weather forecast for tonight and tomorrow', that is rarely used in isolation from other sentences. Thus functions are sometimes attributed to sentences, though such an attribution is an occasional and contingent feature of discourse about sentences while it is a universal and necessary feature of the way in which lexicographers normally discuss word-meaning. The purpose one knows how to use a given sentence in achieving is normally just one particular kind of purpose whether it be of magic, of political propaganda, of engineering, or of broadcasting, while knowing how to use a word is knowing how to use it in a wide variety of sentences appropriate to many different purposes.

Before examining this important conception of word-function further, and showing how it links together the verbal and conceptual planes of semantic discourse, it will be useful to consider two possible objections to what has been said so far.

First, someone may object that the theory advanced is neutral in regard to long-standing controversies in the philosophy of mind. 'Despite its claim', he may say, 'that temporal semantics is often concerned with the role of words in achieving purposes and expressing or promoting states of mind, the theory never penetrates more deeply into the analysis of these mental concepts. It neither accepts a behaviourist account of purposes like E. C. Tolman's nor a non-behaviourist account

[1] 'Ordinary Language', *Philosophical Review*, lxii (1953), p. 178.

of intentions like G. E. M. Anscombe's. It takes no side in the recurrent tournaments of those who fight under the banners of "psycho-physical parallelism", "materialism", "idealism", "interactionism" and other metaphysical doctrines.'

But it does not need to do so. Victory in these tournaments may be important for those interested in supporting or attacking certain religious doctrines, like those of purgatory or transmigration, or psychological hypotheses of certain kinds, like some of those favoured by Freud, Jung or Watson. It is not important for lexicographers or grammarians. In practice many of the latter have been attracted by various philosophies of mind. But their work gains nothing, and loses a great deal, if they allow such an attraction to colour their professional discourse and affect what their theories imply. An academic lexicographer or grammarian does not need to declare his own allegiance in the philosophy of mind through each statement he makes about the meaning of a word, phrase or sentence. He hardly wants every such statement to seem a philosophical blunder to readers of an opposite allegiance and thus to expose himself gratuitously to adverse criticism. He is probably open to enough criticism already, irrespective of philosophy, for the factual claims he makes about meanings. A theory about how lexicographers and grammarians, as such, conceive meaning, or should conceive it, does well to be neutral in regard to competing accounts of the relations which hold, or should hold, between our concepts of mental events and attributes and our concepts of physical ones. It cannot justify rejecting a behaviourist account, as Popper seems to suppose that it can,[1] nor can it justify accepting one.

The underlying reason for this is that while we do not use motor-cars in describing the purposes for which motor-cars, say, are used we must use words in describing the causes, effects or purposes of uttering words. Indeed, the more accurately we describe the normal cause, effect or purpose of uttering a particular sentence the more closely do we reproduce its meaning in our own words. If we can we simply mention another sentence that has precisely the same causes, effects and purposes. 'Charles est chez lui', we say, means the same as 'Charles is at home.' When we have to describe the sentence's causes, effects or purposes in a roundabout way – 'They utter this in order to placate the

---

[1] 'Language and the Body-Mind problem', *Proc. XI Int. Cong. Phil.* (1953), vol. VII, pp. 101 ff.

rain-deity'– because we know of no familiar equivalent, it seems a poor second-best: the sentence's vital spark has been put out. Of course, we must be careful to distinguish what people cannot but achieve in uttering a sentence from what they normally seek to achieve as a result of uttering it. Anyone who utters the sentence 'Charles est chez lui', except in some special game or code, does so with the purpose, in a sense, of stating that a person called Charles is at home. But this is a wholly immanent purpose. It is achieved, and cannot but be achieved, in the very act of utterance. Hence to describe this purpose, though it seems like giving the sentence's meaning, is not to elucidate the utterance-type by placing it in its context. To do that we must describe what the normal purpose of (further end achieved by) stating such a thing would be, viz. to convey the information to someone else, not-withstanding that the same thing might often be said instead or as well with some special purpose, such as to remind, warn, cheer, rebuke, advise, invite, etc. But, since the concept of stating is far too familiar a one for it to require this kind of elucidation very often, the sentence's meaning will for the most part be described quite adequately by the mention of an equivalent sentence without any explicit description of the further end for which such sentences are normally used.

Accordingly in the actual discourse of lexicographers and gram-marians 'purpose' and other concepts of mental life are largely im-plicit rather than explicit, and constitute the framework of discussion rather than a part of its content. A grammarian who implicitly utilizes such a concept in reporting the equivalence of two sentences no more needs to answer the questions raised about it by the body-mind prob-lem than the Londoner who goes to work in a bus needs to worry about the religion of the driver. The controversies about meaning that most affect a contemporary philologist's work do not concern relations of that concept with other concepts outside his special field, but rather its relations with other concepts inside his field, as in the still active dis-pute about whether the concept of a phoneme can be usefully defined in terms that do not involve a concept of meaning, so that the forms and structure of a language may be studied in complete independence of its meanings. If a philologist as such has nothing to gain in the simplicity, penetration and comprehensiveness of his theories by allegiance to one solution of a problem rather than another, the problem is irrelevant to his interest. He can afford to operate with a concept of purpose that is insufficiently specific to commit him either to acceptance or rejection of behaviourism.

Suppose even that there is a sense in which a word may sometimes be said to have one or more private meanings within the minds of individual persons – like associated imagery, for instance – that differ from the public meanings attested by the linguistic and non-linguistic contexts of its use. These private meanings would still do nothing to force students of language into opposition to behaviourism. They might interest a biographer, but not a lexicographer or grammarian. The latter's province is the language of a community. One must however beware against concluding that language is all right as it is just because its words have no private meanings against which public usage may be checked. For instead many extra-linguistic considerations, of a kind discussed in §§10–12 below, may turn out to be relevant to the question whether an existing usage is a good one or a bad one.

Someone might now object that there is no need to attribute to most philological semantics even an implicit concern with mental attitudes like the beliefs, desires and intentions of purposive activity, let alone to determine in this connection the precise analysis of such attitudes. 'The linguist entering on the study of a hitherto unknown language observes', it may be argued, 'the correlations or causal connections between the sounds its speakers make and the observable circumstances of these sounds. Sometimes, as with words for pain or hunger, the causally relevant circumstances will be features of the speaker's own appearance or behaviour, like grimaces or voracious feeding. But more often they will be features of his immediate environment, and in particular what Quine has called "conspicuously segregated objects",[1] such as domestic animals or pieces of fruit. To assert that a given sentence in the language investigated is equivalent in meaning to some specified sentence in the investigator's own language is to claim that a similar correlation holds in both cases. But it need not always be mental attitudes that are thus held to be connected with the utterance of sentences. Indeed, since a person's desires, intentions, feelings and other mental processes become patterned by the language that he learns to speak, it must always be viciously circular to analyse statements about meaning in terms of statements about mental phenomena.'

The threat of circularity here is unimportant. Elementary circularity,

---

[1] *From a Logical Point of View*, p. 62.

as in the English sentence 'The English expression "Thanks!" is uttered in order to convey thanks', is avoided by using a different language or different words of the same language, in describing the purpose or function concerned. Nor, if one accepts a reciprocal interdependence between word-meanings and mental phenomena, is one barred from explaining how languages are ever learned at all. Children's speech does not begin with utterances that have the fully fledged meanings of adult word-use any more than their mental life begins with the same experiences and attitudes as adults have. Instead speech and mind develop gradually and interdependently, aided by whatever primitive forms of non-linguistic conception may exist.[1]

Moreover, even if meanings were largely to be elucidated in terms of non-mental happenings, these latter would still only be conceived or described with any degree of accuracy through the means of some language. Few story-telling pictures, for instance, can avoid being vague, ambiguous or over-assertive in some respects, if they do not rely at all on quasi-linguistic customs of representing particular kinds of events in particular kinds of way. What is the difference between a picture of a man climbing up a tree and of a man climbing down? If we are given a row of pictures of a man on higher and higher branches of a tree, how are we to tell whether these pictures should be scanned from left to right or right to left? How are we to tell whether they are pictures of the same man or of different men? And how is the artist to avoid ascribing the man or the tree some characteristic that was not mentioned in the sentence to be elucidated, such as the number of the man's limbs or the tree's branches? A request that all meanings should be analysed in ways that are utterly untainted by language is doomed to disappointment.

However perhaps all that is being objected here is not that meanings may always be analysed by pointings, picturings, etc., that are utterly untainted by language, but merely that statements about meanings in a language need not be either implicitly or explicitly about mental phenomena of any kind. Certainly the mental reference of temporal semantics has often been wrongly conceived. In particular it has sometimes been thought that the meanings of sentences are mental processes

[1] Cf. F. Fearing, 'An Examination of the Conceptions of Benjamin Whorf in the Light of Theories of Perception and Cognition', *Language and Culture*, ed. H. Hoijer (1954), pp. 47 ff.

that shadow, or can shadow, them almost word for word as they are uttered. Locke held that a man's words have no meaning other than his own ideas,[1] though the abstract ideas in which Locke believed are notoriously difficult to conceive, as Berkeley pointed out. Berkeley himself thought it was their ability to suggest appropriate mental imagery that made the sentences we utter informatively meaningful,[2] though this theory condemns those congenitally incapable of such imagery to be ignorant of all meanings. It is true too that just as a child may learn its first sentence by the mother's constant repetition of 'dada' when the father appears, or by the mother's constantly repeated smile when the child's babbling approximates in sound to 'mama', so too the discovery of *prima facie* correlations between the utterance of certain sounds and the presence of certain conspicuously segregated objects is what may well set the linguist on the road to formulating his first conclusions about the sentences of a hitherto unknown language. But one should not conclude that the existence of such correlations is what these conclusions themselves claim or imply. The linguist is not seeking in the end to correlate the utterance of some sentence like 'Here is an apple' and the presence of an apple. Such an utterance is not always serious, honest and well-informed. The meaning of a sentence is not exhausted by its utterance in true affirmative statements. Whatever *prima facie* correlations the dictionary-maker takes as his starting-point, the conclusions at which he aims cannot avoid an implicit concern with mental attitudes. The meanings he seeks to identify are the functions of words in all forms of unpurposed self-expression or purposed communication, not merely in the processes by which a newly found language is first investigated.

§8. Meanings in a culture

One of the many things wrong with Wittgenstein's influential recommendation to look at words as tools[3] is that it muddies the path to understanding how lexicographers conceive of a word's meaning as a *de facto* function rather than a purpose or rule. We are told that the analogy with tools reminds us how different uses of words shade into

[1] *Essay*, III, ii, 8.
[2] *Principles of Human Knowledge*, intro., paras. 6–10, 19.
[3] E.g. *Philosophical Investigations* (1953), p. 113. Cf. Plato, *Cratylus*, 388.

each other and 'how close the connection is between doing things with words and doing them with smiles, nods, winks and gestures', as distinct from doing them with labels.[1] We are told that it reminds us to use clean tools, 'to know what we mean and what we do not'.[2] But these reminders can be achieved without the mischief created by the tool-use analogy.

The trouble with this analogy is partly that in reality words are not artifacts, to be operated in accordance with craft-rules or manufacturers' instructions, and that speech is not exactly a technique, but rather something that can itself be either technical or non-technical. By treating speech as a technique the tool-use analogy encourages a normative attitude to language, when philologists themselves have long since abandoned any such attitude in order to do justice to all social levels of speech. Similarly Plato's comparison of ruling to a technique best exercised by experts, like helmsmanship or medicine, supported reversion to a non-democratic conception of government that had long since been abandoned by the majority of his contemporaries. But this implicit myth of a universal speech-guild, with philosophers as self-appointed wardens, is not the only thing wrong with the tool-use analogy. It also blurs the difference between word-meaning and sentence-meaning by fitting the latter rather better than it fits the former, for which it was primarily intended. The sentences of a language, not the words, are like tools in being either the stock means to certain frequently desired ends or the *ad hoc* means, specially constructed, to ends that may or may not be so frequently desired. Sentences sometimes, and only sometimes, have functions in a ritual or other form of human activity, just as tools sometimes, and only sometimes, have functions in a particular tool-kit: about potato-peelers and coal-choppers no question of function normally arises to imply their use along with other tools in some combined operation. Moreover, while any single individual can in principle design or construct as wide a variety of tools and sentences, and operate with them in as wide a variety of ways as they admit of, he cannot be so easily prolific in adding new words to his language. Though an inventor often cannot in practice get others to use his new tool, their reluctance to do so does not gainsay the fact that a new tool is now in existence. But it takes considerably more than just

[1] P. H. Nowell-Smith, *Ethics* (1954), pp. 96 ff.
[2] J. L. Austin, 'A Plea for Excuses', *Proc. Arist. Soc.*, lvii (1957), p. 7.

my inventiveness and utterances, or just yours, to add a new word or a new word-meaning to English. Social inertia always has the opportunity to obstruct linguistic reform, and the tool-use analogy makes the problem of initiating language-change seem far too simple.

Wittgenstein did, of course, emphasize the social quality of language and the relevance of a word's context to its meaning; he often spoke, appropriately enough, of a word's 'function' or 'role'; he sometimes referred to its use as an institution; and he even pointed out, in the course of comparing language to games, that in some games we alter the rules as we go along.[1] But by recommending analogies like the one with tools, by saying next to nothing about changes in concepts as distinct from changes in their popularity, and by talking so often about the 'rules' of a language,[2] some of his later writings give the impression that he conceived of a word's functions as *de jure* rather than *de facto*.

If words, lexicographically conceived, are to be assigned to some category of things more comprehensive than language itself, we should classify them (not their uses) as social institutions rather than compare them to tools, though as social institutions generated more by need, like law-courts, than by demand, like luxury trades, and constituted more by habit, like the August rush to the seaside, than by rule, like law-courts. The way in which a social institution operates, like the way in which a word does, is not fully understood unless one is conscious of the ways in which it is often employed for particular purposes in combination with some institutions, and seldom or never employed in combination with others. News agencies and the press; royalty, flags and anthems; police, bench, bar and prison – are all obvious examples of common combinations: law-courts and national dances, dog shows and parliaments, of rare ones. Indeed the more one knows about the customariness or rarity of such combinations the more one also knows about which institutions are capable of deputizing for which. To know just when 'He is a brother but not a male sibling of mine' is uttered with the purpose of communicating something, is to know the extent to which 'brother' and 'male sibling' do not perform precisely the same function, and by implication the extent to which they do. Moreover, by classifying words as institutions, just as well as by the tool-use

[1] E.g. *Phil. Inv.*, pp. 8, 11, 20, 39, 73, 81, 88.
[2] E.g. *Phil. Inv.*, pp. 6, 39, 45, 47.

analogy, we emphasize the diversity and flexibility of human word-use, and especially the existence of prepositions, conjunctions, pronouns and articles as well as of nouns, verbs, adjectives and adverbs; and we thus counter the pernicious tendency to identify all of human word-use with naming or labelling. Wine festivals, hand-shakes and general elections perform very different functions in a community. Just as different meanings often shade into one another, so too do the functions of institutions, like the respective roles of embassies and legations or the preventive and detective duties of a police force. The contrast between using words technically and non-technically can be brought out by distinguishing between the specialized and non-specialized functioning of institutions – the policeman directing traffic at a busy cross-roads and the policeman on his beat. Social inertia can obstruct the alteration of political institutions in much the same way as it can obstruct linguistic change. Would-be reformers cannot get the people concerned to change their habits of thought or action.

The classification of words as social institutions also does more justice than the tool-use analogy to the number, heterogeneity and interdependence of the factors that philologists need to treat as causes or effects of changes in word-use. In any synchronous state of a language, we are told, 'the various semantic factors are indissolubly intermixed: conventionality and motivation, onomatopoeia and popular etymology, emotive meaning, synonymy, polysemy, and homonymy, form one organic whole. . . . Moreover, they are interlinked with the phonological, morphological and syntactic system, with the stratification of the vocabulary, with the social and dialectal structure prevailing at that given time, with foreign influences, standards of style, modes of spelling, and even punning technique; and, transcending the boundaries of language, with the general "atmosphere", cultural aspirations and moral outlook peculiar to the age.'[1] Words are exposed to the influence of not only a multitude of purely linguistic factors but also an equally important multitude of factors that are outside the exclusive concern of linguists. In short, they are conceived as having functions not only in language-sentences but also in culture-sentences and thus as liable to be affected in their uses by any features not only of their language, but also of their culture. In this they are quite like other social institutions.

[1] S. Ullmann, *The Principles of Semantics* (1951), p. 137. Cf. G. Stern, 'Meaning and Change of Meaning', *Göteborgs Högskolas Arsskrift*, xxxviii (1932), pp. 161 ff.

Just as language-words are defined in terms of their form and culture-words in terms of their use, so too a police force may be identified either by its uniform or by its duties, and a law-court either by its court-room and personnel or by its jurisdiction. Just as words are elements not only in language-sentences and culture-sentences, but also in the language and culture as a whole, so too police and law-courts are not only elements in particular social operations, such as the punishment of traffic-offenders, but also in the general life of the community. Just as the notion of a concept as a continuant with changing states is integral to the history of ideas, so too a political scientist can often not discuss changes in the function of government unless he has an analogous notion of that function. Otherwise he risks exaggerating discontinuities in the process, say, by which modern welfare-states have emerged in north-western Europe, just as a historian of ideas does in connection with the Renaissance or the rise of modern science. At the centre of power there may be a core of institutions – the legislature in particular – that have gradually extended their functions, rather than one set of institutions that has replaced another. Thus there is nothing specially mysterious about the conceptual plane of semantics or the relation of the history of ideas to history in general. It is one case among many of discourse about the functions of institutions where particular functions rather than particular institutional forms are the topic of discussion.

Appreciating that if words have functions in sentences they must also be conceived as having functions in their language, Saussure compared a language with a game of chess in that at each momentary stage of the game the values of the pieces depend on their positions with respect to one another. But he thought that in diachronistic, as distinct from synchronistic, study words should not be treated as elements in an interlocking system, and he compared the way in which only one chess-piece need be moved in order to pass from one state of the game to the next.[1] However it seems that just here the parallel with a game of chess may sometimes obstruct enquiry and the comparison of words with other social institutions may be more fruitful. Jost Trier's theory of linguistic fields has given a considerable impetus to the substitution of a holistic for an atomistic approach even in historical studies of language. He has shown how useful it may be to study the history not just

[1] *Cours de Linguistique Générale*, pp. 44, 129.

of one word at a time, but of whole sections of a language's vocabulary.[1]

Trier thinks that every such field, like the German vocabulary of mental comprehension which he himself has investigated so thoroughly, should be regarded as being contained within larger and larger fields until the totality of the language is reached. When one discovers that in 1300 'wisheit' no longer expressed the unity of intellectual, technical, courtly and religious knowledge that it did in 1200, nor has any other word taken its place, the change to be noted is an integral change in Middle High German. Not only that: it is also a change in the outlook and attitudes of the medieval German community. The history of a linguistic field embraces the history of several words mutually related in use, together with the story of their synonyms, antonyms and associations. It is therefore, as Trier sees, a contribution to the history of ideas, albeit the ideas of a single speech-community, whereas the old history of word-meanings, as conceived by Saussure, belonged wholly on the verbal plane.

Admittedly, just as the meanings of some words may be much less context-dependent than those of others, so too a holistic approach to their history may be less valuable. A philologist's history of word-meanings will merge into or separate from the history of ideas just as far as he finds interconnections of synonymy, antonymy, etc., to be relevant or irrelevant, respectively, to his enquiry. It might therefore seem that on many occasions it would be a mistake to think of statements about word-meanings on the verbal plane as statements about the functions of social institutions. But to accept a functional theory of word-meaning is not to claim that the histories of single word-meanings can never be written in comparative isolation from one another. Almost any paragraph of the Oxford *New English Dictionary* would suffice to refute this claim. What the conception of words as institutions implies is rather that the understanding of such individual histories and the explanation of their details can in principle always be facilitated by exploring their interconnections, though the results of such an exploration

---

[1] Cf. *Der Deutsche Wortschatz im Sinnbezirk des Verstandes*, vol. I (1931), esp. pp. 1–4; 'Deutsche Bedeutungsforschung', *Germanische Philologie: Ergebnisse und Aufgaben: Festschrift für O. Behaghel*, ed. A. Götze *et al.* (1934), pp. 173–200, esp. p. 188; and 'Das Sprachliche Feld', *Neue Jahrbücher für Wissenschaft und Jugendbildung* (1934), pp. 428–49.

may conceivably not always be so interesting as those of Trier's researches in the German vocabulary of mental comprehension.

Morphemes are not quite on the same footing as words here. The meanings of some morphemes admit of discussion only on the verbal, and not at all on the conceptual, plane. Certain noun-endings in Central Algonquian, for instance, are described by J. H. Greenberg as having a linguistic function but no ethnic one.[1] We should not expect to find any direct connections between changes in their use and changes in the non-linguistic aspects of the community's life, in the way that a decline in the importance of pastoral wealth altered the meaning of the Latin word 'pecunia'. But, if the term 'word' is confined to forms that sometimes constitute an utterance when not combined with one or more other words, all words must in principle admit of discussion on the conceptual plane. A speech-form that sometimes makes up the whole of a sentence, with its characteristic cause, effect or purpose of utterance, has some part to play in the life of the community, and its meaning is therefore open to conceptual discussion. Correspondingly all sentences admit of both verbal and conceptual discourse about their meanings: every language-sentence is an example of a culture-sentence. Just as on the verbal plane one can discuss the syntax of a sentence or how its utterance should be paraphrased in its own language or translated into another, so too on the conceptual plane one can discuss what other characteristic causes, effects or purposes of utterance are related to its own (what other statements, commands, questions, etc., its utterance implies) and when the purpose of the sentence is appropriate (when it would make a true statement, a reasonable command, a relevant question, etc.).

More will be said about the semantics of sentences in §§16–19, since saying-sentences are on the whole of greater interest than saying-words, whereas culture-sentences are less interesting than culture-words. But the sense in which one should say that temporal discourse about word-meanings is primarily concerned with functions rather than with causes, effects, purposes or rules may be further clarified by comparison with the way in which biologists often find it convenient to talk about functions. In both cases questions about function concern the contribution of mutually interconnected factors to the existence of a whole that is considered to be relatively invariant under different conditions.

[1] 'Concerning Inferences from Linguistic to Non-Linguistic Data', *Language in Culture*, ed. H. Hoijer (1954), pp. 14 f.

In the one case this whole is either a living organism, when the elements about which questions of function arise are its organs, like the heart, veins and arteries, or its normal activities and body-processes, like the consumption of sugar; or the whole is some animal community like a beehive and questions arise about the functions of activities like the worker-bee's homecoming dance. In the other case the whole is either a sentence and its meaning, that is relatively invariant from speaker to speaker, or a language and culture that are relatively invariant through-out a given region and period. Just as we can ask about the function of a mammal's heart where it would seem odd or misleading to ask about its cause, effect or purpose, so too with questions about words and other social institutions. Just as the physiologist only distinguishes as organs those features of an organism that have identifiable functions in its life under normal conditions, so too the philologist only analyses out as words or morphemes, and the historian of ideas is only interested in, those recurrent sound-patterns that have an identifiable function in normal utterances.

Yet there are some important differences between semantic and biological discourse about functions, even apart from their different subject-matter. Perhaps the most obvious is that the function of an organ is that contribution to the organism's life for which the organ, in the organism's normal circumstances, is physically indispensable, whereas languages often provide partial synonyms that enable a sentence to replace this or that word by another in a given kind of context and yet to retain the same meaning. Only to the richness of a culture as a whole may individual words be regarded as indispensable and then only so far as complete synonyms are taken to be so rare and imperma-nent as to be negligible.

It is also worth noticing that, if words are to be conceived as social institutions, there can be no such thing as a language that only one per-son ever speaks. What useful purpose would be served by the concep-tion of a private language? Private codes and shorthand notations are common enough as measures to ensure the secrecy of personal diaries. But by calling them private languages one would confuse a language like English or French with a method of writing it. A castaway infant might at least conceivably grow up on an otherwise uninhabited island to devise memory-aids for himself and even instruments of calculation. By notching sticks according to self-set and faithfully observed rules he could count the number of days in each lunar month and in each solar year as they passed, and the ratio between any two of these numbers would become apparent to him by a comparison of the two relevant sticks. But by calling these devices a language we should confuse speech with the use of tallies and abaci. The castaway might even make a similar noise each time he saw a certain bird or felt a certain kind of pain. But this would be a habit of voice production, not of soliloquy. To soliloquize is to say something to oneself in private that others would understand if it were said in public. Words are social institutions that are similar to certain religious rituals in their ability to be operated both privately and publicly: to say that something is a social institution is not to imply that it only functions in a crowd.

One of the strongest temptations to insist, implicitly or explicitly, on the possibility of a private language has perhaps been the classical desire of empiricist philosophers to deny that any of a man's thoughts or thoughtways are innate. When Locke argued that all a man's ideas were the fabric of that man's own experience, he naturally came to exclude the possibility that much of a man's conceptual system was inherited from the culture of his community in the process of learning its language. Children only come to use words, Locke maintained, when thay have 'by repeated sensations got ideas fixed in their memories' and 'these verbal signs they sometimes borrow from others and sometimes make themselves'. Moreover each child builds up for itself its own stock of general ideas by abstraction from the memorized data of sensation and reflection, and then the words naming such data become general by attachment to these general ideas.[1] Thus at each stage, on Locke's view, the ideas are fundamental and the word-meanings derivative: the meaning of words is to be understood solely in terms of the ideas their utterance evokes, and the ideas may be very different from person to person. Hence in order to deny the possibility of a man's thoughtways' being anything but the fabric of his own experience Locke was led to imply the theoretical possibility of an entirely private language – a language that was idiosyncratic both in its forms and in its meanings. The practical need to communicate with one another is apparently all, on Locke's view, that ever prevents men from having and using such languages.[2] But the untenability of a theory of meaning like Locke's, and the extent to which a man's conceptual system must be regarded as

---

[1] *Essay*, II, xi, 8–9; III, iii, 6.   [2]*Essay*, III, ii, 8.

consisting essentially in his habits of word-use, force us to recognize at least one respect in which the denial of innate ideas should be carefully qualified. Anyone who denies them should be prepared to acknowledge the extent to which a man's thoughtways are not solely the fabric of his own experience but are also the heritage of his community, which teaches him, in effect, to discriminate those elements in his experience for which its language affords descriptions. On the normal individual's debt to his community here Hegel is a better guide than Locke.

Recent discussion about the possibility of a private language has had a recognizably connected starting-point.[1] For its main point of departure has been Carnap's *Der Logische Aufbau der Welt*, which was an attempt at the rational reconstruction of human knowledge from the data of a single individual's consciousness; and Locke's denial of innate ideas had led him on to imply the possibility of just such a reconstruction. However the question attracting most attention in recent years has been about the nature of statement rather than of language: can we make statements about intrinsically private experiences in the manner suggested by Carnap's book? It is a mistake to confuse this question with the question whether meanings are to be understood, in the way that Locke or Berkeley suggested, as intrinsically private experiences. To classify words as social institutions is not to exclude the same notion of a private language as is entailed by the acceptance of statements about such private experiences. Even if one grants that every language is spoken by at least two persons one has not thereby committed oneself to the thesis that utterances like 'I have a pain in my lower jaw' are to be regarded as mere avowals, rather than as descriptions that the speaker alone can verify. A language is no less a system of social institutions if the appropriateness with which some of these institutions operate can sometimes be checked by only one person. Confession and penitence are institutions of many religions, but their appropriateness in particular cases is often known only to the sinner, especially where sins of motivation are alleged. Hence the question whether statements about intrinsically private experiences are possible must be settled by considering what is to count as a statement and be entitled to possess a truth-value, not what is to count as a language. The system of Carnap's *Aufbau* is a theory, not a language. Here as

[1] Cf. e.g. A. J. Ayer, 'Can there be a private language?', *Proc. Arist. Soc.*, Supp. Vol. xxviii (1954), pp. 63 ff.

elsewhere the philosophy of historical and lexicographical semantics is neutral in regard to rival philosophies of mind.

§9. Can a language be a prison?

It appears no small convenience of the rules-of-use theory that it offers an elucidation of impossibilities like Wittgenstein's 'The colours green and blue can't be in the same place simultaneously.' What can or cannot be so, in these cases of *a priori* truth, is said to be determined by the rules of word-use, and in particular by rules permitting or forbidding the conjoint predication of certain words, such as 'green' and 'blue'. The green-blue impossibility, and even perhaps the necessities of logic and mathematics, are all to be accounted for without the assumption of what Kant called synthetic *a priori* knowledge. So that if the propositions of metaphysics are synthetic *a priori* they have no respectable bedfellows.

But here again it is hard on lexicographers and grammarians that they should be forced to take sides on so weighty an issue. If the rules-of-use theory of meaning commits them to a linguistic theory of *a priori* truth and thus to the repudiation of Kantian metaphysics, so much the worse for the rules-of-use theory as an account of how these particular experts in the study of meaning should discuss it. A *de facto* theory of philological semantics implies instead that in statements about what cannot be said in a given language or culture at a given date the impossibility should be taken to depend on the uniformities of speech-custom that exist in that community at that date. It is more like a political impossibility than a logical one, more like a very great difficulty than an outright impossibility. If the language or culture develops suitably, it might well become a possibility at a later date. The history of grammar or of ideas would be devoid of subject-matter if there were not thus strings of words that could readily constitute sentences at one date but not at another. But these varying difficulties in combining words into language-sentences or culture-sentences can hardly be quite the impossibilities with which a theory of *a priori* truth is concerned. Philosophers who instance the impossibility of anything being both green and blue all over as an item of *a priori* truth do not take this impossibility to be one that may conceivably vanish at some stage in the life of their language or culture. No rules-of-word-use theory can solve their problem in the way that M. Schlick[1] and others thought it could, unless the theory is of the old pre-Herder kind and conceives meanings to be timeless and unchangeable (compare §20 below).

Not that the possibility of sentence-construction is in every respect a perspicuous notion in the *de facto* semantics of philologists. Difficulties of translation between certain languages were familiar both to Lucretius and to Locke, as was remarked in §4. Locke put these difficulties down to differences between some of the ideas prevalent in different communities, and he thought these differences due in turn to differences of custom or way of life. But what Locke and Lucretius remarked on was the frequent difficulty of finding a word in one language to correspond exactly with a given word in another. They were not apparently worried by the possibility of grammatical, as distinct from merely lexical, bars to translation, nor were they interested in the causes or effects of such grammatical difficulties. However during the last two centuries there has been a debate of no little fruitfulness about how far, and in what sense, both the lexical and grammatical possibilities of constructing language-sentences are interdependent with the possibilities of constructing culture-sentences. The subject of this debate was succinctly set out in 1759 by the Berlin Academy's question for its prize essay in that year: what is the mutual influence of popular opinions on language and of language on popular opinions? Awareness of the problem was an active factor in the intellectual ferment from which modern linguistics developed. If American Indians obviously lacked many thoughtways of civilized Europe, it became plausible to assume that their languages might also lack some of the grammatical forms that were familiar in European languages. At any rate it would clearly beg an important question to suppose from the start that their languages possessed all these forms. Hence arose C. W. von Humboldt's influential recommendation that a philologist should not take the grammar of his own language or of Latin as his point of departure in studying a new language.[2] But von Humboldt emphasized that the structure of a

---

[1] 'Gibt es ein materiales *A priori*?', *Gesammelte Aufsätze* (1938), pp. 19 ff.

[2] 'Über das Entstehen der grammatischen Formen, und ihren Einfluss auf die Ideenentwicklung', *Werke*, ed. A. Leitzmann, vol. iv (1905), pp. 285 ff. J. L. Austin's 'fifty years or more' is something of an understatement with regard to the period in which such recommendations have been made or followed: cf. 'Ifs and Cans', *Proc. Brit. Acad.*, xlii (1956), p. 131.

language was no more static than the ideas of its speakers. For example, he attacked the division of languages into agglutinative and inflected ones on the ground that whether agglutination or inflection prevails is often a matter of the stage of development that the language has reached rather than of some inner necessity peculiar to the language throughout its history. He was convinced, rightly or wrongly, that all languages began agglutinatively, that as they develop inflection increases, and therewith they become more favourable for the development of abstract thought.

Most modern discussions of this subject, though more sophisticated than von Humboldt's, are equally concerned to treat the problem as a factual one: when one has abstracted both the grammatical uniformities in the patterns on which language-sentences are constructed and the conceptual uniformities in the patterns on which culture-sentences are constructed, what kinds of correlation, if any, emerge between the two sets of uniformities in different communities? Admittedly B. L. Whorf called it a 'new principle of relativity' that all observers are not led by the same physical evidence to the same picture of the universe, 'unless their linguistic backgrounds are similar, or can in some way be calibrated'. Whorf's thesis that no individual is free to describe nature with absolute impartiality, but 'is constrained to certain modes of interpretation even while he thinks himself most free',[1] has an air of suggesting that facts may only illustrate what is claimed and cannot conceivably refute it. He is asserting that marked differences of grammar must always influence conception, not merely that they sometimes do and sometimes do not. But it turns out very hard even to find incontrovertible illustrations of Whorf's thesis, let alone a demonstration of it.

Clearly people who have a word for lions in their language will be able to think about them much more easily than those who have not, and people who have no numerical expressions except 'one', 'two' and 'many' will be unable to develop a general theory of numbers. But lexical impediments of this kind are comparatively unimportant because they can so easily be remedied by additions to a language's vocabulary when cross-cultural contacts or other historical developments make the need felt. George Orwell too, in the appendix to his *1984*, sketched a language in which he claimed the expression of unorthodox opinions

[1] *Collected Papers on Metalinguistics* (1952), pp. 5 ff.

would be 'wellnigh impossible'. But the sanctions against its use to express political discontent were purely lexical, determining resources of vocabulary, compatibilities and incompatibilities of predication, and nothing else. Orwell assumed that even when Newspeak began to be spoken these restrictions would be inherent in the language, as if the identity of a language through time were determined by an unchanging system of rules for word-use rather than by continuities of developing custom. But he needed the old, discredited normative conception of word-meanings in order thus to justify supposing that Newspeak could be kept static by anything but the omnipresent efficiency of Big Brother's police force. As Saussure put it, anyone who pretends to compose an unalterable language, a language that posterity must accept as it is, resembles the hen that sat on a duck's egg: as soon as an artificial language, like Esperanto, passes into circulation it becomes subject to change.[1]

A radical reform of grammar, however, is much more difficult to achieve, since the speech-habits that constitute grammatical uniformities are much more pervasive than particular items of vocabulary. They constitute the general patterns of sentence-construction, rather than the detailed content of particular sentences, and grammatical obstructions to thought, if they existed, would therefore be much more important. But how could we ever establish that a people's thoughts were thus imprisoned by their grammar? Certainly a man could never discover this about his own current language, without thinking on both sides of the prison wall at once. Whorf's claim to have discovered ways in which the Hopi conceive things but English-speakers cannot is intrinsically incapable of illustration in the language in which Whorf himself wrote. Nor is it clear how a man could ever establish that there are ways in which English-speakers conceive things and Hopi cannot – that there are English sentences untranslatable into Hopi. He would always risk the objection that if he does not know how to put such-and-such a conception across to a Hopi he cannot have learnt the Hopi language well enough. A real master of a language would mould it to his purposes, as missionary translators of the Bible have often done. Hence most linguists who have discussed this problem, from Humboldt's time to the present day, find it best to assume with E. Sapir that 'all languages are set to do all the symbolic and expressive work that language

[1] *Cours de Linguistique Générale*, p. 113.

is good for, either actually or potentially', and that if any question arises about differences in the potential of different languages it should rather be about the ease or difficulty with which they lend themselves to the expression of different ideas than about the permanent possibilities and impossibilities that Whorf claimed to exist.[1] When Hobbes asks whether in a language in which predication was expressed by the adjunction of subject and predicate rather than by a copula there would be any terms equivalent to 'entity', 'essence', 'essential' or 'essentiality',[2] it is better to answer that in such a language it would be relatively more difficult to develop such a vocabulary than that it would be impossible.

Even then it is clearer how a negative thesis might be established than a positive one. If the languages of two speech-communities had their main grammatical features in common, the conceptual differences between the two cultures must obviously be explained otherwise than by reference to grammatical considerations. But when one considers all the many differences between ancient China on the one hand, and ancient Greece and India on the other, how could one become reasonably sure that it was primarily differences of grammar which accounted for the comparative paucity of metaphysical and formal-logical thinking in ancient China? The diversity and complexity of conceivably relevant factors is so great, the opportunities for experimental variation of them so restricted, and the number of comparable cultures so small, that the grounds for selecting grammar to be the fundamental variable in explaining these cultural facts are very poor. Perhaps languages that operate successfully with a high proportion of what Ryle has called 'systematically misleading expressions',[3] as in the grammatical similarity between 'Mr Pickwick is a fiction' and 'Mr Baldwin is a statesman', are languages that in the past have lent themselves most readily to the expression of radically new conceptions. But there is still the problem of establishing that grammar is the fundamental variable in such cases and not just one of many ways in which some other social factor shows its influence.

[1] Cf. *Selected Writings of E. Sapir*, ed. D. G. Mandelbaum (1949), pp. 153 ff., and C. F. Hockett in *Language in Culture*, ed. H. Hoijer (1954), pp. 127 f.

[2] *Leviathan*, IV, xlvi (Everyman edition, p. 368).

[3] 'Systematically Misleading Expressions', *Proc. Arist. Soc.*, xxxii (1932), pp. 139 ff.

In sociology, therefore, the fruitfulness of this grammar-culture problem has lain rather in the reverse direction. Linguistic differences have been assumed accountable for by cultural ones, not cultural by linguistic, and the study of primitive people's languages thus came to be taken – no doubt with varying degrees of caution – as one legitimate avenue of research in cultural anthropology by L. Lévy-Bruhl, Ernst Cassirer, and many others. By investigating the Ewe language, for instance, where the same adverb designates both yesterday and to-morrow, one was said to discover a culture that lacks the European consciousness of temporal continuity.[1] But, though such studies have not always been fortified by sufficient study of the interdependence in function between a community's linguistic and non-linguistic institutions, nevertheless the mere difficulty of saying something in a language is sufficient to be of note here: one does not need to discover an out-right impossibility. A *de jure* theory of philological semantics is therefore as pointless in this connection as in its encouragement of fantasies like those of Orwell.

Nor is a *de jure* theory the only kind of mistake about philological semantics that can generate trouble here, as is evident from Quine's treatment of the problem. Quine builds his discussion[2] around the imaginary investigation of a hitherto quite unknown language on the basis of what he calls 'stimulus meaning'. He defines the affirmative stimulus meaning of a sentence for a speaker at a date, and relative to a maximum period of stimulation, as the class of all stimulations at the date that would prompt his assent to the sentence within the period. Negative stimulus meaning is defined similarly, but with 'dissent' for 'assent', and stimulus meaning is then defined as the ordered pair of affirmative and negative stimulus meanings. Quine then points out that the concept of stimulus meaning fails to satisfy certain intuitive – habitual but unexamined – demands on the notion of sentence-meaning. For example, 'there may be a local rabbit-fly unknown to the linguist, and recognizable some way off by its long wings and erratic movements; and seeing such a fly in the neighbourhood of an ill-glimpsed animal could help a native to recognize the latter as a rabbit' and assent to the appropriate sentence, even though the linguist might remain

[1] E. Cassirer, *The Philosophy of Symbolic Forms*, tr. R. Manheim (1953), vol. I, pp. 220 ff.

[2] *Word and Object* (1960), pp. 26–79.

unaware of the rabbit's presence. Thus at the level of investigation into a sentence's stimulus meaning no experimental sense can be attached to a 'distinction between what goes into a native's learning to apply an expression' and what goes into his learning supplementary information about the objects concerned. Quine's way round this difficulty is to suggest that a translation between the investigator's language and the investigated one should be conceived to rely not on an identity of the relevant stimulus meanings but on a significant tendency of these meanings to approximate one another when circumstances and informants are appropriately varied.

Truth-functional connectives also should present no difficulty, if signs of assent and dissent are understood. A negating expression will turn an assented-to sentence into a dissented-from one, and vice versa, and a conjunctive expression will produce assent when and only when the conjoined sentences both do so. Quine is prepared thus to exclude the possibility of a pre-logical mentality in the people investigated, because in general a mistake in translation is much likelier than mere silliness in the native speaker.

Trouble begins, according to Quine, when the investigator comes on certain sentences, like 'Bachelor' and unlike 'Red' or 'Rabbit', that are inculcated through their connections with other sentences and link up thus indirectly with past stimulations of other sorts than those that serve directly to prompt assent to them. The stimulus meaning of a comparatively non-observational sentence like 'Bachelor' will vary with the speaker's past, and constitutes no basis for general principles of translation. What then can an investigator do about these non-observational sentences? Moreover, even translation in terms like 'rabbit' may be similarly under-determined. The synonym for 'Rabbit' as a sentence is fixed by considerations of prompted assent, but a synonym for 'rabbit' as a term cannot be so fixed. Does the local word denote an enduring whole rabbit, or a temporal slice of such an enduring whole, or the sum of a rabbit's undetached parts, or the attribute of rabbithood, or the aggregate of rabbits? An investigator cannot decide this, Quine points out, unless he has 'decided what native devices to view as doing in their devious ways the work of our own various auxiliaries to objective reference: our articles and pronouns, our singular and plural, our copula, our identity predicate'. Here stimulus meaning has failed us again.

Quine grants that for any one speaker at any one time a non-observational sentence may have detectably the same stimulus meaning as some other sentence, as in the case of 'Bachelor' and 'Unmarried man'. If the two expressions are also such that the speaker would assent at the same time to a sentence of the form 'All bachelors are unmarried men, and vice versa', Quine calls them stimulus-synonymous. In certain cases this synonymy will be due to the speaker's possessing some special information, as when he responds identically to 'Everest' and 'Gaurisanker' because he has discovered that these expressions name the same mountain. But where a stimulus synonymy has been found to hold under varying conditions throughout the community, a fact has been established about the language. Moreover the investigator is then in a position to pick out certain sentences as being 'stimulus analytic', viz. those that are formed by concatenating two stimulus-synonymous sentences with the truth-functional connective that is equivalent to 'if and only if'.

But how can an investigator go beyond these somewhat limited achievements and establish the translation of relatively non-observational sentences? It is natural to suggest, Quine thinks, that on the basis of what he has already established he should seek to compile 'analytical hypotheses', i.e. hypothetical equations of words and phrases in his own language with hypothetically segmented parts of sentences in the local language. No outright equation of each local word with any one English word or phrase is required. The hypothetical equations may be relative to the contexts of the words concerned, and further hypotheses about word-order and syntax may be needed. But what is essential is that the sentence-translations derivable from these analytical hypotheses should include all those already established by approximations of stimulus meaning, together with truth-functional compounds of these, and at the same time should maintain invariant any stimulus-synonymy or stimulus-analyticity that is noted in the original. The investigator might then expect, with the help of his analytical hypotheses, to be able to extrapolate from what he has already established to what is as yet undetermined.

Quine argues, however, that this expectation is doomed to disappointment. The linguist's analytical hypotheses may certainly yield an infinite correlation of sentences between the two languages. But the further we get away from sentences with visibly direct conditioning to non-verbal stimuli, and the remoter the culture with which we are dealing, the less sense there is in saying what is good translation and what is bad. This is because 'there can be no doubt that rival systems of analytical hypotheses can fit the totality of speech behaviour to perfection, and can fit the totality of dispositions to speech behaviour as well, and still specify mutually incompatible translations of countless sentences insusceptible of independent control'. One might think of objecting that the linguist can at least in principle learn the local language as a native child does, by putting his past knowledge of language out of mind, and he will then be as good a speaker of the language as anyone native to the community. But, Quine answers, when such a bilingual investigator comes to translate, he must still compile his grammar and dictionary – his analytical hypotheses – and the same trouble will recur. He is introspecting his experiments instead of staging them, but the hypotheses are still under-determined by the evidence. Another bilingual could have a semantic correlation incompatible with his, and yet not deviate detectably from him in speech dispositions within either language, except in his dispositions to translate.

This argument of Quine's for the indeterminacy of translation, here summarized only in outline, is the most elaborate defence of Whorf's thesis that has yet been advocated. Nevertheless the argument is invalidated by a mistake about what concept of meaning is most suited to the kind of philological enterprise under discussion. Quine assumes that the concept of stimulus meaning which the investigator might find useful at the outset of an enquiry is also, in effect, the only concept of meaning that is relevant to assessing its final success. He has not shown, as he claims, that two mutually incompatible sets of analytical hypotheses can fit any totality of native dispositions to speech behaviour just as well as one another, but only that two such sets of hypotheses can fit any totality of communally shared stimulus meanings. But if sentences of certain kinds have no common stimulus meaning throughout a community, it is hardly surprising that stimulus meanings on their own should fail to supply us with sufficient grounds for choosing between certain rival translations of such sentences.

Suppose instead we take the concept of stimulus meaning to be merely an initial tool, helping the investigator to formulate his first grammatical and lexicographical hypotheses, just as the one-word sentences of the nursery, with their indicatable correlates, belong to a very primitive stage of speech in the life of any individual. Suppose we take the concepts of sentence-meaning proposed earlier in the present chapter to supply the final criteria by which the correctness of these hypotheses is to be judged. Then we shall take a sentence in one language to mean the same as a sentence in another so far as its utterance has not only the same kinds of cause and effect in both communities but also, and more importantly, the same purposes. But how can the investigator detect, it may be objected, the extent to which two sentences are characteristically uttered with the same purpose? Is not the concept of purpose too nebulous and unempirical to give him any firm foundation for a final decision on the correctness of his hypotheses? Not at all: the purpose theory of meaning points exactly to the way in which such hypotheses normally are, and should be, tested for their power to produce correct translations in fields of discourse different from those initially studied. The investigator tests his hypotheses by using them. He tries to find out whether the sentences they lead him to construct will achieve the same purposes in utterance as the correlated sentences of his own language. He does not confine himself to the neat and tidy experimental procedure of testing for stimulus meanings, which is comparatively sterile, as Quine correctly points out, beyond a certain limited range of sentences. He must instead go and live with the community, taking an active part in all its many-sided cycle of activities. If he succeeds in communicating with its members over a sufficiently long period in sentences homophonous with theirs; if they come to appreciate the purposes of his utterances and he of theirs; if he is not ridiculed for calling the tribe's champion polygamist a bachelor, or for smoking out two rabbits only when he was asked to smoke out two rabbit-warrens; then his grammatical and lexicographical hypotheses cannot be far wrong. Much may need amending as he goes along, and deep-seated misunderstandings may only come to light after many years. But in principle this is the way in which most exotic languages have yielded up their secrets to investigators, whether these investigators have been missionaries, traders, administrators, anthropologists or professional linguists. The long toils of the early Jesuits in China are a notable example.[1]

The problem is partially analogous to that faced by cryptographers

[1] For references cf. J. R. Firth, *Papers in Linguistics 1934–1951* (1957), pp. 104 f.

who can guess the gist of some, but not all, messages in the code they are trying to break and who then find that the guessed messages, and collateral information, leave open a choice between rival hypotheses about the contents of the code-book, which mere reading of the remaining messages that are available cannot determine. They must then find out what happens when they (or persons instructed by them) act on one or other interpretation of these remaining messages, or elicit a new message, or when they contrive themselves to send a message encoded on one or other of the hypotheses. They must enter actively into situations of the kind in which the coded messages are being exchanged, and must not be content with the role of merely passive, nonparticipant observers.

After all, Quine admits that there is sense in saying that a child has mastered its own native language and even in saying that an investigator can, up to a point, 'simulate the infantile situation' and so learn to become as fluent in the investigated language as in his own. Yet by standards built on a study of stimulus meaning alone we could as little appraise success in language-learning of this kind as in the more theoretical enterprise of interlingual lexicography. We could have no conceivable evidence for saying that the child or investigator had got beyond the primitive one-word sentences of the nursery, with their indicatable correlates. It would make no sense either to say or to deny that a child has learnt to utter relatively non-observational sentences according to the community's customary usage, because to this field of discourse the concept of customary usage would be irrelevant. No speech-community would exist anywhere except in regard to sentences asserting the immediate presence of conspicuously segregated objects or conspicuously demarcated characteristics, and their truth-functional compounds. In short, Quine's arguments for the indeterminacy of translation not only destroy the major part of the concept of language that is commonly in use among philologists, but also render pointless any human communication of other than the simplest kind. To avoid such a sweeping paradox he must accept some other concept of sentence-meaning, some other criterion of language-learning, than the one on which his main argument is based. But whatever this alternative to stimulus meaning be, if it is in general adequate to the task of appraising a man's success at speaking his native language, it must also be adequate to the task of appraising his success at speaking any foreign language, however exotic, that he has learnt via the analytical hypotheses of a philological investigator from his own community. And if these hypotheses enable him thus to render his own sentences into foreign ones successfully, what more can be required of them?

Indeed, one may note *ad hominem* that Quine elsewhere employs just the criterion of comparison between one sentence and another that does the job which stimulus meaning cannot do in this connection. In discussing alternative proposals for analysing or explicating the logic of indirect discourse he remarks of one sentence he mentions that it 'well enough serves any purposes of' another mentioned sentence 'that seem worth serving'; and in general he asserts that, when some puzzling or troublesome form of expression serves certain purposes that are not to be abandoned, philosophical explication consists in finding 'a way of accomplishing those same purposes through other channels, using other and less troublesome forms of expression'. 'We fix on the particular functions of the unclear expression that make it worth troubling about, and then devise a substitute, clear and couched in terms to our liking, that fills those functions.'[1] Certainly he explicitly repudiates the view that philosophical explication should seek and claim the discovery of synonymies.[2] For him the sameness of the purpose that two sentences normally accomplish, or the sameness of function that two expressions normally fulfil, is no measure of their sameness of meaning. But all that this boils down to is that, if one refuses to adopt an appropriate account of sentence- and word-meaning, and relies on the jejune and unfertile concept of stimulus meaning instead of on a purpose-and-function theory, then one can generate any number of paradoxes and puzzles about what other philosophers say who are using, whether they are fully aware of it or not, a purposive concept of sentence-meaning.

Moreover what happens in philosophical explication, as Quine describes it, runs partially parallel to what happens in translation from one language to another. Admittedly the criteria of merit are different. The explicator seeks a better instrument for the same purposes, the translator one that is neither better nor worse. But in both cases it is sometimes relatively easy to find how a sentence may be formulated in a different idiom that will accomplish the same purpose, sometimes relatively difficult, and sometimes, at the time, impossible. In both cases

[1] *Word and Object*, pp. 214, 260, 258 f.
[2] Ibid.

73

such an impossibility calls for and generally achieves some extension of, or alteration in, the paraphrasing idiom. What is wrong with Whorf's thesis is that it represents temporary difficulties of this kind as permanent impossibilities.

III

Meanings Conceived as Topics for
Philosophical Investigation

§10. What room is there for a specifically philosophical study of meanings?

The past generation has seen many pronouncements of what ought to be the business of philosophers with language. But the extent to which these programmes already compete or conflict with one another measures the futility of proposing another. It is more fruitful of agreement to examine first what ought not to be the special business of philosophers because it is already adequately supplied with expert attention, and then to see what problems are left over for philosophers to tackle. The question to be asked is not what they must do or what they actually do, but rather what they may legitimately do without risk of exposure to the charge of amateurism. What room is there for a specifically philosophical concern with particular meanings, let alone for a kind of concern with meanings that should constitute the distinguishing characteristic of all genuinely philosophical enquiry? What can philosophers find to study in meanings that philologists, historians, sociologists and other specialists in semantics omit to study?

The preoccupation of most modern British philosophers with a study of meanings received some considerable impetus from G. E. Moore's devastatingly minute analyses of statements made by nineteenth-century British Hegelians. By revealing hitherto unnoticed ambiguities and obscurities in their writings Moore not only undermined their arguments and destroyed the predominance of Hegelian idealism in Britain, but also directed the attention of his colleagues towards the profits to be gained by a painstaking exactness of concern for the meanings of familiar words and sentences. But though this aspect of Moore's work has been a very powerful source of inspiration for linguistic philosophers it does not supply an answer to the question asked in the present chapter. When Moore puzzled over the meaning of F. H. Bradley's remark that time is unreal, or H. H. Joachim's that no relations are purely external, the starting-point at least of his enquiry was another philosopher's utterance-sentence or saying-sentence; and far too many different kinds of intellectual controversy require a participant to pay close attention to the meaning of what his opponents say for this requirement in itself to be a specially philosophical one. The meanings of utterance-sentences or saying-sentences are of too general an interest for any of them to constitute the particular province of philosophical semantics. It must be a way of approaching these meanings, rather than any study of the meanings themselves, that is peculiarly philosophical, and since one always has to approach the meanings of particular remarks through meanings in a language or culture it must *somehow* be the latter rather than the former that are of immediate philosophical concern. But how?

One of the obvious questions to settle here is whether philosophical discussion of meanings should be conducted on the verbal or on the conceptual plane. So let us first see what can be said in favour of a verbal approach here.

J. L. Austin, apart from making some very illuminating contributions to certain ranges of genuinely philosophical controversy, also recommended philosophers, in his Presidential Address to the Aristotelian Society, to study language-words on the ground that the ordinary language of, say, the English speech-community embodies 'the inherited experience and acumen of many generations of men'. By finding out what distinctions are implicitly present in the English vocabulary of some non-technical activity, like that of making excuses, we are sure, he said, to discover something worth knowing, however much we may also need to study the technical requirements of jurisprudence or psychology. Hence we can do well to begin by consulting some fairly concise English dictionary, so as to make a complete list of the terms relevant to our chosen topic. In this way we may perhaps come across such facts as that a high percentage of the terms connected with excuses prove to be adverbs. We may then need warning to take care in observing the precise position of an adverbial expression. Similarly we are advised to ask ourselves such questions as why English nouns in one group are governed by the preposition 'under' and in another by 'on'. Nor can we afford to ignore the etymology of a word

76

because 'a word never – well, hardly ever – shakes off its etymology'.[1]

Austin recommended philosophers, in effect, to ask themselves what exactly are the ways of thinking about a topic like excuses to which the English language, in its contemporary form, most easily lends itself. In pursuit of such an enquiry they may expect 'the fun of discovery, the pleasures of co-operation, and the satisfaction of reaching agreement'. Unfortunately, however, these joys have long since been experienced by others in the same pursuit. For nearly a century and a half, as mentioned in §9, C. W. von Humboldt's example has encouraged linguists and anthropologists to investigate what are the ways of thinking to which this or that language most easily lends itself. Moreover, they have often tried to distinguish, as Austin seemed reluctant to do, those features of a language that have an important social function from those that have little or none, like Greenberg's noun-endings in Central Algonquian that were mentioned in §8. Even though in English 'I went' is closer to 'he went' than 'I go' to 'he goes', this fact hardly represents any great inheritance of acumen or experience but merely requires an explanation in Teutonic philology. In fact the volume of books and papers on this and related topics that was accumulated by A. Warburg was so immense that Ernst Cassirer was almost deterred from entering the subject at all.[2] Perhaps this material lacks such startling discoveries as that a word never or hardly ever shakes off its etymology. But in default of numerical data, or of any stipulation about how far back the history of a word's component morphemes is to count as its etymology, Austin's readers may wonder why 'pecuniary' should be considered an example of a much rarer phenomenon than 'accident'. Perhaps middle-class British English of the twentieth century has not yet received as much attention by anthropologists, or formed the subject of so many cross-cultural comparisons, as the languages of some more primitive communities. But it is not easy to see how the facts about it, once established, can form a basis for any distinctively philosophical conclusion.

The only reason why such a conclusion seems available to Austin is that he conceives ordinary English to embody 'the inherited experience

---

[1] 'A Plea for Excuses', *Proc. Arist. Soc.*, lvii (1957), pp. 1 ff.

[2] F. Saxl, 'Ernst Cassirer', in *The Philosophy of Ernst Cassirer*, ed. P. A. Schilpp (1949), pp. 47 ff.

and acumen of many generations of men'. He expressly admits that it incorporates some superstition, error and fantasy, and even some 'back-seepage of jargon' – usages produced by the theories they appear to support. But he seems to assume, at least in his Presidential Address, that all reasonable men would agree in condemning these features when detected, and that ordinary language lacks the intermingled mass of lumber – customs once generally agreed to be useful but now more controversial – that accumulates around human institutions of other kinds, like armies or building-styles, if their functions are not periodically revalued. He also apparently assumed ordinary language to preserve in unimpaired vitality all the gains ever achieved in the course of its development. He did not express any fear that some laziness, carelessness or intellectual short-sightedness may lose a people part of its cultural inheritance. He implicitly rejected the view, maintained by J. S. Mill,[1] that in the long history of human language word-uses sometimes slowly deteriorate and experience is as often lost as preserved. In short in his Presidential Address he applied the eighteenth-century notion of enlightened progress to the particular case of ordinary language. He assumed, whether aware of his assumption or not, that ordinary language has moved, is moving and presumably will move in a desirable direction.

Herder encouraged historians and anthropologists to detach themselves as much as possible from evaluation of the word-uses they study and to concentrate on description and explanation. Only by attaching equal *prima facie* value to the institutions of every period and every country would they ever be able to surmount the limits imposed on their perception by the prejudices of their own cultures. Though the difficulties of complete objectivity and impartiality in this field are notorious, Herder at least warned people against some of the more obvious biases. Hence it is only by reverting to a conception of language more like Condorcet's than like Herder's that Austin made it seem plausible to expect philosophical conclusions from a kind of study that on Herder's assumptions must, at its most general, issue in nothing more than cross-cultural comparisons. But if questions of value are to be raised at all, it is better not to beg them quite so sweepingly, even if they are begged with the wit and sparkle that were customary to Austin. Why may we not keep our minds open to ask what is gained or lost by

[1] *System of Logic*, IV, iv, 6.

each word-use that interests us, instead of being forced by an underlying presupposition of progress to suppose that almost every word-
use existing in our language is of established value? There is no more
reason to suppose our language all right as it is, than to suppose it not
all right.

In view of this and of the wide range of experts who have long
preceded them in the study of language-words, it is not surprising that
most modern philosophers have in fact directed their own concern with
meanings to culture-words instead. Their theses are fully translatable
from one language to another, and some of their works, such as Wittgenstein's, are even better known in translation than in their original
language. They have tended to emphasize the potentially misleading
character of grammatical similarities, rather than, like Austin, their
potential revealingness. In some cases their work has generated the
so-called paradox of analysis[1] just because an equivalence was being
asserted on the conceptual plane that was not assertable on the verbal
one: 'Brothers are male siblings' is not a trivial identity just because,
though the concept of a brother is the concept of a male sibling, the
French translation of 'brother' is not the French translation of 'male
sibling'. But even when the conceptual character of philosophical
semantics is fully recognized, there still turns out to be some risk of
trespassing in fields more competently cultivated by others, and a *de
jure* theory makes this risk particularly acute. It will therefore be useful
first to sketch and criticize a widely held *de jure* theory of philosophical
semantics that confines the province of philosophers to culture-words
as distinct from language-words, before going on to distinguish within
the study of culture-words that particular form of concern for their
meanings that is in fact left for a philosopher to exercise.

§11. The doctrine of logical grammar

It is often said that a philosopher's characteristic concern with language
is with its 'logical grammar', with a vitally important range of 'logical'
rules for word-use that somehow overlay ordinary lexical and grammatical rules both in everyday usage and in any technical parlance. If a
sentence of normal grammar is said nevertheless not to make good

[1] Cf. C. H. Langford, 'The notion of Analysis in Moore's Philosophy', *The
Philosophy of G. E. Moore*, ed. P. A. Schilpp (1942), p. 323.

sense, like 'My head remembers' or 'My brain does long division', it is one or more of these logical rules that has been broken. 'The task of philosophy', we are told, 'is to examine different classes of sentences and formulate the rules of the correct employment of the words which compose them' – the rules that make it possible to construct 'meaningful sentences'.[1] If a philosopher is accused of a 'howler' or 'solecism' or of 'misusing' words, what is implied is that he has uttered some such sentence and so disobeyed these rules. Nor is there any room for permanent differences of opinion between reasonable people about the content of such rules, however opposed to one another people may be in their views on religion, politics, art or ethics. If a man does not like a logical rule of language his remedy is to propose its reform, not to pretend that it does not exist.

I shall call this theory the doctrine of logical grammar. But if I quote someone's words as an instance of it I do not want to imply that he has always adhered to it or accepted its consequences or even that he now does. I am content to criticize the theory, not the theorists. It is true that a great deal of recent philosophy, such as Ryle's *Concept of Mind*, has been cast in the mould of contributions to the study of logical grammar. But it is fortunate that much of this does not stand or fall with its mould, since the whole doctrine of logical grammar is a mistake. Its *de jure* theory of meaning points to the existence of a muddle in connection with philosophical semantics of the same sort as that which began to be cleared up in connection with philological semantics at the end of the eighteenth and the beginning of the nineteenth century. The old philologists thought of language not as a welter of heterogeneous dialects – metropolitan and provincial, slang and polite – but as a pure and unitary system of speech compared with which all dialects were deviations or corruptions. Analogously logical grammarians think of ordinary usage not as a mixture of clarity and confusion, consistency and inconsistency, usefulness and futility, but rather as a single system of worthwhile rules. The old confusion between factual and normative linguistics – the confusion found in Panini, Valla, Vaugelas, and the rest – has the doctrine of logical grammar as its analogue on the conceptual plane. Just as verbal studies have profited immensely by the separation of grammar and lexicography,

[1] Cf. J. L. Evans, 'On Meaning and Verification', *Mind*, lxii (1953), pp. 11, 13, 18.

on the one hand, from the critique of good style on the other, so too conceptual studies may be expected to profit if descriptive surveys of ideas are clearly distinguished and separated from the critique of good sense. The rules-of-word-use theory does double harm in that it obscures both distinctions. It is true that some philosophers have strongly criticized the doctrine of logical grammar, or are at least at variance with its conception of the philosopher's task, without themselves abandoning a rules-of-word-use theory of meaning.[1] But I do not think such a point of view can be altogether consistent.

The most obvious fault in the doctrine of logical grammar is that it suggests the conceptual study of meanings to be concerned with something that is timeless and unchanging. Exponents of the doctrine have no doubt not intended to imply that there is no room for a history of ideas. But if conceptual talk about word-uses is said to be talk about 'the logic of ordinary language', 'the logic of moral discourse', 'the correct logic of mental conduct concepts', 'the logic of personality', 'the logic of mortality',[2] and so on, that must be part of what is implied. I do not want to object merely, as has often been objected, that the term 'logic' is better confined, at least in any technical use, to the comparatively narrow range of topics studied by formal logicians. This might suggest that we may speak, as Ryle does, about the logic of 'and' and 'some', but not about the logic of 'pleasure' and 'seeing', as Ryle also does.[3] Yet the former is just as misleading a metaphor as the latter in one important respect. The meanings of the culture-words 'and' and 'some', like the meanings of 'pleasure' and 'seeing', may change, whereas the literal use of 'logic' or 'logical', when it refers not to a discipline but to a subject-matter, implies timelessness. The logic of an argument cannot change, any more than the meanings of the (perhaps fifty-odd) utterance-words in which its author expressed it: otherwise its formal validity could never be finally assessed. But ordinary language changes and the meanings of a people's (hundred thousand or so) language-words, including the English word 'logic', have only a

---

[1] E.g., respectively, E. Gellner, *Words and Things* (1959), pp. 44, 139, 232, and S. Hampshire, *Thought and Action* (1959), pp. 136 f.

[2] Cf. P. F. Strawson, *Introduction to Logical Theory*, p. 230; title of a book by P. Edwards (1955); G. Ryle, *The Concept of Mind* (1949), p. 23; title of a book by B. Mayo (1952); title of a book projected by A. G. N. Flew, *A New Approach to Psychical Research* (1953), p. 3, respectively.

[3] *Dilemmas* (1954), p. 119.

relative stability. A logical implication cannot be dated, any more than can the meanings of statements implying one another. But the various forms of mental conduct concepts may be dated to the periods in which they prevail and so too may the meanings of the words expressing them. The logical consistency of a speech has no duration, short or long. But different patterns of moral discourse have prevailed for different lengths of time in the course of human history. In short, the metaphorical use of 'logic' in phrases like 'the logic of ordinary language' or 'the logic of mental conduct concepts' suggests that relations between the meanings of culture-words in ordinary conversation or in discourse about mental conduct are to be conceived as timelessly and unhistorically as those relations between meanings which are called logical in a literal sense.

If logical grammarians expressly disclaimed any such suggestion of timelessness, the harm done would be minimized. But not only is the suggestion rarely disclaimed.[1] It is sometimes even reinforced. It is sometimes expressly asserted, as by P. F. Strawson in his book about the concept of an individual, that 'there is a massive central core of human thinking which has no history – or none recorded in histories of thought; there are categories and concepts which in their most fundamental character change not at all'.[2] But unfortunately these assertions are not documented, and they are not easy to believe (if intended as statements of fact rather than as definitions of 'thinking') when one compares, for example, the Renaissance conception of an individual human being with the Greco-Roman, or contrasts the medieval European conception of a soul with the modern one. Even the most well-structed arguments to show that such-and-such is the only clear and consistent way of thinking about human beings are not sufficient to establish that it is the only way of thinking about human beings that has ever been practised.

Further reinforcement for the doctine's suggestion that the meanings of many important culture-words are timeless comes from the often explicit claim that, as Wittgenstein put it, 'philosophy is a battle against the bewitchment of our intelligence by means of language'.[3] It is often

[1] Cf., however, *Logic and Language* (2nd series, 1955), ed. A. Flew, introduction, p. 8.

[2] *Individuals* (1959), p. 10.

[3] *Philosophical Investigations*, p. 47.

asserted that the misuses of words embodied in false philosophical theories are due solely to mistaken linguistic analogies. We are encouraged to explain metaphysical theories of particular and universal, for instance, or of substance and attribute, as 'pseudo-material shadows, cast by the grammar of the conventional sentence, in which separable expressions play distinguishable roles'.[1] But it is only if we suppose the principles of correct word-use to be timelessly insulated, like the logic of an argument, from the ebb and flow of historical forces that such a diagnosis of philosophical maladies becomes plausible. If instead objectionable word-uses, and theories supporting them, are conceived of as occurring in a specific historical or sociological context, other factors than mere linguistic confusions must appear capable of influencing their occurrence. Trinitarian worship, eucharistic ritual, and belief in the moral sanction of life everlasting, can then be recognized as the potent non-linguistic factors in seventeenth-century controversies about substance which Locke's correspondence with Stillingfleet and much other evidence confirm them to have been.[2] No doubt the grammar of a language must lend itself to accommodating a doctrine of substance if the doctrine is to find a ready welcome among those who speak the language, and when the relevant grammatical analogies are present in many languages the doctrine will come easily to the lips of many peoples. But the soil on which a plant feeds is not the seed from which it germinates. The doctrine of logical grammar encourages the view that the history of philosophy is to be explained almost entirely in terms of standing linguistic problems and the genealogy of attempts to solve them, and scarcely at all in terms of changing political, religious and scientific problems and the relations between them. But Berkeley, for instance, did not introduce his notion of Deity into his *Principles* in order to underpin his phenomenalist analysis of ordinary language. Rather, he propounded the phenomenalism in order to defend his notion of Deity, as is indicated by the sub-titles of his *Principles* and *Three Dialogues* and by the concluding paragraphs of his *Principles*.

This illusion about the history of philosophy is further fostered by the criteria of identity and difference that the doctrine tends to impose on concepts and meanings. If there are logical rules of word-use we describe a concept – the meaning of a culture-word – by deploying a

[1] P. F. Strawson, 'On Referring', *Mind*, lix (1950), p. 336.
[2] Cf. J. W. Yolton, *John Locke and the Way of Ideas* (1956), pp. 132 ff.

certain nexus of rules. We do not have to endorse some forms of the concept and condemn others, since the existence of logical rules ensures that only one form exists: the rest is merely linguistic solecism or a different concept. The dichotomy between the use and misuse of a culture-word tends to deprive of philosophical value, and eliminate from philosophical parlance, any distinction between one form of a concept and another. It becomes possible to regard the units of philosophical study as *infimae species* of usage and to speak as if concepts are indivisible. Thus Ryle talks not about the different forms of the same concept that exist in different disciplines but rather about the different concepts that exist in different studies of the same subject-matter.[1] I do not mean that whenever anyone has supported the doctrine of logical grammar he has always implicitly adopted this atomist theory of concepts, only that the doctrine makes this theory seem practicable, and for simplicity's sake preferable, in philosophical semantics. But the theory has at least two important drawbacks.

First, it encourages confusion between such highly specific meanings of culture-words and the fully determinate meanings that particular occurrences of the word have in actual speech. The difference of a non-empty *infima species* from an individual is notoriously slight in any case. If an individual is distinguished from any other individual by its characteristics, then only one individual has all those characteristics and the species constituted by them is for practical purposes not further divisible: every proper sub-species of it is empty, and we can thus identify the individual by reference to such a species or the species by reference to the individual. Hence a theory of atomic concepts enables the meaning of a culture-word to be too easily equated with the meaning of a saying-word and thus conceived timelessly instead of temporally. Indeed, a clearly temporal conception of meaning is only achieved, as was shown in §4, when it becomes possible to treat meanings as continuants with changeable states or contents, which a theory of atomic concepts prevents. Of course, the assigning of particular semantic statements to particular levels of specificity may vary with the purpose in hand and the development of human thought. But for a historian's purposes no concept can be an *infima species*, if it is to form a topic of his narrative. A historian of ideas always needs to be able to narrate how at an earlier period one particular form of a concept was

[1] *Dilemmas*, pp. 6 ff.

84

jostling others for popularity and at a later period supplanted them. Otherwise his account of such events as the Renaissance or the rise of modern science may be distorted in certain characteristic ways by placing too much emphasis on discontinuities and too little on continuities. Moreover, a historian is often especially interested, like A. O. Lovejoy,[1] in just those concepts that have had an important role in more than one branch of human thought. By surveying the various forms of the concept of nature, say, in philosophy, science, poetry, art, religion and politics he can show its cardinal influence on the whole life of an epoch. But a theory of atomic concepts renders all such surveys and narratives impossible. This kind of theory is thus just what one might expect from a doctrine that reverts to the normative notion of meaning prevalent up to Herder's day. Atomic concepts are as timeless and unchanging as the logical relations with which the doctrine of logical grammar wrongly compares relations between culture-words. The thesis that there is a massive central core of human thinking which has no history is made true by definition.

Not only does an atomist theory tend to make all meanings timeless, none temporal. It has a second serious drawback in that it tends to push philosophical semantics over on to the verbal plane. The doctrine of logical grammar sets out with the express purpose of distinguishing the logical rules of word-use from the non-logical rules and so of setting philosophical semantics unmistakably on the conceptual plane of discourse. But because it also supports a theory of atomic concepts it has an internal incoherence which tends to vitiate that purpose. The trouble is this. Either a philosopher assumes that cross-bearings on a meaning are available, as described in §4, or he does not. If he does, then he can say something about it on the conceptual plane, since he can refer to it by one of the two or more considerations identifying the meaning and then discuss how far some other consideration identifies the same meaning more clearly or more conveniently. But the meaning is then not being regarded as an *infima species* since it has been thought at least possible to delimit it more precisely or to prefer one form of it to another. On the other hand, if he assumes no cross-bearings on a meaning to be available, he thereby takes it to be an *infima species*. But then he has no way of making a non-trivial statement about it on the conceptual plane. He can indicate the meaning on this plane,

[1] Cf. *The Great Chain of Being* (1936), p. 15.

but so far as no other bearing on it is available he can say nothing about it. He is restricted on the assumption that no cross-bearings are available on what he isolates as distinct meanings, either to a mere listing of concepts, with nothing said about them, or, if he does want to say something, what he says must be on the verbal plane. In the latter case he will remark that certain words in certain languages are, or should be, used in such-and-such ways. He can talk about different uses of the same language-word, but not of the same culture-word. Only thus can one explain how some adherents to the doctrine of logical grammar seem able to slide so easily into the outwardly very different doctrine that was advocated by Austin. The path is greased for them by an atomist theory of concepts.

The conjunction of these two drawbacks in an atomist theory of concepts may be further illustrated by a historical comparison. In the centuries before Herder, when all semantic discourse was normally assumed timeless, it was also normally confined to the verbal plane. When seventeenth-century language-planners, like Descartes, Dalgarno, Wilkins and Leibniz, sought to combine a new international auxiliary with a systematically precise terminology for natural science, they could only think such a combination possible because they did not distinguish the conceptual plane of semantic discourse from the verbal one. A new international auxiliary required the assignment of new word-forms to familiar tasks, while an improved scientific terminology required a new arrangement of word-tasks. The former is essentially a project for language-words, the latter for culture-words. But it was characteristic of seventeenth-century thinking to suppose only one problem here. Similarly, instead of suggesting that people talk about word-meaning in two different ways, even so hard-headed a philosopher as Hobbes distinguished instead between 'mental discourse' and 'verbal discourse', and conceived of speech as transferring a train of thoughts, imaginations or 'decaying sense', as he called it, into a train of words.[1] Though philosophers often differed from one another about the nature of thought, a nominalist theory of universals did not generally carry with it a nominalist theory of thinking. To say that people speaking different languages often had the same ideas or concepts, or made the same judgements, was to imply something not so much about their speech-habits, but rather about their visual imagery or about some other

[1] *Leviathan*, I, iv (Everyman edition, p. 13), and *De Corpore*, II, iv.

intrinsically private feature of their mental life. As Ryle has acutely observed, people often supposed there to be a special mystery about how we publish our thoughts instead of realizing that (at least in most cases) we employ a special artifice to keep them to ourselves.[1] But, *pace* Ryle, this mistake was as much bound up with the poverty of people's concepts of language and meaning as with extravagances in their concept of mind.

It is an irony of philosophical history that many of those who were keenest to reject the theories of atomic facts at one time propounded by Russell and Wittgenstein fell unawares into an equally fallacious theory of atomic concepts. The rules-of-word-use philosophy, which largely under Wittgenstein's later influence was to replace the reductionist approach of an earlier generation, led through its doctrine of logical grammar to another kind of atomism that now stands in equal need of repudiation. Such a repudiation might be achieved by affirming that the culture-words of a community stand in internal relations to one another: we must so conceive their meanings that none could have been different without all the rest – no doubt in varying measure – also being different. But the same point is perhaps made more clearly by emphasizing, as suggested in §8, that the meanings of culture-words should be conceived as their functions in their community. One then implies that these functions, like those of other social institutions, are so interconnected that cross-bearings on any one of them are always available. In principle there are no *infimae species* of word-use.

Of course, just as logical grammarians could expressly disclaim any implications of timelessness in talking about what they call the logic of ordinary language, so too they could expressly disclaim any implications of atomicity in what they say about concepts. But in fact the doctrine of logical grammar has not normally been advocated in this qualified form; and in any case the doctrine makes yet another unfortunate suggestion which is too intrinsic to it to be easily repudiated.

If the alleged logical rules of word-use really exist, one must judge by reference to them whether a man's remark is in fact meaningful and what it actually means. Hence, if two philosophical theories offer conflicting accounts of precisely the same concept the evidence of actual usage can never be divided, part of it favouring one account and part of it the other. If one of the two theories offers the correct account because

[1] *The Concept of Mind*, p. 27.

it correctly describes the relevant logical rules, any actual utterances that seem to illustrate the other account, because they purport to use words in accordance with what it claims to be logical rules of usage, must be regarded either as meaningless or as not actually meaning what their authors apparently intend them to mean. For example, it has been argued that a correct analysis of the concepts concerned shows the description 'conscious machine' to have no proper use.[1] What then are we to say, if we accept such an analysis, of a cyberneticist who deliberately uses such a phrase?[2] According to the doctrine of logical grammar, either the remarks he makes with it can have no meaning at all, because he is seeking to say something that cannot be said, or at best he does not really mean what he thinks he means.

No doubt this consequence of the doctrine helps its supporters to believe that sufficiently well-informed and intelligent people should never have any legitimate grounds for ultimate disagreement about the validity of this or that thesis in philosophical semantics. But the consequence is nevertheless unwelcome. It implies that, where such disagreements persist in all good faith, at least one of the disputants is as ignorant, though he does not know it, about some of the concepts he actually uses in his own culture as perhaps he knows he is in regard to the concepts, which he never uses, of Hopi Indians or Melanesian islanders; and when the disputants are equally well educated it seems hardly likely that they should have this degree of disparity in conceptual understanding.

Worse still, if the doctrine of logical grammar is right, at least one of any two such disputants is altogether debarred from saying some of the things that, when he is not talking *about* saying them, he wants to say. Twist and turn his phrases as he may every utterance he makes on a certain topic is either meaningless or illustrates a philosophical thesis with which he disagrees. He is powerless to use words meaningfully in accordance with his own theories about meaningful word-use. Enmeshed in the net of logical grammar he has to choose between saying nothing at all or giving away his own case. His situation is partly analogous to that in which over-zealous adherents of certain theological,

[1] M. Scriven, 'The Mechanical Concept of Mind', *Mind*, lxii (1953), pp. 230 ff., esp. p. 236.

[2] Like K. W. Deutsch, 'Some Notes on Research on the Role of Models in the Natural and Social Sciences', *Synthese*, vii (1948–9), pp. 521 ff.

socio-economic or psychological theories often think their opponents involved: anything their opponents say they take to illustrate their own theory because it fits in with the opposition which that theory leads them to expect from devils, from vested interests, or from deep-rooted mental inhibitions. So far as the doctrine of logical grammar is concerned, the philosopher who persists in using words the way his theory wrongly claims to be correct is not showing at least the practicability of his own theory but merely illustrating some deep-seated bewitchment of his intelligence by human language. His usage constitutes what Austin – writing perhaps under the influence of the doctrine in this respect though not in explicit support of it – called a 'back-seepage of jargon'.[1]

An advocate of a genuinely well-founded theory can afford to refrain from dealing with his opponents in this summary and question-begging way. He can afford to take objections seriously because they are refutable on independent grounds. Conversely, if he does not take them seriously, he suggests that they are not so refutable. Hence a philosopher who holds that the description 'conscious machine' has no proper use would do well to construe this impropriety otherwise than in terms of disobedience to some supposed logical rules of word-use. He would do well to regard the cyberneticist's use of such a description as intelligible, even though he rejects the theory which that use illustrates, and to locate the usage's impropriety in, say, the social harm it does by rendering the notion of having a mind of one's own compatible with the notion of thinking wholly according to preimposed rules.[2] In short he should repudiate the doctrine of logical grammar, and hold it as legitimate to appeal to non-linguistic considerations in arguments against an error of philosophical semantics as to cite non-linguistic factors in the historical explanation of such an error. If language is not a system of rules it does not contain within itself the criteria of good word-use.

§12. The critique of good sense

If a concept has several forms in current use, it is at worst mere journalism and at best no more than a preliminary clearing of the ground, just

---

[1] 'A Plea for Excuses', *Proc. Arist. Soc.*, lvii (1957), pp. 17 ff.
[2] Cf. L. J. Cohen, 'Can there be Artificial Minds?', *Analysis*, xvi (1955), pp. 36 ff.

to report this fact and list the forms. Serious study of the concept only begins when we ask in turn how important each of these forms is. But is that a question about the form's influence or its value? Two quite different kinds of question emerge. First, how many people use the concept in that form, in what cultures or sub-cultures are they mostly found, is their number increasing or decreasing, and what are the distinctive causes and effects of their usage? Secondly, how valuable is that form of the concept compared with the others, by what other patterns of usage are people committed to it, and what is gained or lost by adopting it?

The former question has often occupied sociologists, and in the literature of the subject its fundamentally quantitative character is quite apparent. In studying the actual functions in a community of words like 'senator', 'communist' or 'Negro' a sociologist must at least find out if any stereotype images or attitudes are generally associated with a given word among people of this or that occupation, income-level, skin-colour, etc.[1] For such a purpose he needs to poll a reasonably large number of individuals and to state the results of his interrogations in numerical terms so that the relative significance of each result can be properly assessed: perhaps four out of every five members of a certain community conceive of all Negroes as superstitious while only half of them conceive of all Italians as artistic.[2] Nor is interest in opinion-polling and numerical data confined to sociologists studying associations of ideas like these, as distinct from literal synonymies or antonymies. Arne Naess has argued that unless one uses such methods even in the study of scientists' ways of thinking one cannot secure any properly founded descriptions.[3] By his standards descriptions that lack such a foundation, as do Cassirer's anthropological surveys, are to be condemned as methodologically unreliable – unless they may be excused as preliminary surveys of a vast field where the discovery of adequately substantiated conclusions requires research on a scale that is too enormous and unprofitable to attract ready sponsors or interested participants. Similarly, if a man is being prosecuted under a law requiring disseminators of antidemocratic propaganda to disclose their identity, it

---

[1] Cf. K. Young, *Handbook of Social Psychology* (1946), pp. 189 ff.

[2] D. Katz and K. Braly, 'Racial Stereotypes of 100 College Students', *Journal of Abnormal and Social Psychology*, xxviii (1933), pp. 280 ff.

[3] *Interpretation and Preciseness* (1947–51), vol. I, pp. 14 f., etc.

is unsatisfactory to have his guilt or innocence depend on the un-methodical impressions of inexpert witnesses. In several such cases United States courts have therefore accepted evidence that relies on H. D. Lasswell's quantitative techniques for describing the meanings of culture-words. There is nothing more remarkable in this (even if Lass-well sometimes claims too much for his techniques) than in using counts of language-word occurrences to confirm or refute disputed literary authorship.[1] By the former technique one compares the fre-quencies with which a given word is used in certain ways in two or more texts of agreed authorship, by the latter the frequencies with which different words or phrases occur in two or more texts of dis-puted authorship. The former technique establishes the function of a given culture-word by reference to the kind of people who use it, the latter establishes who has written a given text by reference to the kinds of language-words or language-phrases he has used. The former achieves a quantitative foundation for the sociology of ideas, the latter for descriptive stylistics.

It is true that a few workers in these fields sometimes call their work philosophy. Many of Cassirer's anthropological surveys occur in a book entitled *The Philosophy of Symbolic Forms*, and Naess claims that his research procedures afford a sure method for the conduct of philoso-phical analysis. But this nomenclature is comparatively rare for cross-cultural and quantitative studies of ideas, and is belied by the close interconnections of method and topic such studies have with admitted branches of sociology. Even Naess defines a community's ideology – its central core of thoughtways – so as not to require clarity or self-consistency of it.[2] But a theory of philosophical semantics which does not allow at least for that requirement would be altogether too in-applicable to the kind of discourse about word-uses with which rival theories, like the doctrine of logical grammar, have in fact been con-cerned. By defining his notion of ideology so as not to require clarity or consistency a sociologist puts himself in a position to examine the extent to which people's actual usage conforms to that endorsed by such-or-such a philosophical thesis, but at the same time distinguishes his interest in this usage from a philosopher's.

[1] H. D. Lasswell, N. Leites, *et al.*, *Language of Politics* (1949), esp. ch. iv and ix. Cf. G. U. Yule, *The Statistical Study of Literary Vocabulary* (1944).
[2] *Democracy, Ideology and Objectivity* (1956), p. 183.

What is left to constitute the distinctive province of philosophical semantics is the question of value. Extent of prevalence no more measures the value of a culture-word than of any other social institution, so that quantitative data are characteristically irrelevant to philosophical discourse about meanings. By confounding together descriptive and evaluative modes of semantics the doctrine of logical grammar makes it particularly easy for sociologists to miss this irrelevance, and tempts them to protest that those who claim to solve the problems of philosophical analysis without using quantitative techniques of experiment and observation are 'guilty of grossly unempirical and unscientific procedures'.[1] To avoid such a confusion one must reject a *de jure* theory of conceptual semantics altogether, just as philologists have in practice long since rejected a *de jure* theory of verbal semantics. There are no rules of word-use, but only the *de facto* functions of words in a language or community and these can be either described or evaluated.

Indeed, the distinctive features of philosophical semantics are best brought out by comparison with the analogously evaluative mode of discourse on the verbal plane that is familiar from handbooks of good style like H. W. Fowler's *Dictionary of Modern English Usage*. But philosophers have said so much about the principles and methods of philosophical semantics, and so little about those of works like Fowler's, that the ground for any such comparison needs preparing by an investigation of the latter in some detail. This will help to confirm the existence of a middle way between describing current usage and proposing innovations; for the doctrine of logical grammar often confuses philosophers into ignoring the existence of any such third possibility.[2]

In the Oxford *New English Dictionary* statements that it is better to use a word this way rather than that are found rarely if at all: in Fowler's *Dictionary* they are a principal feature of the book. The former normally purports to set out with complete impartiality the different ways in which English words are known to have been used. The latter again and again selects one usage as better than another. Of course, just as the *N.E.D.* includes a great deal of etymology, orthography and quotation, and even a certain amount of implicit selection, especially in

[1] H. Tönnessen, 'The Fight against Revelation in Semantical Studies', *Synthese*, viii (1950–1), pp. 225 ff.

[2] E.g. A. G. N. Flew, *Logic and Language* (2nd series, 1953), editorial introduction, p. 9; and P. Edwards, *The Logic of Moral Discourse* (1955), p. 41.

regard to pronunciation, so too stylistic reviews like Fowler's do a great deal more than just discuss the meanings that particular words should preferably be used to express and the patterns of order in which particular kinds of words are best combined. When a word is commonly spelt or pronounced in more ways than one they often tell us how they think this should be done. When some particular feature of a language is going through a marked period of change they tell us the direction in which they think the change is going.[1] Above all they provide arguments to support, and examples to illustrate, their criticisms.

These arguments perhaps exhibit more clearly than anything else the characteristic tenor of a work like Fowler's. They appeal to a wide variety of considerations. Sometimes they invoke the practice of a writer commonly recognized as a master of prose style, like Lord Morley or Edmund Burke if English is the language under consideration. Generally they prefer a prevailing usage to one that is comparatively rare. But they sometimes treat the superior quality of authorities favouring one view as outbalancing the larger quantity of those favouring another, especially when the former are works of corporate authorship like *The Times* or *The Encyclopaedia Britannica*, or the edicts of a corporate body like the French Academy.[2] Often they make their points by quoting a series of passages that exhibit the fault of style under criticism in a glaringly clumsy form, so that a reader's intuitive sensitivity will then suffice to convince him of a principle which from more casual and inoffensive examples would have been less obvious to him. Fowler makes a most effective use of this method in reproving the tendency of 'second-rate writers' to think use of a synonym always more elegant than repetition of a word or reference back to it by a personal pronoun: he quotes a score of sentences, like 'They spend a few weeks longer in their winter *home* than in their summer *habitat*', that have obviously been made affected or inelegant by such a variation of terms. Often, too, certain commonly recognized values are invoked, like the dangers of obscurity and ambiguity, even against good authorities or a majority of writers. But sectional values, like the genteelism that would say 'lady-dog' instead of 'bitch', may

[1] *Dictionary of Modern English Usage* (1926), s.v. 'caddis', 'badinage', 'transference', 'either', etc.

[2] Ibid., s.v. 'which) (that) (who', 'which with and or but', 'concernment', '-ize, -ise, in verbs', etc.

be ridiculed for their pretentiousness.[1] Again, it may be shown that use of two particular words as total synonyms, like 'elemental' and 'elementary' or 'economic' and 'economical', will tend to impoverish the language's resources. Or it may be argued that new compounds in '-less', say, should maintain the principle that in prose, as distinct from poetry, this suffix should be added to nouns only, so as to have regard for the long-term interests of the language rather than for its pliability to purposes immediately in hand. Or sometimes the historical origin of an expression like 'Frankenstein' or 'the gentle art' may be cited in order to deter the ill-read from its abuse.

Though many others also occur, these are perhaps the most typical forms of argument that any expert on good style in a particular language can employ to support his evaluations. Of course, we may sometimes think such arguments pedantic. It is difficult to see why one should agree with Fowler, for instance, that the 'real meaning' of the English phrase 'idols of the market-place' was settled once and for all by Francis Bacon's quaint metaphor and that the phrase's widespread modern use in a less metaphorical and much more readily intelligible way is to be condemned as a 'misuse'. When those who use it in the latter way intend no allusion to Bacon's classification of fallacies, one would do better to admit that the proper meaning of the phrase has at last slipped out of the conservative grip which the dead hand of Bacon's metaphor may once have exercised. But in thus condemning one argument of Fowler's as pedantic we should be arguing against him within his own frame of reference. We should be appealing to some general principle, like the danger of impoverishing the language, which Fowler himself would wish to apply in many other contexts. In condemning one view of his as 'pedantic' we should be using that term in just the same way as he himself wants to use it of many views advanced by other critics of English prose style.[2]

It is a very different matter, however, to condemn all such evaluations of word-use as being pedantic or otherwise unacceptable. Despite the constant risk of pedantry in detail this mode of verbal semantics is not one with which we can profitably dispense. It is integral to our self-conscious involvement with language. We are agents in, as well as spectators of, linguistic activity, and accordingly we may from time to

[1] Ibid., s.v. 'Elegant variation', 'that', 'genteelism'.
[2] Ibid., s.v. 'Pedantry'.

time need to talk about our own several languages in another fashion than that of dictionaries and descriptive grammars. We may need to discuss which locutions, out of the multitude we know of as native speakers of the language, will most effectively express what we now want to say. Or we may need to discuss how we can best say what we want to say at the moment without thereby restricting the ways open to us for saying other things in the future. Thus evaluations that can occur as major premises in such discussions, and can themselves be defended in turn by arguments of the kind already considered, constitute a by no means unprofitable mode of temporal semantics on the verbal plane.

Someone may object to calling these evaluative statements 'temporal', because he thinks that they claim to determine the correct meaning of an English or French word for all time. He may point, in support of his objection, to the way in which a man like Fowler talks about 'the true meanings of "polity"', 'the real meaning of "farouche"', or claims that it is 'meaningless' to answer an unpleasantly pointed interrogator by 'That is a leading question', as if the very nature of the word or phrase permitted only one use for it. But though these idioms – 'true meaning', 'real meaning', etc. – originated in close connection with the older conception of meaning, whereby the meaning of words and sentences in a language were thought of as timeless and unchanging, it would be a mistake to conclude that using such idioms today still commits one to such a conception or to the *de jure* theory that goes with it. Fowler, for example, though he sometimes used the word 'grammar' in the old-fashioned, normative way, knew well the importance of semantic change and the consequent relativity of what he said to the changing facts of actual usage.[1] In order to help solve the ordinary writer's practical problems of word selection what are needed are evaluations of usage that may be thought of as valid for the writer's own generation. To seek advice on means of expression that will be equally effective for all time is to seek a style that belongs to no period at all and a language that has neither life nor death. It makes sense to conceive of certain stylistic values as unchanging, like the requirement of maximum lucidity or the need to avoid impoverishing the language, and to conceive of certain others as matters of changing fashion, like the virtue of echoing Ciceronian phraseology, though experts have often

[1] Ibid., s.v. 'fine', 'lay and lie', etc.

differed about which principles should be assigned to which category. But one must treat all the evaluative consequences that principles of either category have for a given language as being open to change, if one so treats the language itself. If the range of actual usage alters, the same principles may come to justify a different selection from it. Hence, modern evaluative discourse about the meanings of particular language-words should conceive these meanings temporally, even if a survival of the old confusion between factual and normative linguistics occasionally leads people to indulge in linguistic evaluations that claim a timelessly unchanging validity.

If lexicographers and grammarians are mainly concerned, as was argued in §7, with describing the functions of words, and the purposes of sentences, in human speech, it follows that it is these functions and purposes which experts on good style are evaluating. One should therefore not be surprised to find such evaluations often expressed as statements about the 'real' or 'true' meaning of a word or even to find the word 'meaning' itself used without qualification as a partially evaluative term, since the words 'function' and 'purpose' are also often used in this way. When a left-wing politician claims that the function (true function, real function) of general elections in twentieth-century Britain is chiefly to provide the House of Commons with a fresh mandate, or a right-wing politician claims that the purpose (true purpose, real purpose) of voting at such elections is to choose the House's personnel, he is generally concerned with how he thinks the existing constitution ought to work, not with the various purposes that people in fact aim to achieve by operating it nor with some pro-posal for constitutional reform.

Hence the critique of good style is as different on one side from ordinary lexicography, grammar or descriptive stylistics as it is on the other from the proposal of occasional neologisms or of wholesale linguistic novelties like C. K. Ogden's Basic English. Analogously the critique of good sense, evaluating meanings on the conceptual plane, differs as much from the history or sociology of ideas as from the pro-posal of conceptual innovations. Not that philosophers are in any way excluded from making such proposals. But conceptual innovation stands to selection from existing thoughtways as a proposal to substi-tute plebiscites for general elections stands to an assertion about the latter's true function. It gains an audience only where people have a much more radical discontent than they can satisfy through expressing a selective preference for certain of the many functions currently performed by linguistic institutions.

It is not always easy to decide in particular cases whether adopting a purged and regulated way of thinking about a topic should be considered an innovatory reform, or merely a selective refinement, of existing concepts. It depends on whether we treat some pre-existing complex of linguistic custom as a single concept requiring reform or as an amalgam of sound and unsound features. But even though one might debate whether Hume's analysis of causation should be classed in the former category or the latter, one could hardly deny Newton the credit of an innovation in the concept of mass nor Locke the role of an underlabourer to Newton. On the whole philosophers have been more concerned with elaborating and criticizing what is implied by the conceptual innovations of lawyers, statesmen, mathematicians, natural scientists and others than with initiating such revolutions themselves. Theirs has been a reflective, second-order concern with language. Even when they do make innovating proposals of their own, as particularly in what philosophers like Carnap and Quine call 'explications',[1] it is in the evaluation of these proposals rather than in the proposals themselves that one finds the patterns of argument characteristic of philosophical semantics. A theory that explicates a concept by constituting a more exact, less troublesome, system for accomplishing the same purposes as the explicandum, is not itself necessarily the product of philosophical interest. Whenever any physicist, mathematician or philologist sharpens up some element in his conceptual apparatus that has hitherto operated too loosely, he carries out an explication. What is characteristically philosophical (or at any rate needs some distinguishing name) is the activity of comparing this explicating theory with the explicandum and evaluating their respective merits. One may also note that so far as both this theory and the explicandum must be capable of accomplishing some of the same purposes of sentence-utterance, they must be regarded as constituting alternative forms of the same concept. No one can support the enterprise of explication without implicitly rejecting an atomist theory of concepts.

The kinds of argument used in justifying evaluations of style are

[1] Cf. R. Carnap, *Logical Foundations of Probability* (1950), pp. 3 ff., and W. V. Quine, *Word and Object* (1960), pp. 258 ff.

closely paralleled by many of those used to substantiate theses in philosophical semantics. Just as writers of acknowledged repute are cited by stylists, so too are thinkers by philosophers. One important prop of Schlick's verificationist analysis for the concept of meaning is his claim to 'stick consistently to Einstein's position'.[1] On both the verbal and conceptual planes of evaluative semantics, too, a prevailing usage is generally preferred to one that is comparatively rare, since an overriding purpose of most discourse is to be as readily intelligible as possible. But the authority of one man like Einstein may be sufficient to outweigh that of his numerous critics. That is why the quantitative techniques so important in the sociology of ideas are largely irrelevant to philosophical semantics.

Again, a well-chosen set of quoted passages may exhibit a fault of style in such an outstandingly glaring and clumsy form that a reader's intuitive sensitivity will suffice to convince him of a stylistic principle which from more casual and inoffensive examples would have been less obvious to him. So too a philosopher often seeks to support a theory by showing how odd or absurd may be the consequences, in the form of actual or imaginary utterances, of not accepting it: they serve no conceivable purposes of discourse. Ryle defends the thesis that to talk about myself is not necessarily to talk about my body by pointing out how absurd it would be in some cases to substitute for the personal pronoun a reference to a part of one's body and to speak of 'my head remembering' or 'my brain doing long division'.[2] On both the verbal and conceptual planes of evaluative semantics this kind of argument rests ultimately on an appeal to the individual's sensitivity, much as an argument for the mandate-giving function of general elections might end with the appeal 'Surely you can see that it's wrong for parliament to bind people by laws to which they have not consented?' Indeed, in all fields appeals of this sort are often a legitimately ultimate resort in the reasoned defence of evaluations. To suppose that one can always go beyond such an appeal to the evidence of observation, experiment and quantitative assessment, replacing argument from the appeal itself by argument from a survey of its actual or probable results, is to confuse the merit of an opinion with its popularity. But it is necessary to remember that what seems at one time or place to be self-evidently

---

[1] 'Meaning and Verification', *Gesammelte Aufsätze* (1938), p. 341.
[2] *The Concept of Mind* (1949), p. 189.

pointless or purposeless may nevertheless have a valued function in the activities of another.

On both the verbal and conceptual planes of evaluative semantics certain commonly recognized values and certain important purposes that human discourse can achieve, or help to achieve, are often implicitly or explicitly invoked. On the one hand, obscurity and ambiguity of expression are condemned, on the other, conceptual fuzziness and inconsistency. Just as the resources of a particular language must not be impoverished, neither must the resources of our conceptual inheritance. On the one hand the long-term interests of a language must be kept in mind and nothing done to block its future development. On the other the expansion of our conceptual horizon must not be circumscribed by restrictive definitions that block the paths of enquiry, industry, art or other developing forms of human activity. Physical theory, for instance, must not be thought essentially deterministic or we shall be unable to treat as an empirical question the problem of how far non-deterministic theories like quantum theory should be accepted into physics.[1] Not all values, however, are so universally admitted nor are all purposes so universally esteemed. Just as a sectional value, like genteelism, is sometimes rejected in the critique of style, so too the religious value of facilitating belief in miracles did not weigh with Hume in his analysis of causal connection.

The historical origins of concepts may be as relevant to their analysis as the etymology of a word, or the origin of a phrase, to opinions about its proper use. If at one period the point of a word-use has come to be easily blurred, forgotten or misunderstood, a historical account of its origins may serve to sharpen and re-establish it. But of course this historical mode of argument always risks the rejoinder that the original form of the concept is no longer appropriate. R. G. Collingwood was at one time so taken up with this form of argument – well illustrated in his distinction of three different senses for the word 'cause' – that he came to make the mistake of conceiving the analysis of fundamental concepts simply as a branch of historical enquiry.[2] One may compare the way in which Naess and Tönnessen are so preoccupied with those arguments in favour of philosophical statements which appeal to

---

[1] Cf. H. Feigl, 'Logical Empiricism', *Readings in Philosophical Analysis*, ed. H. Feigl and W. Sellars (1949), p. 21.

[2] *An Essay on Metaphysics* (1940), pp. 285 ff.

prevalent usage that they mistakenly conceive of philosophical semantics as a branch of sociology. Rather, the various kinds of relevant argument should at best complement and reinforce each other. Where their conclusions conflict one or more must be subordinated to the rest, or the philosopher can content himself with pointing out which conclusions are justified on which principles of argument. But to suppose that only one kind of argument is ever relevant is to have a misleadingly oversimplified conception of philosophical semantics and to miss a crucial range of facets in the analogy between them and statements about good style.

This diversity is perhaps best illustrated here by the present book's arguments about the meaning of 'meaning'. Lovejoy and Cassirer have been cited as thinkers of repute in the history of ideas, Lasswell and Naess in the sociology of ideas, Fowler in the critique of style, the Oxford *New English Dictionary* in lexicography, and Saussure and Trier in linguistics. But on topics that do not constitute an established subject-matter for specialized academic enquiry, such as the timeless meanings of particular remarks, it has been worth while to cite prevalent patterns of usage or to appeal to the reader's intuitive sense of pointlessness. Clarity and consistency demand that word-use should not be likened to tool-use if a word's meaning in a sentence is the function it performs there. But it is primarily to leave an open road for the history of ideas that one must reject an atomist theory of concepts, and because it thus becomes possible to discuss meanings at different levels of specificity one need not suppose that philologists should be as specific in their use of mental-conduct words like 'purpose' or 'intention' as psychologists or theologians. Finally, in investigating the meanings of 'meaning', 'concept', and similar words, it helps us to have some understanding of their history: hence the utility of occasional references to Phrynichus, Vaugelas, Herder and others.

The fact that a man like Fowler normally expresses views on good style about no language but his own is paralleled by the way in which philosophers normally evaluate concepts in no culture but their own. On both planes the need for an evaluative mode of temporal semantics arises because each of us is an agent in a particular *milieu* – not just a spectator of it – with an embarrassing profusion of inherited words or concepts at his disposal. Within any one such verbal or conceptual *milieu* we all have both an interest in, and at least some qualification for, arguing with one another about the selections we should make from this inheritance and from proposals for its reform. But it would be odd for a Frenchman to argue with Fowler how English should best be written. We are wise to confine our advice about the writing of other languages than our own to comparatively elementary manuals of instruction designed for those who are also foreigners to those languages. Analogously a European anthropologist who sought to go beyond a merely descriptive survey of Hopi thought to an analysis corrective of certain conceptual confusions which perhaps commonly occur in it, could hardly hope to say anything of importance unless either he had so absorbed Hopi standards and interests that he would now be said to share their culture or, alternatively, he had decided to govern his analytical selections by European standards and interests and so to treat Hopi life as a sub-culture within his own community. Moreover, just as the stylist's statements about the 'true' or 'real' meaning of a word are relative to the range of his generation's vocabulary and accepted stylistic values, so too the philosopher's are relative to the range of his generation's conceptual resources and its accepted interests. Only so far as his successors share these resources and interests may they be able to learn from him. That is why the problems of philosophical semantics often seem to demand new solutions in every age.

A further helpful feature of the analogy between philosophical semantics and the critique of style is the way in which it elucidates, as the doctrine of logical grammar cannot, how equally honest, reasonable, well-informed and intelligent members of the same culture, even when contemporaries of one another, may have legitimate grounds for disagreement in particular cases. Employing different, but equally relevant, principles of argument – one appealing to prevalent usage, say, and another to the purpose of furthering scientific enquiry or religious belief – they may understandably diverge as much from one another in their conclusions about the proper functions of words as in their political controversies about the proper functions of constables, stock-exchanges, national flags or general elections. The doctrine of logical grammar implies that at least one of two such parties is as ignorant, though he does not know it, about some concepts of his own culture as perhaps most Europeans know they are in regard to Hopi thought. But if philosophical semantics is evaluative such a disagreement can more readily be thought compatible with both sides being equally well-informed.

Indeed, if the doctrine of logical grammar is right, at least one of any two such disputants is altogether debarred from using words in some of the ways that, when he is not talking *about* so using them, he wants to do. Enmeshed in the net of logical grammar he has to choose, as was argued in §11, between saying nothing at all on certain topics and giving away his own case. But the comparison of philosophical semantics to discourse about good style shows how this kind of question-begging is in practice avoided. Just as on the verbal plane the evaluative senses of 'meaning', 'meaningful', etc., used by men like Fowler must be distinguished from the purely factual ones that occur implicitly or explicitly in dictionaries or descriptive grammars, so too on the conceptual plane there are evaluative senses of 'meaning' and 'meaningful' as well as factual ones. When Fowler calls it 'meaningless' to 'object as people do when they are challenged to deny or confirm an imputation, "That is a leading question" ', he is obviously not using 'meaningless' in the same way as a descriptive grammarian who declares 'If a goes the but' to be a meaningless string of English words. Analogously a philosopher may evaluate a sentence about conscious machines as 'meaningless' though for the historian or sociologist who seeks to record the vagaries of thought among twentieth-century cyberneticists it is perfectly meaningful. Evaluative ascriptions of meaningfulness cannot be valid unless the corresponding factual ones are also true, even if only within the limits of some novel theory. But a sentence can be factually meaningful though evaluatively meaningless, because such an evaluation normally presents a choice from the variety of available usages. It is a major fault in the doctrine of logical grammar, as it also was in the old pre-Herder confusion of factual and normative linguistics, that we are not allowed to distinguish these two senses of 'meaning' and its compounds and so to regard the conceptions of our philosophical opponents as meaningful in the former sense though meaningless in the latter. Questions like 'What does *x* mean?' are thus liable to be misleading in more ways than one. Not only is it a mistake, as logical grammarians rightly emphasize, to take the transitiveness of the verb as implying that the answer should always name an entity meant. It is equally a mistake to suppose, as logical grammarians too often do, that the question's indicative mood implies the correct answer always to be one which all honest, reasonable, well-informed and intelligent people will accept.

Consequently, if one says that a philosophical thesis articulates its author's knowledge how to operate with a certain concept or category of concepts, or his understanding of what words mean when used in certain ways, what one calls knowledge here is wisdom rather than technique and what one calls understanding is more like a good essayist's understanding how to write prose than a good pupil's understanding of the Latin vocabulary he acquires at school. If a philosopher condemns some word-use as a misuse or howler, one should compare this with criticizing a bad essayist's lapses in linguistic taste rather than to a bad pupil's mistakes in Latin composition. Or, if one compares the communication of thought with the commerce of goods, philosophical semantics should not be likened to a geographical survey of existing commercial arrangements but rather to a political discussion of the merits of such arrangements as against perhaps some programme for rationalizing them. The question at issue is not so much 'What jobs are at present being done by words?' but rather 'How can words do their present jobs better (more clearly, more consistently, more profitably) than they sometimes seem to do?' Philosophical semantics does not spring from the disinterested pursuit of truth about word-use, but from the interested pursuit of consistency in it. With regard to the customary usages of ordinary language the job of a philosopher is rather to seek for their own justification, if any, than to seek in them for a justification or refutation of philosophical theses.

No doubt a philosopher will often find himself fighting against ways of thinking so strongly favoured by familiar grammatical similarities and analogies that much of his attack will be concentrated on a purely linguistic front. No doubt he will often occupy himself more with certain very general or categorial concepts like 'animal', 'cause' or 'time', than with details of usage that are peculiar to much more specific concepts, like 'ant', 'glue' or 'noon'. No doubt the main technical problems of philosophical semantics, the major difficulties to be encountered, the focal opportunities of analytical prowess, are all in the application of conceptual values, rather than in debate about what they are or should be. But the underlying evaluative character of philosophical semantics cannot be gainsaid. It is here alone that room can be found for a specifically philosophical concern with particular meanings. Moreover, where any of the issues determining the best way to think about a certain topic have ever been controversial a philosopher ought not to avoid considering matters of substance within the mode of discourse he is investigating. Unless, for example, he pays some attention to recent controversy about continuities and discontinuities in the Renaissance and the rise of modern science he cannot see quite how badly an atomic theory of concepts fits the history of ideas. The boundary between arguments about a mode of discourse and arguments within it is thus not as clearly marked as the doctrine of logical grammar implies. Even if the critique of concepts were the only proper concern of a philosopher it should nevertheless sometimes lead him to a consideration of wider, non-linguistic issues. Something ought sometimes to stand or fall with what he says that is not itself a philosophical theory.

Indeed, the doctrine of logical grammar has sometimes been attacked solely on the grounds that it confines philosophical thinking within artificially narrow limits by locating within language itself both the origins of all genuine philosophical problems and also the data for solving them. But there are good reasons for not spending too much time in criticizing logical grammarians on these grounds alone.

First, most of what they have said about particular meanings can be recast without difficulty in the mould endorsed here. It is their conception of meaning that I am criticizing, not their appeals to clarity, consistency or prevalent usage, even if other modes of argument might justify other conclusions. This is true even for F. Sommers's ingenious theory of the 'ordinary language tree' where each pair of concepts is ordered according to whether or not the two concepts can appear as subject and predicate of a meaningful sentence.[1] One can take such meaningfulness to be determined not by ordinary usage, as Sommers assumes, but rather by principles of evaluative semantics. Certainly, if philosophical semantics uses arguments from clarity, consistency and prevalent usage too exclusively, it runs the risk of degenerating into a barren and uninteresting scholasticism. But the opposite course also has its dangers. If a professional philosopher relies too much on arguments involving matters of substance within the mode of discourse he is investigating, he easily exposes himself to the charge of amateurish

[1] 'The Ordinary Language Tree', *Mind*, lxviii (1959), pp. 160 ff.

interference in a field of specialist study. The path between these two pitfalls is not very wide.

Secondly, a philosophical school is best overthrown by attack on its strong or central points, not on its weak or peripheral ones, since only the former kind of attack can shed direct light on the main problems that interest the school. No one ever gave up being a logical positivist because he was told that his philosophy had the consequence of excluding all metaphysical argument and perhaps all moral argument too. Support for logical positivism declined when it became apparent that its central doctrine – its neat dichotomous classification of intelligent discourse into empirical and analytic statements – did justice neither to the protean variety of linguistic usage Wittgenstein later succeeded in revealing to philosophers (though it was well-known to linguists)[1] nor to the discoveries of Church and Gödel in metamathematics nor to the difficulties of establishing an adequate criterion of empiricalness. Similarly no one will ever give up being a logical grammarian because he is told: 'Your belief that you are concerned solely with linguistic problems conceals your real motives and principles and prevents you from discussing the real issues that determine how people think.' The strength of his philosophy lies in the informal rules-of-word-use account of meaning that enabled him to surmount the earlier crudities of logical positivism, and only by convincing him that that account is wrong can one expect to dissuade him from his over-narrow conception of philosophy in general. Moreover, to support this dissuasion one needs to replace the logical grammarian's rules-of-word-use theory, which was a good deal more subtle and sophisticated than what logical positivists had to say about meaning, by a theory that in its turn does even more justice to the complexity of the central problem. An attack on the philosophy of logical grammar runs the risk of degenerating into unconstructive polemic if it still shares the Schlick-Ryle assumption that queries about meanings should be treated as queries about rules of word-use.

Such unity of theme as the present book has springs from its attempt to show that any single theory of meaning, such as the rules-of-use theory, is bound to do less than justice to the complexity of problems

[1] Cf., e.g., Karl Brugmann, *Verschiedenheiten der Satzgestaltung nach Massgabe der seelischen Grundfunktionen in der indogermanischen Sprachen* (Berichte über die Verhandlungen der Sächsichen Gesellschaft der Wissenschaften, lxx, 6: 1918).

about meaning. Instead it seems that there are several importantly different ways of talking about meanings and correspondingly there are several importantly different kinds of query about meanings. Perhaps the way in which that thesis is most relevant here is in its implications for the concept of meaninglessness or what is sometimes called 'logical oddity'. This concept is an old weapon in the armoury of philosophical argument. It was used, for instance, by Berkeley against Locke. But it seemed to acquire a new force when Russell used it to solve certain logical paradoxes like those about the class of all classes not members of themselves or the man who says that he always lies. It seemed as though Russell's theory of types could be generalized in such a way that other and quite different philosophical problems could be solved. Just as Russell excluded from legitimacy any sentence purporting to assert or deny that a class of some given type was a member of a class of the same type, so too perhaps all concepts could be assigned to types or categories, according to supposed rules of word-use, such that mistakes or muddles about their correct assignment would issue in philosophical theories attributing meaning to sentences that had none. But this analogy breaks down at both ends. In the first place Zermelo showed that the Class paradox could be solved without using a theory of types to exclude certain expressions as illegitimate, and Ramsey pointed out the extent of the difference between formal antinomies like the Class paradox and semantical antinomies like the Liar.[1] Secondly, it seems evident that when a man claims to discern meaninglessness he may have discerned one or other of several very different things, depending on the context of his claim. This is true even if we disregard statements on the verbal plane of semantics, as when he has seen that a particular string of language-words instantiates no customary pattern of sentence-construction, such as 'If a the goes but' in English, or when he has seen that a particular use of some language-phrase, like 'leading question', is undesirable. Perhaps he has seen that a certain combination of words has no function in the culture of a certain community, like the expression 'empty term' in ancient Greek logic. Perhaps he thinks that no conceivable purpose is achieved by uttering a certain sentence, such as 'Edinburgh is between Glasgow.' Or perhaps he thinks that no

---

[1] Cf. E. Zermelo, 'Untersuchungen über die Grundlagen der Mengenlehre', *Mathematische Annalen*, lxv (1908), pp. 261 ff., and F. Ramsey, *The Foundations of Mathematics* (1931), pp. 20 f.

desirable purpose is served by uttering some other, such as 'Some machines can think for themselves.' In addition to these various possibilities about meaning in a language or culture, there are yet others, which will emerge from §§16–19, about meaning in communication. When a man claims that a remark is meaningless he may have seen that it is self-contradictory, or that it has no implications whatever. He may have seen that though it is apparently a statement its truth-value is in principle quite unascertainable (cf. §22). Or he may have seen that it is not a statement at all, like the habitual liar's remark 'I always lie', in so far as it cannot even have a truth-value (cf. §26). This is by no means a complete list, but it at least serves to show that the concept of nonsense is too multiform to be much illuminated by any single theory of meaning, like the rules-of-word-use theory, even when that theory is supplemented by a doctrine of linguistic types or categories.

IV

The Concept of Meaning in the
Problem of Universals

§13. The problem conceived as insoluble

If the evaluative theory of philosophical semantics is true to itself, one cannot always draw a sharp line between questions about the concept of meaning in philosophical semantics and questions of philosophical semantics about particular meanings. Some solutions of first-order philosophical puzzles ought to stand or fall with the solution of the second-order puzzle about philosophical puzzlement. Hence one cannot properly assess the merits or demerits of the evaluative theory of philosophical semantics without examining at least some of its commitments within philosophy and comparing these with those of the principal theory it seeks to supplant – the doctrine of logical grammar. The present chapter will attempt such a comparison in regard to the problem of universals.

There is a certain treatment of that problem which the doctrine of logical grammar encourages. I do not mean that all who have so treated the problem[1] have been or still are logical grammarians, or that all logical grammarians have so treated it. But anyone who accepts the doctrine of logical grammar will naturally be inclined to say certain things about classical theories of universals. In particular he will seek to trace the origin of these theories to confusions or mistakes about language since they are clearly not philosophical theories of the sole legitimate kind. They do not articulate logical rules for using particular class-names and attribute-words.

First, the logical grammarian must identify one or more questions which appear to be answered by classical theories of universals but which in reality are unanswerable, or at least are better not asked in the form in which the theories seem to answer them. He must then aim to show that these questions arise naturally in a philosophically unsophis-

[1] E.g. D. F. Pears, 'Universals', *Philosophical Quarterly*, i (1951), pp. 218 ff.

ticated mind, since only thus can the problem of universals be traced to mistakes about language and not to mistakes of other kinds. For this role of pseudo-question two candidates are especially apt here: 'Why are things what they are?' and 'Why are we able to name things as we do?'

The former question has a quite uncontroversial use to express the general spirit of human enquiry. But if a man has not yet learned to be satisfied with the fragmentary answers that gradually emerge from the detailed researches of scientists and historians, it is obvious that he may be tempted to propose a once-and-for-all answer like the theory of universals in Plato's *Phaedo*. He may be led by the grammar of 'Why are things what they are?' into thinking that, like any ordinary interrogative sentence, this is a question admitting of an immediate answer, whereas in fact it merely expresses the spirit in which a whole category of more detailed questions are asked. However, this can hardly be the pseudo-question that more recent theories of universals have been designed to answer. The rise of modern science has shown how much more fruitful it is to ask for particular explanations of particular phenomena. The pseudo-question that generates the modern problem of universals must be one that is not so obviously replaceable by the detailed enquiries of science. If therefore it does not request an explanation of things, what seems left for it is to ask about their names. If it is not about the world, it must seek an explanation of the language with which we describe the world: 'Why are we able to name things as we do?'

The logical grammarian has then to argue that any comprehensive explanation of naming is as vacuous as any comprehensive explanation of events. The realist, he will claim, tries to explain the applicability of a general name by the existence of a generic entity – a universal. The explanation looks informative, he will say, because it shifts to another level. But unfortunately universals are themselves specifiable only by reference to words. One cannot point them out. So the realist theory opens up no 'exit from the maze of words'.[1] Universals are just the shadows cast by names in a twilight of philosophical confusion. The realistic theory is inherently circular. Nor can other theories fare any better, if the logical grammarian is to make out his case. Locke's abstract general idea and Berkeley's representative image, it will be said, are completely identifiable only by their use. No doubt we can

[1] Ibid., p. 220.

partly identify images by describing their features and certain images most naturally stand for certain things. But thought may not follow the most natural course, nor is it always clear which course is most natural.[1] Hence a mental tool, like a concept or an image, can be completely identified only by referring to the things that evoke its use. But for such a reference we have to use the name. So conceptualist and imagist theories are as circular as realist ones. Similarly the nominalist who explains naming by a likeness in the things named is immediately open to the objection that likeness is an incomplete predicate. Anything is like anything in some positive or negative way. But to specify the relevant kind of likeness one must again use a name, since in most cases one cannot enumerate all the members of the class named, and even when one can enumerate them they may be alike in more than one respect. Here too there is no exit from the maze of words.

A skilful logical grammarian will not be quite content yet. The victory must not be too easily won, or it will not seem plausible that so many intelligent people should have taken the problem of universals seriously. Perhaps many theorists were not exactly seeking a comprehensive explanation of particular facts. Perhaps they were not trying to explain the possibility of naming in every case where names are actually in use, but rather were trying to characterize the process of naming by some general analogy. But no analogy, it will be claimed, can be sufficiently close to satisfy philosophers without being too close.[2] What is needed is a visible process that is analogous to the way in which a name is connected with the things it names, like the presence of a single ingredient in several dishes. But any such process is either a natural one or an artificial one. In the former case the analogy is too distant to be illuminating. In the latter case some class of things must be chosen on the ground of something they have in common other than their connection with the focal entity that corresponds in the analogy to a name. But it is just this kind of choice which the analogy itself is designed to elucidate. Here again therefore theories of universals fall inevitably into circularity. In short, when such attempts at analogical characterizations of naming have been mentioned, along with detailed reasons why why we call particular things by particular names, and the psychological background of all this, nothing is left but a futile metaphysical urge to transcend language.[3]

[1] Ibid., p. 221.   [2] Ibid., p. 224.   [3] Ibid., p. 227.

§14. The problem conceived as soluble

So many different kinds of argument have at different times been used to support theories of universals, that no attempt to define the problem at issue can avoid being historically selective. But even if all such definitions are equally selective from the past they may not all be equally fruitful for the future. No doubt some theorists have sometimes seemed to want nothing but an explanation or characterization of naming, of a kind that can be shown to be in principle unobtainable. No doubt this unobtainability is worth demonstrating. But to leave the problem there is like killing the weeds in a garden without watering the flowers. The doctrine of logical grammar encourages one to look for linguistic folly in traditional theories of universals but not for signs of non-linguistic wisdom. Its approach is intrinsically sterile. Indeed, since it allows no room for differences of philosophical opinion between reasonable men, the traditional controversies about universals cannot in its view represent differences of opinion that are worth respecting, let alone perpetuating. Yet on a different selection from the historical evidence those controversies reveal elements of continuity with several issues that are still worth disputing about. The logical grammarian is prevented from seeing this by his inability to look outside language for the seeds of philosophical theory. Even Locke, who at one point is certainly asking 'how general words come to be made', at another point examines whether the supposition of real essences is serviceable to any part of human knowledge.[1]

Suppose we extract a third question from the traditional problem of universals. Suppose we ask not 'Why are things as they are?' nor 'Why are we able to name things as we do?' but rather 'What do names mean?' If we still had the old pre-Herder conception of meaning we should assume that each name-use is invariant. It cannot have different forms, of which now some are prevalent now others. Hence if one theory says that the use of a certain name implies the existence of a universal and another that it implies only the existence of a similarity between particulars, one or both of the two theories must in all cases be false. The problem of universals, in the shape we have just given it, would have a single true answer for which it was worth contesting,

[1] *Essay*, III, iii, 6 and 17.

though the contest would be as open to the logical grammarian who denies that name-use has any such implications as to the traditional theories which assert them. The contest would be won by the philosopher whose account of naming fitted closest to the true nature of language. Thus the logical grammarian would have at least one thing in common here with the realists, conceptualists and nominalists whom he derides. They would all assume the true nature of language, against which the theories are to be checked, to be utterly independent of those theories. It would be inconceivable that in the normal course of events a word might sometimes be used realistically, sometimes conceptualistically, sometimes nominalistically, and sometimes neutrally.

But in fact the old pre-Herder approach to language and the closely analogous doctrine of logical grammar are blinkers which prevent one from seeing that name-use might conceivably vary in just this way. If one does not assume a single set of correct rules for using words, or take all concepts to be atomic and unchanging, there is no true nature of language against which all theories are to be checked. So the basic issue becomes not so much 'Do universals exist?' but rather 'Do, or should, people speak as if they existed?' In this way the question 'What do names mean?' opens up two main dimensions of enquiry in the problem of universals. There is a historical and sociological problem about the extent to which different theories of universals are implicit in the discourse of different groups at different times and places, and a philosophical problem about the value of this or that theory's being so. My object here will be not to make any contribution towards the solution of these problems but merely to show that they are genuine, in the sense that something important may be at stake in their solution.

Quine has suggested that recent researches in the foundations of mathematics display some broad affiliations to the three traditional theories of universals.[1] A system like Whitehead and Russell's *Principia Mathematica* shows it realist sympathies by using bound variables to refer to non-enumerably many sets or attributes. Brouwer, Heyting and others are seen to have kept the conceptualist flag flying by restricting the criteria of proof in various ways that would make mathematics more a matter of invention than of discovery. Hilbert brought a kind of nominalism into twentieth-century mathematics by encouraging

[1] *From a Logical Point of View* (1953), pp. 14 f.

people to conceive of classical mathematics more as a set of rules for manipulating a notation than as a set of meaningful statements about abstract entities or mental constructs.

But what is relevant here is that the effective differences between these attitudes or approaches are important ones, and cannot be explained away as idle variations in the answer to an unanswerable question. They are important just because something within the discipline stands or falls with these different philosophies of mathematics. The mathematician is encouraged to conduct his researches on the assumption that numerals denote abstract entities, or that they denote mental constructs, or that they are notational tools, respectively. He is encouraged to use his terms in one way rather than another, to operate with one form of number-concept rather than another. He is not being offered an explanation of naming that is futile and circular because the explanans cannot be conceived except through the explanandum. Instead he is offered a programme of enquiry that is sharply distinguished by the boundaries that its conceptual equipment imposes. At the very least a conceptualist has to exclude all but the lowest of Cantor's ascending orders of infinity, and a nominalist has no reason to take any system seriously until it has been proved consistent. No doubt a simple trichotomy has long since ceased to be adequate here. Hybrid systems of various kinds have been developed, and many more subtle distinctions have been drawn. Moreover the feeling that rival schools are contesting with one another about the true nature of mathematics has often been replaced by acceptance of each attitude or programme as being itself a contribution both to the progress of mathematical studies and to the understanding of the fundamental concepts with which mathematicians operate. But a growing tolerance and sophistication does not suffice to break off all continuity with the traditional problem of universals, where in any case there have often been more than just three contestants. After all, it was Plato who launched this old problem into European philosophy, and one cannot understand Plato's solution of it at any period of his life without understanding the status he assigned to numbers and geometrical figures, and the way in which he thought mathematical studies could open people's minds to the apprehension of real universals.

Here therefore we have at least one area of discourse in which people have not only sometimes used words realistically, sometimes conceptualistically, sometimes nominalistically, and sometimes – especially in the historical building up of classical mathematics – neutrally, but also canvassed the various merits and demerits of so using them. It may be objected that numerical expressions and other mathematical terms are too unlike the ordinary run of names in human language for these modern developments in metamathematics to be sufficient confirmation of my present thesis. It is certainly true that metamathematics can tell us nothing about how non-mathematical names should be used. But my thesis does not entail that the right way to use names in any one kind of discourse is the right way to use them everywhere. Perhaps also the whole subject of metamathematics will be thought too technical to be cited in an argument about so eminently non-technical an issue as the traditional problem of universals. But analogous controversies can be shown to arise in other fields as well.

Traditionally there are said to be two kinds of realist theory – the Platonic one that universals exist independently of their instances and the Aristotelian one that they exist only in their instances. These are regarded as the two main ways in which the question 'Do universals exist?' can be answered affirmatively. Accordingly, if one is to show overall continuity between traditional discussions of the question and some live controversies of more recent date, one must at least find as close an heir to the dispute about Aristotelian realism as metamathematics is to that about Platonism. Aristotle's own special interests afford a good clue to the direction in which to look for such an heir. If Plato's well-known reverence for mathematics predisposed him towards the realism of his *Republic*, it is not unreasonable to suppose that Aristotle was confirmed in a very different form of realism by his keen interest and marked ability in the observation and classification of biological phenomena. What seems to count for a taxonomic science is the species, not the individual, just as arithmetic seems to be concerned with the numbers one, two, three, etc., not with units, couples, trios, etc. But since a species of plants or animals is only to be studied by observation of its instances nothing is gained by assuming it to exist independently of them, whereas numbers might plausibly be so regarded by someone who was struck by the non-empirical character of arithmetical study. Correspondingly the realism that has been controversial in modern botanical taxonomy is of an Aristotelian variety, while metamathematical realism is Platonic. It is worth retelling in this light a tale that is well known to historians of botany,[1] but even in a short and necessarily oversimplified form is as relevant as the history of modern meta-mathematics to any enquiry about the best way to conceive meaning in the problem of universals.

For at least the greater part of his life Linnaeus held, as in his *System of Nature*, that in a systematic arrangement of all natural bodies 'the classes and orders are arbitrary; the genera and species are natural'.[2] He was convinced that the number of species was the same as the number of forms created from the beginning, and that plant hybrids, like animal ones, were incapable of reproducing themselves. He specifically repudiated interest in the new varieties of plants that gardeners managed to produce, on the ground that they were not true species created by God and could only boast a short life.[3] In effect, therefore, he held that class-names and order-names should be used according to a conceptualist theory of universals, but genus-names and species-names according to an Aristotelian realism, and he believed that taxonomists should be guided, in what they accepted or rejected, by these principles of thought.

De Candolle and some other nineteenth-century botanists accepted from Linnaeus the dogmas about special creation and the constancy of species that were fortified by the first chapter of *Genesis*. But they thought it artificial, rather than natural, to classify plants, as Linnaeus had done, according to sexual characteristics like the number of stamens or carpels. Single characteristics, chosen mainly for convenience in identifying unknown plants, could not supply the basis for a perfect classification. The true natural affinities of plants could only be exposed by a detailed study of the forms and functions of all their parts, and the right way of grouping plants was the one which placed together those with the greatest number of similarities to one another.[4] In effect, therefore, these botanists were criticizing Linnaeus for not being sufficiently consistent in his realism. Moreover their insistence on a doctrine of fixed types implied that any one member of a species represented it as well as any other. So that the most natural way to facilitate identification of unknown plants was by collecting single

---

[1] Cf. esp. J. Heslop-Harrison, *New Concepts in Flowering-Plant Taxonomy* (1953) – a book to which I am much indebted on the subject.
[2] *Systema Naturae*, tr. W. Turton (1806), vol. I, p. 3.
[3] *Critica Botanica*, tr. A. Hort (1938), pp. 150 f.
[4] A. de Candolle, *Introduction à l'Étude de la Botanique* (1835), vol. ii, pp. 387 ff.

specimens of every known species. The principal herbaria of Europe and America are solid monuments to the popularity once enjoyed by this rigorous Aristotelianism, and the International Rules of Botanical Nomenclature are founded on its premisses.

The results these classical taxonomists obtained were an important source of evidence for the evolutionary doctrines of men like Darwin, and were in part explained by them. But Darwin's point of view was essentially at odds with that of his predecessors. His belief in the variability of species was incompatible with the presupposition of constancy that underlay the old taxonomy. The morphological differences with which the taxonomists had been preoccupied were for him merely by-products in a process of adaptation for survival. It is true that, in default of an adequate fossil record, the genealogy of plants cannot itself form a basis for classifying them. But the theory of evolution has come to sponsor a new group of experimental sciences that have not been slow to propose radical reforms in the old taxonomy. Genetics, cytology and ecology have combined in supporting an approach to classification that assumes the existence, not of real universals, but merely of human ability to design discriminatory experiments. To these experiments the static and lifeless specimens of a herbarium are necessarily irrelevant. Darwin's work has led to the emergence of a botanical conceptualism to oppose Linnaeus's and de Candolle's realism, which has thus been challenged in a much more fundamental way than by any trouble about the discovery of borderline cases between established categories – a discovery that realists can always accommodate by a revision of categories without having to change their philosophical position.

This new conceptualism is perhaps most evident in the issues raised by the proposals of Turesson and others to base the classification of plants on their capacity to interbreed, so as to make it easier to study the relation between the genetical composition of plant populations and their environment.[1] Such a classification may show no correlation whatever with one based on a morphological criterion, since similarities or dissimilarities of form may be due to environmental rather than genetic factors. Nevertheless from an evolutionary point of view reproductive isolation is a property of fundamental importance. Its attainment may be taken to mark a cardinal point in the history of two

[1] Cf. e.g. G. Turesson, 'The species and the variety as ecological units', *Hereditas*, iii (1922), pp. 100 ff.

diverging populations, since these can afterwards grow side by side within one in the same area and beget further lines of diverging populations. Hence the question arises: how far is the experimenter justified in intervening to bring about a crossing that natural circumstances prevent? No doubt it is reasonable to circumvent the isolating effects of spatial separation by growing plants together. But what other bars to crossing are to be removed artificially? It may well be informative to test the use of artificial pollination. But if this circumvents a genetically determined selectivity for pollination by particular kinds of insects, one can hardly avoid admitting that the resultant classification depends to a certain extent on the choice of experimental design. There will be much else, too, to compel that admission, such as the frequently different results for different individual members of a population and the fact that hybrids may be viable under some culture conditions but not under others. The influence of all this on orthodox taxonomy has been limited both by the relative fewness of the plant-groups amenable to present methods of experimental study and by the existence of a ceiling – the level at which no interchange of genes whatever takes place – in any experimentally based system of taxonomic concepts. So that there seems no chance of producing an all-embracing classification that is based on experimental methods alone. In botany, as in mathematics, a thorough-going conceptualism will not take us all the way, despite its great fruitfulness for research. Accordingly it is not surprising to find many botanists now adopting a tolerant and eclectic attitude analogous to that which has recently developed in meta-mathematics. Experimentally based classifications are no longer taken to conflict with the orthodox ones, where the two differ. Rather they are seen as the by-product of a mode of enquiry that aims primarily at studying dynamic processes of natural variation and is not at all concerned to produce a static taxonomic system that will have practical value in the current technology of farming, gardening and forestry.

Nevertheless the progress of this experimental work has helped to spread the belief that all taxonomic systems are conventional, whether or not they are governed by the choice of experimental design. Nor is that belief an idle one. Its general consequence is that taxonomists should be much more flexible in their approach than were men like Linnaeus and de Candolle. They should not expect all variations to fit neatly into any single framework of terms. More particularly, if universals do not exist in nature and the identification of unknown plants may be more a matter of terminological invention and re-arrangement than of discovering some unmistakable marks of kinship, then the idea of selecting a single individual to represent a species loses much of its point. Accordingly du Rietz and others have proposed to take concrete populations rather than abstract species as their taxonomic units, with the consequence that distribution as well as morphology must be taken into account in framing the lower units.[1] Du Rietz could hardly be truer to the traditional spirit of nominalism.

This botanical story is not the only relevant story that is available. It is easy to find other illustrations of the various ways in which the problem of universals, appropriately construed, can become a live and genuine topic of intellectual controversy, with important issues at stake. In jurisprudence, for instance, the doctrine of logical grammar promotes the belief that definitions of fundamental legal terms like 'right' and 'corporation' need not fall into any of the three traditional categories of theory. A logical grammarian is led to believe that he can achieve a satisfactory definition by describing merely how such a term is used in legal discourse, without assuming that it stands for entities of any kind, whether subsistent, fictitious or collective. But the only neutral definition obtainable turns out to be one that just would not dissipate the kind of perplexity which classical definitions of these terms, albeit with sometimes oversimplified metaphor, are designed to meet. It would neither hint how the law should be developed or interpreted in doubtful cases, nor would it do justice to the variety of usage and attitude that exists among practising judges and lawyers.[2]

Even the hard-headed authors of current medical textbooks sometimes find it necessary to inform their readers that 'there is no disease, only the diseased', and to insist that 'it is not just idle philosophizing to say . . . that *disease* has no real existence'.[3] The difference such a conception makes to the classification, diagnosis and treatment of certain epidemic infections has long since been noted.[4]

[1] G. E. du Rietz, 'The Fundamental Units of Biological Taxonomy', *Svensk Botanisk Tidskrift*, xxiv (1930), pp. 333 ff.

[2] Cf. L. J. Cohen, 'Theory and Definition in Jurisprudence', *Proc. Arist. Soc.*, Supp. Vol. xxix (1955), pp. 213 ff.

[3] *Medicine*, ed. H. G. Garland, W. Phillips and F. A. E. Crew (1953), pp. 8 f.

[4] Cf. F. G. Crookshank's supplement to C. K. Ogden and I. A. Richards, *The Meaning of Meaning* (1949), pp. 337 ff.

Thus the old question 'What do names mean?', the very generality of which was an encouragement to metaphysics, splits into an indefinite number of more specialized but more profitable enquiries, as new lines of scientific knowledge emerge. It fares no differently in this respect from its old associate 'Why are things as they are?' Even the classification of the special sciences themselves, which was long reserved for philosophers or polymaths like Aristotle, Francis Bacon or John Wilkins, is now a serious concern mainly to bibliographers, librarians and university planners, and in their thinking the old problem of universals is not dead yet.[1] Are there necessary lines of division in human knowledge, discoverable by epistemologists and perhaps based ultimately on divisions in reality itself, to which library classifications should conform? Or is it better to take one's system for arranging and cataloguing information to be essentially artificial, so that borderline cases are not treated as intellectual freaks but as reasons for revising the system? Or is it best simply to have some central body, like the British Museum or the National Library of Congress, govern the whole issue by its decisions in each individual case?

Not that the old problem of universals, as here construed, has wholly passed into fields where a mere philosopher can note its presence but is incompetent to propose how it should be solved. In §19, for instance, it is seen to bear on the question whether propositions exist. Certain current controversies in moral philosophy, too, still have the old problem at their heart. Are principles of justice determined by a superhuman Reality or are they a matter for human choice? Is there any worthwhile meaning in a concept of moral justice outside the framework of belief in a God-given law? Those who find such a concept unintelligible will not accept some of the opportunities for qualifying moral prohibitions that are accepted by their opponents.[2] Correspondingly, if a man conceives of moral justice in such a way as to imply neither a belief in supernatural commandments nor acceptance of any other reality besides language and observable facts, he cannot avoid the conclusion that moral arguments between quite reasonable people are always liable to break down

[1] Cf. H. J. T. Ellingham, 'Divisions of Natural Science and Technology', and J. E. Holmstrom, 'A Classification of Classifications', in *Proceedings of the Royal Society Scientific Information Conference* (1948), pp. 477 ff. and 501 ff. respectively.

[2] Cf. G. E. M. Anscombe, 'Modern Moral Philosophy', *Philosophy*, xxxiii (1958), pp. 5 ff.

since he has no reason to suppose that people will always agree just how moral prohibitions should be qualified.[1] In both ways nominalism tends to support a tolerant and easygoing morality that realists, or conceptualists of the Kantian school, would find it more natural to repudiate. If the philosophical study of moral concepts cannot avoid some participation in the more general judgements of everyday moralizing, it is largely because the problem of universals is not as dead as the doctrine of logical grammar would lead one to believe.

§15. How should the problem be conceived?

To rehearse all these various controversies in detail would be quite out of place in an essay on the concept of meaning. It is enough to remark how again and again they belie the logical grammarian's thesis that theories of universals are attempts to explain the possibility of naming where no conceivable explanation can avoid circularity and escape the maze of words. The controversies just do not arise from a failure to understand the limits of worthwhile enquiry about name-use, and the problems are not solved – or the arguments even weighed – without some understanding of the non-linguistic issues at stake.

Indeed, the logical grammarian's account of universals finds no exit from the maze of words because his very conception of the problem shuts off all such exits. Not only does his atomic theory of meaning exclude any element of selection or evaluation in the study of name-use, so that the general question at issue becomes 'How can we name?' rather than 'How should we name?' But he is also deterred from breaking up the generality of the question. Since he believes all traditional philosophy originates in mistakes about language, he will be disinclined to look for examples of this philosophy in the work of mathematicians or botanists who have obviously been puzzled by other things besides language. Instead he will look inwards into his own profession for a definition of the problem, and since in each generation some of his less wide-awake predecessors have looked in just the same direction the result is that the problem as he eventually defines it is characteristically unspecialized and metaphysical in character. He will see it as 'How can we name?' rather than 'How can we count?', 'How can we classify

[1] Cf. L. J. Cohen, 'Are Moral Arguments always Liable to Break Down?', *Mind*, lxviii (1959), pp. 530 ff.

plants?', and so on. Hence there is not merely nothing valuable at stake in the solution of the problem as he defines it, because no opportunity for choice between alternative usages is made available. But also no detailed and definite lines of enquiry are distinguished which different choices might be seen to promote or obstruct. Then, for a problem that is thus utterly cut off from the particular needs and interests of contemporary civilization, for a problem that makes no difference to us whichever way it is solved or not solved, the logical grammarian correctly points out that there is no non-circular solution. It would be very surprising if there were.

It might be objected that the problem of universals is a problem about names, and that the numerals of arithmetic, the fundamental words of law and ethics, and the words for botanical species, human diseases and scientific specializations, are too heterogeneous a crowd of expressions to be grouped together under this heading. But to maintain that the problem of universals arises in one way or another for each of these categories is not to extend it much beyond the range of concerns that generated it in ancient Greece. The scope of the problem has not shifted: the lines along which it splits up have merely become more marked. A growth-conscious history of ideas will take this as a fruitful new development in the concept of the problem rather than as a total breach of continuity. It is a development precisely parallel to that which has taken place in the other main part of the old problem, the question 'Why are things what they are?' Nor are all cases of the question 'How should we name?' equally separate from one another. If two neighbouring fields of study, like botany and zoology, have no sharp boundary, it will be difficult to justify being a realist in one and a nominalist in the other. It is true that Platonism in metamathematics does not commit a man to Platonism in moral philosophy, since the effective arguments for these two theories are mutually irrelevant. But any two such theories can still offer each other an opportunity for some degree of clarification by analogy.

A logical grammarian might, however, claim that at least he is still left with a problem amenable to his methods in those unspecialized areas of discourse where the content of what is said does nothing to determine the precise form of the concepts involved in saying it. Here, he might affirm, no question arises about how people should speak, but only about how they do or can speak. But he would be mistaken to affirm this. Just as in some fields it might turn out profitable to speak in accordance with a nominalist theory of universals rather than a realist one, or vice versa, so too in others it might be unprofitable to presuppose any such theory at all. In such a case it might be better to employ concepts that are insufficiently specific to commit their user to any side in the traditional controversy. But there is still a balance of profit and loss to be reckoned. The fact that people have often employed concepts of this kind in many fields is probably one of the reasons why the logical grammarian, like the theorists he criticizes, assumes that some pure usage exists, uncontaminated by theory, against which philosophical accounts of name-use are to be checked. But where such usage does exist it serves his purposes no better than it serves those of the theories he rejects, since what is at stake is not the mere existence of such usage but its value.

Certainly a very strong case could be made out for saying that modern controversies in metamathematics and botanical taxonomy do not touch the metaphysical problem of universals. The issue the logical grammarian wants to consider still arises in all fields of discourse. One has not *explained* Linnaeus's ability to use species-names if one asserts the advantage, for identification purposes, of assuming that real species exist, nor yet if one asserts that the opposite assumption is more congenial to an experimental study of natural variation. For to identify a plant is to assign it to some type and to study variation is to study the development of varieties. One cannot avoid using classification concepts of some kind here, where what is to be explained is one's very ability to use any such concepts. So nothing that is said in these modern controversies can provide a non-circular solution of what the logical grammarian takes to be the problem of universals. But so much the worse for his conception of the problem. The philosophical semantics of mathematicians, botanists and other specialists is at least concerned with a series of live issues. Even if professional philosophers can no longer be expected to offer their own theories of universals in many of these fields, they are at least in a better position than others to embrace the current state of the whole problem within a philosophy of meaning that makes useful sense of it.

V

Meanings Conceived as what are Understood
in an Act of Communication

§16. Meanings, uses and subsistent entities

In the last three chapters the rules-of-use theory has been found want-
ing again and again. It has been shown to serve the purposes of the
schoolroom or of explicit agreements for technical nomenclature, but to
fit no other worthwhile concept of meaning. Yet its fault has lain in
relating meanings to rules rather than in relating them to use. Wittgenstein's well-known advice, to ask for the use, not the meaning, of a
word, does not run counter to anything that has been said so far about
language-words or culture-words, and indeed this book has often
talked about the uses of these words as if their uses – their functions in
achieving the characteristic or primary purposes of discourse – were
indistinguishable from their meanings. A critic might therefore perhaps
object that some writers on language and literature sometimes find it
convenient to distinguish between the uses and the meanings of
language-words. Edmund Wilson, for example, has written about
words 'which have been undergoing a change of use that sometimes
amounts to a change of meaning'.[1] But Wilson could just as well have
said that the use of some words has changed sufficiently to deserve mention in dictionaries – which on the whole give less specific accounts of
word-use and draw fewer distinctions than do historians of ideas. So we
do not here encounter a sense of 'meaning' that is unobtainable from
'use'.

But however much the functions of language-words and culture-
words are illuminated by Wittgenstein's advice to ask for the use rather
than the meaning, the position is very different with utterance-words
and saying-words. Where we do speak about the use of an utterance-
word or a saying-word, the use does not constitute one of the standing

[1] In *The New Statesman and Nation* of 13th September 1958. Cf. also L. Wittgenstein, *Philosophical Investigations*, p. 20 (para. 43).

speech-habits that go to make up a language. It is normally just a single event. A man may use the first few words of his speech to strike a key-note for the rest or to arouse the attention of his audience. Moreover, his success in achieving such a purpose depends on what the words actually mean, so that the purpose cannot be identified with this meaning. We could know the use without the meaning or the meaning without the use, and often there is no such use to be mentioned at all.

Perhaps it might be claimed that even though the meaning of an utterance-word cannot be identified with the use of the utterance-word, it is nevertheless precisely the same as the use of the corresponding language-word in that kind of context. Analogously the meaning of a saying-word will be the use of the corresponding culture-word. It will then still be right to ask for the use rather than the meaning, though the meaning of the first word in someone's remark will be the normal use of an English, French or European word rather than of the word in the remark itself. But even in this way one cannot make Wittgenstein's advice apply to questions about the meanings that are understood in a normal act of communication. If I correctly understand the first word of your remark, I have grasped a meaning that does not change, whereas the English or French words you used may come to mean something different even in the same context. What you said, correctly understood, is for ever true, or for ever false. No change in the language can come to affect your meaning.

It might seem preferable therefore to equate the meaning of your first word with the normal use of the corresponding English or French word at that period and in that social group. But there is still trouble here. The use of a word at a given period and in a given group may be fairly stable or it may be rather variable and unsteady: the word may or may not be experiencing a phase of transition from one settled use to another. If the use in question is said to be the normal one, we can always say 'Yes, but just how normal is it?' But though the meaning of an utterance-word may be either more, or less, typical of the language-word instantiated, and may even be ambiguous, it cannot be either stable or unstable since change is inconceivable for it. The synchronous facts about normal usage supply the premises from which we infer to the actual meaning of a particular utterance-word or saying-word. They are not to be identified with that meaning.

Nor are they even instantiated by it. For they are facts about the function of a word in involuntary self-expression or in achieving the purposes of utterance, and consequently they are instantiated by individual performances of this function. But the words a man utters do not always perform their intended functions. Sometimes, through a lapse of tongue or memory, through ignorance of the context in which they will be heard or read, through faulty knowledge of the language, or some other such cause, a word in his remark does not actually mean what he intends it to mean. His utterance of it is not then a piece of evidence for the normal use of the word at that period, and does not instantiate that use. Hence it is about the intended meaning of an utterance-word or saying-word that the question arises whether it does or does not instantiate normal usage. To the word's actual meaning this question would simply not apply.

Indeed, no *de facto* theory of the ordinary, temporal kind could hope to fit the timeless meanings of the words or sentences of a remark. These meanings are neither physical events, processes or dispositions, nor mental ones. But that is not a good reason for proposing a *de facto* theory of an extraordinary, timeless kind in this connection. We must reject Frege's theory that the meaning of a man's remark, or the thought he thinks, is an eternal entity existing in a third realm which is neither mental nor physical but similar to both in being factual and different from both in being timeless.[1] Why is Frege's theory unsound, like Meinong's somewhat similar belief that the content of an assertion in indirect discourse is a subsistent 'objective'?[2] Commonly the argument against it rests on a general preference for economy over extravagance in ontology, or for empiricism over rationalism in epistemology. But those general considerations prove too much in this kind of case. They cannot be invoked as a matter of course to solve the problem of selecting the most convenient way to carry on a familiar mode of everyday discourse. Certain modes of everyday discourse, like those of religion, mythology or ghost-story fiction, often deliberately take mysterious, non-natural and even eternal entities for their topic, so that it would be ridiculous for a philosopher to deny there that the relevant concepts are concepts of just such entities. We need therefore an argument to suit the particular case of expository semantics. We

[1] 'The Thought: a Logical Inquiry', tr. A. M. and M. Quinton, *Mind*, lxv (1956), p. 302.

[2] Cf. J. N. Findlay, *Meinong's Theory of Objects* (1933), pp. 59 ff.

need an argument to show that the concept of a remark's meaning should not be of such a mysterious kind. Nor is it difficult to find this argument. Questions about the meaning of what a man says seek typically to remove some form of puzzlement or mystification in the questioner. They are asking for the less familiar to be interpreted in terms of the more familiar, not to have attention directed to something that is completely unfamiliar, like a subsistent entity. Hence theories like Frege's or Meinong's miss the whole spirit of expository semantics. Nothing is gained for that mode of discourse, and a good deal is lost, by conceiving meanings as eternal denizens of Frege's third realm. Just as lexicographical semantics has no business to involve commitment to any theory about the body-mind problem that philosophers like Popper try to read into it (see §7), so too expository semantics is no place for the metaphysics of subsistent entities.

Instead, the timelessness of these meanings may conveniently be accounted for by a *de jure* theory of an appropriate sort. The point begins to emerge when one considers just why it is that a mistake about the meaning of an utterance-word cannot affect that meaning though mistakes about the current meaning of a language-word sometimes cause that very word to change its meaning. J. S. Mill tells us that the ordinary use of 'utilitarian', contrasting that which is agreeable or ornamental with that which is utilitarian, arose through a vulgar error of the latter kind.[1] If enough people speaking a language accept as true a false statement about some current word-use and act in accordance with their beliefs, a description of the word's meaning similar to the one that is now still false can come to be true for a later date. But no such result can follow from an error of expository semantics. Since the meanings of utterance-words are conceived of as timeless and unchanging, no amount of true or false beliefs of any sort, or of action in accordance with those beliefs, could ever change the meanings concerned. It is, of course, a moot point how we should interpret the meaning of a remark about some architectural design, in which the word 'utilitarian' was for the first time intended to mean 'non-ornamental'. Should we say that though its actual meaning was to call the designs in keeping with the philosophy of the greatest-happiness principle, its intended meaning was to call them non-ornamental? Or should we say that, though its actual meaning was to call the designs

[1] *Utilitarianism* (Everyman edition, 1910), pp. 5 f.

non-ornamental, it would at its time of utterance have been taken by most educated people to be calling them in keeping with the greatest-happiness principle? If we allow ourselves to be guided by subsequently published dictionaries, we shall take the latter alternative: if we look at the matter from the point of view of the speaker's contemporaries we shall take the former. But whether or not we think that a new word-meaning should be read back into the first instance of the word's use with that intended meaning, we shall not in either case conclude that subsequent events have altered the actual meaning of an utterance-word. At worst the actual meaning is vague or ambiguous. All that can be altered is what people take this meaning to be.

There is, then, one type of mistaken belief about meaning such that if people behave in accordance with their beliefs their behaviour may cause the meaning in question to alter, and there is another type such that analogously based behaviour can produce no corresponding change. It is not difficult for a *de facto* theory to elucidate how the first type of belief can have this effect. If the meaning of a language-sentence is rightly conceived of as the connection between the sentence's utterance and a habit of mind or kind of situation, beliefs about a meaning are obviously one of the things likely to change it, just as beliefs about what clothes are being normally worn are one of the main influences on how people in fact normally dress. On the other hand meanings that cannot conceivably be affected by mistakes about them call for a *de jure* theory. A principle unaffected by its breach is a principle about what may or ought to happen, not about what does in fact happen, and there are rules of many kinds that stand immune to revision even under the pressure of mass disobedience. This is not, of course, how Vaugelas or the modern logical grammarians conceive the rules of word-use. They take those rules to be malleable, as in a game like chess where the content of the rules depends largely on the practice and tradition of those who are reputed good players. When Louis XIV's courtiers began to break one of Vaugelas's rules they were, in his view, setting up a new rule, like the famous Rugbeian who took up the ball and ran with it. But the prescription for translating some particular remark into twentieth-century French, for arguing validly from it, or for representing its meaning in some other way is not malleable at all. It is more like a rule of arithmetical calculation that tells us, say, to add the logarithms of multiplicands. Its content depends on considerations integral to the matters with which it deals rather than on the practice of those reputed expert at obeying it, although this practice is often a good guide for those in doubt about the content. It is a rule that is discovered rather than invented, not self-imposed by those who want to obey it but imposed on them willy-nilly, once they accept the subject-matter with which it deals. The meaning of Lincoln's speech at Gettysburg depends on the word-uses and grammatical constructions current in the American English of his day, not on the practices of those who try to translate his utterance-sentences into modern French or to elicit the implications of his saying-sentences. No amount of mistranslation or invalid argument will ever alter the meaning of his speech.

Again, we may ask about the date at which a particular rule was introduced into football and about the period it lasted. But there is no point in asking such questions about a rule specifying how Lincoln's speech may be translated into twentieth-century French or how we ought to state its implications. Though the first statement of such a rule or the first occasion on which it was obeyed may be datable, the validity of the rule itself depends not on the datable practice of those who follow it but on the nature of the task it tells us how to accomplish. Whenever that task is to be accomplished, the same rule serves our purpose. The rule itself has no date or duration.

In short, only a *de jure* theory of an appropriate sort can do justice – without mystification – to the timeless and unchanging meanings that form the topic of expository semantics. The rules-of-use theory failed to fit lexicographical, historical or philosophical semantics, because it was undesirable there to talk about rules though convenient to talk about uses, and it fails to fit expository semantics because it is out of place here to talk about uses though quite in point to talk about rules. Perhaps much of the rules-of-use theory's plausibility is due to the way in which it thus achieves a kind of semi-adequacy in both fields. But two half-truths do not make a whole one. The theory's emphasis on use enables it to discourage the hypostatization of meanings in philosophical semantics, and its reference to rules seems to take account of the fact that in discussing what a remark implies we are discussing what may or ought to be said by way of inference from it, not what is in fact said. But a single theory cannot possibly fit both temporal and timeless meanings.

§17. The meaning of a remark in a particular language

'Don't ask for the meaning: ask for a translation or paraphrase.' This, then – not 'ask for the use' – is the main advice one should give people who are at all puzzled or confused about the status of meanings on the verbal plane of expository semantics and inclined to suppose that those meanings must be subsistent entities of the kind that Frege or Meinong postulated. Sometimes however all that is needed is for an utterance-sentence to be parsed or the syntactical function of an utterance-word made plain. Even where translation is in point many requests for the meaning of an utterance-sentence neither expect nor receive as answer the specific statement of a rule like 'One may translate it into English by ". . .".' Such a rule is often followed rather than stated, as by the subordinate clause in 'His secretary's remark "Il est chez lui" means that he is at home', and then the rule followed may vary when the semantic statement is itself translated. It will always be a rule for translating or paraphrasing the same English, say, or French utterance, but the language of the translation or paraphrase which it authorizes will vary with that of the semantic utterance in which it is followed. Nevertheless to say anything *about* the meaning of an utterance-sentence, such as that it is difficult to discover, is to speak about a contextually relevant rule for translating, paraphrasing, or perhaps parsing, that sentence.

It is true that a man may know a rule for translating some English utterance-sentence into French and yet claim that he does not understand its meaning. But then either he is uncertain about this meaning on the conceptual rather than the verbal plane or he is ignorant of both English and French and would be better off if he knew a rule for translating the sentence into his own language. After all, to say that a translation or paraphrase correctly represents the meaning of an utterance-sentence is not to say that it accords with some single, uniquely relevant rule. What it accords with, if correct, is rather one or other of an indefinitely large disjunction of rules for translating or paraphrasing the sentence. Many languages are so rich and flexible that in fact linguists can rarely if ever list all the different ways of paraphrasing a remark in its own language or of translating it into some required one. Still less can they give an exhaustive list of all the importantly distinct languages, past, present and future, into which it could be translated. But in practice when we ask on the verbal plane for the meaning of a particular remark, or for that of its fourth word, we want to be told the rule most germane to our own interests. If the original remark was in our own language we want to know how it may be paraphrased into more familiar terminology. If it was in a foreign language we want to know how it may be translated into our own, not into some other foreign one. Or if poverty of vocabulary impedes direct translation or paraphrase we want to know how this may be got round by means of some suitable periphrasis.

What is the genesis of such rules? It is obvious that an utterance-word depends for its meaning on the meaning of the language-word that it instantiates. But what precisely is the connection between these two meanings? How is the temporal meaning connected with the timeless one? How do the facts of lexicographical semantics generate the rules of expository semantics on the verbal plane? This question is worth while answering not only for its own intrinsic interest but also for the analogy it offers to the philosophically more important question about the rules of expository semantics on the conceptual plane – rules that regulate the truth-values of statements, the validity of arguments and the commonly acknowledged possibilities and necessities of *a priori* knowledge.

The first key factor here is that, though the meaning of a language-word is its function in unpurposed self-expression and in achieving the normal purposes of utterance, such a function is most conveniently described by mentioning another language-word or language-phrase that functions identically in some or all contexts. Hence, though a language-word's meaning is basically a fact about human behaviour, it may correctly be given by a sentence that makes no explicit reference whatever to human behaviour and merely puts one word or phrase equivalent to another. Secondly, though lexicons and grammars are compiled as records of fact and may be read or verified as such, they may also be used as sources of instruction. Hence the pocket-dictionary's formula 'chat : cat' tells an English-speaker not only that 'chat' has much the same function in French utterances as 'cat' in English ones, but also that he should put 'cat' for 'chat' in his translations from French into English. If we are strangers to a language dictionaries and grammars tell us how to begin to speak it. If we already speak it they introduce us to the use of rare words or unfamiliar idioms and remind us how familiar ones are spelt and pronounced. So that from sufficiently up-to-date grammars and dictionaries we can learn in general how to paraphrase remarks in other words of the same language or to translate them into another language. One cannot exactly say that they tell us how to speak a language, for this would imply that the language was incapable of development beyond the stage at which some particular grammar and dictionary were compiled. The adult natives of a country who constantly adapt their language in new ways to their changing purposes of communication are reckoned to speak the language better, not worse, than foreigners who take care to stay within the boundaries of already recorded usage. Nevertheless where what is at stake is not how to make a remark on some perhaps novel occasion in the future, but how to paraphrase or translate a remark already made, it is in principle possible to read complete instructions for so doing out of sufficiently comprehensive grammars and dictionaries. So far as one is interested in the contents of dictionary and grammar for their relevance to given tasks of translation or paraphrase, one treats the meanings listed therein not as facts about how people have normally used words but as general rules for showing how they have done so. To claim one knows the meaning of a foreign word is very often to claim that one knows in general how to translate it.

These general rules for translating French, say, into English will change as the French and English languages change, and in some periods will be more stable than in others. But, when we apply them to the task of translating a particular utterance-sentence of Lincoln's, say, from nineteenth-century American English into twentieth-century French, any one rule we derive for accomplishing that particular task cannot itself change. Nor has its validity any date or duration. The same task may always be accomplished in that way. We cannot even ask how stable the rule is, since being one out of many available rules its identity is inseparable from its content: it has no room to fluctuate, yet in the relevant context it fully suffices to constitute the meaning at issue. Moreover, not only is the rule timeless in this quite unmysterious way. One can also see that its identity would be destroyed if the quoted passages in any statement of it were assumed to be translatable. To enunciate such a rule is thus unmistakably to represent a timeless meaning on the verbal plane.

Nor does any factual statement correspond to such a rule in the way that factual descriptions of normal usage correspond to general rules of translation or paraphrase. If anyone tries to pinpoint a factual form of timeless semantics by arguing that writing the French words 'Il y a quatre-vingt sept ans que' is a means to the end of translating the first few words of Lincoln's speech, he is open to the rejoinder that this is like saying 'Moving the king one square at a time is a means to the end of playing chess.' Just as one has already made a move in chess when one has obeyed the rule prescribing how a king or some other piece may be moved, so too Lincoln's words have already been translated when 'Il y a quatre-vingt sept ans que', or an equivalent phrase in any language other than English, has been substituted for them. The means in such cases is not distinguishable from the end. No factual connection is at stake but only conformity to a rule. We cannot get away from the need for a *de jure* theory of timeless semantics.

Perhaps someone will object that translation or paraphrase is often too delicate and subtle a task to be accomplished by mechanical obedience to stated rules. 'To convey in another language the psychological nuances of a novel or the imagery and associations of a poem', he might say, 'is a task requiring the creative sensitivity of an artist. We should criticize it, if at all, as we criticize a symphony or statue, but not just mark it correct or incorrect like a schoolboy's construe or a signal-clerk's decoding. The King James Bible, Urquhart's Rabelais, Pope's Homer, or Scott-Moncrieff's Proust could never have been produced by translation-machines. There is an obvious level of achievement in translation – and why not also in paraphrase? – at which the dichotomy of accordance or discordance with equivalence-rules no longer affords an appropriate mode of appraisal. Indeed a well-known linguist[1] has remarked – perhaps a little sweepingly since so many scientific, industrial, commercial, financial, diplomatic and military ideas are in international currency today – that "except in the rarest of instances there are only two types of translation: a wooden version which mechanically reproduces the original without regard to its native shadings or literary style; or a more or less periphrastic rendering which represents the spirit rather than the letter of its source".'

It would be absurd to suppose that Scott-Moncrieff deliberately set himself to follow a series of particular rules after conscientiously de-

---

[1] L. H. Gray, *Foundations of Language* (1939), p. 141.

ducing them from certain general rules for translating modern French into modern English. No doubt his renderings came to him in many different ways: sometimes with a smooth and effortless fluency, sometimes in a sudden flash of inspiration, sometimes as the result of laborious experiment. Nevertheless it is trivially true, so far as he made no howlers, that one could read off from his translation and its original a set of rules which would tell just how to represent Proust's meaning, sentence by sentence. It is also trivially true that by the standard of those rules Scott-Moncrieff's version would be a hundred per cent correct. But in claiming that such rules are conceivable, and are implicitly what should be conceived when we discuss this meaning on the verbal plane, we are not committed to the view that Scott-Moncrieff obeyed them. All we claim is that his translation conforms to some such rules, and to those general rules of French-English translation of which these may be viewed as a particular application. Moreover, when one concentrates on the appraisal of literary merits, like elegance of construction, freshness of idiom or economy of resources, as distinct from the pedestrian though often difficult question of verbal fidelity, one is no longer concerned just with conformity or non-conformity to some general equivalence-rules out of the indeterminately large disjunction of relevant ones, but much more with how good a selection from that disjunction has been exemplified. It is somewhat like the difference between checking the legitimacy of a player's moves at chess and appraising his brilliance.

This element of selection is especially prominent where the translator has to choose between the spirit and the letter of his original, as is often the case in translation from particularly exotic languages. On the one hand there are rules connecting words or idioms that perform broadly analogous functions in the two speech-communities, on the other rules connecting words or idioms that perform superficially more similar functions but have widely disparate associations. Of course, it is a mark of creative genius to devise a way of escaping between the horns of such a dilemma by developing the potentialities of one's own language in the very act of translation to a stage at which a more exact rendering is readily seen to be available. But even that kind of achievement should not altogether escape description within the conceptual framework endorsed by a *de jure* theory. For in effect it extends the list of general translation-rules that could be read off a sufficiently up-to-date grammar or dictionary, or used for programming a translation-machine. The meanings of language-words themselves are not determined by rules of use because they are thus indefinitely adaptable. Each new usage as it arises is neither correct nor incorrect: it is just new. But a new usage in one language may nevertheless be correct or incorrect as a translation of an old usage in another, or even as a paraphrase of an old usage in the same language.

§18. The meaning of a remark in any language

On the verbal plane, then, we expound the meaning of a particular remark, when communication seems blocked, by implicitly or explicitly describing rules for parsing, paraphrasing or translating it. We can thus achieve our point on this plane in either of two main ways. The first is to show how the grammar of the given utterance-sentence should be construed by explaining which adjectives qualify which nouns, which nouns govern which verbs, and so on. If this outline guide is insufficient to clear the stoppage of communication, we can go on to a second mode of exposition, in which we fill in the details by showing specifically how more familiar words, phrases or sentences in the same language or another, may be substituted for the given remark. In the first case we stay within the sentence to be expounded, in the second we go outside it to one or more other sentences.

Conceptual exposition is achieved in analogously divergent ways, though the rules concerned must themselves be invariant under translation or paraphrase. We can either stay within the passage to be expounded and indicate the logical interrelations of its parts by explaining which clauses are conditional on which, which expressions are contraries of one another, and so on. Or, if this is insufficient, we can go outside the passage itself by showing what is partially or totally inter-substitutable, though not inter-translatable or inter-paraphrasable, with it, which amounts to showing from what it may be inferred, or what may be inferred from it alone or from it conjoined with other premises or from statements about it. The more we know of a culture-word's function in our community – the more cross-bearings we can cite – the better-equipped we are thus to deploy the inference-liaisons of any saying-sentence in which the word occurs.

Suppose an English reader is for the moment puzzled about what was meant when on 21st January 1955 *The Times* called Baghdad 'a western city'. Suppose too, as is not unlikely, that no obvious paraphrase like 'an urban centre of the west', and no translation into another familiar language, like 'une cité occidentale', seems any more enlightening. What the reader wants to know is how to get beyond these comparatively trivial substitutions, which are all equally puzzling in the context, to a representation of the meaning that would belong to a different set of mutually inter-translatable or inter-paraphrasable expressions. He would probably be satisfied when told that *The Times*'s remark necessarily implies and is implied by any remark that the authorities in Baghdad are anti-Communist. That is, he would probably be satisfied when told that the latter remark is substitutable for the former because either is arguable *a priori* from the other.

Of course, this is only a very simple paradigm for the myriad more or less similar ways in which the meaning of a person's saying-sentence or saying-word can be indicated. If the remark at issue is a question or command, rather than a statement, we may be more interested to hear what is implied by a report that it has been asked or made, answered or obeyed. Moreover, a straightforwardly equivalent expression is not always available to be substituted for the one that created particular puzzlement in the original remark, as 'anti-communist' for 'western'. But certain sections of our descriptive vocabulary are largely taught us at second-hand, as it were, through the medium of other words, rather than directly and by ostensive example, and these fields are rich in synonyms. For instance, the names for days of the week give us 'Tuesday' for 'the day after Monday'; the avoirdupois scale gives us 'one ton' for '2240 pounds' and the terminology for family relations gives us 'brother' for 'male sibling'. Even these synonymies are not always in point. If an English poet likens his beloved to a June day one does not say much about his meaning by pointing out that he is implicitly likening her to a day in the month that follows May and precedes July. In such a case the arguments to be indicated depend more on the popular associations of a word than on relations of literal synonymy or antonymy.

Elsewhere we may have to fall back on a more or less elaborate account of the sole conditions under which the saying-sentence is to be taken as true, if a statement, or in point, if a question, command or other form of non-statement-making utterance. We shall then be building on knowledge about the normal purpose of the corresponding culture-sentence that is knowledge of the circumstances to which the purpose is appropriate rather than knowledge of other sentences capable of fulfilling the same purpose. It would be legitimate here to speak of a rule for appraising truth or appropriateness, rather than a rule of argument. But the description of the relevant circumstances will still be capable of standing in for the original remark, though perhaps forming a much less concise or complete substitute for it than one achieved with the aid of synonymous expressions. There may be several alternative conditions under which it is true, so that the stand-in statement is a fairly lengthy disjunction. Baghdad is a western city if and only if the Baghdad authorities are members of such-and-such an alliance, or permit such-and-such political activities, or proclaim such-and-such principles, and so on. Or perhaps we may cite the evidence we should require before accepting some causal generalization as true, such as the kind of clinical trials necessary to establish that quinine is a prophylactic against malaria. Or perhaps we may say 'He wants you to buy tickets from him for your journey' to people who have never before travelled in a London bus and are puzzled by the conductor's request 'Fares, please'; and then we have substituted a report on the conductor's state of mind for the actual text of the original saying-sentence. The relevant inference is not so much from the content of the utterance as from the presumption of its candour.

One must, however, be careful to distinguish here between two different kinds of rule for appraising the truth of a saying-sentence. The rules in question are those that a knowledge either of the language or of the speaker's own stipulations is sufficient to establish, and the truth of a sentence cannot be ascertained without ascertaining that the relevant rule has been satisfied, though a man might know something that in fact evidenced some conclusion without realizing that it did so. But there are many other truth-rules – and corresponding argument-rules – that, at least at a given time and place, cannot be established in this way. Those who live in a town without watering-carts generally know that it is true that it has recently been raining if and only if the streets are still wet. But if someone there says 'It has recently been raining', we could reasonably be taken here to confuse his evidence with his meaning if we commented 'This remark means that the streets are still wet.' For we could ascertain that it had recently been raining without ascertaining that the streets were still wet. Perhaps it is partly because these two forms of truth-appraisal are superficially so alike that at times discoveries of fact and judgements of value are so easily absorbed into human language. Philosophers have often remarked how an observed property of phosphorus, say, such as its melting-point at 44° C. may come to be included in the commonly accepted definition of 'phosphorus', or our changing moral sensitivity may come to affect the descriptive implications of words like 'virtue' in ordinary usage.[1] The new belief becomes so firmly entrenched that it begins to operate as a normal principle of inference – a rock against which the truth of other statements may be tested – and from this relatively *a priori* status it passes easily first into the language of small groups and thence into that of the whole community, where, if it does not dislodge other built-in beliefs about phosphorus, say, or justice, it at least comes to live alongside them as one among several forms of the relevant concept. This process will be further discussed in §38. Here it will be sufficient to emphasize that these linguistically entrenched rules of argument are not to be conceived of as rules of word-use. Their entrenchment does not consist in the making of additions or alterations to existing rules of language, like the entrenching of new clauses in a legal constitution, for there are no such rules of language. Rather, it consists in the fact that in certain contexts the purposes for which certain culture-sentences are uttered have become indistinguishable from the purposes for which certain others are uttered. In certain contexts the purpose of uttering the sentence 'This is phosphorus' has become indistinguishable from the purpose of uttering 'This is phosphorus and melts at 44° C.', so that if the former purpose is appropriate we may infer *a priori* that the latter is also. The former kind of statement has come to imply the latter.

Finally, some assertive saying-sentences have a meaning that no ordinary rule of substitution can represent. If the saying-sentence itself embodies a linguistically entrenched rule of argument like 'Tuesday is the day after Monday', we cannot replace it by a sentence embodying some other rule of argument, such as 'Tuesday is the day before Wednesday.' But we can say that the saying-sentence as a whole is true if and only if the saying-word 'Tuesday' means the same as the saying-phrase 'the day after Monday', i.e. if and only if the saying-sentence

[1] E.g. G. H. von Wright, *The Logical Problem of Induction* (1957), pp. 41 ff., and J. S. Mill, *A System of Logic*, IV, iv, 6.

does indeed embody a linguistically or stipulatively entrenched rule of argument.

Thus expository semantics itself, unlike the history of ideas, has no essential concern with causes, effects or purposes or with the description of mental attitudes or experiences of any sort, since it is concerned, on the conceptual plane, with the permissibility of an inference or truth-claim, not with its actual occurrence. Admittedly, one is often more interested in the meaning a writer or speaker intends than in the actual meaning of what he says, especially if his remark is vague or ambiguous as it stands, and requires amplification. Sometimes this intended meaning is called just 'his meaning', which may seem to describe a mere state of mind, as in 'he means to go'. But though a man may forget, conceal, regret, state, or take time to show what he intended to convey when he wrote a certain sentence, his intended meaning is no more of a fact than his actual meaning. For this intended meaning is just the actual meaning of any remark that would have made his intention clear – by being the utterance of a culture-sentence with his kind of purpose as its normal one. Though scholars or commentators may discuss what the man intended to convey *when* he wrote the sentence and search for evidence of these intentions elsewhere than in the sentence itself, no question normally arises for them about the date or duration of the meaning he intended. No *de facto* theory is applicable here.

Instead, if a man is worried about the meaning of a saying-sentence and inclined to look for some correlated fact, we should advise him: 'Don't ask for the meaning – ask how to argue in connection with it or how to appraise its truth-value.' It would be quite wrong to advise him: 'Ask for the use.' If we doubt whether a man's saying-sentence has any clear meaning at all, we are entitled to ask him for a rule by which to understand it. But this would be a rule of argument or truth-appraisal, not a rule of usage. Insistence on the conception of meaning as use in such contexts blocks the way to seeing an important part of what is involved in understanding a communication. Even when the author or speaker has stipulated special meanings for certain words, to expound any particular occurrence of such a word is to show how the saying-word should be taken, not how the culture-word should be used. One can be perfectly well acquainted with a language and with an author's idiosyncrasies of usage and yet still be puzzled by the meaning of a particular passage. Such puzzlement arises more or less as often from a temporary incapacity to apply the basic linguistic knowledge that one already has as from a total or partial lack of relevant knowledge. Nor does one show that one can apply such knowledge to the understanding of a saying-sentence unless one indicates at least a few of the relevant deductive liaisons and truth-conditions or behaves as if one could indicate them.

Correspondingly, if a man argues invalidly from what he himself, or someone else, has said, he breaks a rule of argument, not a rule of word-use – a rule of correct exposition, not a rule of language. He may be a very skilful manipulator of words who has deliberately taken advantage of his skill in order to propound a plausible fallacy. To say that he has used words incorrectly would be to moralize, not to appraise his linguistic facility. Similarly if he commits himself to asserting something which is in fact false, he has implicitly broken the rules for appraising the truth of what he says. But he need not have done anything that could plausibly be reckoned a breach of some rule of word-use in his language. He may be as fully conscious as his critics of the functions normally performed by the words he uses, and he may also carefully refrain from innovations of usage. The falsity of his assertion may be due instead to factual ignorance or to an intention to deceive.

Perhaps someone will object to any *de jure* theory for expository semantics on the ground that it is only in special contexts that one can actually talk about meanings as if they were rules. 'Though a translation is sometimes said to conform or not to conform to a meaning, as to a rule', he may point out, 'it is never said to break a meaning in the way in which it is often said to break a rule. Similarly, though a man is sometimes said to obey the literal meaning of a command, one would have to admit, strictly speaking, that the command was being obeyed, not the meaning. One never says of a valid argument "It has obeyed the meaning of its premisses." Yet it would surely be quite in order to say this if the meaning of any particular remark may be conceived of as a rule for arguing from it.'

But my theory of expository semantics is a thesis about the best form for the *concept* of meaning it employs, not about the best use for some language-word, such as the English word 'meaning'. It is a philosophical, not a stylistic, thesis. What are at stake therefore are the conceptual implications of certain statements about meanings, not the verbal inter-substitutability of language-words or language-phrases that occur in the expression of such statements. It is true that 'represent' cannot be paraphrased by 'obey' when the representation of a meaning is under discussion. But this does not prevent statements about any such representations from implying and being implied by statements about conformity to certain rules, any more than the unsuitability of 'Today is Tuesday' as a paraphrase for 'Tomorrow is Wednesday' prevents an assertion of the former sentence from being conceptually equivalent to an assertion of the latter on the same day. Indeed when one language-sentence does turn out in general to be paraphrasable by another – i.e. when a single sentence, or string of sentences, in another language will translate either of them – the equivalence between the statement expressed on a given occasion by the one and that expressed by the other is trivial because it is the equivalence of identicals. There are two language-sentences, but only one culture-sentence. To avoid such triviality is a merit, not a flaw, in a philosophical thesis – as the so-called 'paradox of analysis' made plain.

It is certainly possible that an equivalence should seem to some people to be trivial when asserted in one language and yet non-trivial when asserted in another. In the first the two sentences concerned each appear to express the same statement and therefore to be inter-paraphrasable, while in the second the two sentences appear to express different though still equivalent statements and so to be no longer inter-paraphrasable. But either one or the other of these appearances should be rejected. Correct translation should always maintain invariant whatever qualities of triviality or non-triviality pertain to assertions of equivalence in their original form. A difficulty in maintaining such invariance indicates that the languages concerned are spoken by communities which do not share precisely the same stock of concepts, though they may have closely similar ones. If we do not conceive correct translation in this way, we commit ourselves to at least two unfortunate consequences. First, we sanction a form of translation that may lead to the substitution of admittedly false statements for admittedly true ones when indirect discourse is being translated, as if 'He says that a western city is an anti-communist town' were substitutable for 'Il dit qu'une cité occidentale est une ville de l'ouest.' Secondly, we blind ourselves to a particularly subtle form of cultural change or differentiation. For if two sentences that were once capable of expressing non-trivially equivalent statements have come to be inter-paraphrasable, or a reverse process has taken place, a historian of ideas will do well to note the change and ponder on its causes and effects. A historian of logic, for instance, may remark how emphasis on the importance of the distinction between using words and mentioning them has tended to transform the relation between any two sentences like 'It is not the case that today is Tuesday' and 'The statement that today is Tuesday is false', or 'If today is Tuesday, tomorrow is Wednesday' and 'The statement that today is Tuesday implies the statement that tomorrow is Wednesday.' In *Principia Mathematica* Whitehead and Russell regarded each member of such a sentence-pair simply as a way of paraphrasing, or expressing the same statement as, the other. But W. V. Quine and most other modern logicians think of them rather as expressing different though equivalent statements. The pairs are now pairs of culture-sentences, rather than pairs of language-sentences instantiating one and the same culture-sentence.

§19. Do propositions exist?

I have argued that though we sometimes need to conceive meanings timelessly we do not therefore need to conceive them as subsistent entities. The meanings of the words or sentences of a particular remark are timeless, but they are rules, not entities. However, I have not yet discussed the concept of timeless meaning that is perhaps the most potent temptation to a doctrine of subsistent entities in this field.

What is it that a man can repeat to himself every day, pass on to his friends, and treat now as a conclusion from evidence now as a premiss for further argument? How should we conceive that which men born a thousand years or miles apart may equally well believe true? What is it that thus articulates the content of a belief, the matter of a communication, or the elements of a theory? It is not a language-sentence or culture-sentence, for its meaning must be invariant under change of time or place. Neither is it an utterance-sentence or saying-sentence. For these may be identified by their original position of occurrence in a particular book, speech or remark. They are your saying-sentences, or mine, at a particular point in a particular conversation or chain of reasoning, rather than something that does not intrinsically belong even to any one person, let alone to any one remark. We need here a way of conceiving a saying-sentence in which we abstract from its original event of utterance and from certain peculiarities of wording that vary with this rather than with its meaning, just as the concept of a saying-sentence was achieved from that of an utterance-sentence by abstraction from its language, and the concept of an utterance-sentence from that of a sentence-token by abstraction from the number of printings, recordings, recitals, etc., that reproduce it.

Let us refer to saying-sentences or saying-clauses so conceived as *sayings*, and to their saying-words or saying-phrases as *terms*. Two tokens are the same saying or term, as the case may be, if and only if they have the same meaning as saying-expressions and either they admit of identically worded reformulations, or one is itself a reformulation of the other, in indirect speech. Conditions for identity of saying are thus partly analogous to those identifying as the same utterance-sentence any two sentence-tokens such that both are copies of the same original or one is a copy of the other, and also to those identifying as the same saying-sentence any two utterance-sentences such that both admit of an identical translation in some other natural language or one is itself a translation of the other. My remark to Smith 'You look tired' and your remark about his appearance on the same occasion 'He looks tired' are the same saying, because we could both be truly reported to have said that he looked tired. But if someone else had said 'Smith looks tired', that would have been a different saying. For to report of you and me that we had said that Smith looked tired would be incorrect, or at least misleading, since it would suggest that we knew Smith's name at the time, which we might not have done. Also, if you and I both utter assertively the sentence 'I have brown eyes' our remarks are not both the same saying, since they have a different meaning. Yours means that you have brown eyes and mine means that I have. The rules for appraising the truth of your remark or for arguing from it differ from the rules for mine. Again, my remark yesterday 'It will rain tomorrow' is not the same saying as my identically worded remark today. For the former meant that it would rain today and the latter that it would rain tomorrow. It has sometimes been maintained that two such remarks differ only in their context of reference, and not in their meaning.[1] But this seems to confound expositions of what has been said with expositions of what has been said about a given context. Similarly your saying-word 'I' is a different term from mine, because their meanings

[1] E.g. P. T. Geach, *Mental Acts* (1957), pp. 65 f.

differ. Not that their meanings are the people they severally refer to, for their meanings do not walk about, wear clothes and eat food. But the criteria for identifying you are different from the criteria for identifying me. On the other hand if you define a special sense of your own for some ordinary word that occurs in your remark, the latter is the same saying as a remark that differs from it only in using the definiens of your definition instead of the definiendum. Indirect discourse need not acknowledge differences of wording that have no roots in customary usage or association: such acknowledgements are best left a task of direct quotation.

Thus what a man can repeat to himself, communicate to others, or treat now as a premiss now as a conclusion is a saying. Often assertive sayings – sayings that can be regarded as either true or false – have been called propositions or statements. They are the domain of standard propositional logic (despite certain theories to the contrary that are discussed in §§31–33). But we need a more comprehensive name than 'proposition' here, since there are so many other forms of discourse besides assertion. Commands, questions, promises, wishes, recipes, etc., can be repeated and communicated just as well as statements, and their logic also requires investigation. Moreover the word 'proposition' has been used in so many different ways that it lends itself all too easily to a confusion between sayings and their meanings. Though propositions are often said to be true or false, which meanings can hardly be, they are also commonly said to be expressed by people's words, much as meanings are. Church indeed has defined the word 'proposition' so that it comes to denote something that is both the meaning of a culture-sentence and also the concept of a truth-value rather than the possessor of one.[1] But in §24 and §31 below I shall give reasons for rejecting the analysis of non-extensional discourse that requires this definition.

Perhaps someone will object: 'Why try to distinguish sayings or propositions from their meanings? After all the common feature of my remark to Smith "You look tired" and your remark about him "He looks tired" is just that they do have the same meaning and make the same point. So if a saying is identified and differentiated solely by its meaning, and is in any case as little tied to time and place as the latter, nothing seems to be gained by distinguishing sayings from their meanings.'

[1] *Introduction to Mathematical Logic* (1956), vol. I, pp. 26 f.

But, first, sayings cannot be identified and differentiated solely by their meanings. To state the meaning of a saying is presumably to state certain timeless rules of *a priori* valid argument, truth-appraisal, etc., that apply to all its saying-sentences. Hence if some people say 'George is her only brother' and others say 'George is her parents' only son' the two sayings have precisely the same meaning because they are true under precisely the same circumstances and justify precisely the same *a priori* valid arguments (at least so long as we accept the usual formal-logical convention that even the trivial step from, e.g., 'George is her only brother' to 'George is her only brother' is to be reckoned as an argument). But though they have the same meaning the two sayings are by no means identical. For of the first set of speakers it would be true to report 'They say that George is her only brother'. But it would be false to report this of the second set: they only imply that George is her only brother, and do not actually say it. The point is that in the individuation of sayings their wording counts as well as their meaning, though it counts in a way that transcends not only differences of language and trivial variations of phrase, as with saying-sentences, but also certain differences in the immediate context of utterance. For if you say to George about his sister 'You are her only brother', and you also say to his sister about him, appropriately varying your pronouns, 'He is your only brother' your two saying-sentences are the same saying since not only do they have the same meaning but also their wording differs only in certain permitted respects. You could report truly 'I said both to George and to his sister that he was her only brother', even though in thus reporting what you said you use yet a third pair of pronouns and a different verb-tense.

Secondly, sayings are not free of spatiotemporal ties in quite the same way as their meanings are. Certainly none of them belong intrinsically to any one person or any one remark. Many of them also have no orientation in time or space whatever. This is true, for example, of most generalizations in natural science or moral codes, and of appraisals of a saying's truth-value or of an argument's validity. But some sayings, unlike their meanings, readily admit of being partially identified by their most characteristic time and place of utterance. This is true of sayings in which culture-words like 'this', 'that', 'here', 'there', 'come', 'go', 'today' or 'tomorrow' occur, or in which verb-tenses are used to indicate a past, present or future occasion. Today's forecast

'It will rain in the afternoon' is not the same saying as yesterday's forecast in the same words. Certainly modern logicians have often sought an equivalent with timeless verbs, etc., for any saying that is itself spatiotemporally orientated by its wording in one of these ways. Systems for the logically articulate reconstruction of everyday arguments often, in effect, prefer to represent a temporal saying like today's forecast that it will rain in the afternoon by a timeless ascription of raininess to the afternoon of 4th April 1960. But we cannot hope to estimate the success or failure of this logical enterprise unless we have first formed a clear notion of its subject-matter, viz. sayings that can be partially identified by some reference to their most characteristic time and place of utterance. We cannot gauge the alleged identity of meaning unless we acknowledge both sides of the equation to refer to a permissible form of saying.

If despite these evident differences between a saying and its meaning the two are neverthless equated, the temptation to treat the amalgam as a subsistent entity is easy to see. While the meaning on its own might conveniently be conceived merely as a rule, the saying seems something more substantial. It can be analysed or summarized, appears, disappears and reappears in the course of a conversation, incites mobs to riot as they reflect on it, or inspires lovers to reconciliation when it occurs to them. Yet according to many formal logicians it either has no ties in time or space itself or at least has a spatiotemporally untied equivalent that is logically more respectable than it. If it is also to be identified with a meaning that cannot conceivably have any mental or physical existence, what else can this timeless substance be but a denizen of a Fregean third realm?

Once sayings are safely distinguished from their meanings, however, a less mysterious account of them becomes possible. Sayings are not a different kind of thing from saying-sentences, as tables are from chairs, but just the same kind of thing differently conceived. If a man eats supper in a certain house, in a certain town, in a certain country, he has eaten one meal not three. Analogously if he asserts something it is both an utterance-sentence, a saying-sentence, and a saying. These are just different and progressively more abstract ways of describing the same thing. What he utters is also describable as a language-sentence and a culture-sentence, though that is in a different dimension of description with which I am not at the moment concerned. Hence sayings do not belong to a mysterious realm of subsistent being but are just sentence-tokens described under a certain determinable. A term or a saying may be said to exist if a token of it has been, is being or will be uttered, or if rules have been, are being or will be given for forming tokens of it, like the formation and semantical rules of a formalized language, or rules for constructing numerals in the decimal notation, or rules for constructing map-references from a co-ordinate system. When you repeat your friend's advice to yourself or pass on his report, the sense in which what you say is the same as what you have heard is the sense in which your sentence-token has at least one property – the property of being such-and-such a saying – which your friend's original sentence-token also had. There is not a single, mysteriously non-physical and non-mental entity, like a Fregean thought, that has the property of being entertained or expressed by you at one time plus the property of being entertained or expressed by me at another, but rather two physical or mental entities sharing a common property: not just one entity with at least two properties, but just one property that is relevant and at least two entities. You have not, as it were, reposted the missive your friend had addressed to you, but posted another letter in identical terms.

Nor is the property of being such-and-such a saying a property to the description of which some realist theory of universals should apply. We must not eliminate mystery from the concept of a saying merely for it to reappear in the concept of the property of being such-and-such a saying. Once theories about the divine origin of language have been abandoned, along with the old, pre-Herder assumption of a changeless stock of concepts and meanings, there is no longer any reason for applying a realist theory to terms for the classification of individual human utterances. The way these group themselves into language-sentences, culture-sentences, utterance-sentences, saying-sentences and sayings is as much a product of human decisions, habits and attitudes as is the formation and conduct of political institutions. Perhaps classifiers have a somewhat greater range of discretion with the terms 'same language-sentence' and 'same culture-sentence' than with 'same saying'. Perhaps linguists and historians of ideas enjoy greater opportunities for taxonomic inventiveness than do translators, commentators, editors, logicians and other expositors. But there still remains a certain room for discretion in setting up the criteria for sameness and difference of saying.

The best way to show this is to examine some of the issues at stake in deciding what differences of wording are to be stipulated as permissible between saying-sentences that are to count as the same saying. Whatever course we take we seem to be committed to a thesis that is at least in some respects controversial.

By my criterion no saying-sentence today could be the same saying as yesterday's 'It will rain tomorrow.' But it might seem paradoxical to imply thus that a man can never rethink many even of his own recent thoughts, so far as these are verbal in form, let alone the thoughts of others long since dead. After all, one of the purposes of defining the concept of a saying was to elucidate what men born a thousand years or miles apart may equally well believe true. Some philosophers of history, like R. G. Collingwood, have argued that a historian must always seek to re-enact the thoughts expressed in the documents he studies.[1] To mitigate this paradox, if it be one, it should be noted that though a man cannot later rethink such a thought, according to my theory, he can at least recall it or think something equivalent to it. He can then recall *that* he thought it, or think instead 'It will rain today', and analogously the historian must often be content with discovering merely *that* the author of his document thought such-and-such. Certainly, in translating the author's utterance-sentences he would be producing further utterance-sentences of his own. But even the latter are the author's saying-sentences, not the historian's: the historian has not produced a saying-sentence of his own that is the same saying as the author's. Whether or not this is felt as a restriction on our freedom of speech or thought, it does at least fit the assumption of a temporal order in which no precognitive or retrocognitive telepathy in verbalized form is possible. Were that assumption abandoned, either my definition of 'saying' or the ordinary use of tensed verbs would need to be changed.

On the other hand my criterion for identity of saying makes differences of pronoun irrelevant so long as the meaning is the same. Against this someone might object that, if orientation from a different time or place suffices to distinguish one saying from another, so too should orientation from or towards a different person. Unless we do assume the possibility of verbalized telepathy, how can one man ever be said to repeat exactly the thought of another: 'I am on the brink of a precipice'?

[1] *The Idea of History* (1946), pp. 282 ff.

147

In any case, must we not distinguish what a man says about his own inner experiences from what his friends say about these? Is their report 'He is in pain' backed by the same anguish or the same possibilities of authentication as his own 'I am in pain'?

My reply here might be to insist that if there were differences of this kind worth noting they would be differences of meaning as well as of wording and therefore covered by my definition. But then my reply would suggest that even yesterday's 'It will rain tomorrow afternoon' and today's 'It will rain this afternoon' could be taken to differ in meaning, because they differ in orientation, so that any requirement about similarities and dissimilarities of wording would begin to seem otiose. Nor is it easy to see what differences of meaning could exist in such cases that would jibe with my account of the meanings of saying-sentences. The state of mind accompanying a man's 'I am in pain' is very likely to differ from that accompanying his friend's 'He is in pain.' But the former saying-sentence would normally be true in precisely the same circumstances as the latter and justify precisely the same inferences.

Accordingly I shall be more consistent if I offer some reason for not treating variations from 'I' to 'he' or from 'him' to 'you' in quite the same way as variations from 'come' to 'go' or 'now' to 'then'. In fact, an adequate reason for so doing is that in human speech variation of pronoun without change of meaning is not under our own control to quite the same extent as variations in these other words and morphemes. Short of verbalized telepathy or demonic possession I cannot, except in mimicry or quotation, make first-person utterances with the same meaning as yours. But within certain limits, set by factors like the length of my life, the impossibility of being in two places at once, and the non-existence of verbalized telepathy or a Wellsian time-machine, I can word some of my utterances with 'now' that have the same meaning as later utterances worded with 'then'. Rather than conceive this as a restriction on the variety of what we can say that is present in the one case and absent in the other, it is better to suppose that difference of pronoun does not necessitate difference of saying. Those who are contemporaries and neighbours of one another are then conceived in principle to share very nearly the same saying-potential, instead of losing much of this common lot merely by being a plurality of persons. Between any two people there are a sufficient number of practical obstacles to communication that result from differences of language, education, culture, temperament, etc., for it to be worth while not imposing more *a priori* restrictions on identity of saying than we can conveniently avoid.

'By all means', someone might say, 'let us maximize the extent to which different people can utter the same saying. We should therefore free all sayings, and not just some, from spatiotemporal ties. If, for reasons already given, this is not to be done by conceiving today's forecast "It will rain in the afternoon" to be the same saying as a timeless ascription of raininess to the afternoon of 4th April 1960, then at least it can be done by dropping the assumption that every assertive saying's truth-value, every interrogative saying's correct answer, and every wish's gratification or disappointment, is invariant under change of time or place. Many ancient logicians, like Diodorus of Megara, many medievals, like William of Ockham, and some moderns, like A. N. Prior, have taken truth-values to be temporal and changeable characteristics of what they characterize rather than timeless and unchanging ones.[1] On that assumption yesterday's saying-sentence "It will rain this afternoon" is the same saying as today's identically worded remark. It is just that the saying turned out to be true yesterday and false today.'

But this conception of sayings is neither necessary nor desirable. Even the best of Prior's arguments[2] in its favour rely on assumptions that we can readily reject. He argues, for example, that we ought to distinguish the form 'It was not true that *p*' from 'It was true that not *p*', holding that when three particular conditions are jointly satisfied a man may truly assert the former though it might well be false for him to assert the latter. The three conditions are: '*p*' is 'I exist', meaning 'There are facts about me'; the time referred to is a hundred years ago; and there being no facts about a person at a certain time is taken to be itself a fact about him at that time. It then follows that if it were true for me to say that a hundred years ago it was not true that there were any facts about me, not even the fact that there were no facts, it would be false to say that it was true, i.e. a fact, that there were no facts about me

---

[1] Cf. B. Mates, 'Diodorean Implication', *Philosophical Review*, lviii (1949), pp. 234 ff.; E. A. Moody, *Truth and Consequence in Medieval Logic* (1953), p. 66; and A. N. Prior, *Time and Modality* (1957).

[2] Cf. my review of Prior's book in *Philosophical Quarterly*, viii (1958), pp. 266 ff.

then. So that we have a case in which 'It was not true that p' is true while 'It was true that not p' is false, and Prior implies that a logic of timeless truth-values could apparently not represent this difference. But we can easily avoid being thus forced into a modal logic of temporal truth-values. We have merely to reject the assumption that all facts are of the same type or order, and insist that the order of facts referred to in 'p' be specified. Let us suppose that if there are or are not first-order facts about a person at a certain time, i.e. facts describable without use of the word 'fact' or a synonym, this itself is only a second-order fact about him, and in general that if there is or is not some nth order fact about him this itself is an $n+$ 1th order fact about him. Then whether we take 'p' as 'There are first-order facts about me', or whether we take it as 'There are second-order facts about me', the two forms 'It was not true that p' and 'It was true that not p' come to mean not only the same as one another but also the same as 'It is (timelessly) true that not p', where 'were' has replaced 'are' in 'p'.

Prior also argues that when temporal truth-values are iterated, as in 'It was true $m+n$ days ago that it will be true n days hence that p', they are not even reducible to single temporal truth-evaluations like 'It was true m days ago that p', let alone to timeless ones. But his argument rests on the assumption that contingent statements about the future should be considered neither true nor false but indeterminate. On this assumption, even if it was the case m days ago that p, it might not have been true $m+n$ days ago that it was going to be the case n days later that p, since $m+n$ days ago the issue might still have been indeterminate. But to make such an assumption is to introduce a metaphysical commitment where it has no place. To maximize the possibilities of communication our logic should remain an impartial arbiter of rationality in the arguments of determinists and indeterminists alike. In fact a logic of timeless truth-values does not take sides in such controversies. The saying 'It is (timelessly) true that it will rain tomorrow' does not imply that something has already happened or will happen to ensure that it will rain tomorrow, nor does it imply that no such thing has happened or will happen, but merely that it will rain tomorrow. If in fact the monsoon has broken or clouds have been seeded and we believe in an appropriate causal law, we can always say instead: 'Something has happened to ensure that it will rain tomorrow.' But it will be factual beliefs that commit us to this, not timeless truth-evaluations.

Moreover, the theory of temporal truth-values is not merely unnecessary to logic. It is also an undesirable extravagance. For even if we accept a sense of 'saying' in which sayings can change their truth-values we still have to accept another sense in which they cannot. In a continuous piece of argumentation several of our saying-sentences may have exactly the same meaning and wording. The sentence 'It will rain tomorrow' may occur now as a premiss, now as a conclusion, now as a categorical assertion, now as the antecedent or consequent of a conditional, in a single series of arguments. In such a context the sentence must be supposed to have the same truth-value at each occurrence, even if we attribute it a different truth-value in yesterday's argumentation. Correspondingly, for any one interpretation of a formula or derivation, however long, in our logical calculus we must suppose that on any one occasion each propositional symbol or other well-formed part has just one truth-value throughout, and these occasions must each be at least as long as it takes to read the interpreted formula or string of formulas. To take a very simple case, the law of *modus ponens* 'If p only if q, and p, then q' would be no use at all if, by the time we got from the first occurrence of 'q' to the second, 'q' could change its truth-value. So even for Prior's various logical systems of temporal truth-values we need to determine the conditions under which different-tensed saying-sentences in the same chain of reasoning may be represented by the same symbol within a single formula, deduction or proof. But in determining this we shall in effect define a sense of 'saying' in which the truth-value of a saying is unchangeable. Why go on then to define another sense in which its truth-value can change? A more economical policy is to rely wholly on timeless truth-evaluations and therefore on criteria for sameness and difference of saying like those proposed above.

No doubt people do sometimes say 'The statement "It will rain in the afternoon" was true if uttered here yesterday morning and false if uttered today.' But when they use the word 'statement' thus we should suppose them to be referring to a culture-sentence, not to a saying. For, *pace* Prior, they would not in the same sense go over into indirect discourse and say 'It was true here yesterday morning that it was about to rain in the afternoon, and false today', but rather 'It was true that it rained here yesterday afternoon and false that it rained this afternoon', where the 'was' could equally well have been a timeless 'is'. The idiom

'It was true that such-and-such was about to happen' is reserved for special cases like prevented or nearly prevented accidents and frustrated or nearly frustrated intentions. Nor will the concept of a culture-sentence bear the weight of logical requirements (see further §§31–33), even in a logic of temporal truth-values, because a culture-sentence is essentially something that has a history. From yesterday to today a culture-sentence may plausibly be conceived to change the truth-value of its utterance in a given place and to retain its meaning unchanged. But over longer periods the meaning can change too. So that if the prediction 'It will rain here a thousand years from now' is taken to be equivalent to 'The culture-sentence "It is raining" will be true here a thousand years from now', our meteorological predictions are all put in double jeopardy. They run the risk of falsification by changes in the pattern of linguistic usage as well as by changes in the pattern of rainfall.

In sum, there are strong arguments against so defining 'saying' that the same saying may be now true, now false. But the arguments are not of a kind to suggest that the property of being such-and-such a saying is a property to which some realist theory of universals should apply. They are arguments for constructing one definition rather than another, not arguments for saying that one thing is the case rather than another.

VI

Meaning and the *a priori*

§20. Are all *a priori* truths analytic?

Some true sayings are commonly held to be *a priori* in that, though true, they are not exposed to verification or falsification by the evidence of a person's senses or powers of introspection. To claim that a saying is *a priori* true is to claim both that it is true and that no one should ever take any experiences to verify or falsify it. This characterization of the *a priori* suffers from any element of imprecision that is present in the notion of empirical verification and falsification. But for present purposes that difficulty about the connotation of the term '*a priori*' may be disregarded if one can assume some measure of agreement about the term's denotation. Let us assume for the moment, first, that among *a priori* truths are to be included at least the accepted truths of unformalized logic and mathematics, everyday truisms like 'Nothing is both green and blue all over at the same time', and any true statements that may be made about supernatural entities, and, secondly, that the term '*a priori* truth' can be defined otherwise than in terms of a disjunction (or equivalent function) of such kinds of statement: see further §38.

How are such truths validated? Notoriously it has been the misfortune of philosophers that their answers to this question have too often been overtaken by the progress of science. Kant's complex theory that synthetic *a priori* truths were grounded in the very structure of the human mind was discredited by the failure of Aristotelian logic, Euclidean geometry, and Newtonian mechanics to retain the unique status which Kant's theory supposed they must always have. Frege believed it probable that the propositions of arithmetic are analytic in the sense that if we trace back their proof we need come on nothing but general logical laws and definitions.[1] But when Whitehead and Russell attempted to carry out this tracing back they came on non-logical laws, like the axiom of infinity, and Gödel even showed that no system of

[1] *Foundations of Arithmetic*, tr. J. L. Austin (1950), pp. 99 ff.

postulates could trap all arithmetical truths.[1] A. J. Ayer, holding that all *a priori* truths are analytic, argued that the validity of an analytic proposition did not depend on its deducibility from other analytic propositions but followed immediately from the definitions of its terms.[2] But no one has ever yet achieved a rigorous validation of this kind in formal logic unless it be by the use of truth-tables, and Church has shown that the truths of relational logic are not all discoverable by any such automatic decision-procedure.[3] Indeed even if a criterion of analyticity could be proposed by which all the truths of unformalized logic and mathematics would be correctly adjudged analytic, it is doubtful whether this would achieve any other result than to obscure the important differences that exist in regard to decidability and completeness between different branches of logic and mathematics.

Hence if someone still wanted to maintain a linguistic theory of *a priori* truth he would probably confine it to the familiar truisms of everyday discourse, where the concept of validation has not been absorbed into the technical vocabulary of metamathematics. Of course, if the theory no longer applied to mathematical systems, it would lose much of its anti-metaphysical and anti-Kantian force. If mathematical truths at least are not indisputably analytic, the category of synthetic *a priori* statement may turn out to be more respectable than was supposed. But some interest, and especially some anti-Husserlian interest,[4] would still lie in the claim that familiar *a priori* necessities and impossibilities, like the impossibility of the same thing's being green and blue all over at the same time, are validated by meanings alone. I want to argue that this claim too is unfounded, though my argument will be sufficiently general to exclude a linguistic validation for any kind of *a priori* truth whatever.

It is essential to bear in mind that the whole problem collapses if the analytic-synthetic dichotomy is not defined independently of the *a priori*-empirical one. The thesis that all *a priori* truths are analytic cannot articulate the way in which *a priori* truths are validated, if our

---

[1] *Principia Mathematica* (1910), vol. II, p. 210; and K. Gödel, 'Ueber formal unentscheidbare Sätze der Principia Mathematica und verwandter Systeme', *Monatshefte für Mathematik und Physik*, xxxviii (1931), pp. 173 ff.

[2] *Language, Truth and Logic* (1936), pp. 71 ff.

[3] 'A note on the Entscheidungsproblem', *Journal of Symbolic Logic*, i (1936), pp. 40 f. and 101 f.

[4] Cf. M. Schlick, 'Gibt es ein materiales *A priori*' in *Gesammelte Aufsätze* (1938), pp. 19 ff.

definition of analyticity presupposes a concept of *a priori* truth; and the question will be begged against opponents of the thesis if the analytic-synthetic dichotomy is not distinguished even in sense, let alone in actual working, from the *a priori*-empirical one. It is not easy to see what is gained by a defence of these two dichotomies that confounds a defence of one with a defence of the other[1] and thus excludes all communication and controversy between Kantians and logical positivists.

What then are the meanings that are supposed to validate these *a priori* necessities? Let us suppose first that they are the meanings of sayings and their terms. To state the meaning of a saying is to state a timeless rule of argument, truth-appraisal, etc., that is shared by all its saying-sentences. Hence, if a rule for arguing from the description of things as blue permits the inference that they are not green, it looks as though one may reasonably claim the impossibility of a thing's being both green and blue all over at the same time to be determined by the meanings of the terms 'green' and 'blue'. Certainly one cannot know these meanings without knowing the truth of the statement about the green-blue impossibility. Certainly, too, the impossibility has been elucidated, up to a point, when it has been related to such a rule. The concept of such a rule is a concept of something strong enough to determine possibilities and necessities (what may or must be inferred) as distinct from mere matters of fact. But can this fairly be called a validation of the *a priori* truth? To elucidate here is hardly to validate. The trouble is that in ordinary speech arguments are of more than one kind. Some depend for their validity on a supposed matter of empirical fact that determines the scope of a causal generalization or of a corresponding material principle of inference. It is valid to argue from wet streets to recent rain if the streets are never wetted in any other way. Other arguments, like 'There are ten lamps on each side of the street and therefore twenty in all', have no such dependence: if the conclusion were false we should always reject one or more of the premises rather than the principle of inference itself. Hence we cannot say what kind of argument-rule we are equating with the meaning of a saying or saying-sentence – we cannot make this concept of meaning clear – unless we introduce some such term as '*a priori*' or 'non-empirical' in order to

[1] E.g. H. P. Grice and P. F. Strawson, 'In Defence of a Dogma', *Philosophical Review*, lxv (1956), p. 142, and J. Bennett, 'Analytic-Synthetic', *Proc. Arist. Soc.*, lix (1959), pp. 163 ff.

name the relevant kind of argument-rule. We have then merely moved from an *a priori* statement to the corresponding *a priori* rule of inference, and have done nothing better to validate that statement than we should have done for the statement 'If the streets are wet it has recently rained' by moving to the corresponding rule 'From wet streets one may infer recent rain.' We have not achieved a validation that is in any way comparable with the procedures of observation and experiment by which we should establish a statable or inferable connection between wet streets and rain. In sum, we have not defined a concept of analyticity that is sufficiently independent of the concept of *a priori*. *A priori* truths cannot be seen to be validated when they are seen to be analytic, if their analyticity can only be seen when their *a priori* character has already been grasped.

An analogous point has been made by Quine with regard to one of Carnap's attempts to define the concept of analytic truth for a formalized language.[1] If certain postulates of the language-system are singled out as meaning-postulates, Carnap in effect suggested, then theorems that depend for their proof solely on these postulates may be termed 'analytic'. But we have not in this way displayed some special technique for defining analytic truths through which their true nature is clarified. The mere choice of certain postulates as those labelled 'meaning-postulates' does nothing but pose a fresh problem. Why should just these postulates be so chosen?

Nor is it an improvement to copy Frege here and say that any statement is analytic if and only if when we trace back its proof we need come on nothing but general logical laws and definitions. Not only, as Quine long ago pointed out, is the term 'definition' question-begging in this context, because the nature of the meaning-identity involved still remains to be settled.[2] But also, and just as unfortunately, this criterion of analyticity takes for granted that truths of logic are analytic. It begs the question against those who, like Aristotle, wish to take the law of non-contradiction as a first law of being – as a thesis of ontology. The question whether or not all truths of logic are analytic is a philosophically controversial one. Even if Kant, Schlick and Ayer, despite

---

[1] *From a Logical Point of View* (1953), pp. 32 ff. Cf. R. Carnap, *Meaning and Necessity* (2nd ed., 1956), pp. 223 ff.

[2] 'Truth by Convention' in *Philosophical Essays for A. N. Whitehead*, ed. O. H. Lee (1936), pp. 90 ff.

their other differences, were all on the same side in that controversy, the question should not be begged in setting up a criterion of analyticity for the purposes of discussing whether or not all *a priori* truths are analytic.

No attempt to define the concept of analyticity, so as to make everyday truisms analytic, can escape these various kinds of question-begging unless the meanings supposed to validate an analytic truth are the meanings of culture-words and culture-sentences rather than of terms and sayings. We have to escape from talking about meanings that are themselves nothing but *a priori* rules of argument, to talking about meanings in a way that is not thus the mere equivalent of what it is supposed to validate. We must recognize, in our definition of analyticity, that an analytically true saying is normally a truth that has become part of someone's cultural inheritance and was imparted to him, whether or not he fully recognized it, when he learnt the relevant sections of his language. The classical examples of analyticity, like Kant's 'All bodies are extended', are all of this nature. So too are those cases where a culture-sentence that would not normally express an analytic truth is made to do so by special stipulation. If someone stipulates that as he uses the phrase 'cousin german' it is to mean only what is normally meant by 'father's brother's son', then any remark of his that all his cousins german are male is an analytic saying. But what ultimately confirms its analyticity is not so much his own stipulative definition as the normal usage of the undefined culture-words occurring in his definiens. By the criteria set up in §19 the man's remark 'All my cousins german are male' would be the same statement or saying as his friend's 'All your father's brothers' sons are male', since both remarks admit of an identical reformulation in indirect discourse.

Hence any attempt to define analyticity within the study of formalized languages is doomed to failure. If a philosopher ignores the connection with natural language and seeks a definition of analyticity through the study of artificial language-systems, i.e. a definition in the semantical meta-language of a calculus, he should not hope to reach a definition that would enable him to formulate a linguistic theory of the *a priori* without circularity. Whatever the value of such studies by Carnap, Kemeny, Martin[1] and others, they have no bearing on the classical thesis that all

---

[1] Cf. J. G. Kemeny, 'A New Approach to Semantics', *Journal of Symbolic Logic*, xxi (1956), pp. 1 ff. and 149 ff., and R. M. Martin, *The Notion of Analytic Truth* (1959).

a priori truths are analytic. Certainly the concept of analyticity might profit from further refinement than is here in point. But the study of how to refine it belongs to the methodology of research into the sociology of ideas, not the semantics of calculi. It is work for men like Lasswell, Naess, etc., not men like Carnap.[1] The main problem is to determine under what circumstances a sociologist of ideas should treat two sentences as serving the same purpose, or two phrases as performing the same function, in a community. How should he formulate his questionnaires, whom should he question, by what criteria should he assess the significance of the answers he receives? It is not merely a matter of hitting on a few stock forms of question like 'Would you mention this to a foreigner if you were teaching him the language?', 'Would you fail to understand its denial?', or 'Would you say that if a child denied it he must be ignorant of his own language?' Rather a whole strategy of research is involved, in terms of which a preciser concept of analyticity is to be operationally defined.

All that is required for present purposes, however, is the assumption that such research is practicable. It does not matter if different research procedures, or the same procedures in different sections of a community, tend to net different though overlapping ranges of analyticity. For useful sense to be given to the analytic-synthetic distinction it is not required that there should never be any controversy as to exactly which culture-sentences are analytic in normal utterance in a given culture or sub-culture. One proviso, however, must be made. Empirical research of this kind is to be conceived as netting only those culture-sentences that are capable of general recognition as being true-by-meaning, or false-by-meaning in normal utterance. Suppose we call the statements these sentences normally make *self-evidently analytic*. There are likely also to be many other sayings, probably very complex ones, that are not themselves self-evidently analytic but can be derived in one or more steps from one or more sayings that are so, by rules of argument that correspond to self-evidently analytic sayings. Since all self-evidently analytic sayings are *a priori* because their meaning leaves nothing to be settled by empirical evidence, the sayings thus derived from them will also be *a priori*. Unless, therefore, we include these derived sayings under the general term 'analytic', along with the self-

[1] Though cf. Carnap's 'Meaning and Synonymy in Natural Languages'. *Philosophical Studies*, vi (1955), pp. 33 ff.

evidently analytic ones, we shall make it too easy to say that some *a priori* truths are not analytic.

In general, then, if a saying is analytic it is *a priori*, but it is not *a priori* that it is analytic, since the establishment of its analyticity in a given culture requires sociological research. Hence it is not analytic that, if it is analytic that so-and-so, it is analytic that it is analytic that so-and-so. The opposite theory, like Lemmon's,[1] that 'It is analytic that so-and-so' does imply 'It is analytic that it is analytic that so-and-so', depends on the relatively obstructive assumption that an analytically true saying is one that is true solely in virtue of the meanings of its terms, not of its culture-words, even though the phrasing of Lemmon's own definition – 'in virtue of the meanings of the words in the sentence used to make the statement' – suggests rather that he has language-words or culture-words in mind.

It would therefore be easy to ensure by our definitions of the terms that it is at least not analytic that all *a priori* truths are analytic. All we have to do, after defining analyticity as above, is to stipulate a sense for '*a priori*' in which, if a saying is *a priori* true, then it is *a priori* true that it is *a priori* true. This would immediately rule out any analytically true equivalence between 'analytic' and '*a priori*'. But our discussion of the thesis that all *a priori* truths are analytic will be of more general application if we no more assume that the thesis is not analytically true than that it is. As it turns out, in whichever of these two senses the thesis is asserted, it could, if true, solve the problem of *a priori* truth only under one or other of two equally unsatisfactory conditions.

The first condition is if the main problem is taken to be one of fact rather than of validation. For to show that a certain saying is an analytic truth is certainly to show that the corresponding culture-sentence is *a priori* true in the normal usage of those who speak one of the languages in which the saying can be easily expressed. But justification from linguistic evidence for the claim that a certain culture-sentence is *a priori* true in normal use is by no means the same as a justification of that use. In this connection Kant rightly distinguished the question *quid juris* from the question *quid facti*.[2] The former generates a philosophical problem, the latter a sociological one.

---

[1] 'Is there only One Correct System of Modal Logic?', *Proc. Arist. Soc.*, Supp. Vol. xxxiii (1959), pp. 35 f.

[2] *Critique of Pure Reason*, tr. N. Kemp Smith (1950), p. 120.

Secondly, even the question *quid juris* could be solved by reference to customary ways of thinking if any attempt to probe beyond existing custom is blocked, as it was for both Kant and Schlick, by some restrictive theory of thought and meaning. If concepts are atomic and unchanging, as Kant seems to have supposed, we cannot ask whether one form of a certain concept is better than another. Every analytic truth remains on an equal footing in regard to the justifiability of the thoughtway that makes it analytic rather than synthetic. If it is validated at all, it is validated, as Kant puts it, by what we always think.[1] Similarly a *de jure* theory of culture-words permits a purely linguistic solution for the philosophical problem of the *a priori*. If there are rules of word-use, as Schlick suggests,[2] then *a priori* acceptance of a culture-sentence is justified by pointing to the rule that forbids its denial. Language is conceived to contain its own criteria of correctness and incorrectness in word-use, and analytic truths are validated by these criteria. Or again, a progress theory of language serves much the same purpose. If linguistic custom at any one date embodies the total mass of relevant experience hitherto, in the way that philosophers like Condorcet and Austin have believed, then no one at that date can have any grounds for passing an adverse judgement on any feature of existing usage. Analytically true statements then appear to be self-validating in their period of currency because the usage that generates them seems unimpugnable.

But if no such restrictive theory about thought and meaning is tenable, as has been argued in the preceding chapters, then the problem of how *a priori* truths are validated cannot be solved in any field by a reference to linguistic custom. For we can always go behind such customs to enquire whether or not they are justified. We can bring all our inherited ways of thinking, though not all at once, before the bar of philosophical criticism. If a concept can change and may occur in several different forms, we can always ask whether it should be used in the form that makes a given culture-sentence constitute an analytic statement, or a synthetic one. Moreover, the same difference between *a priori* and empirical, that was to be clarified at the level of statement-making by equation with the difference between analytic and synthetic, now reappears at the level of philosophical semantics. There seem to be both *a priori* and empirical kinds of argument for the preferability of

[1] Op. cit., p. 49.
[2] Loc. cit.

one conceptual form to another. An algebraist's argument[1] that a^0 should be defined equal to 1, since $1 = a^m/a^m = a^{m-m} = a^0$, has at least the appearance of enjoying a wholly *a priori* status. But the empirical arguments for Newton's theory of motion as against Aristotle's are also arguments for a concept of the moon that assumes this planet to have fundamentally the same material character as an apple, rather than to differ from the apple in being animate and indestructible. So that even when analyticity is defined independently of the concept of *a priori*, any discussion of the variety of ways in which analyticity is justified comes up against that same concept once again.

In short, the thesis that all *a priori* truths are analytic can shed no very penetrating light on the way in which *a priori* truths are validated. But the philosophy of language that implies this anti-positivist conclusion has just as much an anti-Husserlian and anti-Kantian implication also. If the meanings of culture-words are temporal and changeable, it would be of no great moment if certain *a priori* truths turned out to be synthetic. Suppose that, as a people's word-uses stand, 'Every event has a cause' makes a synthetic statement. This need not stop them from taking it also to make an *a priori* true one. But it would then have a strong tendency to pass into their posterity's cultural inheritance as an analytic truth. The onus of making its *a priori* character evident is readily shifted from the individual speaker and borne by the language itself, and to know its meaning becomes to know its truth, even if the reasons for maintaining this *a priori* character remain the same. Hence the main trouble with the concept of synthetic *a priori* truth is not that it is empty. If it were empty it could easily, too easily, be filled by a reverse process of linguistic revision. The trouble is rather that the concept is too unenlightening for the purpose it is normally intended to serve. It is of very little philosophical interest whether a given culture-sentence is normally asserted as an analytic or as a synthetic saying. What is important is the nature of the reasons why it should or should not be so asserted. This issue would not even be affected if everyone accepted the logical positivist thesis in the form of a recommendation that all normally accepted *a priori* truths ought to be entrenched in human language, rather than as the statement that they are already so. There would still remain the root problem whether any features of the

[1] Cf. A. Ambrose, 'Proof and the Theorem Proved', *Mind*, lxviii (1959), p. 441.

resultant conceptual system would be such that wholly *a priori* arguments can justify them – a problem discussed in regard to logical concepts in §§31–33 below. The *a priori*-empirical dichotomy is fundamentally important in a way in which the analytic-synthetic one is not.

It would probably not be fair to blame Kant for failing to see this since he wrote at a period when the new conception of concepts, as temporal continuants with changeable states or forms, was only just beginning to emerge. One can hardly complain that in neither the 1781 nor the 1787 edition of his *Critique of Pure Reason* did Kant show any signs of acknowledging that conception, let alone of reckoning with its impact on his philosophy of fixed categories. But modern champions of exact metaphysics would be well advised to seek sharper instruments than the concept of synthetic *a priori* truth, just as modern positivists need to develop a more penetrating counter-attack than is made by the assertion that all *a priori* truths are analytic.

§21. Is analytic truth a matter of degree?

The dichotomy between what is *a priori* and what is not is nevertheless oversimplified in some respects. I do not quite want to claim, like Quine, that our statements 'face the tribunal of sense experience not individually but as a corporate body' and that therefore there is no sharp line between those statements that have an *a priori* truth-value and those that have not – only a varying reluctance on our part to call them in question.[1] But there is a point worth noting here which has got overlaid by a confusion, under the umbrella-term 'statement', between assertive culture-sentences and assertive sayings. Quine's thesis applies to all the former but not to all the latter.

If we just mention a culture-sentence like 'Phosphorus melts at 44° C.' we have not specified whether a saying that instantiates it is analytic (linguistically *a priori*) or not. We have not been specific enough to determine whether the culture-word 'phosphorus' is being used in such a way as to imply that anything called 'phosphorus' melts at 44° C. or in such a way that the sentence could be uttered with the purpose of communicating a discovery about the melting-point of a substance. Of course, we could instead talk about another culture-sentence which is a more specific form of this one and would be

[1] *Methods of Logic* (1952), p. xii.

sayings instantiated just by analytic, or just by synthetic ones. But if we keep above that level of specificity we can confine ourselves in our talk about culture-sentences to a conception of them that is as yet indeterminate in such respects. With sufficient ingenuity and imagination we can suggest circumstances in which even old favourites like 'It is both green and blue all over' or 'Brothers are not male siblings' might have an intelligible instantiation as non-analytic truths, let alone the more obvious candidates for informative status like 'My brother is not an only child.' Moreover, this is not only a possible level of conception for assertive culture-sentences. It is also often a useful one. Without it we could not discuss whether 'Phosphorus melts at 44° C.' has changed, or should change, from being normally uttered in an *a priori* sense to being normally uttered in an *a posteriori* sense, or vice versa. It follows that at this level of conception – if these assertive culture-sentences are what he means by 'statements' – Quine's thesis must hold for culture-sentences. There is no sharp dichotomy between sheep and goats, but only a varying degree of reluctance, which changes as knowledge increases or as opinions fluctuate from culture to culture, to utter them in one sense rather than in the other. To describe the meaning of a particular culture-sentence at any one period we must assess just how strong is this reluctance in its case at that period.

Correspondingly, if by 'statements' Quine means the sayings that these culture-sentences themselves, rather than one of their more specific forms, would assert, his thesis is also true. Since the culture-sentence is insufficiently specific the saying it makes will be indeterminate in regard to analyticity or syntheticity. It is then reasonable to remark of this saying that it is more, or less, *a priori* true than another, in the sense that its truth has more, or less, deserved or achieved entrenchment in the language.

But we can only go thus far with Quine when we admit that his thesis cannot hold if by 'statements' he means fully determinate assertive sayings. A saying of this kind is either analytic or not. Its analyticity, or non-analyticity, as the case may be, is absolute, and cannot vary from culture to culture, though in some cultures the saying may be much easier to express than in others and to know whether or not it is analytic we must know something about the culture or language in which it has been described or asserted to us. We can only talk about a varying degree of reluctance to utter culture-sentences in an analytic sense rather than in a synthetic one, if the dichotomy between those two senses is sharp and absolute for all assertive sayings that are neither vague nor ambiguous. It is rather like the way in which we can only talk about the varying degree of reluctance with which different people will cast their vote at a general election if we presuppose a clear distinction between voting and not voting. The difference of degree between temporal meanings requires a difference of kind between exact timeless ones.

The 'sweeping epistemological dichotomy' to which Quine[1] objects is therefore valid for fully determinate sayings once a workable procedure for the identification of analytic-making synonymies and contradictions has been selected, but not valid for culture-sentences or certain indeterminate sayings. No doubt Quine would object that he wishes to dispense altogether with any concept like that of a saying, and to rely wholly on that of a culture-sentence or language-sentence. But the need for some concept like that of a saying emerges unmistakably from enquiry into the logic of indirect discourse and into the requirements of formal logic in general, as §§23-33 will show. Meanwhile, it is worth pointing out that two factors help to explain the ease with which culture-sentences are sometimes confused here with 'sayings', under the loose name of 'statements'.

First, if a culture-sentence contains proper names, personal or demonstrative pronouns, or references to time and place that are relative to the time and place of the sentence's utterance, its difference from a saying is obvious to anyone. When you remark today 'It has just stopped raining', you are obviously not asserting the same saying as when you uttered the same culture-sentence yesterday. But many culture-sentences, especially the generalizations that occur in scientific theories or in legal codes, lack any such words or inflections that force a saying to be more determinate than the culture-sentence it instantiates. A sufficiently specific sentence of this kind is easily confused with the saying that is it sole instance, and a sufficiently specific culture-word in it is easily confused with the corresponding term. Indeed perhaps the doctrine of logical grammar acquires some of its plausibility by philosophers' sometimes confusing the meanings of terms with the meanings of culture-words and then supposing that the latter, instead of the

[1] *Word and Object* (1960), p. 67.

former, are determined by rules which generate proprieties and improprieties of statement.

Secondly, whenever we test a physical or chemical hypothesis we are implicitly testing along with it certain auxiliary hypotheses about the reliability and interpretation of our measuring instruments or other experimental apparatus, as Duhem did well to emphasize.[1] If at the time we seem to be testing the main hypothesis alone, this is merely because at the time we are readier to sacrifice it than the auxiliary hypotheses in the face of adverse evidence. But on any occasion on which we were not thus prejudiced we must regard ourselves as exposing a whole theory, or group of theories, rather than just this or that individual saying, to the test of experiment and observation. In such cases we should conceive all the hypotheses or all the sentences of the theory as combining to form a single conjunctive saying that has a non-analytic sense. Each component saying within it is neither analytic nor synthetic but harmlessly ambiguous in this respect. Hence a philosopher may be tempted to assimilate the system of sentences in a culture to the system of sentences in such a theory or conjunction of hypotheses, and to equate attitudes to the former with attitudes to the latter. But he would then be destroying two useful distinctions. He would be confusing the temporal meanings of culture-sentences with the timeless meanings of sayings. And he would be treating the incoherent mass of partly connected, partly unconnected statements that members of a culture actually make from day to day on all sorts of subjects as if they were no less interdependent than the laws or hypotheses in a system of physical or chemical theory.

It is quite true that the culture-sentences of a community face the tribunal of its experience not individually but as a corporate body. This is a consequence of what was argued in §§8 and 11 towards the thesis that the meanings of culture-words are their functions in a community, that all the words of a language form a single field, in Trier's sense, and that the doctrine of atomic concepts is valueless and obstructive. If the meaning of any one word in a given culture has changed under the influence of events, then the meanings of all the others must also have changed since its relevance for each of them is now different. Admittedly, this difference will often be very slight, so that the history of ideas can in practice be split up into relatively independent studies in different

[1] *The Aim and Structure of Physical Theory*, tr. P. P. Wiener (1954), pp. 144 ff.

fields. For most purposes one can describe the modern concept of friend-ship without having to describe also the arithmetical concept of zero. But something is always said about the meanings of any two culture-words when it is said whether, or in what ways, they are combined in any single culture-sentence. Indeed, the extent to which the description of any one culture-word's meaning is normally relevant to the descrip-tion of another's varies up to a point with our readiness to ascribe an *a priori* truth-value to saying-sentences in which the two words or phrases occur as predicate and subject respectively. Compare 'The melting-point of phosphorus is a certain degree of temperature', 'The melting-point of phosphorus is 44° C.', 'The melting-point of phos-phorus is something known to every schoolboy', and 'The melting-point of phosphorus is a banana.' Hence a correct philosophy of concepts must lead to precisely the same conclusion about culture-sentences as that already reached. The distinction between analytic and synthetic is a matter of degree in their case, not of kind.

But, though the meanings of all a community's culture-sentences are thus to be viewed as interdependent on one another, it does not follow that the meanings of all its sayings should be conceived likewise and that every assertive saying is therefore part of a single system of saying-sentences, like an all-embracing scientific theory that is to be tested against experience not in separate bits but as a corporate whole. If the meaning of the culture-phrase 'melting-point of phosphorus' is not much elucidated by its relation to the meaning of 'something known to every schoolboy', it must be comparatively easy to construct two sayings that differ from one another only in that one has the former phrase where the other has the latter, such that at least *a priori* the two sayings stand or fall in truth-value quite independently of one another. Only so far as this was difficult to contrive would one want to hold that the meanings of the two culture-phrases were closely connected. Hence the theory that all meanings in a culture stand in varying degrees of interdependence to one another implies that some saying-meanings are interdependent and some are not. Though no words have simple, indefinable meanings in a culture, terms often have simple un-defined meanings in a theory. The position with regard to dependence here is analogous to that with regard to analytic truth. The difference of degree in the mutual dependence (in regard to complete description) that pertains between temporal meanings requires a difference of kind among the relations of dependence or independence (in *a priori* valid argument) that pertains between timeless meanings.

§22. Can meaning be the method of verification?

The anti-metaphysical doctrine that all *a priori* truths are analytic has often been conjoined with the thesis that questions about the meaning of a non-analytic proposition are questions about its method of verification. For if this thesis is true in the required empirical sense of 'verification', all non-analytic truths must be *a posteriori* and therefore all *a priori* ones analytic: the elimination of *a priori* metaphysics has thus acquired a new foundation.

Here again, however, as with the emotive-cognitive distinction discussed in §7, controversy has been bedevilled by a general failure to make it clear whether the doctrine concerned was primarily a theory about how we should discuss meanings or about what we should say of them. As the former the doctrine can, in an appropriate context, perform the useful task of contrasting one important mode of semantic discourse with another: as the latter it does great harm by obscuring the variety of ways in which we use words to compose our utterances. Bridgman, for example, contrasted Einstein's operational attitude towards concepts with Newton's tendency to define them in a manner more appropriate to pure mathematics than to physics. Einstein, he says, achieved a scientifically fruitful critique of statements asserting simultaneity by identifying their meaning with the way in which they are verified, while one can only expound Newton's phrase 'absolute time' by showing what it is that statements using the phrase imply.[1] 'At two distant points', as Einstein once expounded his own view, 'we have two perfect clocks showing exactly the same time. This statement should be true regardless of the care with which we verify it. But what does it really mean? How can we make sure that distant clocks always show exactly the same time? . . .'[2]

But in 1936 Schlick was not content, like Bridgman in 1927, to contrast different modes of semantic discourse in their application to physical theories. Though he claimed that all he was trying to do was 'to stick consistently to Einstein's position and to admit no exceptions

[1] *The Logic of Modern Physics* (1927), pp. 4 f.
[2] *The Evolution of Physics* (1938), p. 189.

from it', in fact he maintained that there is not and never has been any other way of talking about meaning than Einstein's, whether in regard to physics or any other topic. From this generalized form of the verificationist doctrine it followed immediately that any sentence which seemed to express an unverifiable statement was either meaningless, like many metaphysical utterances, or perhaps the expression of a rule rather than a statement, like our assertions of natural laws.[1] From being an attack on a certain mode of discourse about the meaning of physical statements, the verificationist doctrine became an attack on the claim of many sentences to express statements at all. From implying that a few of the sentences normally reckoned useful in pre-Einsteinian physical discourse were in fact meaningless, because they included phrases like 'absolute time' or 'absolute simultaneity', it came to imply that all sentences belonging to certain categories of discourse were meaningless. So the doctrine slid into being a theory primarily about the meanings that different categories of sentences have or lack, and became open to all the obvious objections about how it makes future verificationist procedures the content of historical narrative, how it fails to do justice to the nature of moral or metaphysical discourse by writing it all off indiscriminately as 'nonsense', how it fails to produce a sufficiently precise criterion of verifiability, and so on. The facts now cited against it were not about how people normally discuss meaning, but about what they normally intend to convey by their use of words in historical narrative or moral judgement.[2] From being an analysis of semantic discourse about physical statements in certain contexts – an analysis that may plausibly be defended by references to what some physicists themselves have said about meanings in those contexts – it had become a generalization about how words are used to make statements in any field whatever. Such a sweeping paradox lay wide open to being classified finally by Wittgensteinians in 1938 as a piece of positivist, or anti-metaphysical, metaphysics in the tradition of David Hume.[3]

But critics of verificationism are mistaken if they think that this classification disposes of every sense in which the sentence 'The meaning of a statement is its method of verification' may be worthwhile consider-

[1] Cf. 'Meaning and Verification', and 'Der Kausalität in der gegenwärtigen Physic', in *Ges. Aufsätze* (1938), pp. 341 and 68 respectively

[2] Cf. e.g. I. Berlin, 'Verification', *Proc. Arist. Soc.*, xxxix (1939), p. 230.

[3] J. Wisdom, 'Metaphysics and Verification', in *Philosophy and Psychoanalysis* (1953), pp. 51 ff.

ing. When discussing semantics one has always to bear in mind that different modes of discourse about meaning should be expected to produce different results. Different concepts of meaning enable one to ask different, though related, questions about linguistic activity. It is particularly easy to confuse these questions if, as ordinarily, a single word 'meaning' occurs in all of them. One may feel inclined to say that the meaning of a generalization like 'Friction always causes heat' cannot be identified with the rule for appraising its truth because the logical consequences of such a generalization with regard to all future time are part of its meaning though not of the evidence normally taken to justify its assertion, which is the extent to which it has already stood up to test. One might be reluctant to identify the meaning of a historical statement like 'Picts once lived at Tullybaccart' with a rule specifying the archaeological finds that would justify accepting it, because the statement itself implies nothing whatever about the present existence of weems and earth-houses. Yet in both cases one would be guilty of confusing the answers to two different questions – a question about meaning conceived as an operational rule of truth-appraisal and a question about meaning conceived as a rule of argument from synonyms to synonyms. It would be like saying that the cause of a match's bursting into flames is not a chemical process, but a movement of the hand that strikes it, or not a movement of the striker's hand but a motive in his mind. There are many different ways of conceiving causal relations though one way may in some contexts be more fruitful than another: so too there are many different ways of conceiving meaning, and what is true of a meaning in one conception is often false in another. Indeed, verificationist semantics is of prime interest in connection with those kinds of terms and assertive sayings for which it does produce different results from what is produced by the conception of meanings as *a priori* rules of argument. Einstein's famous use of it is a typical example, and similarly it is better, not worse, occupied with sayings about the past or future, or about other people's minds, than with sentences about natural processes occurring before the present gaze of the speaker. A contrast between the results produced by these two different modes of semantics brings home to us the measure of our intellectual responsibility in asserting the sayings in question. By genuinely historical statements about the past, for example, we do commit ourselves about the present. To say 'Picts once lived at Tullybaccart, but without leaving any trace of it anywhere' is about as otiose and pointless as to say that two given events are absolutely simultaneous.

In short there is one mode in the semantics of sayings in which it is a truism, and another in which it is absurd or off the point, to claim 'The meaning of a sentence is the rule specifying criteria for the truth or appropriateness of its utterance.' This claim will only deviate into metaphysical paradox when it purports – a part being taken for the whole – to express the sole worthwhile conception of meaning.

Against such a paradox the rules-of-use doctrine of meaning was a salutary reaction. By stressing that there are very many different ways of using words meaningfully it countered the claim made by verificationism, in its metaphysical phase, that apart from analytic truths only empirical statements are meaningful. It rightly opposed the view that philosophers could determine some single criterion of meaningfulness for all utterances. But in place of verificationism as a thesis about one of the ways in which it is useful to discuss the meanings of terms and sayings, especially in science, the rules-of-use doctrine has nothing of value to offer. Not merely does it have all the drawbacks that have already been noted. It is also exposed to a special kind of criticism from historians and philosophers of science.

The word 'velocity', we are told by way of example,[1] has a constant meaning in both classical and modern theories of mechanics: 'velocity at a point' always means the unattained limit of the ratio of a distance to a time as the time is made shorter and shorter. But the relative velocity of two trains approaching one another is obtained differently in classical and relativity mechanics. In the former their velocities are added together, in the latter they are not. This change in such a fundamental procedure as that of compounding velocities might lead one to say that 'velocity' has a new use, and therefore, according to the rules-of-use doctrine, a new meaning in relativity mechanics. But what has happened, a historian of science might prefer to say, is that a new theory has replaced an old theory about the relations between velocities understood in the same sense. If there is a new use of 'velocity' it is only a by-product of this change of theory, not vice versa.

The trouble here arises through applying the use-meaning equation outside its proper field. Such a conception of meaning has considerable advantages in the semantics of language-words and culture-words, but

[1] Cf. J. O. Wisdom, 'Esotericism', *Philosophy*, xxxiv (1959), p. 343.

none in that of utterance-words and saying-words. Accordingly it is also of no advantage in the semantics of terms. But for two reasons the temptation to employ it there is particularly strong in the study of scientific theories. First, a term can occur more than once in a saying, and normally does so in a scientific theory, though each saying-word has only one occurrence in its saying-sentence; and it is more natural to speak of something as a use if it can, at least in principle, happen more than once. Secondly, the difference between a saying and the culture-sentence it instantiates is so easily missed when the culture-sentence contains no proper names, no personal or demonstrative pronouns, and no references to time and place that are relative to the time and place of utterance. As a result it becomes very plausible to suggest that the meaning of a term in such a saying or theory is identical with the meaning of the corresponding word or phrase in the corresponding culture-sentence or culture-sentences, and that if the latter is a matter of use so is the former. The trouble about terms like 'velocity' is then generated.

What we must say instead is that the meaning of the term 'velocity at a point' is given by its defining criterion, viz. the truth-rule for sayings that such-and-such is the velocity of such-and-such at such-and-such a point. We have then satisfied the desire of a historian of science to describe the situation as one in which a new theory has replaced an old one about the relations between velocities understood in the same sense. But we have not excluded a historian of ideas from enquiring whether the change of theory brought about a change in the meaning of the culture-word 'velocity'. If he were to find that the postulates of relativity mechanics had come to be taken for granted whenever the word was used by certain people, he would have good ground for claiming such a change. Nor are we committed to the view that within any scientific theory, and without reference to any outside considerations, we can distinguish between those sayings that are analytic and those that are not. If the definition of 'velocity at a point' appears as a postulate of the theory we must be content with distinguishing merely between those theorems that are provable from it alone and those that require other postulates also. The theory as a whole can only be said to contain new theorems *about* the relations between velocities, so far as the appearance of this postulate in both the earlier and the later theory shows the reluctance of physicists to discard it and thus establishes the relatively *a priori* character of the corresponding culture-sentence.

VII

Meaning and the Law of Extensionality

---

§23. The problem of non-extensional discourse

In §20 I argued that a distinction between analytic and synthetic truths is much less important than one between what is *a priori* and what is not. But I have not yet considered one of the most powerful arguments for the former dichotomy. 'The case for the analytic-synthetic distinction', I may be told, 'does not stand or fall with its relevance to controversy between metaphysicians and positivists. Kant and Ayer have not exhausted its utility. We also cannot avoid assigning it, or something very like it, an important role in formal logic. Any defence of the analytic-synthetic distinction that does not at least discuss this role borders on the superficial, because it ignores the only case for the dichotomy that arises from a solidly developed body of uncontroversial truths – the truths of logic.'

'Notoriously,' such an objector will continue, 'the law of extensionality fails for some passages of human discourse. Though the Morning Star is in fact the same planet as the Evening Star yet it may be true that a man believes the Morning Star is not the Evening Star, while false that he believes the Morning Star is not the Morning Star. Where substitution of identically referring terms for one another, like "the Morning Star" for "the Evening Star", fails to preserve truth-value, we need a way of describing the reason for that failure. One good way of describing this is via a distinction between the extension, denotation or reference of a term, on the one hand, and its intension, connotation or meaning, on the other. We can say that in all such passages the meaning of a term is as relevant as its reference, and that is why mere identity of reference is insufficient to license substitution. But the analytic-synthetic dichotomy is then just what we need in order to distinguish between those identity-statements that do license substitution in non-extensional passages and those that do not, respectively. For in any analytic statement the meaning of the predicate term is the same as, or part of, the meaning of the subject term. Hence we cannot do without some such dichotomy if we are to make a serious attempt at articulating the logic of non-extensional discourse. It is well known that a wholly extensional logic is adequate to the needs of classical mathematics. But we should not pay too much heed here to Quine's point that mathematics is the branch of science whose logical needs are most clearly understood.[1] We might just as well argue that theorists in other fields are more likely than mathematicians to be deficient in logical rigour and intuition, so that the need for a system of logic to cover their patterns of discourse is more pressing. And it seems most unlikely that such a system could be constructed without making crucial use of some dichotomy like that of analytic and synthetic.'

To refute the main point of this objection I shall have to make a somewhat detailed investigation of the logical issues at stake. I shall first argue that, apart from a general distinction between extensional and non-extensional forms of discourse, no dichotomy is of much value here. The various forms of non-extensional discourse are too heterogeneous in character for Frege's dichotomy of sense and reference, or Kant's of analytic and synthetic, to be of any systematic use. I shall then show that, even without relying on such a distinction, one can formalize all non-extensional statements of informal discourse within standard, extensional, truth-functional logic as well as within an appropriate modal logic. So far is a sense-reference, or analytic-synthetic, dichotomy from being essential to formal logic that, para-doxical as it may seem, one can formalize all non-extensional passages on the basis of standard, non-modal calculi and yet avoid paralogism. However, such a formalization does not axiomatize any of the inter-relations between different kinds of non-extensional discourse: it reproduces their heterogeneities to the exclusion of homogeneities. I shall finally, therefore, develop several systems in which some of these interrelations are axiomatized and some scales of non-extensionality are represented that might replace the old analytic-synthetic dichotomy.

§24. Why is Frege's distinction insufficient?

In his famous essay 'Ueber Sinn und Bedeutung'[2] Frege began by

[1] *From a Logical Point of View* (1953), p. 159.

[2] *Zeitschrift für Philosophie und philosophische Kritik*, c (1892), pp. 25 ff., tr. in *Translations from the Philosophical Writings of Gottlob Frege*, P. Geach and M. Black (1952), pp. 56 ff.

pointing out that statements of the form $a = a$ and $a = b$ are 'obviously statements of differing cognitive value'. It is an important astronomical discovery that the Morning Star is the Evening Star, but not that the Morning Star is the Morning Star. He therefore proposed to distinguish between the reference of a term (i.e. what it refers to) and its sense (i.e. the manner in which it designates). The reference of 'Morning Star' is the same as that of 'Evening Star', but not the sense, and in reported speech one talks about the sense of a person's remarks, not their reference. Frege then drew a further distinction. Since in reported speech words do not have their customary reference, but designate what is usually their sense, he spoke of this as an *indirect* use of words. That is, he distinguished the customary from the indirect reference of a word, and its customary sense from its indirect sense, and identified the indirect reference with the customary sense. He then went on to apply the sense-reference distinction to declarative sentences and clauses as well as to terms, and to identify the customary reference of a sentence or clause with its truth-value and the customary sense with the thought it expresses. But a subordinate clause in indirect speech has its customary sense as reference. Hence in all such cases 'it is not permissible to replace one expression in the subordinate clause by another having the same customary reference, but only by one having the same indirect reference, i.e. the same customary sense'.

It would be an easy, but superficial, criticism of Frege's essay that he conceives us capable of referring equally well, and in the same sense of 'refer', to such very disparate things as planets, truth-values and modes of designation. After all, this ontological extravagance – this characteristically Fregean expansion of our domain of reference to include a third realm of subsistent entities besides the familiar realms of mind and matter – might be justified if no better account of non-extensional discourse could be obtained. The real trouble with Frege's theory here is rather that it is inadequate to the facts. It amounts to saying that wherever the law of extensionality seems to fail – wherever terms identical in customary reference, or statements identical in truth-value, may not be substituted for one another *salva veritate* – statements identical in customary sense may nevertheless be so substituted. But what is to count as identity of sense? Whatever criterion we adopt a great deal is going to be left out of account.

Let us first adopt the strongest criterion possible, and postulate that if two expression-tokens differ in sound or shape they do not designate their references in the same manner. Then the only things an expression-token will have the same sense as will be other expression-tokens of the same type, and Frege's theory will permit no substitution whatever of one expression-type for another in non-extensional passages. Frege himself would not have accepted so strong a criterion when he wrote 'Ueber Sinn und Bedeutung', since it amounts to distinguishing between two expression-tokens only as objects, and not as signs, whereas he explicitly preferred to distinguish between them as signs, i.e. in respect of the manner in which they designated their references. Elsewhere he pointed out that if no two expressions ever had the same sense or embodied the same thought as one another no translation would be possible, all definitions would be false, and logic itself would be radically crippled.[1] But, whatever Frege's views, it is in any case clear that this criterion would be far too strict. We should not even be able to infer from

(1) He implied that he would come the day after Monday

to

(2) He implied that he would come on Tuesday.

Let us therefore relax the criterion a bit and postulate that any two expressions have the same customary sense if their equivalence is demonstrable *a priori*. This too does not seem to be quite what Frege had in mind. Where *a*, *b*, *c* are the lines connecting the vertices of a Euclidean triangle with the mid-points of the opposite sides, it is demonstrable *a priori* that the point of intersection of *a* and *b* is the same as the point of intersection of *b* and *c*. But Frege thought that a statement of this identity contains actual knowledge, as he put it, and therefore that 'point of intersection of *a* and *b*' has a different sense from 'point of intersection of *b* and *c*'. Though he held the truths of arithmetic to be analytic, he nevertheless agreed with Kant that the truths of geometry were synthetic *a priori*.[2] Hence the criterion of *a priori* equivalence would have been too weak for Frege. Yet it is not as

---

[1] 'Begriff und Gegenstand', *Vierteljahrsschrift für wissenschaftliche Philosophie*, xvi (1892), p. 196. Cf. *Translations*, p. 46.

[2] *Foundations of Arithmetic*, tr. J. L. Austin (1950), pp. 101 f.

weak as it might have been. Such equivalences still have to be distinguished from purely extensional ones. Though twelve was the number of tablets on which the old Roman law was engraved we cannot infer from

(3) It is demonstrable *a priori* that 12 is 7 + 5

to

It is demonstrable *a priori* that the number of tablets on which the old Roman law was engraved is 7 + 5.

Perhaps instead we should seek a criterion about midway between the two so far considered, one of which seems too strong and the other too weak. Let us postulate that any two expressions have the same customary sense if their equivalence is analytic – i.e. an *a priori* truth embodied in linguistic usage. We may suppose that 'Tuesday' is equivalent to 'the day after Monday' in this way, and then Frege's theory will come to justify the inference from (1) to (2). I think that this comes close to what Frege had in mind, though his own use of the word 'analytic' in *The Foundations of Arithmetic* is somewhat wider, since it embraces all statements provable by reference to definitions and logical laws alone and many such are undiscoverable by empirical methods of linguistic enquiry like those suggested in §20. Nevertheless this is too weak a criterion for some cases and too strong for others. It is too weak where it would allow us to infer from

(4) They explicitly said that George was her only brother

to

They explicitly said that George was her parents' only son

or from

(5) It is logically true that either today is Tuesday or today is not Tuesday

to

(6) It is logically true that either today is Tuesday or today is not the day after Monday.

is too strong for non-extensional passages of discourse in which not only analytic statements license substitution but also certain kinds of non-analytic ones. Consider, for example,

(7) It is chemically certain that if this substance were common salt it would have dissolved in pure water.

The chemical discovery that pure water is a compound of two parts of hydrogen to one of oxygen licenses us to infer by substitution in (7) to

It is chemically certain that if this substance were common salt it would have dissolved in a compound of two parts of hydrogen to one of oxygen.

But though substitution in the subordinate clause of (7) is thus licensed by certain synthetic statements as well as by any relevant analytic ones, the clause is nevertheless clearly non-extensional in its logical character. The statement 'The earth is flat' has the same truth-value as the consequent of the conditional sentence in (7). But we should obviously do wrong to infer from (7) to

(8) It is chemically certain that if this substance were common salt the earth is flat

since flatness of the earth is not a natural consequence of any substance's being common salt. No equivalence that is merely truth-functional will license substitution in (7): all express statements of causal connections and their implications are, *pace* Frege,[1] non-extensional forms of discourse (see also §§37–40 below).

In short, however we define identity of sense, Frege's theory does a very great deal less than justice to the variety and heterogeneity of non-extensional discourse. Implicitly, and at its outset even explicitly, the theory relies on Kant's dichotomy between analytic and synthetic statements, between statements that do not extend our knowledge and statements that do. It suggests that wherever all synthetic identity-statements fail to license substitution any appropriately worded analytic one will succeed, and that wherever analytic statements are not needed to licence substitution any appropriately worded synthetic statement of identity or equivalence will do so. Both suggestions turn out to be false. 'It is analytic that' and 'it is synthetic that' are just two out of very

[1] Cf. *Begriffsschrift* (1879), ch. i, *Translations*, p. 20.

many expressions that generate non-extensionality. They have no special logical status among these expressions.

Perhaps someone will object that even if 'analytic' is not a sufficient addition to the vocabulary of formal logic it is at least a necessary one. 'Maybe we must add several other such terms', he will say, 'if our logic is to do justice to the full variety and heterogeneity of non-extensional discourse. For example, some concept like Carnap's intensional isomorphism[1] seems to be required in order to specify the type of sense-identity that licenses substitution in passages of reported speech like the subordinate clause of (4), or we might use here the identity of what Frege called indirect sense. Indeed, Frege's own theory, as Church has shown,[2] lends itself to the development of a logical system acknowledging an infinite number of kinds of sense and, correspondingly, of sense-identity. For if we are to acknowledge an indirect kind of sense, that is the sense of an expression when referring to its own customary sense, we might as well go on to acknowledge a further kind of sense that is the sense of an expression when referring to its own indirect sense, and so on indefinitely.

But the logic of non-extensional discourse is too complex to be netted in either of these ways. One main drawback to Church's hierarchy of sense-types is that it extends the range of varieties of sense-identity upwards from analyticity, as it were, but not downwards or sideways. Just as identity of customary sense is a stronger, i.e. more restrictive, criterion of intersubstitutability than identity of reference, so too identity of indirect sense is a stronger one than identity of customary sense, and so on. Hence Church's hierarchy allows for no simple forms of identity that are stronger than identity of reference but weaker than identity of customary sense. In particular, it does not provide for a form of statement that will license substitution in (7) but not in (1). Moreover it is by no means the case that all important forms of identity-statement are ordered by a serial relation of being stronger than. One form of identity-statement may be said with some convenience to provide a stronger criterion of intersubstitutability than another if and only if appropriately worded statements of the first form license substitution in all passages where appropriately worded statements of

[1] R. Carnap, *Meaning and Necessity* (1947), p. 59.
[2] 'A Formulation of the Logic of Sense and Denotation' in *Structure, Method and Meaning*, ed. P. Henle *et al.* (1951), pp. 3 ff.

the second form do, and there are some passages where the former license substitution and the latter do not. But, though this relation is clearly transitive and irreflexive, it does not conform to the third requirement for a serial relation: it is not connected. Pairs of identity-forms exist such that neither member of the pair bears this relation to the other. One pair of this kind is constituted by identity-statements of the forms 'It is demonstrable from Peano's axioms for arithmetic that . . .' and 'It is demonstrable from the Lewis-Barcan axioms for the S4 system of strict implication that . . .' Another pair is constituted by those of the forms 'It is chemically certain that . . .' and 'It is a principle of English law that . . .' One has only to consider the extent to which truth-preserving substitution is licensed in statements of these very forms in order to see the force of such examples. Hence no single serial order of strength can fit all the relevant identity-forms. Church's hierarchy of sense-types not only fails to allow for some identity-forms that are stronger than the weakest member of the series it does allow for. It also fails to allow for an indefinitely large number of parallel or partially parallel series.

It might therefore be thought that what we need is a theory more like Carnap's, in which each requisite identity-form will be introduced by a string of definitions in terms of appropriately chosen meta-linguistic primitives. But is it the business of *formal* logic to define in turn each requisite variety of identity? Traditionally logic is the study of those arguments that are valid, or of those statements that are true, solely in virtue of their form, not their content. More precisely one may say it is the study of those arguments that are valid, or of those statements that are true, under all uniform replacements of their non-logical terms, where only 'not', 'and', 'if', 'or', 'some', 'all', 'is', 'true', 'false', 'therefore', etc., are to be taken as logical terms. Admittedly there is no *a priori* reason for supposing this list of logical terms to be anything but open-ended. Admittedly it is natural to seek to develop the subject by extending the list, and certain terms have an obvious topic-neutrality that seems to qualify them as *prima facie* candidates for admission. The conjunctival 'that', for example, as in (1), (3), (4), (5) and (7), is a candidate that could hardly be refused. But that term does not characterize any particular form of identity-statement, since it is common to many. Perhaps we should therefore be prepared to consider the claims of 'intensionally', or of a corresponding meta-linguistic term, like 'sense', 'meaning', 'intension', or 'connotation'. 'Extensionally' or 'extension' is another such term, 'intensional-isomorphically' a third, 'it is physically necessary that' yet another. But even supposing all these could be admitted to our logical vocabulary without its formalization's needing to contain more than one or two primitives extra to the requirements of extensional logic, we should still have to add an indefinitely large number of other terms whose topic-neutrality becomes more and more dubious, if our non-extensional logic is to be systematized in this way. We should need the deontic modality of 'it is obligatory that', the epistemic modality of 'it is *a priori* that', the interrogative modality of 'is it the case that', the optative modality of 'would that', the imperative modality of 'bring it about that', and so on.

G. H. von Wright[1] and others have proposed interesting axiom-sets for many of these modalities and have pointed out partial or total isomorphisms between some of the systems thus generated. Moreover among the several current uses of the word 'logic' is certainly one in which it signifies the interpretation of a calculus to constitute a deductive system that deploys in its axioms and theorems a selection of statements that are true, or of arguments that are valid, under all uniform replacements of terms belonging neither to the standard vocabulary of extensional logic nor to some family of word-uses chosen for special study in the system. Von Wright has given the title 'deontic logic' to such a study of the concepts of permission, prohibition, obligation, etc., and he has similarly discussed 'the logic of wishing' and 'the logics of knowledge, certainty, doubt, and belief'.[2] In each case the vocabulary of constants defined by the axioms is the result of adding not more than one or two terms – different terms in different systems – to the vocabulary of extensional logic. Let us call these several studies *special logics*.[3] For in another familiar sense of the word logic is no more concerned with permission than with percussion, no more concerned with wishing than with whistling, no more concerned with doubt than with doublebasses. Instead its distinctive concern is with the topic-neutral conditions of all rational discourse – with the conditions of valid reasoning whether about whistles, wishes, doubts, commands, entreaties, ques-

[1] E.g. *An Essay in Modal Logic* (1951).
[2] 'Deontic Logic', *Mind*, lx (1951), pp. 1 ff., and 'On the Logic of some Axiological and Epistemological Concepts', *Ajatus*, xvii (1952), pp. 213 ff.
[3] Cf. I. Kant, *Critique of Pure Reason*, tr. N. Kemp Smith (1950), p. 93.

tions, etc., or any combination of these. Let us call logic in this sense *general logic*, so that the problem I am discussing here becomes: how can our general logic come to cover all non-extensional as well as extensional discourse?

I do not wish to suggest that the development of special logics is not in most cases at least as worth while an objective as any other project in axiomatization. But it cannot solve the problem which Frege vainly attempted to solve with his dichotomy of sense and reference. Most notably it cannot provide us with a convenient technique for formalizing arguments in which a variety of different modalities occur. In political theory, for example, it is common for physical, epistemic and deontic modalities to occur in the same argument. In private international law obligations under different systems of rules are often compared and related. Sometimes in everyday speech the phrase 'it is obligatory that' will be used to imply the possibility of what is said to be obligatory, sometimes not. No doubt the lowest common multiple of all special logics – the simplest system within which they were all derivable – would have a certain adequacy here. But it would be immensely cumbrous and unwieldy, with very large numbers of axioms and undefined constants. Nor is it at all clear that the expression 'all special logics' has any determinate reference. How many natural languages do we have to scrutinize before we can be sure that just so-and-so many modal operators deserve separate logical study? How can we ever be sure that someone somewhere in some language is not using a new modal operator at this very moment? We can hardly recommend delaying the construction of our general logic until all special logics are completed, if we cannot specify what would count as evidence of this completion. We shall do much better, as often in science, to generalize boldly and challenge the objector to produce his counter-instance.

§25. The problem of non-extensionality as a problem about statement-forming operators on sayings

What is needed for the solution of this problem in general logic is neither the old dichotomy of analytic and synthetic nor yet the new multiplicity of modal logics, but instead a general theory of statement (i.e. true-or-false saying)-forming operators on sayings. All non-extensionality may conveniently be taken to arise from the implicit or

G

explicit occurrence of such operators. Frege's 'The Morning Star is the Evening Star' is no counter-example, because unless we preface some operator like 'it is an astronomical discovery that' or 'it is synthetic that' to this statement there is no lapse from truth to falsehood when we substitute 'Morning Star' for 'Evening Star' in it. The fallacy to be avoided is the inference from

> It is synthetic that the Morning Star is the Evening Star

to

> It is synthetic that the Morning Star is the Morning Star,

not the inference from

> The Morning Star is the Evening Star

to

> The Morning Star is the Morning Star.

The latter is not a fallacy at all. It is true that, if the statement

> (9) The day after Tuesday is Wednesday

is analytic, this is already implicit in it, so far as whether or not it is analytic depends on the meanings of its terms. But by parity of reasoning, if the statement

> (10) The day after Tuesday is market-day

is not analytic, its syntheticity is implicit in it. So that when we infer from (9) to (10) in virtue of the discovery that Wednesday is market-day we commit no fallacy. We have not argued from the analyticity of (9) to the analyticity of (10). Analogously it is fallacious to argue from (7) to (8) on the ground that the consequents of the two conditionals involved are truth-functionally equivalent. But it is not fallacious to argue from the one conditional sentence to the other on this ground, so long as it is clear that the 'if . . . then . . .' of these sentences does not purport to express a natural connection between two facts. What Frege called the 'cognitive value' of a statement is irrelevant to its logic, except so far as it forms part of another statement which implicitly or explicitly ascribes this value to it. There are operators, like 'it is false that' and 'it is the case both that it is raining and also that' which do not generate non-extensionality. But no non-extensionality occurs that cannot conveniently be taken to arise from the occurrence of some statement-forming operator on sayings. Of course, what is non-extensional is not the whole statement in which the operator occurs, like (1) or (7), but only that part of it which is within the scope of the operator. The first occurrence of 'he' in (1) is straightforwardly extensional.

It is true that terms sometimes have a non-extensional occurrence in sayings that contain no explicit statement-forming operator. Consider, for example, the statement

(11) Taking daily doses of mepacrine prevents the onset of malarial fever

and suppose that, as it might quite accidentally happen, all and only inhabitants of Moulmein take daily doses of mepacrine. You can infer that Moulmeiners do not develop malarial fever but not that living in Moulmein prevents this development. What prevents the fever is the dosage, not the accident of residence. Clearly the grammatical subject and object of 'prevents' in (11) are non-extensional, though no statement-forming operator occurs explicitly in (11). But if we say instead

It is a causal law that anyone who takes a daily dose of mepacrine does not suffer from malarial fever

we make a statement that has the same meaning – justifies all and only the same arguments – as (11), and contains an operator of much the same kind as (7). Or consider the statement

(12) A policeman is looking for the thief

and suppose that the thief is, as it happens, the butler's nephew. It would obviously be fallacious to infer that the policeman is looking for the butler's nephew, for he may not believe him to be the thief. Accordingly that part of (12) which is the grammatical object of 'looking for' is non-extensional, though it lacks a statement-forming operator. But (12) has the same meaning as[1]

(13) A policeman is endeavouring that he finds the thief

which does contain an appropriate operator. Again, the statement

---

[1] I owe the suggestion of this equivalence to W. V. Quine, *Word and Object*, p. 152.

> The characteristic of being a featherless biped is not to be identified with the characteristic of being a rational animal

is non-extensional except in respect of the term 'characteristic'. But it is equivalent to some such statement as

> It is not analytic that all and only featherless bipeds are rational animals.

Similarly

> Someone is here who, you say, sells ice-cream

is equivalent to

> (14) Someone is here of whom you say that he sells ice-cream.

On the other hand certain statements sometimes cited in this connection do not lend themselves to such a reformulation. For example, Quine once considered the two statements

> (15) Giorgione was so called because of his size

and

> (16) 'Cicero' contains six letters

to be typically non-extensional,[1] and no appropriate 'that . . .' clause can plausibly be teased out of either statement. Just to call a man by a name is not to say anything, nor is the naming of a word's written form the naming of a saying. Hence either these statements are not non-extensional at all, or we must abandon the theory – call it *the theory of operators* for short – that the logical problem of non-extensionality is essentially a problem about the logic of statement-forming operators on sayings. But the former alternative is the correct one. The term 'Cicero' does not occur in (16), but only the language-word 'Cicero'. So that if identically referring terms are to be substituted for one another in (16) 'Tully' would not be put for 'Cicero', replacing a true statement by a false one, but rather 'Tully's family name' for " 'Cicero' ", replacing one true statement by another. To put the same point in Frege's terminology: Cicero is neither directly nor indirectly referred to in (16), but only the expression 'Cicero'. Though Quine has now

---

[1] E.g. W. V. Quine, *From a Logical Point of View*, p. 139.

in effect acknowledged this regarding statements like (16), he still takes (15) to be genuinely non-extensional.[1] Yet (15) is a telescoped version of

> The name 'Giorgione' was given to Giorgione because of his size

where the substitution of the term 'Barbarelli' for the term 'Giorgione' creates no paralogism because " 'Giorgione' " is here a term for a language-word, not for a term. Hence both (15) and (16) are straightforwardly extensional. What causes most confusion, perhaps, in such contexts is the fact that quotation-marks can be used equally well to indicate language-words, culture-words, utterance-words, saying-words, and terms, and not only these but also the corresponding phrases, clauses, and sentences as well. But if that fact is borne in mind, and it is accepted (as will be further argued in §§31–33) that formal-logical analysis is concerned with terms and sayings, not with language-words and language-sentences, statements like (15) and (16) will not be reckoned as counter-examples to the theory of operators.

Now compare this theory with Frege's. Frege's theory requires us in effect to distinguish between two different versions of the law of extensionality for informal discourse. According to the stronger version terms identical in what would customarily be taken as their reference, or statements identical in truth-value, may be substituted for one another in any statement without affecting its truth-value. According to the weaker version it is identically referring expressions *simpliciter* that may be so substituted. In its stronger version – the one hitherto considered – Frege recognized that the law is patently unsound for informal discourse, applying only to some statements and not to all, but it does serve to define a problem. The logical problem of non-extensionality is the problem of how to articulate and systematize the general logic of those statements to which the law, in this stronger version, does not apply. In its weaker version, however, the law is not so evidently unsound, as Frege has shown. For what Frege tried to do, in effect, was to maintain the law in this weaker version and to adapt the understanding of human discourse so as to fit it. If we grant that in the troublesome contexts our expressions do not in fact refer to what, on Frege's view, they would customarily refer to, but refer instead to something else, then the weaker law of extensionality might perhaps be

[1] *Word and Object*, pp. 141 ff.

saved. Thus on Frege's theory these contexts do not require a non-extensional system like Church's for their formalization. Frege's theory of sense and reference is tailored to fit his own *Begriffsschrift*, so long as an expression of informal discourse has one symbol or formula of the calculus to represent it in its customarily referring occurrences and another in its indirectly referring ones. But all this is only achieved at the cost of altering the sense in which the latter occurrences are to be understood. If they do not refer as they usually do, their sense is not what their sense usually is, but instead is what Frege calls their indirect sense. Hence Frege's solution of the problem is not merely inadequate in scope, as has already been shown. Even where it does work it achieves success by moulding the facts to the law, rather than the law to the facts, and for that purpose it requires us to make a distinction between two different concepts of meaning which has no utility outside the solution of this very problem.

In contrast with Frege's thesis the theory of operators implies no recondite difference of meaning between one occurrence of an expression and another. According to it the problem of non-extensionality does not force us to recognize any other modes of sense-differentiation than those with which we are ordinarily familiar. The expression 'the thief' turns out to have precisely the same sense in the butler's statement

> If he finds someone with a squint and size-twelve boots, he finds the thief

as in (13), because the very same saying, 'He finds the thief', occurs both in (13) and here. If we suppose that, implicitly or explicitly, all informal non-extensionality arises from the addition of certain operators to sayings, we must suppose that the identity of the sayings involved is unaffected by this addition. The same sayings occur, now in an extensional context, now in a non-extensional one, and since the sayings are the same so too are their meanings and the meanings of their terms.

Indeed, how unfortunate it would be if, as Frege's theory implies, we could never report exactly what a man said! How unfortunate if somehow, through the very act of trying to report him in indirect speech, our words were forced to bear a different meaning from his! How frustrating if one cannot refer to what he actually said but only to its meaning! How frustrating if one can never say, without self-contradiction, 'The editor wrote that Baghdad is a western city, I know, but I do not know the meaning of his remark'! How odd too if the very meanings of 'brother', 'male' and 'sibling' that make the saying 'Brothers are male siblings' analytically true were not the meanings these words had in

It is an analytic truth that brothers are male siblings!

How unfortunate, finally, if there were as many different types of sense an expression could have as there are logically different forms of non-extensional discourse! For this is what would be required for a satisfactorily comprehensive solution of the problem along Frege's lines. It is difficult enough for children and lexicographers to master the variety of customary senses in which words are used, but perhaps they should consider it a mercy that they are not condemned to a much vaster task, as they apparently would be if a Fregean solution of the whole problem were unavoidable.

Because the theory of operators does not suppose the meanings of expressions to vary with the extensionality or non-extensionality of their occurrence it does not lead to any of these paradoxes, let alone to the further paradox of enlarging our domain of reference to include meanings and truth-values in precisely the same sense in which it already includes planets and people. Rather than maintain a law of extensionality for unformalized statements by modifying their normal interpretation, the theory maintains instead the normal interpretation of these statements and is content to accept that the law of extensionality does not apply to them even in its weaker version.

Nevertheless, when it comes to formalization, the theory of operators permits us to be even more extensional than Frege. The general logic of statement-forming operators on sayings turns out to admit of representation in a formal system for which the law of extensionality is provable in its stronger version. In a logically idealized reconstruction of ordinary human discourse no non-extensionality need occur at all. But to see this we must first observe that the reduction of all non-extensional contexts to statements containing statement-forming operators on sayings is only a half-way stage. There is a logically simpler form of statement that is equivalent to this one. Any such statement turns out to have an equivalent in meaning that predicates something of either some or all tokens of its constituent saying.

This is obvious enough in the case of statements formed by operators like 'he said that'. If, and only if, he said that either today is Tuesday or today is not Tuesday, some token of the saying

(17) Either today is Tuesday or today is not Tuesday

was uttered by him. But we may equally well accept that if, and only if, it is logically true that either today is Tuesday or today is not Tuesday, any token of (17) is logically true. In the former case the operator refers to a particular event and the equivalent subject-and-predicate statement is particular in its logical quantity. In the latter case the operator makes no such reference to a particular event and its generality requires the equivalent statement to be a universal one.

Certain familiar objections to admitting predicational equivalents for these operators deserve attention. First, an objector would gain nothing here by applying the translatability criterion with which Church attacked Carnap's analysis of indirect discourse in terms of statements about sentences.[1] For when one ascribes to a token the property of being such-and-such a saying one does not specify its language, as one would when mentioning the language-sentence or utterance-sentence it instantiates. Hence the equivalence claimed is unaffected by the language in which it happens to be expressed and remains invariant under translation. It is true that sameness of reformulation in indirect speech was invoked in §19 as a criterion for sameness of saying, and this might suggest that any analysis of indirect speech in terms of statements about sayings must be circular. But the circularity can easily be avoided if, instead of referring to reformulation in indirect speech, we list in detail just those variations of wording that reformulation in indirect speech normally requires, such as the change of pronoun and verb-form in certain cases, and stipulate that these variations alone leave sameness of saying unaffected. All that is needed are lists of instructions for the schoolboy exercise of putting *oratio recta* into *oratio obliqua*. Such a list can in principle be given for any sufficiently rich natural language, and our logical analyses will not suffer in practice if we confine our concept of saying to sentence-tokens of known languages. If a new language is discovered, the definition of 'same saying as' can be enlarged appropriately.

[1] 'On Carnap's Analysis of Statements of Assertion and Belief', *Analysis*, x (1950), pp. 97 ff.

Secondly, Prior has pointed out that one is plainly not talking about the sentence 'Socrates is dead' when one says

(18) I wish that Socrates were dead

and he argues that an ordinary modal assertion cannot therefore be treated as a statement about a form of words.[1] This is true. But what is at stake is not whether (18) is the same saying as

(19) Some token of the saying 'Would that Socrates were dead!' expresses a wish of mine

but merely whether it has the same meaning, in the sense of being true under the same conditions and of justifying the same arguments. Prior's criterion for equivalence here is too strong. If applied to equivalence of meaning it would make even 'He is my brother' have a different meaning from 'He is my parents' son', for in saying 'He is my brother' a man no more says anything about his parents than he says anything about a form of words when he asserts (18). Perhaps it will be objected that what we do require in a formal representation of an informal statement is sameness of saying, and not merely equivalence of meaning. But this would cut us off from making any non-trivial simplifications in any field of logical analysis. We could not even use truth-functional conditionals. For when one says

If he is my brother he is my friend

one is certainly not saying that it is false that it is both true that he is my brother and false that he is my friend.

There might however appear to be a difference here between operators referring to a particular event and operators not so referring. Perhaps no one can wish that Socrates were dead unless such a phenomenon as vocal or sub-vocal speech exists, so that there is no paradox in supposing (18) to be equivalent in meaning to (19). But, as Prior has also pointed out,[2] it would be impossible for Socrates to be dead without being dead even if there were no such phenomenon as speech, so that there does seem to be a paradox in supposing that the saying

(20) It is impossible for Socrates to be dead without being dead

[1] *Formal Logic* (1955), pp. 219 f.
[2] Ibid.

has the same meaning as

> (21) Any token of the saying 'Socrates is dead without being dead' is a necessary falsehood.

There seem to be conceivable circumstances, such as the non-existence of speech, or even just the non-existence of any token of 'Socrates is dead without being dead', in which the predicate of (21) could be replaced by any term whatever, such as 'necessarily true', without this making (21) false. Though statements like (21) might thus turn out to be vacuously and therefore trivially true if they are truth-functional conditionals, statements like (20) could not so turn out. It cannot be necessarily true that Socrates is dead without being dead. Nor can we evade this apparent paradox by comparing statements like (21) to laws of nature like Newton's first law of motion, which are none the worse for being uninstantiated. Statements of natural laws present well-known obstacles to truth-functional analysis, and are a standard form of non-extensional discourse. But, if (21) cannot be a truth-functional conditional, then in many fields our analysis of operators in terms of predicates has not brought us any nearer to an extensional formalization of non-extensional discourse.

The solution of this apparent paradox lies in recognizing that when one asserts an identity of meaning between (20) and (21) one cannot normally avoid uttering, in the quotation of (21), a token of the saying 'Socrates is dead without being dead.' Statements like (21) cannot be trivially, because vacuously, true, since in the very act of asserting or quoting them one renders them non-vacuous. The assumption that they are truth-functional will therefore never lead us to draw false conclusions from true premises. Of course, by virtue of some code or coincidence of language two sayings might have precisely the same set of sentence-tokens – each token intentionally conveying one message to me and another to you – which would again seem to suggest that sameness of saying cannot be guaranteed by specifying a certain class of sentence-tokens. But any such parallelism in the case of, say, 'Socrates is dead without being dead' is destroyed by the logician who reformulates (20) as (21), since in order to do this he must utter an unambiguous token of that saying.

A complexity arises if we accept that a man's hopes, fears, beliefs or other mental attitudes sometimes remain unverbalized. We cannot then suppose that some particular token of the relevant saying is uttered either aloud or in sub-vocal speech. But there is a corresponding universal statement that will save our formal-logical purposes. We may suppose that any token of that saying which the man had heard, seen or felt would have been likely, in suitable conditions, to elicit from him an appropriate response. Such a statement of likelihoods would not itself be a truth-functional generalization. But we can describe its true nature, whatever that be, in a further statement – a truth-functional generalization about all its tokens. This statement will be true if and only if the original mental attitude statement is true, however much the two may differ as sayings. So that the substitution of the one for the other as a premiss or conclusion of an argument will never lead to the deduction of a false conclusion from true premisses, even if for other than formal-logical purposes, as in psychological enquiry, it may be unsatisfactory to treat hopes, fears, beliefs, etc., simply as dispositions to react to certain utterances in certain ways.

Once we grant that every statement containing a statement-forming operator on sayings has an equivalent which predicates something of some or all of a saying's tokens, we can easily see why there are so many different kinds and degrees of non-extensionality in informal discourse. Different predicates apply to sayings in virtue of different kinds of feature in them, just as 'hot', 'cold', etc., apply to an object in virtue of its temperature and 'red', 'yellow', etc., in virtue of its colour. Change an object's temperature beyond a certain point and it may no longer be truly described as hot: change a sentence's wording in any other than trivial respects and it may no longer be truly described as the saying uttered by a certain person on a certain occasion. Similarly if a saying like (17) is correctly described as a logical truth, this is because the saying remains true under all uniform replacements of its non-logical terms. Hence certain substitutions may be made in a statement like (5) without changing its truth-value, but not, say, the non-uniform replacement of terms that turns (5) into (6). Again, if a saying is truly described as analytic this is because of something about the meanings of its constituent culture-words, irrespective of its language-words. Hence in the statement

It is analytic that a man's brother is his parents' son,

unlike (5), any term in any of its occurrences may be replaced by another term of the same meaning. But if a saying is correctly described as false, only its truth-value matters for this description, so that in a statement like

It is false that the earth is flat

we may substitute any saying of similar truth-value for 'the earth is flat'. Certainly it is not always quite as evident as in these cases just what kind of feature in the saying justifies its predicate, and so we may not always see quite so easily why just such-and-such restrictions are imposed on substitution in the corresponding operator-formed statement. For example, the non-extensionality generated by 'it is a law of nature that' or 'it is physically necessary that' has often been found puzzling, and some elucidation of it is offered in §§37–40 below. Such difficulties create a series of particular problems in philosophical semantics: how should we conceive such-and-such an operator (or predicate), and why? But the general point being made here is merely that for each particular kind of informal non-extensionality the formal-logical problem is best approached by taking the sayings and terms in question to have just the meanings they would normally be taken to have and then enquiring, as appropriate, either what it is about these meanings and their verbal expressions that restricts substitution in statements affirming the true nature of the sayings, or what features of a saying are vital to statements reporting certain events, processes, dispositions, etc., such as the assertion of a belief, in which the saying has figured. The Fregean solution, which takes sayings and terms to have different meanings in their non-extensional occurrence, holds out no clear prospect of being satisfactory in all cases, and even where it does work it works only at the cost of considerable paradox.

§26. The problem of semantical antinomies in the systematized logic of statements about statements

The above treatment of non-extensional contexts in informal discourse prepares them, as it were, for formalization. It reduces them to a certain uniform pattern. But it still remains to be shown that they can then be formalized in at least as simple and extensional a fashion as Frege's theory permits. For if that could not be shown there would still be a strong case for applying Fregean distinctions between different concepts of meaning to as many kinds of informally non-extensional context as possible.

This task of formalization may conveniently be approached via discussion of an issue that is crucial to it. Any attempt to systematize the formal logic of statements about sayings runs up against a well-known risk of antinomy, with which it must somehow come to terms. Such an antinomy arises, for instance, if a formula 'p' is interpreted as the statement " 'p' is not true". For, given only certain elementary rules and the postulate that every statement, including 'p', is either true or not true, we may then prove a contradiction. Four rules that suffice are:

(I) Any statement that the statement '...' is true may be replaced by the statement '...', and any statement that the statement '...' is not true may be replaced by a contradictory of '....'.

(II) Any propositional constant may be replaced by the statement assigned as its interpretation.

(III) The conjunction of a premiss with any statement provable from it is also provable from it.

(IV) Any statement that is provable from each alternate of a disjunction is provable from the disjunction itself.

The proof then runs as follows:

(i)	'p' is true	(hypothesis)
(ii)	" 'p' is not true" is true	(i, II)
(iii)	'p' is not true	(ii, I)
(iv)	'p' is true and 'p' is not true	(i–iii, III)
(v)	'p' is not true	(hypothesis)
(vi)	" 'p' is not true" is not true	(v, II)
(vii)	'p' is true	(vi, I)
(viii)	'p' is true and 'p' is not true	(v–vii, III)
(ix)	'p' is true and 'p' is not true	(postulate, i–iv, v–viii, IV)

It should be noted that this antinomy arises in a semantical metalanguage, i.e. in a deductive system postulating the assignment of meanings and truth-values to the formulas of a calculus. No solution of the problem is achieved, therefore, by arguments, common in recent years,[1] to the effect that such contradictions do not arise or cannot be proved in ordinary language. Our problem here is how to systematize the logic of statements about sayings. So no help can come from theories that are exclusively concerned with how words are actually used in everyday speech, rather than with how they may or must be used in systematizing the laws or truths of formal logic. But an obvious step towards achieving a solution is the Russellian one of rejecting any such interpretation of '*p*'. We maintain the postulate that every statement in our interpreted object language is either true or not true, while barring any of these statements from denying its own truth. But then of course there is the fear that similar antinomies, like the Grelling, may arise from other statements about their own truth-value or meaning, or that they may arise in the meta-meta-language or the meta-meta-meta-language and so on. So the need comes to be felt for some kind of generalized hierarchy policy: the meanings and truth-values of statements on any one level of the hierarchy are only to be discussed at a higher level.

It turns out, however, that this kind of insurance against antinomy is bought at too high a price. In judicial, journalistic or historical fact-finding, as well as in everyday conversation, we frequently cite statements about a witness's truthfulness alongside the report of his testimony as the premises from which we argue about the facts. It is then an essential part of our argument that it should appear to jump from one level of statement to another and perhaps back again. How can the formalization of such an argument adopt any of the usual hierarchy principles as an insurance against semantical antinomies?

Consider, for example,

> (22) If the policeman testifies that anything which the prisoner deposes is false, and the prisoner deposes that something which the policeman testifies is true, then something which the policeman testifies is false and something which the prisoner deposes is true.

The logical form of (22) is exhibited up to a point by

> (23) If A that anything which B is false, and B that something which A is true, then something which A is false and something which B is true.

[1] E.g. R. C. Skinner, 'The Paradox of the Liar', *Mind*, lxviii (1959), pp. 322 ff.

An informal proof that the consequent of a conditional of this form is deducible from its antecedent runs as follows. The premisses are

(24) A that anything which B is false

and

(25) B that something which A is true.

It is required to prove from (24) and (25) that

(26) Something which A is false

and

(27) Something which B is true

are both true. According to (25)

(28) Something which A is true

instantiates the relative clause of

(29) Anything which B is false.

Hence if (29) is true (28) must be false, by universal instantiation, and the contradictory of (28), viz.

(30) Anything which A is false

must be true. According to (24) the relative clause of (30) is instantiated by (29), so that if (30) is true (29) must be false, by universal instantiation. Hence, if (29) is true and therefore also (30), (29) must be false; and so, by truth-functional logic, (29) must be false. If (29) is false, its contradictory (27) is true. Moreover, since according to (24) the relative clause of (26) is instantiated by (29), it follows that since (29) is false (26) is true, by existential generalization. Therefore both (26) and (27) are true.

Since (22) thus remains true under all uniform replacements of its non-logical terms, it is a plausible candidate for acceptance as a logical truth. But no symbolic analysans for it – no sentence on the pattern of (23) – could even be formulated, let alone proved, in a system constructed according to either of the two most familiar proposals for analysing indirect discourse in accordance with a hierarchy principle.

In Church's system – the system mentioned in §24 – the analysans of a statement reporting someone's belief, assertion, etc., in the form of indirect discourse should be formulated in a non-extensional object language. The analysans reports a relation of belief or assertion between a person and an intensional entity like a proposition. Intensional entities are conceived to belong in a hierarchy of successively higher orders, since the name of each such entity must have as its sense an intensional entity of higher order. But it is impossible to assign the proposition that is the sense of an analysans for (29) or (30) to any order whatever in such a hierarchy. For in an analysans of (29) we should quantify over a universe which, as we are told in (25), includes the sense of (28) and therefore also the sense of (30), since (30) is (28)'s contradictory. So that the sense of (29) must belong to an order higher than the sense of (30). At the same time in an analysans of (30) we should quantify over a universe which, as we are told in (24), includes the sense of (29). So that the sense of (30) must belong to an order higher than the sense of (29). And it is impossible for the sense of (29) to belong to an order both higher and lower than that to which the sense of (30) belongs.

According to a proposal of Carnap's the analysans of a statement reporting anything in the form of indirect discourse should be formulated in a meta-language. The analysans reports a relation of some kind, the precise nature of which does not matter here,[1] between a person and a sentence of the object language. On this approach the hierarchy principle adopted is the language-level policy. Each symbol or formula used or mentioned in the analysans must belong to one or more distinct formalized languages which are so constructed, and so assigned to numbered levels, that statements about the truth-values or meanings of expressions in any language assigned to level n may only be formulated in a language assigned to level $n+1$. But according to such a policy, since (25) implies that the truth-value of (28) is a topic of (29), the analysans of (29) must belong to a language of higher level than that of (28) and its contradictory (30). At the same time, since (24) implies that the truth-value of (29) is a topic of (30), the analysans of (30) must belong to a language of higher level than that of (29). But it is impossible for the analysans of (29) to belong to a formalized language of a

[1] Cf. *Meaning and Necessity*, pp. 53 ff., and 'On Belief Sentences' in *Philosophy and Analysis*, ed. M. Macdonald (1954), pp. 128 ff.

level that is both higher and lower than the level of the language to which the analysans of (30) belongs.

Analogous difficulties arise if we substitute a ramified-type structure, like that in Whitehead and Russell's *Principia Mathematica*, for a language-level policy. For then any property designated by a function corresponding to 'A' in (23) must be both lower and higher in order that the property designated by a function corresponding to 'B', which is impossible. Nor would an axiom of reducibility help here, since it would presumably state 'To any function designating a property of any order and any type there corresponds . . .', whereas we could not regard the properties in question as belonging to any order at all. Moreover our axiom would have to be rather stronger than Russell's, and its justification even more questionable,[1] since in order to formalize indirect discourse we should need, for reasons already suggested, an order containing properties designated by functions that were not merely extensionally equivalent to all functions designating properties that belonged to other orders of the same type, but also synonymous, intensionally isomorphic, etc., with them.

It might be objected that (22) is too trivial a truth for us to be seriously worried by its exclusion from a proposed analysis of indirect discourse. But not only is the truth of statements with the form of (23) far from self-evident. They also express logical principles affecting the grounds on which witnesses stand trial for perjury and historians sort out conflicting testimonies in their source material. If a formal logician were to reject such principles as trivial he would depreciate the importance of his own subject over a very wide field of rational discourse. What is needed is a way of analysing indirect discourse that will provide a reasonable degree of insurance against the occurrence of semantical antinomies but does not hinge on a hierarchy principle that would bar the formalization of statements like (22).

Prior, however, has pointed out[2] that if (22) is logically true so is

(31) If the policeman testifies that anything which the prisoner deposes is false, and the prisoner deposes that something which the policeman testifies is true, then either the policeman or the prisoner says something else as well.

[1] Cf. F. P. Ramsey, *The Foundations of Mathematics* (1931), pp. 28 ff.
[2] Cf. A. N. Prior, 'Epimenides the Cretan', *Journal of Symbolic Logic*, xxiii (1958), pp. 261 ff.

And he has claimed that (31), and therefore also (22) which has the same antecedent, is paradoxical in just the same way as he thinks the Epimenides is paradoxical, viz. that if some Cretan does assert that nothing asserted by a Cretan is true, then there must also be, as Church once argued,[1] some true assertion by a Cretan besides this false one. Hence, Prior argues, it is wrong to seek the construction of a system in which (22) can be proved without proving paradoxes, for to prove (22) is to prove a paradox.

But it is important to distinguish a semantical antinomy from a paradox of Prior's kind. The former renders a system worthless by proving a contradiction in it. The latter proves something that is not a logical contradiction but may perhaps be more than we want to prove in that particular system; for Church's argument pointed to the apparent possibility of settling part of the empirical question 'How much does Epimenides say?' on purely logical grounds. Moreover, while a semantical antinomy cannot be admitted into a logical system without utterly vitiating it, a statement like (31) or

(32) If a Cretan says that anything said by a Cretan is false, then something said by a Cretan is true

only seems paradoxical, as Prior himself almost allows, if one does not think the matter through. Let it merely be granted that an operator like 'A says that', 'A asserts that', 'A testifies that', or 'A deposes that' – any operator involving the conjunctival 'that' – is correctly prefaced only to a statement, i.e. to a saying which is either true or false but not both. Then the paradox disappears as soon as one sees what this principle implies. If the antecedent of (32) is true, then according to the principle

(33) Anything said by a Cretan is false

is a statement. But if (33) is true as well as the antecedent of (32), then by universal instantiation (33) is false, and therefore, by truth-functional logic, (33) is false. Hence if the antecedent of (32) is true (33) is false and something said by a Cretan is true. This true statement cannot be (33), since (33) is false and cannot, according to the principle granted, also be true. So a Cretan must have said something else besides (33). On the other hand Epimenides is not condemned to complete silence if no

[1] Review of A. Koyré's 'The Liar', *Jour. Symb. Log.*, xii (1946), p. 131.

Cretan ever says anything true: it is merely that his utterance of (33) cannot be a statement. Similarly, if neither policeman nor prisoner ever says anything else, they have not asserted anything at all: their utterances have not been statements. Of course, this is hard luck for Epimenides if, though a perfectly good logician, he just does not happen to know that he is a Cretan. His utterance of (33) might fall short of being a statement through no apparent fault of his own, just because all Cretans turn out in fact, as he himself seems to say, to speak falsely. But the moral of the apparent paradox is *caveat dictor*. People who utter sayings of the form 'Anything an A says is false' must be particularly sure of their facts. They not only run the usual risk, through factual ignorance, of making a false statement. They also run a special risk, because of the special form of their utterance, of not making a statement at all.

In short, statements like (22), (31) and (32) are not so paradoxical that they must just be written off. Instead we must accept them as logical truths, if we take the conjunctival 'that' to belong in our logical vocabulary alongside 'if', 'or', 'some', 'any', 'true', 'false', etc., and maintain the laws of non-contradiction and excluded middle for statements. For, if it is a statement that must follow 'if' and precede or follow 'or', what other kind of expression should follow 'that'? If a true-or-false statement must follow 'it is not the case that', it must also follow 'he says that'. What is settled on purely logical grounds is not a part of the empirical question 'How much does Epimenides utter?' but a part of the logical question 'How much of what Epimenides utters can count as statement?' Hence no method of formalizing indirect discourse is adequate that relies on a hierarchy principle barring such statements as (22) from being represented at all. We need rather some system, like Prior's or R. L. Goodstein's closely similar one,[1] in which it is possible to represent those statements of informal discourse that are directly or indirectly included in their own domain of reference.

As symbols Prior uses the Łukasiewicz letters 'C', 'K', 'N', etc., for truth-functors; the ordinary statement variables 'p', 'q', 'r', etc.; additional variables 'δ', 'γ', etc., ranging over all monadic statement-forming operators on statements, whether truth-functional or not; and

---

[1] Cf. A. N. Prior, *Time and Modality* (1957), pp. 130 f., and R. L. Goodstein, 'On the Formalisation of Indirect Discourse', *Jour. Symb. Log.*, xxiii (1958), pp. 417 ff.

the quantifiers 'Π' and 'Σ' binding variables of both types. As postulates he subjoins the Łukasiewicz rules for the quantifiers to any postulates sufficient for the ordinary propositional calculus without the variables 'δ', 'γ', etc., and extends substitution, with the usual restrictions in the presence of quantifiers, to these variables. The formal analysans of (32), and statements like it, thus comes to be

(34) CδΠpCδpNpΣpKδpp

and that of (22) is

(35) CKγΠpCδpNpδΣpKγppKΣpKγpNpΣpKδpp

Both of these formulas are theorems in Prior's system, and no antinomies arise within it. Situations that might be suspected of leading to antinomies peter out into theorems like (34).

However, the Prior-Goodstein kind of formalization cannot altogether dispense, *pace* Prior and Goodstein, with a hierarchy principle. Only its object language is protected by theorems like (34). In order to avoid antinomies in its semantical meta-language it needs an overriding meta-meta-linguistic restriction on meaning-assignments, requiring that no well-formed formula of the system is to stand for any statement about the truth-value or meaning of a formula of the system, or for any statement about the truth-value or meaning of a statement about the truth-value or meaning of a formula, or for any statement$_1$ about the truth-value or meaning of a statement$_2$ about . . . of a statement$_n$ about the truth-value or meaning of a wff. We cannot otherwise avoid such an antinomy as would arise in the meta-language if it assigned to a wff W of Prior's system the meaning 'The wff W of Prior's system is false.' It is no use arguing here, analogously to the case of Epimenides, that W may have the above meaning so long as it also has a meaning in which it is true. For if any wff of a calculus, for the purposes of any one exercise in logical analysis, is assigned more than one meaning, we condone the fallacy of equivocation. But since our object is to represent the statements of everyday informal discourse the restriction needed should not worry us too much. We can always use Prior's system to refer to the formulas of Goodstein's, and vice versa. No doubt we need a third system to represent a logical truth of the form of (23) where 'A' is 'a wff of Prior's system states that' and 'B' is 'a wff of Goodstein's system states that'. But these interlocutions between formal systems are hardly as important for any purpose as (22), and I do not see how any consistent formalization can represent them all. The inadequacy of systems like Church's and Carnap's lies in the fact that they apply a hierarchy principle even in their representations of informal statements, when it is only needed in the assignment of meanings to the wff of a formal system.

§27. An extensional formalization of informally non-extensional contexts

Systems like Prior's and Goodstein's have demonstrated the possibility of relaxing the hierarchy principle so as to permit the formalization of a statement like (22). But they are themselves patently non-extensional. We cannot prove

$$\Pi p\Pi q\Pi \delta CEpqE\delta p\delta q$$

in Prior's system. If we could, we should have to restrict the range of substitution-instances for the variable 'δ' to operators that do not generate non-extensionality. Hence, though these calculuses enable us to systematize the general logic of most non-extensional contexts, they do not enable us to simplify it. In that respect they do not achieve as much as Frege's distinction of customary from indirect sense achieves, with its license for extensional formalization. The reason why they fall short of such an achievement is that, in effect, they go only halfway with the theory of operators. Though they treat non-extensionality as the product of statement-forming operators on statements, rather than of words' being used in some non-customary sense, they do not go on to analyse such operators – in the way that was outlined above – into the more general terminology of predicates and quantifiers. Once we accept an analysis of this kind, we need no more as a basis for our formalizations than the standard combination of propositional and predicate calculuses.

Let us gain for our wff the additional perspicuity that punctuation affords and use quantification theory in its Anglo-American rather than in its Polish symbolization, with brackets for punctuation, '$\sim$', '.', '$\supset$', etc., for the usual truth-functional connectives (omitting the dot for conjunction wherever this may be done unambiguously), '($\exists$)' and '( )' for quantifiers, capitals for predicate letters, lower case from the end of the alphabet for individual letters, lower case from the middle of the alphabet for propositional letters, and the usual formation-rules. Assignments of meaning are to be restricted in the way already described. Then a formal analysans for

(36) A Cretan says that it is raining

will be

(37) $(\exists x)((CxRx)(Tx\equiv p))$

where 'C' stands for 'is a statement by a Cretan', 'R' for 'is a statement that it is raining', 'T' for 'is true', 'p' for 'it is raining', and individual letters include sentence-tokens in their domain of reference. For (32) the analysans will be

(38) $(\exists x)((CxFx)(Tx\equiv(x)(Cx\supset\sim Tx)))\supset(\exists x)(CxTx)$

where 'F' stands for 'is a statement that anything said by a Cretan is false' and the rest is as before. Thus the original terms of the reported utterance are preserved by ascription to it of predicates like 'R' or 'F', as proposed by I. Scheffler,[1] and the logical form of the reported statement is articulated in the conjoined rider that the statement uttered is true if and only if . . .

This conjoined rider is needed in order to circumvent Church's valid objection[2] to Scheffler's analysis that it fails to reveal the logical form of what is asserted, believed, etc. – an objection that could equally well be urged against Quine's more recent proposal[3] to analyse expressions like 'believes that Cicero denounced Catiline' as relative general terms of the form 'believes y (y denounced Catiline) of Cicero', where 'y' is to be regarded as a bound variable. No proposal for articulating the logic of indirect discourse can be satisfactory that fails to exhibit either the validity of formally valid arguments constructed on a pattern that essentially involves indirect discourse, or the logical truth of the corresponding statements, like (22) or (32), or like Prior's[4]

---

[1] 'An Inscriptional Approach to Indirect Quotation', *Analysis*, xiv (1954), pp. 83 ff.

[2] 'Propositions and Sentences' in I. M. Bochenski, A. Church, N. Goodman, *The Problem of Universals* (1956), p. 11.

[3] *Word and Object*, p. 216.

[4] *Time and Modality*, pp. 130 f.

(39) If the judge says on Monday that the prisoner will be hanged on Saturday, and the judge also says on Monday that the prisoner will not know on Saturday whether he will be hanged on Saturday, then it is not the case both that whatever the judge says on Monday is true and that whatever the judge says on Monday the prisoner will know on Saturday.

It can readily be seen that (38) is a theorem of ordinary quantification theory. I shall abbreviate the proof by citing meta-theorems from W. V. Quine's *Mathematical Logic* (3rd ed.):

i. $((\exists x)(CxTx)(\exists x)((CxFx)(Tx\equiv(x)(Cx\supset\sim Tx))))\supset$
$(\exists x)(CxTx)$ 100

ii. $(x)(((x)(Cx\supset\sim Tx)((CxFx)(Tx\equiv(x)(Cx\supset\sim Tx))))\supset$
$(CxTx))$ 100, 103, 104

iii. $(x)((\sim(\exists x)(CxTx)((CxFx)(Tx\equiv(x)(Cx\supset\sim Tx))))\supset$
$(CxTx))$ 100, ii, 123, 104

iv. $(\exists x)(\sim(\exists x)(CxTx)((CxFx)(Tx\equiv(x)(Cx\supset\sim Tx))))\supset$
$(\exists x)(CxTx)$ iii, 149, 104

v. $(\sim(\exists x)(CxTx)(\exists x)((CxFx)(Tx\equiv(x)(Cx\supset\sim Tx))))\supset$
$(\exists x)(CxTx)$ 158, iv, 123, 104

vi. $(\exists x)((CxFx)(Tx\equiv(x)(Cx\supset\sim Tx)))\supset(\exists x)(CxTx)$
       100, i, v, 104

Similarly a formal analysans for (22) will be

(40) $((\exists x)((PxGx)(Tx\equiv(x)(Dx\supset\sim Tx)))(\exists x)((DxHx)$
$(Tx\equiv(\exists x)(PxTx))))\supset((\exists x)(Px\sim Tx)(\exists x)(DxTx))$

A proof for (40) is easily obtained if we prove first

$((\exists x)((PxGx)(Tx\equiv(x)(Dx\supset\sim Tx)))(\exists x)(DxTx))$
$\supset(\exists x)(Px\sim Tx)$

next

$(((\exists x)((PxGx)(Tx\equiv(x)(Dx\supset\sim Tx)))\sim(\exists x)(DxTx))$
$(\exists x)((DxHx)(Tx\equiv(\exists x)(PxTx))))\supset(\exists x)(DxTx)$

and then substitute in, and detach from, the truth-functional tautology

$((ps)\supset r)(((p\sim s)q)\supset s))\supset((pq)\supset(rs))$

The corresponding analysans for (39) will be another theorem of quantification theory, viz.

203

(41) $(\exists x)(((JxHx)(Tx\equiv p))(\exists y)((JyNy)(Ty\equiv \sim Kx)))\supset$
$$\sim((x)(Jx\supset Tx)(x)(Jx\supset Kx))$$

We prove first

$$((\exists y)((JyNy)(Ty\equiv \sim Kx))(x)(Jx\supset Tx))\supset \sim Kx$$

then

$(\exists x)((((JxHx)(Tx\equiv p))(\exists y)((JyNy)(Ty\equiv \sim Kx)))$
$$(x)(Jx\supset Tx))\supset (\exists x)(Jx\sim Kx)$$

and then (41).

Indeed, once wff like (37) are accepted as analysing equivalents for statements like (36), one may establish the general reducibility of Prior's system within second-order quantification theory as follows. Consider two calculuses, P and L. P is Prior's, and L is a Łukasiewicz version of quantification theory in which quantifiers may bind propositional, predicate, or individual variables.[1] 'Δ' is syntactical notation for any particular operator variable of P; 'φ', 'χ', 'ψ' ... for any predicate variable of L; 'α' for any individual variable; 'τ' for any wff of P or L; and all quantifiers and truth-functors are self-representing. Then the result of replacing each occurrence of $\Pi\Delta$ by $\Pi\varphi$, each occurrence of $\Sigma\Delta$ by $\Sigma\varphi$, and each wf part $\Delta\tau$ by $\Sigma\alpha KK\varphi\alpha\chi\alpha E\psi\alpha\tau$ in the rules of P for quantifiers binding operator variables, is immediately obtainable from the rules of L for quantifiers binding predicate variables.

Two things are worth noting here. First, quantification over properties need not be regarded as anything particularly mysterious or puzzling in this connection. We may conveniently suppose that a property exists if and only if an instance of it exists. Secondly, though in my informal account I distinguished statements about some token of a saying, like 'I wish that Socrates were dead', from statements about all tokens of a saying, like 'It is impossible for Socrates to be dead without being dead', I do not need to maintain this distinction in my formalizations. If at least one token of a given saying is *a priori* false or is subject to some other similar qualification of its truth-value, then all tokens of that saying are; and we have already seen that the existence of at least one token of each saying may safely be assumed. Hence a formal analysans for (20) will be

$$(\exists x)((SxIx)(\sim Tx(Tx\equiv q)))$$

---

[1] Cf. A. N. Prior, *Formal Logic*, pp. 303 f.

where 'S' stands for 'is a statement that Socrates is dead without being dead', 'I' for 'is incapable of truth', 'T' for 'is true', and 'q' for 'Socrates is dead without being dead'.

Thus the method of formalization proposed contains all the advantages *vis-à-vis* the semantical antinomies that Prior's and Goodstein's systems contain, but is nevertheless based on a standard, well-understood extensional calculus and introduces no special symbolism, formation-rules or postulates. In particular, statements like (22), (31) or (32) turn out to instantiate laws of logic that are of greater generality than the Prior-Goodstein treatment reveals. These laws do not stem from any element of logical form that is peculiar to indirect discourse, as that analysis suggests. Instead they are consequences of the more general principles developed in the standard logic of predicates and propositions. For example, the law instantiated by (32) is equally well instantiated by

(42) If some tall blade of grass is green if and only if any blade of grass is not green, then some blade of grass is green.

For if in (38) 'C' stands for 'is a blade of grass', 'F' for 'is tall', 'T' for 'is green', and individual letters include physical objects in their domain of reference, (38) becomes a formal analysans of (42). It is the superficially paradoxical character of (32), rather than its logical truth, that is peculiarly bound up with indirect discourse. A person of a certain description may well think that he can state anything stated by a person of this description to be false while believing that no person of this description ever states anything else. But he is less likely to think some tall blade of grass to be green if and only if no blade of grass is green, while believing that no blade of grass is green. The contradiction between his beliefs is more evident in the latter case than in the former, because there is nothing in the latter case to parallel the near-statement a man makes when he utters a certain kind of indicative sentence with the intention of making a statement, but fails to state anything through ignorance of logic or of the fact that he is himself a person of the relevant description.

The advantage of so treating statements like (32) emerges with particular clarity when the question is raised whether statements like

(43) If a Cretan says that anything said by a Cretan is true, then something said by a Cretan is false

should also be reckoned as logical truths. Suppose a Cretan does say that anything said by a Cretan is true. Then this would be a perfectly legitimate, though false, statement if some other Cretan statement is false. But if all other Cretan statements were true ones the original statement would depend for its verification on its own truth-value, and the merit of avoiding such circularity might seem to constitute a *prima facie* case for treating (43) as a logical truth.

Certainly the wff corresponding to (43) is not a theorem in Prior's or Goodstein's system. But since such a system is in any case developed by subjoining additional postulates to those of standard logic one might be tempted to add still further postulates to the system in order to make these wff come out as theorems. Yet that would be a mistake, at least so far as general logic is concerned, as is plain from the analysans for (43) in standard quantification theory, viz.

$$(44) \quad (\exists x)((CxVx)(Tx \equiv (x)(Cx \supset Tx))) \supset (\exists x)(Cx \sim Tx)$$

since (44) is not a theorem of quantification theory. Indeed it is easy to imagine other statements of the same logical form as (43) that are evidently not logical truths because they have patently true antecedents and patently false consequents, like

> If something is an English town of ten million inhabitants and is prosperous, and is on the Thames if and only if any English town of ten million inhabitants is on the Thames, then something is an English town of ten million inhabitants and is not on the Thames.

Nor is it at all surprising that an extensional formalization of indirect discourse should thus lead us, whatever our first inclinations, to deny (43) the status of logical truth. For there is no logical bar to a Cretan's saying that anything said by a Cretan is true even if no other Cretan ever says anything. In such circumstances it is possible arbitrarily to assign a truth-value to the statement

> Anything said by a Cretan is true

and whether the truth-value assigned be truth, or falsity, no contradiction results. If the statement is true, it is true, and if false, false. So, since what the Cretan utters is something that can be made to obey the laws of logic, and in particular the laws of excluded middle and non-contradiction, there is no apparent logical reason why he should not be said to state it. An extensional formalization, in virtue of its superior generality, has therefore led us immediately to the correct conclusion about (43), whereas if we were in any case introducing special operator symbols and postulates for the formalization of indirect discourse we should have had to rely solely on *ad hoc* arguments and unsystematized intuitions.

Moreover we can use extensional wff like (37) or (40) for the analysis of statements like (36) or (22), respectively, even if we do not accept the ontologically parsimonious account of sayings and statements that was argued in §19 above. Let us suppose for the moment, whatever it may mean, that statements or propositions are indeed subsistent entities. Then we have merely to specify that the individual letters of (37) include such entities in their domain of reference, and (37) will constitute as good an analysis of (36) as it does when we prefer to quantify over sentence-tokens. Similarly we could talk about judgements here, instead of either sentence-tokens or subsistent propositions. The general formal logic of informally non-extensional discourse turns out to be as impartial as it should be in regard to the familiar controversies between conceptualists, nominalists and realists. It is yet another disadvantage of theories like Frege's or Church's, though not of those like Prior's and Goodstein's, that because of their commitment to quantification over meanings they cannot achieve the level of metaphysical impartiality which befits formal logic as an arbiter of topic-neutral validity throughout human reasoning.

Perhaps there are one or two kinds of statement that seem more amenable to the Frege-Church kind of treatment than to the one suggested here. If we may include propositions in our universe of discourse then a statement like

(45) Brummel believes something George IV does not

comes out simply as

$$(\exists x)(Bxy \sim Bxz)$$

If instead of propositions we have utterance-tokens in our universe of discourse, our analysans must be a little more complex. It cannot be just

$$(\exists F)((x)(Fx \supset Bxy) \sim (\exists x)(FxBxz))$$

since this might be true if all Brummel's utterance-tokens resembled George IV's in being such-and-such sayings and differed only in respect of some other property. But we can exclude this possibility by analysing (45) as

$$(\exists F)((w)(Fw \equiv Sw)((x)(Fx \supset Bxy) \sim (\exists x)(FxBxz)))$$

where 'S' stands for 'is a certain single statement'. Quine, whose method of formalization cannot cope with statements like (45), regards them as 'expendable', since they 'tend anyway to be pretty trivial in what they affirm and useful only in heralding more tangible information'.[1] But (45) is no more or less trivial than

(46) Someone is here who is voting but not a member of the society.

The triviality or importance of these statements depends entirely on their context of utterance and we are no more entitled to regard (45) as expendable than (46): it may be dangerous to have even slightly different beliefs from one's rulers.

§28. A formalization for the general logic of non-assertive sayings

A system like Prior's or Goodstein's is essentially confined to articulating the logic of statement-forming operators on statements. It tells us nothing at all about statement-forming operators on non-assertive sayings, like 'he asks' or 'he orders me to'. In this respect it falls short of being a general logic, and is rather a special logic of assertive discourse. It is on a level with attempts that have sometimes been made to formalize this or that kind of non-assertive discourse and to construct a special logic of, say, imperatives.[2] But we cannot avoid the need for a logical system that will cover both assertive and non-assertive discourse. For commands or questions are often said to imply one another, and factual conclusions are often drawn from reports that they have

---

[1] *Word and Object*, p. 215.

[2] E.g. A. Hofstadter and J. C. C. McKinsey, 'On the Logic of Imperatives', *Philosophy of Science*, vi (1939), pp. 446 ff.; A. Ross, 'Imperatives and Logic', ibid., xi (1944), pp. 30 ff.; T. Storer, 'The Logic of Value Imperatives', ibid., xiii (1946), pp. 25 ff.

been uttered, obeyed or answered. Nor would it do just to lump together such special logics of assertive and non-assertive discourse as we do have, and seek the simplest system within which they are all deducible. For we can put no *a priori* limit on the variety of non-assertive sayings – on the variety of non-assertive purposes that may be fulfilled by the utterance of sentences – any more than on the variety of meanings that individual words may have. The grammatical term 'imperative', for instance, denotes a verb-mood used in a very heterogeneous variety of utterances, such as commands, entreaties, recommendations, and requests, between which it is often important to distinguish. If a man is commanded to vote at a certain election and recommended to vote for Smith if he votes at all, he should not infer that he has been commanded to vote for Smith. Hence the logical vocabulary of general logic should no more include 'is it the case that' and 'let it be the case that' than it includes 'it is obligatory that' or 'it is known that'. Correspondingly, we must seek to avoid introducing into a system of general logic some additional range of logical constants like '?' and '!' to express the difference between different kinds of non-assertive saying, as in H. Reichenbach's analysis of conversational language.[1]

The required analysis of non-assertive sayings, and of statements into which they enter, is readily obtained within standard quantification theory by a simple reinterpretation of wff like (37). If 'C' stands for 'is a command by Jones to Smith', 'R' for 'is a command to vote at the election', 'T' for 'is obeyed' and 'p' for 'Smith votes at the election', then (37) becomes an analysans for the report

Jones commands Smith to vote at the election

and also, if 'Rx' be deleted, for the original command addressed by Jones to Smith just before the last general election

(47) Vote at the election!

Someone may object that this analysis confuses commands with reports of commands, and prescriptive utterances with assertive ones. But the task of a formal-logical analysans is to articulate everything relevant to the formal validity or invalidity of arguments into which the analysandum enters, and what is inferred from a command or request often

---

[1] *Elements of Symbolic Logic* (1948), pp. 336 ff.

depends in part on who gave it. In reasoning out his course of conduct a man may base himself on premises that assign different priorities to fulfilling his wife's requests and his children's, or to obeying his doctor's instructions and his employer's.

It might then be objected that, if the logical analysis of non-assertive sayings replaces them in effect by reports of their utterance, so too should the logical analysis of statements. After all, in reasoning out what he is to believe a man may base himself on premises that assign different credibilities to his wife's utterances and his children's, and different values to weather predictions from meteorological observation and prophecies from tea-leaves. Moreover, if statements too are to be replaced by reports of their own utterance, so again must reports of statements, and our analysans then seems in danger of disappearing down an infinite regress of statements about statements about statements about . . . But this danger is not a serious one. Given that the informal argument we have to analyse in a particular case contains only a finite number of statements as premises, we can always determine whether or not it contains any statements about credibility along with relevant evidence about the authorship of certain sayings. If it does, the analysans will still be of finite length only. If it does not, no premises will need to be replaced by reports of their utterance. The difference in the case of arguments about commands or requests is that there we shall carry out such a replacement even if it is not needed in this way and even if, through ignorance of a command's actual author and addressee, we cannot specify them in the analysans.

The logic of questions admits, with one or two complexities, of being similarly treated, despite the view of some[1] that it is intrinsically anti-symbolic and resistant to formalization. Questions open to the answer 'Yes' or 'No', like

$$\text{Is Smith voting at the election?}$$

are readily seen to be analysable by wff like (37) where 'Rx' is deleted, 'C' stands for 'is a yes-or-no question', 'T' for 'is correctly answered in the affirmative' and 'p' for 'Smith is voting at the election'. A disjunctive question like

---

[1] E.g. Mary Prior and A. N. Prior, 'Erotetic Logic', *Philosophical Review*, xiv (1955), pp. 43 ff.

Is Smith voting properly or spoiling his ballot-paper?

will be represented by a wff like

$$(\exists x)(Dx(Tx\equiv(pvq)))$$

where 'D' stands for 'is a disjunctive question', 'T' for 'is correctly answered by the affirmation of one or other of its disjuncts', 'p' for 'Smith is voting properly' and 'q' for 'Smith is spoiling his ballot-paper'. Conditional questions like

If Smith is voting, is he spoiling his paper?

require an analysans like

$$(\exists x)(Cx((Sx\equiv p)(Tx\equiv q)))$$

where 'C' stands for 'is a conditional question', 'S' for 'is a question that has its condition satisfied', 'p' for 'Smith is voting', 'T' for 'is correctly answered in the affirmative', and 'q' for 'Smith is spoiling his paper'. Finally, questions asking for specific information, such as

Who is voting?

require some such wff as

$$(\exists x)(Wx(y)(Tyx\equiv(\exists z)(VzDyz)))$$

where 'W' stands for 'is a question asking for specific information', 'T' for 'is an expression utterance of which is sufficient to answer correctly', 'V' for 'is voting', and 'D' for 'denotes'. And reports of all these questions in indirect discourse merely require the addition of an appropriate saying-function to the above wff, like 'Rx' in (37).

It is not easy to see what forms of non-assertive utterance could exist that were not open to formal-logical analysis along these lines. But it would be tedious to multiply examples, and no proof of the matter could avoid begging the question of what exactly is to be included in the general logic of sayings.

§29. The problem of quantification into non-extensional contexts

If precautions are not taken, quantification into non-extensional contexts may lead to paradox either through existential generalization from statements about individuals or through universal instantiation from quantifiers binding predicate letters, as Quine has shown. Suppose, first, that 'F' has been assigned the meaning of 'is necessarily the Morning Star'. Then since the Morning Star is necessarily the Morning Star, and the Evening Star is not necessarily the Morning Star, we may infer by existential generalization both $(\exists x)Fx$ and $(\exists x)\sim Fx$, from which it seems to follow that at least two individuals exist in our universe of discourse. What are these individuals? They cannot be physical objects, because conceivably only one physical object might exist at all, viz. the planet in question. But for familiar reasons it is undesirable to have to suppose that they are intensional entities of some kind.[1] Secondly, if the Morning Star is necessarily identical with the Morning Star and the Evening Star is not, then the Morning Star seems to have a property which the Evening Star has not and seems therefore not to be identical with it:[2] the generalization that the Morning Star and the Evening Star have all the same properties is false in at least one instance. Thus, in general, if predicate letters may be assigned non-extensional equivalents like 'is necessarily the Morning Star', the ordinary analysans for the identity of x and y, viz. '$(F)(Fx \equiv Fy)$' puts a condition on assertions of identity that is far too strong for such assertions to be of much use. It makes them assert that x and y share all properties whatever, not only all those ascribable in extensional discourse but also all those that cannot be ascribed except in non-extensional discourse. By these standards even $7+5$ is not identical with 12, since 12 rather than $7+5$ may be what you, but not I, say to be the number of tablets of the old Roman law. Nor is this the description of identity presupposed in the Russellian analysans for a definite description. We cannot reformulate the true statement 'Scott is the author of *Waverley*' as 'Scott wrote *Waverley* and anyone wrote *Waverley* if and only if he is identical with Scott', in this sense of 'identical with', since the biconditional generalization 'Anyone wrote *Waverley* if and only if he is identical with Scott' is then false. It is true that the author of *Waverley* wrote *Waverley*, but false that the author of *Waverley* was as well known to George IV as Scott was.

It follows that in a thoroughly extensional formalization of general

---

[1] Cf. *From a Logical Point of View*, pp. 144 ff.

[2] Cf. an argument of Quine's reported in J. Łukasiewicz, *Aristotle's Syllogistic* (2nd ed., 1957), p. 171.

logic we can never afford to make a non-extensional expression like 'is necessarily the Morning Star' the equivalent of a predicate letter. But we cannot ban all non-extensional equivalents indiscriminately since many of them, like 'is the statement that it is raining' for 'R' in (37), are in fact needed. Hence what is required here is some way of picking out just those expressions that, because they are troublesomely non-extensional, must not be equated in meaning with the predicate letters of our interpreted calculus.

It will suffice to stipulate that no n-adic predicate-letter of the calculus is to be equated in meaning with a predicative term of informal discourse such that for some set of n referring terms $R_1, R_2, \ldots R_n$ a statement formed by concatenating this predicative term with $R_1, R_2, \ldots R_n$ is equivalent in meaning to a statement formed by prefacing some non-truth-functional operator on sayings to a saying that contains referring terms $S_1, S_2, \ldots S_n$ such that S_1 or S_2 or $\ldots S_n$ is R_1 or R_2 or $\ldots R_n$. In effect this bars predicative terms, like 'is necessarily the Morning Star', that contain a non-extensionality-generating expression which would include within its scope any subject- or object-terms supplied to the predicate, as in

(48) The Morning Star is necessarily the Morning Star

Indeed the stipulation is a natural consequence of accepting the general theory that all cases of non-extensionality arise implicitly or explicitly through the occurrence of statement-forming operators on sayings and that they therefore may be viewed as being generated by certain kinds of statements about sayings. For, since 'necessarily', even when inserted thus in the middle, operates on the whole of the saying 'The Morning Star is the Morning Star', we must treat (48) as a statement about this saying, viz. the statement that it is necessary, rather than as a statement about the Morning Star to the effect that it has the property of being necessarily the Morning Star. Thus our general theory of non-extensionality leads directly to a treatment of (48) that averts any paradoxical suggestion that the Morning Star has a property which the Evening Star has not, and is therefore not identical with the Evening Star. But the proposed stipulation does not bar predicative terms, like 'is a statement that it is raining', where a subject-term, if supplied, would fall outside the scope of the non-extensionality-generating expression, as in 'His utterance is a statement

213

H

that it is raining.' These are just the kind of predicative terms, predicating something of some or all tokens of a saying, that our general theory of non-extensionality requires.

Nor does the proposed stipulation prevent us from finding an appropriate formal analysans for any informal statement, like (14), that seems to involve quantification over individuals in non-extensional contexts. These statements seem to be peculiarly hybrid in that, though its context is non-extensional, the pronoun referring back to (i.e. the variable bound by) the quantifier must have a straightforwardly extensional occurrence, like 'he' in (14), since any other pronoun that could make the same reference back would do as well. But such statements are also of two kinds, corresponding to the two kinds of predicative term just considered. Sometimes they arise by quantification into the report of a saying, as in (14), and then they may be formalized without any need to deviate from normal specifications for the values of individual variables. For example, (14) will have as its equivalent the wff

(49) $(\exists x)(\exists y)(YxSx)(Hy(Tx\equiv Iy)))$

where 'Y' stands for 'is asserted by you', 'S' for 'is a statement that a certain person, specified in the statement, sells ice-cream', 'H' for 'is here', 'T' for 'is true' and 'I' for 'sells ice-cream', and individual variables take physical objects or events as values. But if a meaningful statement can be derived by existential generalization from (48) it is of quite a different kind. If the statement

(50) There is something such that it is necessarily the Morning Star

is to be derivable, the term replaced by the existentially quantifying expression must be necessarily equivalent to 'the Morning Star', whereas if (14) is true it would be derivable, whatever words you had used to refer to the ice-cream salesman, from the report of your remark together with a statement, in any terms, that the man in question is here. Hence if a statement like (50) means anything at all it must be taken to mean the same as, say,

> There is a term such that any token is a necessarily true statement if it results from concatenating a token of this term with a token of the term 'is the Morning Star'.

So that in a formal analysans of such a statement we shall quantify predicate letters, denoting the properties of tokens, whereas in (49) we quantify individual ones.

In virtue of thus having a satisfactory mode of analysis for quantifications into the report of a saying, like (14), we also have a satisfactory analysis for certain other kinds of statement which might otherwise appear troublesome. For example, we can now achieve a formal analysans for (12) in virtue of achieving one for (13). For this we can use the wff

$$(\exists x)(\exists y)((PxSy)((Exy(Ty \equiv Fx)))$$

where 'P' stands for 'is a policeman', 'S' for 'is a statement that a certain person, specified in the statement, finds the thief', 'T' for 'is true', 'F' for 'finds the thief' and 'E' for 'endeavours the truth of'. We can deal similarly with statements in which substantival, rather than pronominal, terms occur extensionally in contexts that are otherwise non-extensional. Consider the statement

(51) George IV says that Scott is a great novelist

where the context of utterance makes it plain that the statement is reporting George IV's critical opinion about the man whom he knew only as the author of the Waverley novels and not as Sir Walter Scott. The term 'Scott' here occurs extensionally, though the expression 'says that' normally generates non-extensionality for all terms occurring in its scope. Since (51) is thus equivalent in meaning to

> Someone is both Scott and a man of whom George IV says that he is a great novelist

it has the same logical form as (14). The wff (49), with appropriate re-interpretations, will therefore constitute a formal analysans for it.

It is worth noting that in all such cases the saying on which the non-extensionality-generating expression operates is not the same as that about which the statement as a whole is finally construed, by implication, to say something. In the formal analysans for (51) it is neither the saying 'Scott is a great novelist' nor the saying 'He is a great novelist', but rather George IV's actual saying that is mentioned. The logical form is only made plain when we get beyond the superficial statement-forming-operator-on-saying mode of expression to the underlying statement-about-saying one.

§30. A non-extensional formalization of informally non-extensional contexts

The price inevitably paid for an extensional method of formalization, like the one just described, is that the onus of representing the logical properties of particular modal operators must be borne by formulas that are neither provable nor disprovable within the calculus or its semantical meta-language. The statement, for example, that if each of two statements is necessary, then so is their conjunction, is represented by

$$(x)(y)(z)((((Cxyz(NyNz))((Ty\equiv p)(Tz\equiv q)))\supset(Nx(Tx\equiv(pq)))$$

where 'C' stands for 'is the conjunction of... and', 'N' for 'is necessary' and 'T' for 'is true'. Nor should this limitation be unwelcome in a general logic of informally non-extensional contexts, so long as there are no general, or very widely pervasive, features of non-extensional discourse that thus remain unaxiomatized in our formal system.

It may be felt, however, that some general features of that kind do exist, such as the way in which certain operators generating non-extensionality, like 'it is physically necessary that', 'it is *a priori* true that' and 'it is logically true that', may be arranged in a series, in ascending order of potency, requiring stronger and stronger forms of identity-statement to license substitution in occurrences of sayings that fall within their scope. After all, one sees Frege's theory of sense and reference to be inadequate when one sees that different modal operators impose different conditions on substitution, and it may be felt unreasonable thus to acknowledge the heterogeneity that exists among modal operators without also acknowledging any homogeneity that also exists. There is a certain element of arbitrariness in using the notion of resistance to substitution in order to define what is to count as a non-extensional context, as Quine does, without pointing out that passages closed to some forms of substitution are by no means closed to all, since by varying the form of identity-statement that one uses as a touchstone one also varies the range of contexts that are to be regarded as non-extensional. Even if non-extensionality consists in general of resistance to substitution on the basis of identity statements or bi-conditionals, it may be interesting to develop a general logic in which this kind of resistance is studied systematically. Moreover if a concept or concepts of meaning must have some special part to play in such a system, as it does in Church's, Frege's theory might still be important. I shall therefore now develop such a non-extensional system, and discuss some of its properties, if only to show that Frege's theory is not needed here either. Whether we believe informally non-extensional discourse to require an extensional formalization or a non-extensional one, we may safely suppose that the meaning of an expression does not vary with the extensionality of its occurrence. In both cases we may take it that all non-extensionality arises from the implicit or explicit occurrence of certain statement-forming operators on sayings, though in the non-extensional formalization we do not represent all of these operators by predicate letters, but represent some of them by certain of the system's own operators.

It will be convenient to call the following calculus O4. In it d is some designated positive integer, and unless otherwise specified k, m and n are any non-negative integers that are not greater than d, and h and j are any non-negative integers whatever.

Primitive symbols:

$(\,)$, $\sim$, $.$, $(\exists\,)$	(brackets, tilde, dot, quantifier)
p, q, r, p_1, $\ldots$	(propositional letters)
F^1, G^1, H^1, F_1^1, $\ldots$	(monadic predicate letters)
$F^2 \ldots$	(dyadic predicate letters)
$\vdots$	
$F^j \ldots$	(j-adic predicate letters)
x, y, z, x_1 $\ldots$	(individual letters)
$\square^1$, $\square^2$, $\ldots \square^n$	(square operators)

A *formula* is any finite sequence of primitive symbols.

Syntactic notation:

A, B, Γ, E, Z, H, A_1, $\ldots$	(representing formulas)
φ, χ, ψ, φ_1, $\ldots$	(representing predicate letters)
α, β, γ, α_1, $\ldots$	(representing individual letters)
$(\,)$, $\sim$, $.$, $(\exists\,)$, $\square^1$, $\square^2$, $\ldots \square^n$	(self-representing)

A *well-formed formula* is defined recursively:

A propositional letter is wf.

$\varphi(\alpha_1, \alpha_2, \ldots \alpha_j)$ is wf, where φ is j-adic.

If A and B are wf, so are $\sim$A, (A.B), ($\exists\alpha$)A, $\square^n$A.

There are no other wff besides these.

Upper-case Greek letters hereafter represent wff, and so do '$\varphi(\alpha)$', '$\chi(\alpha)$', '$\psi(\alpha)$', ... '$\varphi(\beta)$', '$\chi(\beta)$', '$\psi(\beta)$' ...

An occurrence of α in A is a *bound occurrence* if in a wf part of A of the form ($\exists\alpha$)B. Otherwise it is free.

Definition-schemata:

$\square^0$A for A
(A$\supset^n$B) for $\square^n\sim$(A.$\sim$B)[1]
(A$\equiv^n$B) for ((A$\supset^n$B).(B$\supset^n$A))
$\lozenge^n$A for $\sim\square^n\sim$A
(α)A for $\sim(\exists\alpha)\sim$A

An occurrence of α, φ, or Γ is an *m*th *grade occurrence* in A if and only if it

(i) forms a proper part of the occurrence in A of a wf part of A of the form $\square^m$B, and
(ii) does not form a proper part of the occurrence in A of a wf part of A of the form $\square^n$E, where $n>m$.

(E.g. 'q', '$\square^2p$' and '($\square^2p$.q)' have 1st grade occurrences in the wff '$\square^1(\square^2p$.$q)$' and 'p' has a 2nd grade occurrence.

Hereafter omit outermost brackets, and also the dot, and the brackets enclosing individual letters, wherever expansion into primitive symbols is fully determined without them.

Axiom-schemata:

1. A$\supset^d$(AA)
2. (AB)$\supset^d$A
3. (AB)$\supset^d$(BA)
4. ((AB)Γ)$\supset^d$(A(BΓ))
5. ((A$\supset^n$B)(B$\supset^n\Gamma$))$\supset^d$(A$\supset^n\Gamma$) where $n>0$
6. $\square^{n+1}$A$\supset^d\square^n$A
7. $\square^n$A$\supset^d\square^n\square^n$A where $n>0$
8. (α)$\square^n$A$\supset^d\square^n$(α)A where $n>0$
9. A$\supset^d$(α)A where α is not free in A

---

[1] I owe this and the following abbreviation to a suggestion of E. J. Lemmon's.

10. $(\alpha)(A\supset{}^{\circ}B)\supset{}^{d}((\alpha)A\supset{}^{\circ}(\alpha)B)$
11. $(\alpha)A\supset{}^{d}B$ where B is like A except for containing free occurrences of β wherever A contains free occurrences of α.

Rules of derivation:

From A and $A\supset{}^{d}B$ derive B. (Mod. pon.)

From A and B derive $(A.B)$. (Adj.)

If A, B and Γ are such that E results from Γ by the substitution of B for one or more occurrences of A in Γ, then from Γ and $A\equiv{}^{d}B$ derive E. (Subst.)

If B is like A except for containing free occurrences of β wherever A contains free occurrences of α, then derive $(\beta)B$ from A. (Gen.)

A *proof* of a wff A is a finite list of wff $A_1, A_2, \ldots A_j$ such that each A_i is an axiom or derivable from the axioms or from the preceding formulas of the list by applying one of the rules of derivation. A is a *theorem* if it is the A_j of such a list. 'A is a theorem' will be abbreviated to ' ⊢A '.

The interpretation envisaged for wff of O_4 is one which rests on the usual formal-logical replacements for all primitive symbols except the quantifier and squares. The initial $(\exists\alpha)$ in each wf part $(\exists\alpha)A$ of a wff is to be replaced by 'something is such that', and free occurrences of α in the wf part A of $(\exists\alpha)A$ by occurrences of a pronoun grammatically connected with this occurrence of 'something'; and 'something is such that —', where '—' stands for the statement replacing A, is understood to be true if and only if there is a term E and an element in the universe of discourse O such that E refers to O and a true statement is got from '—' by putting E for each of the above-mentioned occurrences of a pronoun in '—'. (This method of interpretation, already mentioned in §29, does not subvert the familiar and useful notion of commitment to a domain of discourse through assignment of a range of values for quantified variables. For, if we know what we are talking about on a given occasion, we must at least be able to construct a reference to any part of it, and conversely, if we are able to do this, we must know what we are talking about. If our discourse commits us to the existence of certain referential terms, i.e. to accepting certain rules of construction for referential terms, it also commits us to certain values for our quantified variables, though perhaps to fewer values than terms.) $\Box^1, \Box^2, \ldots \Box^d$ are to be replaced by any set of modal operators that satisfy the axioms, e.g., where $d=3$ by, respectively, 'it is demonstrable that', 'it is *a priori* that', and 'it is logically true that', in appropriate senses.

The following are some theorems of O4:

12. $((A\supset^\circ B)(B\supset^\circ\Gamma))\supset^d(A\supset^\circ\Gamma)$
13. $(A\supset^n B)\supset^d(\sim B\supset^n\sim A)$
14. $((A\supset^n B)(\Gamma\supset^n E))\supset^d((A\Gamma)\supset^n(BE))$
15. $\Box^n A\equiv^d\sim\Diamond^n\sim A$
16. $\Box^n A\supset^d A$
17. $\Box^n A\equiv^d(\sim A\supset^n A)$
18. $(A(A\supset^n B))\supset^d B$
19. $A\supset^d\Diamond^n A$
20. $\Box^n(AB)\equiv^d(\Box^n A\Box^n B)$
21. $\Box^n A\supset^d(B\supset^n A)$
22. $\Box^n\sim A\supset^d(A\supset^n B)$
23. $(A\sim\Box^n A)\equiv^d((A\sim\Box^n A)\sim\Box^n(A\sim\Box^n A))$
24. $\Diamond^n(AB)\supset^d\Diamond^n A$
25. $\Diamond^m\Box^n A\supset^d\Diamond^m A$
26. $(\Box^n A(A\supset^n B))\supset^d\Box^n B$
27. $(A\supset^m B)\supset^d(\Box^n A\supset^k\Box^n B)$ where $k\leq m$ and $m\geq n$
28. $(\alpha_1)(\alpha_2)\ldots(\alpha_j)(A\equiv^m B)\supset^d(\Gamma\equiv^k E)$ where A, B and Γ are such that E results from Γ by substitution of B for each of one or more *n*th grade occurrences of A in Γ; $\alpha_1, \alpha_2, \ldots \alpha_j$ is a complete list of the individual letters occurring freely in Γ and E; and $k\leq m$ and $m\geq n$. (Hence grade of occurrence comes to represent serial degree of non-extensionality so far as non-extensionality depends on any of the operators represented by $\Box^1, \Box^2, \ldots \Box^n$.)
29. $((\alpha_1)(\alpha_2)\ldots(\alpha_j)(A\equiv^m B)\Gamma)\equiv^k((\alpha_1)(\alpha_2)\ldots(\alpha_j)(A\equiv^m B)E)$ where as in 28.

The following are some derived rules:

30. If $\vdash A_1\supset^d A_2$, $\vdash A_2\supset^d A_3$, $\ldots \vdash A_{j-1}\supset^d A_j$, then $\vdash A_1\supset^d A_j$
31. If $\vdash A\supset^d B$, then $\vdash\Box^n A\supset^d\Box^n B$

Proofs of the above are closely analogous to those for theorems in the Lewis-Barcan calculus S4.[1] We may also prove:

32. $\square^m A \equiv^d \square^m \square^n A$ where $m \geqslant n$
    i. $\square^m A \supset^d \square^n A$ where $m \geqslant n$ successive 6, 30, 16
    ii. $\square^m \square^m A \supset^d \square^m \square^n A$ where $m \geqslant n$ i, 31
    iii. $\square^m A \supset^d \square^m \square^n A$ where $m \geqslant n$ 7, ii, 30
    iv. $\square^m \square^n A \supset^d \square^m A$ 16, 31
    v. $\square^m A \equiv^d \square^m \square^n A$ where $m \geqslant n$ iii, iv, adj.

33. If $\vdash A$, then $\vdash \square^d A$.
    This is shown by induction on the length of proof of A.[2]
    Case i. If A is proved in one line, A is $\square^d \Gamma$; and from A and 7 we derive $\square^d A$ by mod. pon.
    Case ii. Hypothesis: if A is proved in j lines, then $\vdash \square^d A$. Suppose B to be the jth line of a proof of E in $j+1$ lines. We show that $\vdash \square^d E$ as follows:
    (*a*) If E is derived by mod. pon. from B and $B \supset^d E$, then by 31 we have $\vdash \square^d B \supset^d \square^d E$, and from this and hyp. we derive $\square^d E$ by mod. pon.
    (*b*) If E is derived by adj. from B and H, then E is (BH) and $\square^d E$ is derived from hyp. and 20 by adj. and subst., since if there is a proof of H in less than j lines there is also one in j lines.
    (*c*) If E is derived by subst. from B and $H \equiv^d Z$, we derive $\square^d E$ by subst. from hyp. and $H \equiv^d Z$.
    (*d*) If E is derived by gen. from B, we derive $\square^d E$ from hyp. by gen., 8, and mod. pon.

The content of O4 may be further clarified by considering a calculus O4^1 that is equivalent to O4. O4^1 has the same symbolism, formation-rules and definition-schemata as O4 and just the following criteria of theoremhood:

i. If A is a truth-functional tautology or an axiom of first-order

[1] Cf. C. I. Lewis and C. H. Langford, *Symbolic Logic* (1932), and R. C. Barcan, 'A Functional Calculus of First Order Based on Strict Implication', *Jour. Symb. Log.*, xi (1946), pp. 1 ff.
[2] I owe this demonstration to a suggestion of M. Dummet's in connection with the analogous theorem for S4.

quantification theory (with tilde, dot, and existential quantifier as primitives, and gen. and detachment as rules), then $\vdash A$.

ii. If $\vdash A$ and $\vdash A \supset^o B$, then $\vdash B$.

iii. If $\vdash A$, then $\vdash (\beta)B$ where as in gen.

iv. If $\vdash A$, then $\vdash \Box^d A$.

v. $\vdash \Box^{n+1} A \supset^o \Box^n A$.

vi. $\vdash (A \supset^n B) \supset^o (\Box^n A \supset^n \Box^n B)$ where $n > 0$.

vii. $\vdash (\alpha)\Box^n A \supset^o \Box^n(\alpha)A$ where $n > 0$.

That $O4^1$ contains $O4$ is readily demonstrated by steps closely analogous to those by which Lemmon[1] has shown P4 to contain S4. That $O4$ contains $O4^1$ is shown as follows: we derive ii from 18 by adj. and mod. pon.; axioms for the classical propositional calculus and for first-order quantification theory (as in i) are easily derived, and with ii derived (and the completeness of the classical propositional calculus) this gives us i; iii is like gen.; iv is like 33; v is proved from 6 and 16, vi from 27 and 16, and vii from 8 and 16.

Moreover, it is evident, where B is like A except in having Γ preceded by n successive occurrences of '$\sim \Diamond \sim$' wherever A has $\Box^n \Gamma$, that if A is an axiom of $O4$ B is a theorem of the Lewis-Barcan calculus S4. Hence it can be shown by induction on the length of proof of A, where B is as before, that if A is a theorem of $O4$ B is a theorem of S4. But the converse apparently does not hold. E.g. $(A \supset^m B) \supset^d (\Box^n A \supset^o \Box^n B)$ and $\Box^m A \supset^d \Box^n A$ seem not provable in $O4$ where $n > m$.[2] Thus S4 is too rich, rather than too poor, to be interpreted as a general logic of non-extensionality.

It is natural to ask whether the general logic of non-extensionality can be as well, or better, articulated in a calculus that stands to some other of the Lewis calculuses as $O4$ stands to S4. We may briefly consider the following, which are all like $O4$ except in lacking 7 and having the specified axioms instead (where $n > 0$):

O1: (none)

O2: $\Box^n(AB) \supset^d \Box^n A$

O3: $(A \supset^n B) \supset^d (\Box^n A \supset^n \Box^n B)$

---

[1] 'New Foundations for Lewis Modal Systems', *Jour. Symb. Log.*, xxii (1957), pp. 176 ff.

[2] This non-provability has been demonstrated by E. E. Dawson in some as yet unpublished work on these systems.

O5: $\Diamond^n A \supset^d \Box^n \Diamond^n A$
O6: as for O2, plus $\Diamond^n \Diamond^n A$
O7: as for O3, plus $\Diamond^n \Diamond^n A$
O8: as for O3, plus $\Box^d \Diamond^n \Diamond^n A$

O1, O2 and O6 are too poor to be of any use for our purposes, since for them there is no meta-theorem like 28 that may be construed as giving the general conditions of substitutivity in non-extensional contexts. O3, O7 and O8 allow such a meta-theorem but seem not so suitable as O4 on other grounds. If $\Box^d A$ is provable in our system of modal logic, it is difficult to see why we should not be entitled to say that it is a truth of modal logic that A is a truth of modal logic, and then it is natural to want this as a theorem just as much as we want $\Box^d A$. Accordingly we need $\Box^n A \supset^d \Box^n \Box^n A$ where $n=d$, and it would be unnecessarily inelegant not to have this also where $n<d$, though it is worth bearing in mind that O3 would allow us to use a square for the representation of 'it is analytic that' in the sense defined in §20 and another square for the representation of 'it is physically necessary that' in the sense elucidated in §38 below. On the other hand O5 seems altogether too strong to be suitable, since $\Diamond^d \Box^d A \supset^d \Box^d A$ is not wanted as a theorem. This becomes evident if you take A to represent some everyday empirical statement – any one you please – such as 'If today is Tuesday, today is market-day.' For such a statement is not logically true, in that replacement of its non-logical terms does not in every case yield a true statement, while the denial that it is logically true is also not logically true. We may note also that the choice of O4 does not preclude us from taking $\Box^n$ to represent 'it is known to any rational man that', where a rational man is assumed to know all the laws of logic. We do not need some other system, analogous to von Wright's M,[1] in order to accommodate this idealized epistemic logic. Lemmon has argued[2] that it is not irrational to have forgotten that one knows something, and hence that even if a rational man knows something he may not know that he knows it. But this argument rests on an equivocation between the occurrent and dispositional senses of 'know'. If a man knows dispositionally that so-and-so he may well not know occurrently

[1] *An Essay in Modal Logic*, pp. 29 ff.
[2] 'Is there only One Correct System of Modal Logic?', *Proc. Arist. Soc.*, Supp. Vol. xxxiii (1959), pp. 38 ff.

that he knows dispositionally that so-and-so. But if he knows anything dispositionally he surely knows dispositionally that he knows it.

The paradoxes that tend to arise in modal identity theory are typified by the material equivalence of material and strict identity that is provable in $S2^2$ and the strict equivalence of these that is provable in $S4^2$.[1] One wants to be able to say that the Morning Star is materially but not strictly identical with the Evening Star, though a man's only brother is strictly identical with his only male sibling. Not that these are different kinds of identity. Rather, they are both instances of the same identity relation, and what differs is the modal operator within the scope of which this relation may be correctly predicated. Similarly 'greater than' is the same relation in both 'It is *a priori* true that 9 is greater than 7' and 'It is *a posteriori* true that the number of planets is greater than 7.' What leads to the kind of trouble in question is the definition of identity in terms of shared predicates where no restriction is placed on the conditions in which these shared predicates may themselves contain modal expressions. But why should *extensional* identity be defined in terms of sharing non-extensional predicates as well as extensional ones? Accordingly, in an enlargement of O4 to include identity theory it seems reasonable to envisage an interpretation of wff in which the assignment of meanings to predicate letters is restricted in the way already described (in §29) as requisite for extensional formalizations. The only difficulty that then remains is to contrive an appropriate treatment of abstracts, as in $O4^2$, which is like O4 except for the following additions:

Primitive symbol: ^ (abstraction operator, self-representing in syntax notation).

If A is *wf*, so are both $(\exists\varphi)$A and $\hat{\alpha}_1, \hat{\alpha}_2 \ldots \hat{\alpha}_j A(\beta_1, \beta_2, \ldots \beta_j)$ where $\alpha_1, \alpha_2, \ldots \alpha_j$ are distinct and $\beta_1, \beta_2, \ldots \beta_j$ are not necessarily distinct.

An occurrence of φ in A is a *bound occurrence* if in a wf part of A of the form $(\exists\varphi)$B. Otherwise it is free. Any occurrence of γ in $\hat{\alpha}_1, \hat{\alpha}_2, \ldots \hat{\alpha}_j A(\beta_1, \beta_2, \ldots \beta_j)$ is bound if γ is one of $\alpha_1, \alpha_2, \ldots \alpha_j$ or is bound in A. Otherwise it is free.

[1] R. C. Barcan, 'The Identity of Individuals in a Strict Functional Calculus of Second Order', *Jour. Symb. Log.*, xii (1947), pp. 12 ff.

Definition-schemata:

$$(\varphi)A \text{ for } \sim(\exists\varphi)\sim A$$
$$(\beta\varepsilon\hat{\alpha}A) \text{ for } \hat{\alpha}A(\beta)$$
$$(\alpha =^n\beta) \text{ for } (\varphi)(\varphi\alpha \supset^n\varphi\beta)$$

If α_i has an mth grade free occurrence in B, and no nth grade free occurrence in B where $n > m$, then any occurrence of β^i to the right of B in a wf part $\hat{\alpha}_1, \hat{\alpha}_2, \ldots \hat{\alpha}_j B(\beta_1, \beta_2, \ldots \beta_j)$ of A is an mth *grade occurrence* of β_i in A.

Axiom-schemata 8, 9 and 10, and gen. are extended over predicate letters. Two further axiom-schemata:

2.12. $(\varphi)A \supset^d B$ where A, B and Γ are wff such that no free occurrence of φ in A is in a wf part of A of the form $(\chi)E$ if χ occurs freely in Γ; any free occurrence of φ in A is of mth grade if some free occurrence of α_i in Γ is of nth grade, where $m \geqslant n$; and B results from A by replacing all free occurrences of φ in A by $\hat{\alpha}_1, \hat{\alpha}_2, \ldots \hat{\alpha}_j \Gamma$.

2.13. $\hat{\alpha}_1, \hat{\alpha}_2, \ldots \hat{\alpha}_j A(\beta_1, \beta_2 \ldots \beta_j) \equiv^d B$ where $\alpha_1, \alpha_2, \ldots \alpha_j$ are distinct and occur freely in A; and B is like A except for containing free occurrences of β_1, where A has free occurrences of α_1, free occurrences of β_2 where A has free occurrences of $\alpha_2, \ldots$ free occurrences of β_j where A has free occurrences of α_j.

Among theorems of $O4^2$ are all the theorems of $O4$ and:

2.14. $(\alpha =^n\beta) \equiv^d (\varphi)(\varphi\alpha \equiv^n\varphi\beta)$

2.15. $\alpha =^n\alpha$

2.16. $(\exists\beta)(\alpha =^n\beta)$

2.17. $((\alpha =^n\beta)(\beta =^n\gamma)) \supset^d (\alpha =^n\gamma)$

2.18. $(\alpha =^m\beta) \supset^d (\varphi)(\square^n\varphi\alpha \equiv^k \square^n\varphi\beta)$ where $k \leqslant m$ and $m \geqslant n$

2.19. $(\alpha =^m\beta) \supset^d (\Gamma \equiv^k E)$ where E is got from Γ by the substitution of a free occurrence of β for each of one or more nth grade free occurrences of α in Γ, and $k \leqslant m$ and $m \geqslant n$

2.20. $(\exists\beta)((\beta =^m\gamma)\square^m(\beta\varepsilon\hat{\alpha}A)) \equiv^d \square^m(\gamma\varepsilon\hat{\alpha}A)$ where β is not free in A and α has no free nth grade occurrence in A such that $n > m$.

But $(\alpha =^m\beta) \supset^0 (\alpha =^n\beta)$ seems not provable where $n > m$.

$O4^2$ has the same relation to $S4^2$ as that of $O4$ to $S4$ which was mentioned above.

On any interpretation of the kind envisaged for $O4$ certain familiar modal operators of informal speech will remain unrepresented by squares, e.g. 'he says that', 'it is a truth of propositional logic that', 'he implies that', and 'it is morally obligatory that'. Of course, all modal operators can be represented in the extensional way described in §§27–29. But such a mode of representation misses the distinctive quality or degree of non-extensionality created by the operator in question. This can often be represented in a wff of the form $(\exists\alpha)(\varphi\alpha(\chi\alpha\equiv^nA))$. E.g. suppose $\Box^1$ is replaced by 'it is demonstrable that' and $\Box^2$ by 'it is demonstrable *a priori* that'. Then for 'He implies that it is raining' φ, χ, and A are replaced as before and $n=2$, while for 'It is morally obligatory that people keep their promises' φ is replaced by 'is a rule of moral obligation', χ by 'is obeyed', A by 'people keep their promises' and $n=1$. However such a mode of representation is not available in $O4$ for certain operators like 'he says that' and 'it is a truth of propositional logic that', which create even stronger kinds of non-extensionality than does 'it is logically true that'. One way of rerpesenting some of these operators (but not 'he says that') is by extending $O4$ into $O4^3$ as follows:

$O4^3$ has all the symbolism of $O4$, together with '$\Box^{d+1}$' and '$\Box^{d+2}$'. It has the same formation rules and definition-schemata as $O4$, where $(d+2)\geqslant n$, and axioms 1, 2, 3, 4, 6, 9, 10, 11, plus:

3.5. $((A\supset^nB)(B\supset^n\Gamma))\supset^d(A\supset^n\Gamma)$ where $(d+2)\geqslant n$ and $n>0$ if no square or individual letter occurs in A, B, or Γ; $(d+1)\geqslant n$ and $n>0$ if no square occurs in A, B, or Γ; and $d\geqslant n$ and $n>0$ if a square occurs in A, B or Γ.

3.7. $\Box^mA\supset^d\Box^n\Box^mA$ where either $m\geqslant d$ and $n=d$, or $d>m$, $m>0$ and $n=m$.

3.8. $(\alpha)\Box^nA\supset^d\Box^n(\alpha)A$ where $(d+1)\geqslant n$ and $n>0$.

3.12. $\Box^d\Diamond^n\Diamond^nA$ where $n>d$.

3.13. $\Box^dA\supset^d(\Diamond^d\Box^nA\supset^0\Box^nA)$ where $n>d$.

3.14. If $A\supset^dB$ is an axiom of $O4$ and no square or individual letter occurs in either A or B, then $A\supset^{d+2}B$ is an axiom of $O4^3$.

3.15. If $A\supset^dB$ is an axiom of $O4$ and no square occurs in either A or B, then $A\supset^{d+1}B$ is an axiom of $O4^3$.

Derivation-rules of $O4^3$ are like those of $O4$ except that instead of subst. $O4^3$ has:

If A, B and Γ are such that E results from Γ by the substitution of B for each of one or more nth grade occurrences of A in Γ, then from Γ and $A\equiv^mB$, where $n\leqslant m$ and $m\geqslant d$, derive E.

The interpretation envisaged for $O_4{}^3$ is one in which $\square^{d+1}$ is replaced by 'it is a truth of first-order predicate logic that', and $\square^{d+2}$ by 'it is a truth of propositional logic that'.

3.16. Meta-theorems 12–33 of O_4 are provable for $O_4{}^3$ where $m\leqslant d$ and $d\geqslant n$; and meta-theorems 12–24 are provable both where $(d+1)\geqslant n$ and no square occurs in A, B, Γ or E, and where $(d+2)\geqslant n$ and no square or individual letter occurs in A, B, Γ or E.

Among other theorems of $O_4{}^3$ are the following:

3.17. If $\vdash A\supset^dB$ and no square occurs in either A or B, then $\vdash A\supset^{d+1}B$.

3.18. If $\vdash A\supset^dB$ and no square or individual letter occurs in either A or B, then $\vdash A\supset^{d+2}B$.

3.19. $(A\supset^{d+1}B)\supset^d(\square^{d+1}A\supset^d\square^{d+1}B)$ where no square occurs in either A or B.

3.20. $(A\supset^{d+2}B)\supset^d(\square^{d+2}A\supset^d\square^{d+2}B)$ where no square or individual letter occurs in either A or B.

3.21. $(\alpha_1)(\alpha_2) \ldots (\alpha_n)(A\equiv^{d+1}B)\supset^d(\Gamma\equiv^dE)$ where A, B and Γ are such that E results from Γ by the substitution of B for each of 1 or more nth grade occurrences of A in Γ; $\alpha_1, \alpha_2, \ldots \alpha_n$ is a complete list of the individual letters occurring freely in Γ and E; no square occurs in either A or B; and $(d+1)\geqslant n$.

3.22. $(A\equiv^{d+2}B)\supset^d(\Gamma\equiv^dE)$ where A, B and Γ are such that E results from Γ by the substitution of B for each of 1 or more nth grade occurrences of A in Γ; and no square or individual letter occurs in either A or B.

3.23. $\square^d\sim\square^n\square^nA$ where $n>d$.

3.24. $(\square^dA\sim\square^nA)\supset^d(\square^d\sim\square^nA)$ where $n>d$.

It can easily be seen, in view of the equivalence of O_4 and $O_4{}^1$, that A is a theorem of the classical propositional calculus (with tilde and dot as primitives) if and only if $\vdash\square^{d+2}A$ in $O_4{}^3$, and that A is a theorem of first-order quantification theory (with tilde, dot and existential quantifier as primitives) if and only if $\vdash\square^{d+1}A$ in $O_4{}^3$. But $O_4{}^3$ has no interpretation into any of the Lewis-Barcan systems S1–S8, since the

Lewis-Barcan, superscript-free analogues for 3.7 and 3.12 are mutually inconsistent.

The consistency of $O4^3$ is established by an arithmetical interpretation. Assign each propositional letter, and each wff of the form $\varphi(\alpha_1, \alpha_2, \ldots \alpha_j)$ the value of 1 or 0. Take tilde to represent subtraction from 1, and dot to represent multiplication. Take $(\exists\alpha)$, $\square^n$ where $d \geqslant n$, and $\square^n$ in each wf part $\square^n A$ where $n > d$ and no square occurs in A, to represent multiplication by 1. Take $\square^n$ in each wf part $\square^n A$ where $n > d$ and a square occurs in A to represent multiplication by 0. Then, if $\vdash A$, A has the value 1; but $(A \sim A)$ has the value 0.

VIII

Meanings Conceived as Topics for
Formal-logical Investigation

§31. What do logical formulas represent?

In §§23–30 it has been argued that the general logic of non-extensional discourse does not require for its own special purposes some concept of meaning that is inessential for extensional logic. Frege's own dichotomy of sense and reference, and even Church's more subtle development of it, are inadequate to the complexity of the problem and generate more paradoxes than they resolve. No term like 'meaning' or 'intension' is required to take its place alongside 'if', 'not', 'and', 'or', 'some', 'all', 'true', 'false', and the other canonical constants of general logic. Yet in another respect all formal logic must, on any account of the subject, have a close concern with meanings. If the onus of determining the validity of people's arguments, or the logical truth of their utterances, is to be shifted from the *ad hoc* intuitions of those who hear, read or utter them to the rules of a logical calculus, then at least there must be some determinate way of correlating the formulas of such a calculus with the utterances of ordinary speech for which they may stand proxy, and clearly this is best achieved by assigning meanings to the formulas. In each case the meaning of the formula must sufficiently resemble that of the utterance for critics to be confident that it is this utterance, and not another, which is thus being tested for logical truth by proxy, or this argument, and not another, which is being proved valid. Quine has denied that likeness of meaning is at all in point here, because he does not believe that any satisfactorily testable criteria for likeness of meaning can be devised, except for a certain very limited field. But, as was argued in §9, he only succeeds in making this position seem plausible by restricting his concept of meaning to what he calls 'stimulus meaning'. Elsewhere, when others would talk about the meanings of sentences and expressions, he talks instead about their purposes and functions, and about resemblances of purpose between sentences of ordinary language and the formulas of an interpreted calculus.[1] If §§7–8 were right to propose a purpose-and-function theory of meaning in a language, this is just another way of talking about meanings. So that for Quine too, in all but name, formal logic is closely concerned with the meanings of human utterances.

But in what sense of 'meaning' is it most directly concerned with these? Or, more precisely, in what sense of 'meaning' does the interpretation of a calculus for general-logical purposes assign meanings to its formulas? A great deal will turn out to stand or fall with the answer to this question.

One answer often given by logicians, probably because the grouping of utterance-tokens into language-sentences is normally so easy an operation and one that is familiar from childhood onwards, is that the meanings concerned are those of language-sentences. The words of some natural or artificial language are assigned to the formal symbols in such a way that the formulas of the calculus are transformed into sentences of the language.[2] But of course many kinds of language-sentence will not do here. What are needed are sentences of a kind that will allow a formula of the calculus to be defined as true (correct, valid) if the sentence or sentences obtained from it under this transformation 'are such that any statement made by using them is true' and as false (incorrect, invalid) if some sentence thus obtained from it is such that some statement made by using it is false.[3] Laws of logical inference, if they are not to be unrewardingly complex, must refer not to mere sentence-tokens but to recurrences of sentences, and assume that a sentence true in one occurrence will also be true in the next, as even in the simple inference from 'p and q' to 'p'.[4] If a sentence makes statements of different truth-value in different contexts it is unsuitable for this role. What seem to be wanted are what Quine has called 'eternal sentences' – sentences 'whose truth-value stays fixed through time and from speaker to speaker'.[5] Theories of temporal and changeable truth-values, like

---

[1] *Word and Object*, pp. 214, 258, 260.

[2] E. J. Lemmon, 'Is there only One Correct System of Modal Logic?', *Proc. Arist. Soc.*, Supp. Vol. xxxiii (1959), p. 25.

[3] Ibid., p. 26.

[4] *Word and Object*, p. 227.

[5] Ibid., pp. 193 f.

the theory of Prior's that was criticized in §19, are rightly rejected. Now pronouns, demonstratives, first names, inflected verbs, and many other words and phrases like 'today', 'next-door', 'the aforementioned', and so on, do in fact vary their reference with their context of utterance, and this variation of reference naturally tends to generate a variation of truth-value in the statements made by sentences in which these expressions occur. Hence it comes to be supposed that eternal sentences are those in which no expressions occur of kinds that are liable to vary their reference with their context of utterance. The referring expressions an eternal sentence does contain – its datings, map-references, etc. – may themselves have been learnt ostensively or with the help of demonstratives, but no actual demonstratives can occur in it. Instead the logician must in principle supply rules for correlating any non-eternal sentence of ordinary language with the various eternal sentences that stand proxy for it in the interpreted calculus. The non-eternal language-sentence 'It rained here this afternoon' must be paraphrased as an indeterminately wide range of eternal sentences, some true and some false, of the form, say, 'Rain present at . . . on . . .', where the blanks are to be filled by map-references and dates, respectively.

Nor do we need to suppose that the existence of an eternal sentence is compromised by failure of utterance. Certainly, if a sentence were taken as the class of its utterances, then all unuttered sentences would reduce to one, viz. the null class. But Quine proposes to 'take each linguistic form as the sequence, in a mathematical sense, of its successive characters or phonemes', and he explains a sequence $a_1, a_2, \ldots a_n$ as the class of the n pairs $(a_1, 1), (a_2, 2), \ldots (a_n, n)$. We can then still take each component character or phoneme a_i as a class of utterance events, since with these few basic elements of the language there is no risk of non-utterance.

An advocate of such a theory, like Quine, may certainly recognize that in practice we do often assign to logical formulas the meanings of sentences whose truth-values vary with time and speaker. We sometimes 'leave temporal and pronominal references unfixed, and even the senses of ambiguous words, simply because the circumstances that would settle these matters on any particular occasion of utterance may be expected to settle them uniformly for the space of the argument'. But occasionally this expectation fails and we are involved in committing the fallacy of equivocation. Hence appliers of logical theory must always keep alert to such a hazard and be prepared, when it threatens, to expand the offending sentences until they are independent of context in the relevant respects. The sentences need not always be replaced by wholly eternal sentences, but at least they must be replaced by sentences that are more eternal than they are themselves. Thus 'the relation of eternal sentences to our logic is like that of silver dollars to our economy: mostly we do not see them, but we reckon in terms of them'. For 'the primary distinction of eternal sentences is that they are the repository of truth itself, and so of all science. In so far as a sentence can be said simply to be true, and not just true now or in this mouth, it is an eternal sentence.'[1]

How unfortunate, then, that there are no indubitably eternal sentences! If eternal sentences are indeed the repository of truth and science, then sceptics have another good reason for saying that that there is no sure truth and no sure science. No language-sentence whatever can be relied on to maintain its truth-value invariant under all circumstances. What lies at the root of the mistaken confidence that eternal language-sentences do exist is an illicit conversion of the statement that all sentences which vary their reference with their context of utterance are also liable to vary their truth-value. From this statement it seems to be inferred – or, at least, this statement expresses the only reason offered for concluding – that all sentences liable to vary their truth-value are those which vary their reference. Belief in the existence of eternal language-sentences rests squarely on the mistaken assumption that contextual variation of reference is the only factor that makes for variation of truth-value.

Indeed that assumption is found not only among logicians like Quine who seek to assign the meanings of language-sentences to logical formulas, but also among others, like Strawson, who oppose such an assignment in order to free the logic of ordinary language from the toils of theoretical regimentation. The latter also hold that a sentence 'entirely free from referring elements', or containing no references dependent on contextual conditions, is such that 'if its utterance at any time, at any place, by any speaker, results in a true statement, then its utterance at any other time, at any other place, by any other speaker, results in a true statement'.[2] Their quarrel with logicians like Quine is

---

[1] Ibid., p. 227.
[2] P. F. Strawson, *Introduction to Logical Theory* (1952), pp. 214 f.

not about the existence of eternal language-sentences, which they fully grant, nor about the consequential possibility of interpreting logical formulas to represent the meanings of such sentences, which they could hardly then deny. Instead it is about whether these sentences should be taken as the canonical repositories of truth, the standard elements of logical argument, the norm rather than the anomaly. Hence what they seek to put in the place of language-sentences, as the basic counters of logic, are not some quite different groupings of sentence-tokens, such as sayings, but rather some refinement on the category of language-sentences. The vast majority of language-sentences tend to vary their truth-value with their reference, they say, and their reference with their circumstances of utterance. So what we must take as the standard possessors of truth-values are not just bare language-sentences with an assertive content, but assertive language-sentences in context. These are what Strawson calls 'statements', though in order not to confuse them with the true-or-false sayings that have been called statements in §§19–30 it will be convenient here to call them 'sentences-in-use'. Variations of reference are eliminated by coupling the wording of the sentence with those circumstances of its utterance that affect its reference, which will be none in the case of eternal sentences. The standard possessors of truth-values are thus to be 'identified, not only by reference to the words used, but also by reference to the circumstances in which they are used, and, sometimes, to the identity of the person using them'.[1] Yet recourse to such sentence-in-use turns out to serve the purposes of general logic no better than recourse to language-sentences that contain no expressions of varying reference, because both doctrines rest on the same false assumption. Both doctrines assume that the occurrence of expressions which characteristically vary their reference, like pronouns and demonstratives, is the sole factor that ever makes a language-sentence vary its truth-value.

This is essentially a pre-Herder assumption. Admittedly homonyms and other trivial ambiguities would create some difficulty for such a view in most natural languages. But they would seldom be sufficient in number to exclude more than a few language-sentences, or sentences-in-use, from the laurels of eternity, since the meaning of a word-form that is equivocal in isolation is often resolved by its setting in the context of the other words that go to make up a many-word sentence

[1] Ibid., p. 4.

with it. What is much more serious is that unless we revert to a pre-Herder philosophy of language we cannot exclude the possibility of meaning-change for any word whatever. Unless we are prepared to jettison the immense advances in linguistic studies and in the history of ideas that presuppose a temporal, non-normative theory of meaning in a language, we must allow that any language-word whatever, and consequently any language-sentence in which it occurs, may change its meaning in the future, even if it has never changed it in the past. Hence change of meaning is another factor, besides variation of reference, that may make a language-sentence vary its truth-value. An expression that is correctly predicated of a subject in one century may not be so in the next. It is naturally easier for logicians like Strawson, who themselves hold a normative, rules-of-use theory of meaning, to ignore this factor, than it is for those who, like Quine, hold some kind of *de facto* theory. Nevertheless the possibility of meaning-change cannot be safely ignored here, and it is a possibility that applies to all words or phrases, not just to some, as does variability of reference, and not only to words themselves but also to the patterns of order in which they compose sentences. Take, for example, the word 'empirical' or 'empiricist' – a familiar enough expression in philosophical writing. Both Francis Bacon and John Stuart Mill would be correctly described as empiricists in the mid-twentieth-century sense of the word. Yet Mill objected to what he called empiricism in science, and Bacon held that 'the Empirical school' of philosophy gave birth to 'deformed and monstrous' opinions.[1] The words 'empirical' and 'empiricist' meant something different before the present century from what they do now. The English sentence 'He is an empiricist' has changed its truth-value not only with the reference of its pronoun but also with the meaning of its predicate. Only the former source of instability in truth-value, not the latter, would be eliminated if we talked instead about sentences-in-use or about sentences without expressions of varying reference.

It is no use objecting that most changes of meaning are slow and that many words never change their meaning in the whole life of a language. The trouble is that the appliers of logical theory can hardly be expected to know the history of each language-word they use. Still less can they hope to know where the vicissitudes of semantic change

[1] J. S. Mill, *System of Logic*, VI, i, 1, and VI, x, 8; F. Bacon, *Novum Organum*, I, lxiv.

will strike next. If an interpreted calculus is to be the final and infallible arbiter of logical truth, consistency, or deducibility, then at least its formulas must have the same truth-value from one year to the next and even from one century to the next. How else can we be sure that when we say 'J. S. Mill is an empiricist' we shall not appear to be contradicting a contemporary of Mill's who said 'J. S. Mill is not an empiricist'? We should do ill to limit our perspective in matters of logical rigour to the present life-span of *homo sapiens*, let alone to the curiosity of the passing day. Moreover, anyone can stipulate what meanings he pleases for the words he uses, and if he does this sparingly and to some point he will still be taken to be speaking in a common language rather than in a code or jargon of his own. The meanings of language-words thus change temporarily and within the confines of a single speech or paragraph, as well as permanently and throughout the community that uses them. If someone utters an English sentence for some such special purpose, its capacity for eternal truth, or eternal falsehood, may well be ruined. In short, for the purposes of general logic we cannot afford a method of interpreting a calculus that assigns its formulas the meanings of language-sentences or of sentences-in-use, since these meanings are in principle always open to change.

Perhaps it will be objected instead that the notion of a language is in any case somewhat indeterminate. 'What are languages,' it may be asked, 'and when do they count as identical or distinct?'[1] Why should we not suppose, for logical purposes, that the life of a language is no longer than the maximum period within which in fact no semantic change occurs? Why should we not suppose that there is not just one English language, lasting from 1500, say, till now, but a hundred English languages in each century since 1500 or twelve in each year, or even more? Then, if we couple our reference to the form of a language-sentence with a reference to some such period, it seems that all this trouble will be avoided. Some language-sentences, and all sentences-in-use, must then be incontrovertibly eternal.

This amplification of the language-sentence theory is not as paradox-free as might appear. Meanings sometimes change very fast in small communities, perhaps even in the space of an afternoon or less. So in interpreting an extensive series of formulas we should soon begin working in a dead language. But perhaps it would be pedantic to boggle at this.

[1] W. V. Quine, *Word and Object*, p. 214.

There is, however, a much more serious trouble. Few changes of meaning proceed uniformly throughout the whole of a speech-community. Normally a word is still being used by some speakers in the old sense when it is already being used by others in the new. We should therefore have to couple a reference to some region of space with our reference to a period of time. But we could still not be sure that all changes of meaning would proceed uniformly within the specified segment of space-time. Even if we tied our concept of language to a single speaker for a single hour, and were content not to worry about the paradoxes inherent in the notion of such a private and idiosyncratic language (§8), there is still a risk that even this single speaker might sometimes speak in the new way, sometimes in the old. No doubt the number of language-sentences affected by the variation would probably be very small. But unless we knew all the man's utterances in the given period we could not be sure just which sentences, or sentences-in-use, were thus deprived of eternal truth-values. Moreover even if we did know all his utterances in the given short period they would not normally be sufficient to constitute a language that would equip the formulas of a logical calculus with all the meanings they need. It is not just that certain sentences would not be uttered. We could easily deal with that difficulty, if it were the only one, by Quine's device of taking each sentence as the sequence, in a mathematical sense, of its successive phonemes or characters. But nothing is achieved by pairing off formulas with given sequences of phonemes if many of these have no more right to be considered meaningful than has 'dorner sug threbble' in English. The pairing off is pointless if there is far too little evidence for a dictionary and grammar to be compiled that would be adequate to the task of translating all these sequences into those of another language. But neither a man's vocabulary during so short a period, nor his range of grammatical constructions, would be large enough to provide such evidence. The trouble is, in fact, that as we progressively restrict the segment of space-time to which all utterances in the relevant language are confined, we are bound to make the language poorer and poorer for the purposes of general logic. We cannot avoid the pitfalls of meaning-change without depriving our logic of its catholicity.

All this is on the dual assumption that logical formulas are to be assigned the meanings of language-sentences or sentences-in-use, and that the sentences concerned in any assignment of meanings to a calculus all belong to one and the same language, be it ever so short-lived. However, perhaps someone who wants very much to retain the first half of this assumption would be content to relinquish the second. Perhaps he would seek to recover catholicity for his logic by choosing the sentences to be correlated with its formulas from a sufficiently wide range of short-lived languages. He might hope thus to avoid the pitfalls of meaning-change and yet still supply his logical formulas with all the meanings he can possibly need. But how is this to be done? If different propositional letters in the propositional calculus are assigned the meanings of sentences or sentences-in-use in different languages, what guarantee can there be that a well-formed formula composed from these letters with the aid of brackets and truth-functional connectives has itself the meaning of a sentence or sentence-in-use in any such language? Or what guarantee can there be for formulas composed analogously from individual and predicate letters in quantification theory? If the symbols and letters of a calculus are to be paired off with the words and sentences, or words-in-use and sentences-in-use, of an ordinary language like modern English, then any well-formed formula, however complex, has a reasonable chance of correlating with a sentence that, however clumsy, would be intelligible in principle to any speaker of modern English. But if, in order to avoid both the pitfalls of meaning-change and the stark poverty of a one-man one-hour language, many different one-hour languages are used, then many of the sentences that will turn out to be correlatable with logical formulas may belong to no language at all.

Of course, it would be natural to select all the languages needed for thus interpreting a calculus from a single common culture. So that if each sentence involved could be considered in abstraction from its own particular language there would be no difficulty in supposing it to be intelligible in principle to any member of the culture. But the original thesis about language-sentences has now been so modified that it is barely recognizable. First, we had to confine ourselves, because of the trouble about meaning-change, to the known utterances of given persons over very short periods. So that we came, in effect, to be dealing with utterance-sentences rather than with language-sentences. Secondly, each of these had to be considered in abstraction from its own particular language. So that we came to be dealing with saying-sentences rather than with utterance-sentences. Thirdly, we have in any case to suppose that the meanings of these sentences are capable of assignment to logical formulas without carrying with them any taint of authorship. The logical validity or invalidity of your argument must not depend in any way on the fact that it was you who uttered it. The logical formula or formulas that represent it must do so quite impersonally. So that in the end we come to be dealing with sayings rather than with saying-sentences. Instead of grouping utterance-tokens into language-sentences, for the purposes of correlation with logical formulas, we have had to group them into sayings. Indeed, though a saying (as defined in §19) may vary its wording to a considerable extent, it can never change either its meaning or its reference, and it is therefore much better qualified for the laurels of eternal truth or eternal falsity than a sentence-in-use or a language-sentence that lacks pronouns, demonstratives, etc. Sayings are the most appropriate groupings of human utterances to have their meanings represented by the formulas of a logical calculus.

It is no use objecting that to apply the definition of a saying requires a knowledge of meaning that is unnecessary for the definition of a language-sentence (except perhaps, according to some linguists, for the discrimination of a community's phonemes). It is quite true, on the one hand, that if two tokens may be correctly described as the same saying they must have the same meaning as saying-sentences or saying-clauses: i.e. the same arguments must lead to or from them. It is also true that if two tokens may be correctly described as the same saying-expression they must have the same meaning as utterance-expressions: i.e. they are either translations of one another or both must admit of identical translation in some other natural language. On the other hand, it is quite true that a language-sentence may be defined without any such requirements as, roughly, a set of phonemes in customary use in a given speech-community, ordered in some customary pattern of self-sufficient utterance. But this bare definition of a language-sentence does not suffice to determine what it is exactly that Quine, let alone Strawson, wishes to correlate with the formulas of a logical calculus. Quine at least needs to find language-sentences without expressions of varying reference that will replace, in cases of equivocation, those sentences that contain such expressions. But this replacement of paper money by silver dollars, in Quine's metaphor, must be underwritten by an identity of purchasing power. The replacing sentence must serve all the worthwhile purposes of the replaced one, as Quine puts it, or, which amounts to the same thing, it must in all important respects be equivalent in meaning. Similarly we cannot differentiate one Strawsonian sentence-in-use from another, so far as just one language-sentence is involved, unless we know what Strawson calls 'the rules for the use' of the referring expressions in the sentence. That is, we must know the meanings of these expressions in the language. In short, some knowledge of meaning is presupposed even by the standard proposals to correlate language-sentences with logical formulas. So that the proposal to correlate sayings instead of language-sentences is at no great disadvantage on this score.

More plausibly it might be objected that the whole point is one of trivial importance only. 'We are all easily taught how to use the propositional calculus', it might be said, 'in order to assess the formal validity of everyday arguments and the logical truth of everyday statements. Even if the textbooks that teach us talk of language-sentences rather than sayings, we in practice soon get the idea of just what is required to match off formulas against arguments. The exact description of what we are doing is therefore a piece of refined pedantry that serves no useful purpose.'

The short answer to this objection is that the overriding aim of formal-logical study is to replace untutored intuitions of validity and logical truth by rigorously controlled operations with the formulas of a calculus. Such an aim is incompatible with any looseness or inaccuracy in the description of those operations that might result in the derivation of a false conclusion from true premisses. But there is also much more to be said. Neither the content of logical theory nor its epistemological credentials remain unaffected by the choice between sayings and language-sentences as correlates of logical formulas.

Consider first the problem of non-extensional discourse, which is closely linked with the present issue. The *prima facie* structure of certain kinds of argument makes it natural to suppose that at least some non-extensional utterance-patterns are formed by concatenating certain operators with elements of just the same category as require to be correlated with logical formulas in the application of logical theory. If, for instance, from the three premisses

(1) He says that all Cretans are liars

and

> Everything he says is true

and

> Epimenides is a Cretan

we may infer the conclusion

> Epimenides is a liar

it is natural to suppose that whatever we take to form the first premiss by concatenation with 'he says that' is as much the possessor of a truth-value, and the owner of logical liaisons, as the three premisses themselves. This supposition is patently accommodated by combining the theory that sayings are the proper correlates of logical formulas with the theory of §25 that all non-extensional utterance-patterns are implicitly or explicitly constituted by statement-forming operators on sayings. Analogously, if language-sentences or sentences-in-use are to be the correlates of logical formulas, it seems that the first premiss of the above inference must be taken as formed by concatenating 'he says that' with a language-sentence or sentence-in-use. Otherwise the logic of indirect discourse must either become unrewardingly complex, as on Quine's proposal to analyse reports of indirect discourse by relative general terms, or unrewardingly paradoxical, as in Church's development of Frege's theory. But there are great difficulties in the way of modelling our formal logic of non-extensional discourse on the assumption that utterance-patterns containing indirect discourse are formed by operations on language-sentences or sentences-in-use. As Church has pointed out,[1] such an analysans does not stand up as well as its analysandum to change of language. It is unsatisfactory to construe (1) as, say,

(2) He asserts a sentence in some language that is intensionally isomorphic with the English sentence 'All Cretans are liars'

because the corresponding all-German analysans for the German version of (1) would not be equivalent to (2). It would imply the existence of a certain German sentence, whereas (2) implies that of a certain English sentence. Quine finds such an argument inconclusive because 'it turns on a notion of likeness of meaning', whereas he himself is only

[1] 'On Carnap's Analysis of Statements of Assertion and Belief', *Analysis*, x (1950), pp. 97 ff.

concerned with whether one sentence serves any purposes of another that seem worth serving.[1] But Church's argument can be formulated just as forcefully about identity of purpose as about likeness of meaning, since with regard to language-sentences these two modes of expression are equivalent.

Moreover all the arguments about change of meaning that showed language-sentences and sentences-in-use to be less fitted than sayings for the role of standard counterparts to logical formulas are equally valid against any proposal to analyse sentences like (1) by sentences like (2). To know just what exactly the speaker did say we should need at least to have the precise period of English specified. Even this might not be enough unless we narrowed our concept of a language to the speaker's own mode of utterance at the time of his remark, and then we seem to be concerned with an utterance-sentence rather than a language-sentence. But the logical liaisons of the speaker's remark with the remarks of others may also be in point, as in the logical truth about the policeman and the prisoner that was cited as (22) in §26. So that we cannot restrict the expression of the speaker's remark to a single one-man language, and must consider it at least as a saying-sentence rather than just as an utterance-sentence. Finally we have to consider it as a saying rather than just as a saying-sentence, because its meaning has to be assignable to a well-formed formula, or to part of a well-formed formula, that owes nothing of the part it plays in logical calculations to any particular person. Thus the same reasons as justify a choice of sayings rather than language-sentences to be the correlates of logical formulas also justify the choice of sayings rather than language-sentences to be the type of expression that formulates the content of indirect discourse – which is only to be expected if the latter expressions are no less the possessors of truth-values and the owners of logical liaisons than the self-sufficient premises of inference that logical formulas must be capable of representing.

It follows from this interconnection that the solution of the problem of non-extensional discourse is, after all, bound up with a certain concept of meaning, though not in the way that Frege proposed. To know the precise sense of 'meaning' in which the interpretation of a calculus for formal-logical purposes assigns meanings to its formulas is to know the type of expression that formulates the content of indirect discourse.

---

[1] *Word and Object*, p. 214.

Nor is it only the logical theory of non-extensional discourse that is affected by the view we take about that concept of meaning. The correlation of language-sentences with logical formulas is an indispensable requirement, for instance, for the kind of *de jure* theory, criticized in §§5–6, which claims that a natural language, like English, does not differ in principle from a formalized one. It is presupposed too by the insistence of some logicians, like Tarski,[1] that the paradoxes of Eubulides and Grelling show the logical inconsistency of ordinary English, Greek, Polish, etc., whereas the correlation of sayings with logical formulas implies that the most these paradoxes can show is the inconsistency of certain statements with one another or the non-statementhood of certain sayings, as suggested in §26. In addition §§34–36 aim to show that unless we correlate sayings rather than language-sentences or culture-sentences with logical formulas the inherent vagueness of language-sentences and culture-sentences force a three-valued logic upon us. Finally, the remainder of the present chapter will be devoted to arguing that two other important issues are also affected, viz. the justification of logical theory and the logical admissibility of an empty universe.

§32. How is logical theory justified?

In §20 it was maintained that the concept of analyticity is no use as a weapon of last resort in problems of justification. On a *de facto* philosophy of meaning in a language, therefore, we cannot hope to justify a logical theory by the claim that it systematizes certain ranges of analytic truths. The sociology of how people in fact use words, like the psychology of how people in fact think, affords no sufficient ground for theories about how they ought to do so. The appeal to language for the justification of logic has to be buttressed, if it is to have any plausibility at all, by some otherwise unsatisfactory doctrine of meaning, such as the view that word-use is controlled by rules. However, if this kind of buttressed appeal to analyticity is reasonably successful in its account of logical truth, we might need to reconsider our attitude to *de jure* theories of meaning in a language. Though such a doctrine has turned out to be harmful and obstructive in philology and philosophy, it might conceivably be of use in logic when combined with

[1] *Logic, Semantics, Metamathematics*, tr. J. H. Woodger (1956), p. 165.

the view that language-sentences or sentences-in-use are the proper correlates of logical formulas. Not that the language-sentence doctrine implies the analyticity doctrine: the former is often advocated by logicians, like Quine, who attack the latter. But the appeal to analyticity does seem to imply that logical formulas should be taken to represent the meanings of language-sentences or sentences-in-use.

Strawson, for example, combines both doctrines. On his view 'rules about words lie behind all statements of logical appraisal', because 'all concepts of logical appraisal may be explained in terms of inconsistency' and behind inconsistencies between sentences-in-use stand rules for the use of expressions, though, of course, these are not generally rules which we draw up and conform our practice to, but rather rules which we extract from our practice. Inconsistencies arise primarily, Strawson thinks, because a word that could be applied to everything without exception would be useless for the purposes of description. When we say what a thing is like, we not only compare it with other things but also distinguish it from yet other things, so that it becomes possible either to assert or to deny its application to a given case or to be inconsistent through both asserting and denying this. It is thus, on Strawson's view, a general feature of all sets of rules for the use of descriptive expressions that they draw boundaries limiting the applicability of the language-words in question; and so far as the consequences of that general feature are articulated by a logical theory – an interpretation of a calculus for logical purposes – the logical theory is ultimately justified.[1]

Perhaps it may seem odd on this view that Church should have been able to prove the impossibility of any comprehensive decision-procedure for the logic of predicates. One might have supposed, if the laws of logic all depend on the rules of language, that any ordinary language-speaker would be as competent to detect all breaches of logical laws as he apparently is to detect all breaches of grammatical ones. But it is probably unfair to make too much of this point. It could always be answered, though Strawson does not in fact discuss the matter, that what Church in effect discovered was just that there was this hitherto unsuspected complexity about the rules of language which determine our logic as distinct from those that determine our grammar: there can be no comprehensive routine for testing whether or not a

[1] *Introduction to Logical Theory*, pp. 2 ff.

given statement is made true by the rules of language governing logical inconsistencies.

A much more serious objection to Strawson's view is that, for reasons already stated, we must take sayings rather than sentences-in-use as the possessors of truth-values and owners of logical liaisons. For it follows from this that the type of expression with which we are primarily dealing in logic is not such that its meaning is given by rules of word-use. Moreover, the capacity of a term to function usefully as a predicate depends precisely on the existence of boundaries to its correct predication. So that the features that in Strawson's view are common to all rules for the use of descriptive language-words are not so much features of language-words (have not anthropologists argued about the existence of pre-logical languages?)[1] as features of description. They are bound up more immediately with the nature of saying than of language. Hence, if sayings are correlated with logical formulas, the axioms of predicate logic may be taken to determine the general conditions of predicability for descriptive terms, just as the axioms of sentential logic may be taken to determine the conditions under which sayings possess truth-values.

It might be objected now: 'What difference does this really make? Are you not just taking in essence the same view as Strawson with the relatively unimportant difference that you write "term" where he writes "expression", you write "saying" where he writes "sentence-in-use", and you avoid taking the concept of consistency as fundamental? In both cases the truths of logic are made dependent on the conditions of predicability and statementhood rather than on what Quine has called "a limning of the most general traits of reality".'[2]

But the difference between Strawson's view and the one suggested here is not so slight. For on his view it is a common feature of all ordinary usage that it justifies certain assertions about the laws of logic, whereas on the view suggested here it is rather the laws of logic that justify certain assertions about ordinary usage. Justification runs in the opposite direction to that suggested by Strawson because justification requires an appeal to norms, and relevant norms are found in the laws of logic, not in the customs of ordinary usage. It is not certain general,

---

[1] Cf. L. Lévy-Bruhl, *How Natives Think*, tr. L. A. Clare (1926), pp. 105 ff., and *Les Carnets de L. Lévy-Bruhl*, ed. M. Leenhardt (1949), pp. 60 ff.

[2] *Word and Object*, p. 161.

boundary-setting features of rules for word-use that are the ultimate backing for logical laws, but rather it is logical laws, articulating the conditions of predicability and statementhood, that support such general features in the customs of word-use. Similarly, the ordinary usage of words like 'inconsistent', 'deducible', 'not', 'if', etc., is not in a position, as Strawson suggests, to justify a logical theory. Rather, if any question arises about the value of such usages, formal logic supplies one important system of criteria, though not the only important system, for judging this value. The extent to which in English, say, the ordinary uses of 'not' and 'and', respectively, approximate to the standard truth-functionally defined constants '$\sim$' and '.' of propositional logic, is one measure of the extent to which ordinary English is primarily adapted to the purposes of articulate reasoning, whereas the extent to which 'and' signifies temporal succession, and in certain English dialects two negative expressions in the same clause fail to cancel one another out, helps to measure the extent to which English is adapted rather to the purposes of rhetoric.

Thus the thesis that logical formulas represent the meanings of sayings rather than language-sentences or sentences-in-use involves the rejection of any attempt to justify logical theory by appeals to analyticity. An enquiry into the purposes of formal-logical system-building will confirm this rejection and shed further light on the actual sources of justification for logical theory.

It is curious that the architects of logical systems seldom say what theoretical profit is gained for logic by constructing them, as opposed to merely cataloguing known patterns of logical truth and deducibility. Great ingenuity is rightly exercised in simplifying their specification – in reducing the number and complexity of axioms, derivation-rules, primitive symbols and so on. Moreover the issues involved in such reductions are often explored, like the way in which a reduction in the number of primitive symbols tends to increase the length or complexity of the axioms. But a satisfactory reason is rarely, if ever, offered for the expenditure of so much effort on this task. One would look in vain for such a reason, or even for a mention of the problem, in standard textbooks like Church's *Introduction to Mathematical Logic*, Quine's *Mathematical Logic* or Prior's *Formal Logic*. When logicians do remark explicitly that formal logic, like any other science, should be organized into a deductive system, and as simple a one as possible, they generally do not say why.[1] Or if they do they give some vague reason like Quine's claim that in logic as in any science the quest for such a system is 'a quest of ultimate categories, a limning of the most general traits of reality', which is little more than a restatement of the problem to be solved: why is it so important to discover the most general laws of logic as distinct from listing their various more specific consequences? At best perhaps they tell us that simplicity is the best evidence of truth, though again without saying why.[2] Nor can it be concluded that the justification of system-building is so obvious to logicians that it is not worth discussing, for they sometimes say or imply that no reason is needed. Quine has on occasion taken conceptual economy as an end in itself, once psychological considerations of manageability have been satisfied. 'Where elegance doesn't matter,' he has written, 'we may and shall, as poets, pursue elegance for elegance's sake.'[3] More specifically Strawson has ascribed to the deductive method of systematizing logic an 'intellectual charm' that lies partly in the exhibition of a set of formulas in an ordered arrangement where each derived formula follows from the ones before it, and partly 'in a feeling of increased control and comprehension, a sense of having reduced a great mass of principles to a handful of premisses and a couple of rules such that, by the application of these to those, the great mass can be re-erected as an orderly structure'.[4] We are apparently to suppose that apart from considerations of manageability the construction of deductive systems merely assists the self-fulfilment of the logician as an artist or satisfies his feelings for order, but that it does not achieve anything intrinsic to the professed object of his enquiry – the determination of logical truth or argument-rules.

No doubt logicians, like many other people, have a certain feeling for order and organization. But it is unsatisfactory to have to conclude that the occurrence of deductive systems in most logical textbooks can be given only a psychological explanation and has no rational defence that is germane to the subject. Here as elsewhere psychological considerations seem irrelevant to the intrinsic nature of formal logic as a theoretical enquiry. No doubt, also, the organization of logical principles into deductive systems enables logicians to study problems about

[1] E.g. I. M. Copi, *Symbolic Logic* (1954), pp. 167 ff.
[2] W. V. Quine, *Word and Object*, p. 250.
[3] *From a Logical Point of View*, p. 79.
[4] *Introduction to Logical Theory*, p. 60.

the completeness, decidability and consistency of such systems. But this is not a sufficient reason for the general policy of systematization, which in any case dates back to the first rough example of a logical system in Aristotle's theory of the syllogism and is thus much older than the discussion of these meta-logical problems. The question whether a given kind of postulate-set is complete, or whether any postulate-set of a given kind can be complete, is only of logical interest if that kind of postulate-set is itself of logical interest, and the issue at stake is just the reason for saying that one postulate-set for logical truth is of more interest than another. Similarly it is only worth while having a mechanical way of deciding whether or not a given statement is provable on certain logical postulates, if simplicity and economy are in any case worth while in logical enquiries. Otherwise, instead of such a general decision-procedure for logical truth, one might just as well have a range of more specific procedures, each appropriate to a particular kind of statement. The central issue at stake reappears here in the form: why is it more valuable to have a general procedure than a range of more specific ones? Finally, an analogous issue emerges in regard to consistency-proofs: why is it more valuable to prove at one swoop, as it were, that our whole catalogue of logical principles is self-consistent, rather than to prove *seriatim* that each is consistent with each? It is no use saying that the saving in time and labour is itself sufficient reason, since this saving would be bought at too high a cost if it involved the sacrifice of reliability. But therein lies the key to the problem in all its forms: economy and simplicity in systematization turn out to increase reliability rather than diminish it.

Suppose we are starting logic from scratch. In general this may be difficult to imagine but within some special, relatively ill-known field, such as the logic of non-extensional discourse, it is not difficult to find oneself apparently in this position. We notice certain patterns like 'If ... that —, and anything which ... is true, then —' that seem to be true for all fillers of their blanks that transform the pattern into a statement. But how can we be rationally justified in relying on their truth in all such cases? How can we be rationally justified in assuming that any saying, whatever its topic, which fills an appropriate blank satisfactorily is a statement, or that any term which does this can function as a predicate? Self-evidence, guesswork or the power of our own imagination affords no such justification. Thumbing through a dictionary and trying to make up all the phrases or sentences that could grammatically fill the blanks is not much better, since new words and idioms are constantly entering our language and in any case there is no limit to the number of words that can occur in a sentence. Scrutiny of the dictionary definitions of words like 'if', 'that', and 'true' is no help, because, even if we suppose logical truths to depend on the meanings of such words, it is logicians not lexicographers who explore the implications of these meanings. Nor is an appeal to logical textbooks of any help if we are genuinely trying to start logic from scratch. Nevertheless after a time perhaps a number of such *prima facie* patterns of logical truth, discovered in mutual independence of one another, can be listed. Can nothing be done to justify greater confidence in their truth than is already justified by whatever combinations of luck, insight, observation, induction, or facility in argument, have led to their detection?

Suppose now that from a very few postulated statement-patterns, which seem themselves to be *prima facie* patterns of logical truth, it is found that all the rest can be demonstrated by following one or other of a very few *prima facie* correct rules of argument. Suppose too that apparently nothing can be thus demonstrated that is false for some fillers of its blanks, like a pattern of conditional statement that for some fillers of its blanks would have a true antecedent and a false consequent. Then, so far as the demonstrable patterns were all initially discovered in independence of one another, they each lend a separate measure of support to the postulated statement-patterns in addition to that which the latter already enjoy on their own merits. Thus much greater confidence comes to be justified in the postulated statement-patterns, and therefore also in the others demonstrable from them. By being organized into such a deductive system our *prima facie* patterns of logical truth have, as it were, corroborated one another. Of course, if the postulates or rules of argument required were relatively numerous, the corroboration achieved would be correspondingly slight, since justifiable confidence in the postulates and rules would be much more thinly distributed. At the limit, indeed, we could put down all our *prima facie* patterns as postulates, and add the rule 'From A infer A'. We should have constructed a deductive system, but the corroboration achieved thereby would be nil. On the other hand if not only are our postulates and rules relatively few and simple, but also some hitherto unnoticed patterns of

logical truth are seen to be demonstrable, then the whole system deserves an additional degree of respect.

All this is only to extend to logic what W. Kneale and others have said
about other sciences.[1] Newton's synthesis of celestial and terrestrial
dynamics gave the laws of seventeenth-century mechanics a legitimate
prestige like that which Euclid had long since given the laws of Greek
geometry. Moreover, just as in natural science and mathematics new
and sharper concepts often require to be introduced, or new and sharper
outlines given to old concepts, in order to achieve this deductive
systematization, so too in formal logic. We can hardly expect that the
inherited concepts of ordinary speech, like 'line', 'move' and 'if',
developed over millennia for the practical purposes of everyday life,
will lend themselves without any alteration at all to the novel and highly
sophisticated purpose of deductive systematization. Just as the points
and lines of Euclidean geometry, or the absolute motion of Newtonian
mechanics are nowhere to be seen by ordinary human beings, so too the
truth-functional conditionals of formal logic are nowhere to be heard in
ordinary speech. The trimming and shaping that need to be done if our
prima facie findings are to be organized into an economical deductive
system produce a theory that may *seem* to have lost touch with the
fields to be surveyed, the eclipses to be predicted, or the reasonings to
be analysed for validity. But that this touch has not really been lost
becomes evident when we learn to treat the theory as a model that
applies to our fields, eclipses or reasonings just so far as the differences
between Euclidean angles and the corners of fields, between absolute
and sensible motion,[2] between truth-functional conditionals and the
conditional statements of ordinary speech, are relatively unimportant
when compared with the similarities. What is important for a conditional statement, for example, so far as it supports a rule of argument
licensing conclusion from its antecedent to its consequent, is just that it
should not have a true antecedent and false consequent and so permit an
inference from a true premiss to a false conclusion: that is why its
similarity to the truth-functional conditionals of propositional logic is
more important than any differences it may have.

[1] *Probability and Induction* (1949), pp. 107 ff., following Whewell.
[2] For purposes of illustration I assume here the general correctness of S.
Toulmin's interpretation of Newton's *Principia* in 'Criticism in the History of
Science: Newton on Absolute Space, Time and Motion', *Philosophical Review*,
lxviii (1959), pp. 1 ff. and 203 ff.

In short the degree of confidence that is rationally justifiable in our logical findings is likely to vary inversely with the extent to which their formulation diverges, under the pressure of deductive economy, from sayings current in ordinary speech. The position resembles a case of complementarity, in the generalized sense that Niels Bohr and some of his followers have given that word. It is unlikely that one can fully assess in the same terms both the extent to which a *prima facie* pattern of logical truth is instantiated in ordinary discourse and also the extent to which it is corroborated by other such patterns.

It follows that if a logician seeks to justify the laws of logic, as he understands them, wholly by reference to the customs of word-use in ordinary language, he cannot pay very much regard to the requirements of deductive systematization. The thesis that logical truths are validated by their analyticity is hardly compatible with the thesis that they are corroborated by systematization. It is not surprising that philosophers like Strawson see no point in such systematization apart from its intellectual charm. To axiomatize logical truth is, for them, to pervert rather than confirm it. But if one rejects the correlation of logical formulas with language-sentences or sentences-in-use, and consequently rejects the appeal to analyticity, one is free to give the builders of logical systems like Aristotle or Russell the credit that is due to them for advancing the study of logical truth. If sayings are the correlates of logical formulas, and logical theories articulate general conditions for sayings to have truth-values and terms to be predicable, thus showing which statements are true, or which arguments are valid, solely in virtue of these general conditions, then the axiomatization of these same conditions achieves a not undesirable sharpening of the relevant concepts – the concepts of statement, predicate, negation, conjunction, and so on. The fact that the ordinary use of English words like 'not' or 'and' differs in certain respects from the role assigned their correlates in the system is evidence not so much of any harm done by the systematization but rather of the harm that might be done by thinking ordinary English the best possible vehicle of rational argument. *Vis-à-vis* ordinary English any systematized logic of sentences and predicates cannot but appear as an explication rather than a mere analysis – a selective refinement rather than a bare description of existing usage.

A familiar illustration of this appears in Russell's treatment of null cases. Suppose you have no dogs: is 'All your dogs are white' true, or is it false? Suppose there is no king of France: is 'The king of France is bald' true, or is it false? Russell took the first kind of statement to be true, the second false, and he was criticized by Strawson on the ground that in ordinary language the existence of some things denoted by the subject of a sentence is a necessary condition of its utterance's being either true or false.[1] But, as Lemmon has shown,[2] Strawson's theory cannot be systematically developed without the assumption of more than two truth-values. This complexity is sufficient to vitiate the theory, from a logical point of view. For when Russell extended the concept of true statement to include vacuous conditionals, and the concept of false statement to include vacuous definite descriptions, he escaped the complexity of a multi-valued logic without in any way licensing the deduction of false conclusions from true premisses. Admittedly Russell himself sometimes seemed to suggest that he was faithfully reproducing, rather than profitably refining, the concepts of everyday usage. In outlining his theory of definite descriptions he professed himself to be concerned with defining what is meant by the word 'the'.[3] But when we cease to treat language-sentences or sentences-in-use as the correlates of logical formulas, we can winnow out what Russell actually achieved from what he thought he was achieving, and recognize that though Strawson's criticisms have some force against the latter they have none against Russell's contribution to formal logic.

More pertinently to the present book someone might object to the logical system O4, developed in the previous chapter, that it cannot represent the ordinary concept of entailment because it embraces the so-called paradoxes of strict implication (meta-theorems 21–22). He might seek an alternative system of non-extensional logic, more faithful to the idiosyncrasies of 'entailment', much as Nelson, von Wright and others have sought to develop systems alternative to the Lewis calculuses.[4] The answer to be made to such an objector is not that there is in fact no discordance between the concept of entailment and that of

[1] *Introduction to Logical Theory*, p. 175.

[2] 'Quantifiers and Modal Operators', *Proc. Arist. Soc.*, lviii (1958), pp. 245 ff.

[3] *Introduction to Mathematical Philosophy* (1920), pp. 167 ff.

[4] Cf. e.g. E. J. Nelson, 'Intensional Relations', *Mind*, xxxix (1930), pp. 440 ff., and G. H. von Wright, *Logical Studies* (1957), pp. 166 ff.

strict implication, as J. Bennett has suggested,[1] but rather that the discordance which does exist is no demerit in Lewis's logic.

The term 'entails' was introduced by Moore to express 'the converse of that relation which we assert to hold between a particular proposition q and a particular proposition p, when we assert that q *follows from* or *is deducible from* p'.[2] Accordingly it is very doubtful whether a statement of which the truth is impossible should be said to entail, and a necessarily true statement to be entailed by, any statement whatever. Though this is implicitly a question about the everyday meaning of the phrases 'follow from' and 'is deducible from', it is nevertheless a question that no survey of everyday linguistic practice could answer affirmatively. For in everyday life as soon as we come to think a statement necessarily true we have no interest in premisses from which to deduce it and as soon as we have come to think a statement self-contradictory it is of no interest to us as a premiss for our further deductions. Even in *reductio ad absurdum* arguments we do not need to make any inference from a statement after we have shown it to be self-contradictory, and before then what we argue from it cannot, without circularity in the argument as a whole, depend on its self-contradictoriness. That is why the so-called paradoxes of strict implication cannot be attacked[3] on the ground that they undermine *reductio ad absurdum* argument by making everything deducible from self-contradictory premisses and not just some particular conclusion that is evidently absurd.

Nevertheless at least two kinds of argument have been advanced in attempts to show that a necessarily false statement does entail, just as it strictly implies, any statement whatever, and that a necessarily true statement is entailed by, just as it is strictly implied by, any statement whatever.

The first kind of argument rests on the claim that if even one self-contradictory statement could be true no restrictions whatever could operate and anything could be true.[4] But, though in everyday speech we normally do aim to operate within the usual restrictions by which to

[1] 'Meaning and Implication', *Mind*, lxiii (1954), pp. 451 ff.

[2] *Philosophical Studies* (1922), pp. 291 f.

[3] *Pace* G. H. von Wright, *Logical Studies* (1957), p. 174, and E. J. Lemmon, 'Quantifiers and Modal Operators', *Proc. Arist. Soc.*, lviii (1958), p. 265.

[4] Cf. e.g. J. Bennett, 'Meaning and Implication', pp. 462 f.

assert a statement to be true is to rule out its contradictory as false, it is nevertheless a moot point whether repudiation of this aim in some one instance implies repudiation of it in every instance.

The second kind of argument rests on an independent proof like Lewis's:[1] assume any self-contradictory statement A.~A; this entails A, and also entails ~A; but A entails AvB, where B is any statement whatever; and the conjunction of ~A and AvB entails B; so A.~A entails B. But it is a moot point whether any such proof can avoid reliance on some questionable assumption about the ordinary use of 'deducible from'. Lewis's proof, for instance, assumes that any conjunction entails each of its conjuncts, and his assumption does not seem to be supported by ordinary usage. If someone said 'I deduce from its being Tuesday today and Alexander's being a great general that it is Tuesday today', it would hardly be a malapropism to complain 'You haven't deduced anything at all, but have merely reiterated one of your premises: a statement can't follow from itself any more than an event can follow itself.' Not that the ordinary use of the phrase 'follow from' definitely excludes a statement from entailing itself in the way that it definitely excludes a statement from entailing its own contradictory: compare how a man can be said to succeed himself in office or to follow his own tracks in a blizzard. But ordinary usage does not definitely include self-entailment either. It is just that a simpler systematization of logic results from assuming that any statement entails itself than from assuming that none does or from making no relevant assumption at all. In short the position with regard to 'A entails A', 'A.B entails A', 'A entails AvB', 'A.B entails B.A', 'if A entails B, then A entails A.B', etc., is no better and no worse than the position with regard to '□~A entails (A entails B)'.

Indeed not only does this trouble about 'A entails A', etc., constitute a weakness in Lewis's alleged proofs of the strict implication paradoxes, and in attempts like Bennett's to refute Lewis's opponents.[2] It also makes the efforts of these opponents fall short of their mark. Von Wright's definition of entailment allows A.B to entail A.[3] Nelson's system is an interesting theory of intensional relations; but it is not the direct analysis of ordinary discourse it claims to be[4] because, while excluding 'A.B entails A' it still includes 'A entails A' among its

---

[1] *Symbolic Logic* (1932), p. 250.   [2] 'Meaning and Implication', p. 457.
[3] *Logical Studies*, pp. 181 and 187.   [4] Op. cit., pp. 440, 443.

theorems. Lewy's paradox[1] shows up an interesting difficulty in a notion of entailment that some logicians have entertained; but it is not a paradox about ordinary usage at all, because it assumes that, if A entails B, A entails the conjunction of A and B. Thus, while the common mistake on the one side has been to suppose that the concept of strict implication does not differ at all from that of entailment, the common mistake on the other has been to suppose that a system can readily be constructed that would both agree in every respect with the ordinary concept of entailment and yet also possess a worthwhile degree of deductive economy.

After all, it would be odd if in this relatively untutored field of linguistic practice a set of usages should exist that without any alteration or refinement serves not only the everyday purpose of ordinary discourse but also the scientific purposes of those who wish to construct a simple deductive system of mutually corroborating truths. Certainly no such set of usages was found by Euclid or Newton in *their* fields of study. Indeed a characteristic and often vital move in the construction of intellectual theories is so to extend or refine a concept that it comes to embrace what before was neither definitely included nor definitely excluded by it, but now appears as a limiting or null case of its previous usage. A line that has length but no breadth, a number that may be added to any number without increasing it, a motion that is insensible, a class that has no members, a vacuously true conditional, an implicate that does not differ from its implicans, an implicans that cannot possibly be true – all these have at different times been important innovations in the interest of theoretical economy. Some of them, like the concept of zero, have now so entered into our cultural heritage that in their cases no divergence of theoretical from ordinary usage is any longer apparent. Perhaps one day the concept of self-implication or of deduction from a statement already known to be self-contradictory will have so entered. If the practical need for an abacus-free system of arithmetical computation forced the concept of zero into everyday European discourse, perhaps the practical need for an intuition-free system of logical computation may one day bring modern formal logic, like Euclidean geometry and Arab arithmetic, into the schoolroom. But until that day those who seek to construct a reasonably economic deductive system in literal fidelity to the everyday usage of 'deducible

[1] 'Entailment', *Proc. Arist. Soc.*, Supp. Vol. xxxii (1958), pp. 123 ff.

from' are probably wasting their time. And even after that day it will be logical theory that will support *a priori* the (new) everyday usage of 'deducible from': the *a posteriori* facts of everyday usage can never do anything to support logical theory. Language may be justified by logic, but not logic by language.

§33. Does logic deny the possibility of an empty universe?

If the meanings that should be assigned to logical formulas are taken to be those of sayings rather than those of language-sentences, it is easier to see why one may disregard certain objections of von Wright, Lejewski and others to the standard calculus of predicates or to its standard interpretation. These objections are plausible, it will emerge, only on the mistaken assumption that it is language-sentences that are correlatable with logical formulas.

Von Wright considers that in the standard calculus of predicates the possibility of an empty universe is wrongly excluded and every property is wrongly ascribed at least one positive or negative instance, in the sense that some sentence attributing the property to a thing is made either true or false. At its bluntest the feature to which he objects is found in the theorem '$(\exists x)(Fxv{\sim}Fx)$', which he implies not to be a truth of logic at all because it 'disagrees with the possibility that the universe may be empty'.[1] He has therefore proposed a calculus of predicates in which neither the supposed analogue of this theorem nor any of its corollaries, such as '$(x)Fx \supset (\exists x)Fx$' is provable.

Whether or not such theorems have a rightful place in a logic of predicates, it is very doubtful whether von Wright's own system is as compatible with the possibility of an empty universe as he supposes. The universality of a property, in his system, is said not to imply its existence. But it is not at all clear why this implication should fail to hold, in view of von Wright's definitions for universality and existence. A property is called universal by him if all instances of it are positive, and is said to exist if at least one instance of it is positive. But a thing is said to be a positive instance of a property if and only if a proposition that attributes the property to the thing is true, and a negative instance if and only if it is false. Hence, so far as von Wright's explicit definitions go, no sense is given to the notion of a property that is both universal

[1] 'On the Idea of Logical Truth' (1948) in *Logical Studies* (1957), pp. 22 ff.

and non-existent. To entertain this notion we require to suppose that if a certain non-existent property had instances they would all be positive ones. But what can this mean for von Wright, unless it be that if certain strings of words expressed propositions, which they do not, the propositions would all be true? Further, why are these strings of words to be supposed incapable of expressing propositions, unless it be that their domain of discourse is supposed to be empty? But, if that is the reason, von Wright's system is not genuinely compatible with the possibility of an empty universe, because the system seems to presuppose that such a universe can never be the topic of propositional discussion.

Lejewski, on the other hand, believes that the standard calculus of predicates is not at fault, but only its standard interpretation.[1] The quantifiers, on his view, should not be assigned any existential significance. Suppose we take '$(\exists x)Fx$' to be equivalent to, or implied by, the expansion '$FavFbvFc\ldots$', and '$(x)Fx$' to be equivalent to, or imply, the expansion '$Fa.Fb.Fc\ldots$' If we then take 'a', 'b', 'c', etc., to designate objects in the universe, we must assign an existential significance to our quantifiers. But Lejewski suggests that if we take 'a', 'b', 'c', etc., merely as meaningful noun-expressions, which may or may not designate objects in the universe, our quantifiers need have no existential import and the controversial formulas will not imply, when interpreted, that something exists. On this interpretation, he believes, all theorems of the standard predicate calculus turn out to be patterns of logical truth that hold as well for reasoning with empty noun-expressions as with non-empty ones, and are as valid for the empty universe as for any other. For example, on the standard interpretation he thinks that '$(x)Fx\supset Fy$' and '$Fy\supset(\exists x)Fx$' are liable to lead to obvious paralogisms when 'Pegasus' is put for 'y', and 'exists' or 'does not exist', respectively, for 'F'. But on his own interpretation Lejewski claims that these formulas can be taken to express logical laws for the safe use of which one does not have to know whether the noun-expressions put for 'y' are empty or not.

Though Lejewski's reinterpretation of the predicate calculus is obviously uneconomical to the extent that it requires some other symbol than a quantifier to express the notion of existence, this lack of

---

[1] 'Logic and Existence', *British Journal for the Philosophy of Science*, v (1955), pp. 104 ff.

economy would be negligible if it were the sole price paid to avert a genuine paralogism. But it turns out that a much heavier price must also be paid.

The trouble is that if we try to interpret the standard predicate calculus along Lejewski's lines we run into paradoxes about predication in the empty universe. Take any empty noun-expression 'y'. On Lejewski's interpretation 'Fyv∼Fy' is a logical truth whatever meaning we assign to 'F', and so is '∼(Fy.∼Fy)'. Of the two statements 'Fy' and '∼Fy' one must be true and the other false. But how are we to tell which is true and which is false, since neither is deducible within the system? If 'exists' is put for 'F' there is no difficulty: 'Fy' is false and '∼Fy' is true, because *ex hypothesi* 'y' is empty. But suppose some other predicate-expression, like 'is winged', 'is unwinged', 'is hot', 'is cold', etc., is put for 'F'. There seems no conceivable reason for assigning one truth-value to 'Fy' and the other to '∼Fy', though perhaps, if it had not been for the theorems 'Fyv∼Fy' and '∼(Fy.∼Fy)', we might plausibly have said that both are equally true, because there can be no evidence against either, or that both are equally false because there can be no evidence in favour of either.

In other words, if the theorems '(x)(Fxv∼Fx)' and '(x)∼(Fx.∼Fx)' are to be valid for the empty universe we have to assume that of every predicate and its contradictory one but not the other holds for the empty universe. But whatever can there be in the empty universe that makes this so for any ordinary pair of mutually contradictory predicates as well as for 'exists' and 'does not exist'? What intelligible truth-conditions can there be for such predicates? We cannot even hope to divide all predicates into two groups, such that truth for the empty universe could be quite arbitrarily assigned to members of one group and falsehood to members of the other. For in order to do this we should need to know the truth-value of every statement of the form '(x)(Fx⊃Gx)', in case we mistakenly decided to make 'F' hold for the empty universe and 'G' not. Nor could we just make all atomic statements, like 'Fy' and 'Gy', false, and their denials correspondingly true, where 'y' is empty. This neat procedure is favoured by Quine where singular terms are retained in a standard interpretation of the predicate calculus,[1] since 'Fy' is certainly false when 'y' is empty and 'F' is read 'exists'. But the trouble for Lejewski with this assignment of truth-

[1] *From a Logical Point of View*, p. 166.

values would be that it would require all generalizations of the form '(x)($\sim$Fx$\supset$Gx)' to be false, if we are not to be plunged in antinomy with regard to the truth-value of 'Ga'. If 'a' is empty, 'Ga' will be false, because atomic; but '$\sim$Fa' will be true and if '(x)($\sim$Fx$\supset$Gx)' is also true, so must 'Ga' be. Can we always expect to be safe in denying, if our domain of discourse is the animal world, for instance, that anything not oviparous is mammalian, or if our domain is the physical universe, that anything not containing carbon is a mineral, or if our domain is even wider, that anything not physical is mental? It is not open to Lejewski, as it is to Quine, to circumvent these difficulties by refusing to apply the principle of universal instantiation in the case of empty noun-expressions, for it is an essential part of his purpose to ensure that all the basic principles of predicate logic are in fact applicable in such cases. Hence, on Lejewski's interpretation, we shall certainly avoid the alleged risk of paralogism in applying certain principles to the predicates 'exist' and 'does not exist' without knowing whether our noun-expressions are empty or not. But we shall do so at the cost of not being able to give the full truth-conditions for any predicate except 'exists' and 'does not exist' without knowing the truth-value of very many generalizations in which it occurs. Lejewski's interpretation simplifies the task of interpreting the quantifiers at the cost of making it wellnigh impossible to interpret fully most of the predicate letters. When this interpretation prevents the quantifiers from representing the notion of existence, it does so at the cost of preventing the predicate letters from representing any other notion as fully.

Nor can Lejewski get out of the difficulty by being content to leave it unspecified how we are to say which predicates, apart from 'exists' and 'does not exist', hold for the empty universe and which do not. For he cannot then claim to have devised a way of interpreting the standard predicate calculus that makes it as valid for the empty universe as for all others. The empty universe would constitute a special case for which a fully adequate interpretation can be given to very few of the calculus's predicate letters. He might just as well admit that as a theory of predicates his system does not apply to the empty universe because it allows nothing meaningful and consistent to be said about the contents of this universe except that they do not exist. Correspondingly he might just as well abandon his claim to accommodate empty noun-expressions. For, where 'y' is an empty but meaningful noun-expression, 'Fy' must now be almost always meaningless, since no rule for appraising its truth-value can be given unless 'F' is read 'exists' or 'does not exist'. Not that a proposal for interpreting the predicate calculus is obliged to give defining conditions of application for every predicate in every universe of discourse where the interpretation is to apply. But it must at least show in principle how this could safely be done without supposing factual omniscience. Admittedly, even when 'y' is empty, 'Fy' is still well-formed and the connectives in such theorems as 'Fyv~Fy' and '~(Fy.~Fy)' still have their meanings as logical constants. But when no truth-conditions can be given for 'Fy', 'F' is not on all fours as a predicate with 'exists', nor is the empty universe on all fours, in regard to the applicability of predicate logic, with non-empty universes.

Hence Lejewski's proposal for interpreting the standard predicate calculus fails to achieve its purpose, and the arguments against Lejewski's proposal would hold equally well against any other proposal to reinterpret the calculus's quantifiers so as to permit quantification over an empty domain. If we think that a logic of predicates should embrace the empty universe in its scope of application, we have no choice but to abandon the standard calculus altogether and to adopt some other basis for our logic, though von Wright's system, as already shown, will not serve the purpose. But there are good reasons to suppose it right for a logic of predicates to exclude, rather than include, the possibility of an empty domain of discourse.

Not that Quine's reasons[1] are adequate for this supposition. Quine points out that quantificational schemata which are valid for all choices of universe of a given size also turn out valid for all smaller universes that are not altogether empty. Thus nothing is gained if in formulating the laws of quantification theory we disregard universes of, say, one to ten objects in the hope of obtaining further laws that will be useful for seriously large universes. For there are no further laws, no laws not holding also for universes of sizes one to ten. It is only when we come to the empty universe that certain laws, holding for all larger universes, fail any longer to hold. Quine argues therefore that we should 'put aside the one relatively inutile case of the empty universe, so as not cut ourselves off from laws applicable in all other cases'. But it is unsatisfactory to have to regard this as the only, or even the main argument, for disregarding the possibility of an empty universe. If there

[1] Ibid., pp. 161 f.

really are logical truths about the empty universe the economies obtained by omitting them from our systematization of logical truth are too dearly bought. If economy may be purchased here at the cost of comprehensiveness, then why not elsewhere also? The road seems open to those who would wish to disregard the logic of non-extensional discourse because all classical mathematics is extensional, and to advocates of other similar economies. Formal logic, so constructed, can no longer claim to be the impartial arbiter of all rational discourse. The problem of systematization is being shirked, not solved, once the ideal of comprehensiveness is sacrificed to considerations of economy. Certainly, in building a logical system we may need to determine the truth-value of certain statements about which ordinary usage is insufficiently explicit, as with vacuous conditionals and the so-called paradoxes of strict implication. But this enriches the system in the very act of simplifying it: to impoverish it for purposes of simplification is a much less profitable procedure.

Fortunately Quine's argument is not needed, because its supposition that there can be logical truths about the empty universe is mistaken. The notion of an empty domain of discourse is self-contradictory. What does it mean to say that such-or-such a term or universe is empty? This question seems *prima facie* answered if we say that a term is empty when it denotes nothing and a class is empty when it has no members. But such an answer would be insufficiently determinate. 'Pegasus' is commonly suggested as an example of a term that denotes nothing, and the class of winged horses as an example of a class that has no members. But these suggestions provide adequate examples only on the assumption that terrestrial, rather than celestial, fauna are the objects of discussion. Certainly classes do not vary their membership in accordance with how they are being discussed, but a language-phrase may vary in the class it denotes in accordance with its context of occurrence. The null class, in particular, is not so often denoted as logicians sometimes seem to suppose. It is fairly safe to say that there are no winged horses – that the class of winged horses is empty – if and only if what is meant is that the class of terrestrial fauna, which are under discussion, and the class of winged horses have no common member, or that the product of these two classes is the null class. Perhaps the word 'Pegasus' itself justifies a presumption that terrestrial fauna are under discussion. But this presumption might be rebutted by the specific assertion that Pegasus is a celestial or supernatural creature. Someone might then want to claim that the term 'celestial fauna' is empty: 'There are no angels, seraphs or Olympian demi-gods,' he will say, 'so Pegasus does not exist after all.' But here again one would want to know exactly what was being claimed. Is it that no such fauna are visible? Then what is meant is that the class of visible objects, which are under discussion, does not intersect with the class of celestial fauna: the two classes have no common member. Or is it rather that celestial fauna are not worth while postulating in scientific theory? Then what is meant is that the class of celestial fauna does not intersect with the class of objects now under discussion, viz. objects that are worth while postulating in scientific theory. In short, all our ordinary, non-analytic assertions of existence and non-existence require the implicit or explicit assumption of a domain of discourse. The invariant element in the meaning of 'there exists' is the assertion of intersection with such a class: the variable element depends on what domain is implicitly or explicitly specified. If a term is said to be empty, this is normally because it denotes no member of the given domain: if a class is said to be empty, this is because it does not intersect with the given domain. What sense therefore could be attached to the notion of such a domain's being empty? Certainly we could at one time take physical objects for our domain of discourse and then later, as followers of Berkeley perhaps, deny that there are any physical objects. But on the later occasion our domain of discourse would have changed to what Berkeley called real things, and we should be claiming that the class of real – perceived or perceiving – things, which are under discussion, did not intersect with that of physical objects. A domain of discourse, as such, is something about which questions of emptiness or non-emptiness do not arise: if you ask whether a certain domain is empty or not, you imply that it is not, at least then, your domain of discourse.

It follows that the formula '$(\exists x)(Fx \vee \sim Fx)$' cannot be interpreted in general as 'The universe of discourse is not empty.' After all, '$(\exists x)Fx$' would not be taken to say that the universe of discourse is not empty, but rather that the class of things that are F is not empty. Similarly '$(\exists x)(Fx \sim Fx)$' means that either the class of things that are F or the class of things that are not F is not empty. Hence it is no use objecting, like von Wright, that the ordinary predicate calculus on its standard interpretation excludes the possibility of an empty universe of discourse, for neither the inclusion nor the exclusion of this is conceivable. More-over the law represented by '$(\exists x)(Fx v \sim Fx)$' is in fact, as it should be, a universal condition on the predicability of terms in statements. No term is truly or falsely predicable within a given domain unless either it or its contradictory picks out the members of a class that intersects with the domain. Again, '$(x)Fx \supset (\exists x)Fx$' seems most objectionable where 'F' is taken to represent the same term as that which denotes the universe of discourse. For then from the truism that anything denoted by this term is denoted by it we seem entitled to infer the apparently contingent fact that the term is not empty. But the non-emptiness of 'F' here stems from our own decision to take as values for quantified variables only those entities that are denoted by 'F': it no longer even appears as a contingent fact when we remember that decision.

Nor are formulas like '$Fy \supset (\exists x)Fx$' likely to lead to paralogism, even when 'F' is taken to mean 'does not exist'. For if 'y' functions here as an individual constant it cannot be an empty term but must denote some element in the universe of discourse. If you want to put 'Pegasus' for 'y' then you must choose celestial fauna or some other suitable class as your domain of discourse. Of course a proper name might be assigned in error. You might assign the name 'Pegasus' to the only winged horse on earth, not knowing that winged horses do not exist on earth. But how could this lead, as Lejewski suggests it does, to paralogism – to the deduction of a false conclusion from true premisses? If you do not know that your term is empty, i.e. denotes no animal, you are not in a position to affirm the antecedent and detach the con-sequent from '$Fy \supset (\exists x)Fx$', where 'y' is read 'Pegasus' and 'F' is read 'does not exist'. If you do know that your term 'Pegasus' is empty on earth you should either refuse to read 'y' or any other in-dividual constant of your system as 'Pegasus', or refuse to confine your universe of discourse – the range of values for your quantified variables – to terrestrial fauna. In other words, for the safe use of '$Fy \supset (\exists x)Fx$' as a principle of inference, where 'F' is read 'does not exist' and quantifiers have their standard interpretation, we do indeed have to know, as Lejewski claims, whether the expression put for 'y' is empty or not relative to the chosen domain of discourse. But in effect this is just a case of the general requirement that, for the safe use of any provable formula $A \supset B$ as a principle of valid inference to the truth of B, we must first know the truth of A.

Why is it then that some logicians have been tempted to suppose that at least some logical laws should be taken to include the empty universe within their scope of application? The origin of the temptation can hardly be a crude confusion between admitting the concept of an empty term or of the null class and admitting the concept of an empty universe of discourse. It is more likely that these logicians have been led astray by the familiar and plausible, but erroneous, assumption that logical formulas primarily represent the meanings of language-sentences that contain no pronouns, demonstratives, forenames, inflected verbs or other expressions which characteristically vary their reference with their context of utterance. They have apparently supposed, to judge from the example offered by both Quine and Lejewski, that a language-word like 'Pegasus' does not vary its reference in this way, and must therefore be either empty or non-empty absolutely, irrespective of its context of utterance. After all, if some eternal language-sentence is correlatable with a logical formula like 'Fy', there must be some proper name of ordinary language that does not vary its reference and so is suited for correlation with an individual constant like 'y'. Hence a language-sentence like 'Pegasus is winged' comes to be thought deserving of correlation with a logical formula like 'Fy', and if 'Pegasus' is indeed absolutely empty, at least one individual letter of the predicate calculus thus comes to be thought entitled to an interpretation that would make it denote nothing. But it also seems a merely contingent fact that a certain array of phonemes or letters, like 'Pegasus', should be empty of denotation, and correspondingly one might be tempted to suppose that the non-emptiness of other noun-expressions, as Lejewski calls them, is equally contingent. Thus it comes to seem quite possible for any individual constant whatever to be empty, and therefore highly paradoxical to have '$(\exists x)(Fx \lor \sim Fx)$' as a theorem in one's predicate logic that is interpreted as 'There exists something which either is F or is not F.' The need seems apparent either for proposals like Quine's to 'put aside the relatively inutile case of the empty universe' and replace individual constants by definite descriptions, or for some new calculus, like von Wright's, or for some new interpretation of the old calculus, like Lejewski's.

On the other hand, once it is recognized that logical formulas must be taken to represent the meanings of sayings, not language-sentences, there is no longer any temptation to admit the possibility of an empty universe of discourse. We do not need to suppose that any language-word or language-phrase has an unchanging reference, and can admit that the same term may be predicated now in one domain of discourse, now in another. Hence no proper name need be absolutely empty, and every proper name may be assumed to denote an element in the domain of discourse in which it occurs. Strawson's sentence-in-use theory would also achieve this result. But it has already been shown to be unsatisfactory on other grounds; and Strawson himself seems to hold that law-sentences in general are independent of context, though in fact they very often vary their domain of discourse with their context, making now one saying now another. Certainly, all sayings that have the same domain of discourse may be regarded as belonging to a single theory. But each assignment of values to the quantified variables of the predicate calculus corresponds to just one such theory, and the predicate calculus may be interpreted by the same man on different occasions to articulate different theories. He need not interpret it once and for all to articulate a single theory – the supposed silver dollar section of the man's natural language. Quine himself emphasizes, it is true, that we should look to variables and quantification 'for evidence as to what a theory says that there is, not for evidence as to what there is'.[1] He does not claim that formal logic itself has any ontological commitments. But if he is right here and if from a logical point of view no one theory's ontology is superior to any other's then we have no *logical* ground for entertaining the possibility that any given theory's universe of discourse is empty or that it is non-empty. One theory may assert that another's universe is empty or non-empty, but it cannot consistently say this of its own. The alleged non-existence of Pegasus, centaurs and the other queer fauna of Greek mythology, is a thesis of zoology, not of Greek mythology. It is therefore not enough to point out that we should look to variables and quantification for evidence as to what a theory says that there is, rather than for evidence as to what there is. One must also avoid any assumption incompatible with this, such as the assumption that language-sentences are correlatable with logical formulas and that some language-words, like 'Pegasus', are absolutely empty.

---

[1] *From a Logical Point of View*, pp. 19, 103. Cf. *Word and Object*, p. 243. Contrast B. Russell, *Introduction to Mathematical Philosophy* (1920), pp. 169 f.

IX

Meaning and Vagueness

§34. Arguments from universal vagueness to universal indeterminacy

One advantage of distinguishing clearly between temporal and timeless semantics, and in particular between culture-sentences and sayings, is that it helps to show up the fallacy in the familiar philosophical argument that, because all, or nearly all, words are vague in meaning, therefore we cannot say definitely of every properly formulated statement whether it is true or false.

This argument appears in a variety of forms from C. S. Peirce's time onward. At its most sweeping it leads to a radical scepticism about the applicability of formal logic. 'All words', Russell once wrote, 'are attributable without doubt over a certain area, but become questionable within a penumbra, outside which they are again certainly not attributable.' The vagueness which belongs to words describing sensible qualities, like 'red', exists also, 'though in a lesser degree, in the quantitative words which science has tried hardest to make precise, such as a metre or a second', since 'all observations have a margin of error'. Because 'all non-logical words have this kind of vagueness, it follows that the conceptions of truth and falsehood, as applied to propositions composed of or containing non-logical words, are themselves more or less vague'. Thus, though the law of excluded middle would be true if precise symbols were employed, 'it is not true when symbols are vague, as in fact all symbols are'. Since 'traditional logic habitually assumes that precise symbols are being employed, . . . it is therefore not applicable to this terrestrial life, but only to an imagined celestial existence'.[1]

On C. S. Peirce's view it had been the law of non-contradiction rather than that of excluded middle which is restricted in scope by the

[1] 'Vagueness', *Australasian Journal of Philosophy*, i (1923), pp. 84 ff.

phenomenon of universal vagueness. In the case of any concept some statements in which it functions are both true and false, rather than, as Russell preferred to put it, neither true nor false. 'Every concept', he wrote, 'that is vague is liable to be self-contradictory in those respects in which it is vague. *No* concept, not even those of mathematics, is absolutely precise; and some of the most important for everyday use are extremely vague.' Peirce seems to have concluded not that formal logic is intrinsically inapplicable to ordinary discourse but rather that a new logic, 'a logic of vagueness', was required, which he said he had 'worked out with something like completeness';[1] and though Peirce's logic of vagueness has never been found various attempts have since been made to replace its loss.[2]

Other philosophers have been more interested in the difficulties they believe such universal vagueness puts in the path of empirical knowledge than in those it puts in the path of formal logic. They have argued, like F. Waismann, that there is something about most 'empirical concepts', even scientific ones, which prevents us from ever verifying conclusively most of our 'empirical statements'. This awkward characteristic is called 'open texture' by Waismann, not vagueness. He reserves 'vague' for what he considers the more familiar sense, in which a word like 'heap' is vague, while one like 'gold' is not. 'Vagueness can be remedied by giving more accurate rules, open texture cannot.' The open texture of a concept consists just in the fact that the concept has not been, and cannot ever be, defined in such a way as to cope with all possibilities of doubt about its usage. 'We introduce a concept and limit it in *some* directions; for instance, we define gold in contrast to some other metals such as alloys. This suffices for our present needs, and we do not probe any farther. We tend to *overlook* the fact that there are always other directions in which the concept has not been defined.' When we use such a concept in making a statement we may not have taken something into account that should after all be considered relevant to its usage. Therefore 'there will always remain a margin of uncertainty' as to the statement's truth-value. Thus on

---

[1] *Collected Papers*, ed. C. Hartshorne and P. Weiss (1931), 6.496, cf. 5.447–50 and 5.506.

[2] E.g. M. Black, 'Vagueness', *Philosophy of Science*, iv (1937), pp. 427 ff., and S. Körner, 'Reference, Vagueness and Necessity', *Philosophical Review*, lxvi (1957), pp. 363 ff.

Waismann's view it is not merely statements about borderline cases that are tainted with indeterminacy, but all or almost all empirical statements. He believes that this is 'rooted in the incompleteness of empirical description'. The moves in a game of chess or the bars of music in a sonata can be completely described from first to last, so that there need never be any indeterminacy about applying a notation for chess or music. But 'however far I go' in describing my hand 'I shall never reach a point where my description will be completed.' I may state 'its size, its shape, its colour, its tissue, the chemical compounds of its bones, its cells, and perhaps add some more particulars', but 'logically speaking, it is always possible to extend the description by adding some detail or other'. Hence we can never describe completely all the characteristics of the situations in which the word 'hand' is correctly used, and our inability to do so accounts for the inconclusiveness with which a statement using the word is verifiable.[1]

§35. The truism of universal vagueness

Waismann's statement of the argument has the merit of admitting a familiar sense of 'vague' in which we accept each other's statements that, relatively to such-and-such a context of use, such-and-such a word is not vague. 'Gold' is not at all a vague word if we are listing the minerals found in a country, though 'much' might be. But Peirce and Russell are right in stressing that in the sense in which all empirical words are vague so are all other words. Concepts like number and proof have shown as marked a tendency to require revision in the development of mathematics as concepts like mass and explanation in physics, and at the points at which they have required revision their application has been doubtful. The standard musical notation of Europe is not at all precise, *pace* Waismann, when it comes to transcribing Indian or African melodies. Even chess-notation becomes imprecise, and shows its open texture, when used to record moves in three-dimensional chess. Conversely our everyday vocabulary would seem as precise as ordinary chess-notation is for two-dimensional chess if we never used it on borderline cases. But it is just these cases that philosophers like Peirce, Russell and Waismann will not let us ignore.

It is perhaps worth adding that the thesis of universal vagueness is

[1] 'Verifiability', *Proc. Arist. Soc.*, Supp. Vol. xix (1945), pp. 119 ff.

asserted on the conceptual, not the verbal, plane of discourse about meaning. Philosophers assert it, not philologists, and the illustrations they give are as apposite in French or Japanese as in English. It is often explicitly to a concept like that of gold, rather than to a French word, like 'or', that they attribute vagueness, and historians of thought, not of language, record the successive redefinitions of 'gold' which this vagueness permits or occasions. For such purposes the normal criteria of verbal semantics for sameness and difference of meaning are insufficiently sharp and subtle, as compared with those of conceptual semantics. Lexicographers cast a net of broader mesh, pulling in the main senses of the language-word, such as mineral, money, value or colour, but letting slip the finer and more specialized variations within these senses that historians of chemistry, economics or literature may choose to explore.

There is thus an obvious way in which the claim that all words are vague or open-textured may be understood to propound a truism. We may take its authors to be asserting that we should regard the meanings of culture-words as open in principle to an endless process of change and development in accordance with human needs. Instead of looking back on past segments of this process, like historians of ideas, they look forward towards that section of it which is still to come. They warn us so to order our thoughts about meaning that we shall always be intellectually prepared for encounters with situations where the applicability of familiar words and phrases is doubtful and where new customs of word-use or new locutions are therefore required. The kind of situation that often provoked changes of meaning in the past may recur again in the future. We are reminded, in effect, that the temporal mode of discourse about word-meanings has a prospective as well as a retrospective aspect. Interpreted in this sense the thesis of universal vagueness helps to define, not to describe, the universe of conceptual semantics.

What is crucial here is the conception of meanings as continuants with changing states or contents. A historian of ideas cannot afford to accept the Fregean theory of timeless meaning, or Moore's dictum that 'to define a concept is the same thing as to give an analysis of it'.[1] He must be able to define a concept that has different analyses at different

---

[1] 'A Reply to my Critics', *The Philosophy of G. E. Moore*, ed. P. A. Schilpp (1942), p. 665.

times. A man studying the transition of a concept from any one stage in its history to the next, or making a synchronous enquiry into the concept's variations between different regions or different social groups, cannot avoid having to find one way of referring to the concept as a continuant and another way of referring to each of its states. He need not seek one strand of meaning that continues throughout the whole history of the concept. The concept may have the unity of a thread spun from a succession of overlapping fibres rather than of a tailor's dummy that wears a succession of fashionable clothes. But for any one stage in the concept's history it must be possible to mention at least two distinct criteria for applying the relevant culture-word. One of these must be a necessary condition of the word's application both at that period and at some other, thus constituting a factor of continuity; and the other must be a sufficient condition of the word's application at that period, so as to constitute a current state of the concept. Because we have such cross-bearings on the modern concept of friendship, for instance, we can see it as a development from the ancient and medieval idea, preserving the factors of association, mutual benevolence and independence of kinship, while replacing those of exclusiveness and aristocratic solidarity by a warmly felt companionship of interests.

The absence of a necessary condition for a word's applying is a sufficient condition for its not applying. So that if in thinking about the meaning of a culture-word a man must be able to conceive distinctly both a continuant and its state he must thereby be able to conceive both a sufficient condition of the word's applying and a sufficient condition of its not applying. But conceivably – or at least, conceivably to a man of sufficiently more sophisticated culture than that he is studying – both these conditions might exist at once. Hence, the use of cross-bearings on a meaning, which is an indispensable feature of temporal semantics on the conceptual plane, always leaves it open in principle to say in a particular case that sufficient conditions are present both for the word to apply and for it not to apply, which is just how trouble arises when people cannot say whether or not a postage-stamp is red or a coin gold. 'In a dull light the stamp looks quite the colour of blood,' they may say, 'but in sunshine it has the glint of a Brazilian orange.' Their difficulty would not have arisen if they had been using just one criterion, not two. Something may evidently satisfy two criteria at once, but one criterion is either evidently satisfied or not. Hence the thesis of universal vagueness could only be opposed with reason by someone who conceived meanings in the old pre-Herder way and therefore denied the need for at least two distinct criteria or by someone who accepted the need for cross-bearings but thought it possible to discover sufficient conditions for a word's applying and for its not applying that could not ever be present in the same case. The latter opponent would be a man who somehow thought, like Descartes or Leibniz, that sooner or later all scientific enquiries will be finally completed and absolutely reliable correlations established between what can or cannot be present with what. It follows that if one does not wish to revert to either of these out-dated positions, both of which in their different ways tend to block the path of intellectual enquiry, one must accept the thesis of universal vagueness.

Indeed, just as rejecting an atomic theory of concepts commits one to the thesis of universal vagueness unless one reverts to the old Descartes-Leibniz conception of science, so too the thesis of universal vagueness commits one to rejecting an atomic theory of concepts as described in §11. For if we can conceive a borderline case for the applicability of a given culture-word we must also be able to conceive a standard case. The borderline case must resemble the standard one in satisfying some sufficient condition of the word's applying, and differ from it in not satisfying some necessary condition. So the word must have at least two criteria of application: it does not express an atomic concept.

§36. The fallacy of universal indeterminacy

It is doubtful, however, whether philosophers like Peirce, Russell and Waismann should be credited with such an innocuous truism when they claim that all words are vague or open-textured, since they take their claim to imply something paradoxical about truth-values or verification. They seem to take a thesis that is necessarily true for the universe of temporal semantics on the conceptual plane to retain its necessary truth in the timeless discourse about meanings in which questions of truth or falsity arise. Any sufficiently concrete example will illustrate the fallacy in their arguments.

Suppose a philatelist in doubt whether to call a new postage-stamp red or not, because it seems to resemble in equal measure a specimen named 'red' on his colour-chart and another named 'orange'. He has sufficient reason to call it red, and sufficient reason not to do so, and his predicament instantiates the truism that all concepts in human use are liable to show their intrinsic vagueness from time to time. What should he do? He could call it red or orange in terms of the existing colour-chart's definition, and what he said would then not be either both true and not-false, or both false and not-true. But he could also change the colour-chart appropriately and therewith his official concept of redness, so that it would now be definitely true or definitely false for him to say 'The stamp is red.' Hence the vagueness ascribable to the concept of redness as to all other concepts from the temporal point of view need not lead to a corresponding indeterminacy of truth-value in all the statements in which the concept is used. The vagueness of the culture-word 'red' does not imply the vagueness of every term or saying-word 'red', at least so far as the latter vagueness creates indeterminacy.

It is a curious fact that philosophers have often been interested in verification and falsification, the procedures by which the truth-value of an assertive saying is established appropriately to an assumed meaning for it, but rarely in the opposite procedure by which the meaning of a sentence is established appropriately to an assumed truth-value. They have been interested in the verification of sayings rather than in the adaptation of culture-sentences to the purposes of true, or false, assertion. Recent philosophical literature is full of distinctions between verification and proof, between weak and strong, direct and indirect, verification, between verifiability and falsifiability, or between what is verifiable or falsifiable and what is not. But little has been said about the various ways of adapting meaning to truth-value or the limits within which meanings are thus adaptable. Yet not only are such precisifications integral to the preparation of any careful statement about a complex or unfamiliar situation, whether it be a judge's interpretation of a difficult part of the law, a botanist's description of a newly discovered species, or an experimenter's specification of margins of error in his measurements. Not only has the concept of precisification an important bearing on the classical problem of induction, as will be shown in §§38–40. Precisification also has a specially useful role in the familiar philosophical solutions of *prima facie* dilemmas through distinctions between the sense in which it is true to say that a man is a free agent and the sense in which it is not, or between the sense in which he sees how things seem and the sense in which he sees them as they are.

Perhaps the failure of most philosophers to take a reflective interest in the process of adapting meanings to truth-values is one reason why some of them have ignored this process in their arguments from the thesis of universal vagueness. Peirce and Russell seem to have supposed, in effect, that the philatelist in a quandary about how to describe the colour of a new stamp can do no better than produce a sentence that breaks the law of non-contradiction or the law of excluded middle. For if he can in principle do better than this why should we accept such a sentence as a statement for the purposes of constructing our formal logic? It is hardly to be expected that sentential logic should include every inchoate attempt at assertion as well as normally determinate statements. If the total absence of a subject or of a predicate, or the vagueness that makes it impossible to say whether the subject of one clause is also the subject of the next, excludes a sentence from the logical domain, it is not unreasonable to suppose that the lack of a definite truth-value does likewise. At any rate it is not evident from the truism of universal vagueness that if we constructed our general logic on this supposition we should ignore anything important. For example, suppose we wished to consider the logic of sayings that are indeterminate with regard to analyticity or syntheticity. Then admittedly, if 'p' were such a saying, the statement 'It is analytic that p' would be neither true nor false. But nothing much is lost for logic by excluding this saying, since 'It is a truth worthy of linguistic entrenchment that p' or 'Any culture-sentence uttered in a statement that p is more normally uttered to make an analytically true statement' could still be either true or false. There do not seem to be any useful patterns of argument in which the argument's validity requires some of the sayings in it to have no definite truth-value just because a culture-word occurring in them has not been defined with sufficient precision. Peirce and Russell have not established that we cannot afford to treat conformity to the laws of non-contradiction and excluded middle as a necessary condition on what is to count as an assertive saying for the purposes of formal logic, at least outside the special field of mathematics. A special logic of vagueness may well be interesting, but it is not indispensable.

In short, it is quite true that for any culture-word a borderline case is always conceivable. But it is equally true that for any conceivable borderline case the culture-word can be redefined so as to preserve the laws of two-valued logic. In this alternating cycle of borderline cases and redefinitions a logician has to decide which phase of the cycle to take as normal and which as deviant. If he views his subject as a descriptive science of all possible worlds he will have to take the border-line cases seriously. But if instead he views it best as prescribing the topic-neutral conditions of statement and predication he can justifiably confine his attention to terms and statements that are precise enough for the requirements of two-valued logic, since the admission of three truth-values is for ordinary purposes an unnecessary and extravagant complication.

Someone may object that, since logic is concerned with the validity of arguments rather than the truth or falsity of their premisses, it is unsatisfactory to require the establishment of some definite truth-value for all the sayings involved before one can apply the technique of logical formalization to a given argument. That is so, but it constitutes no defence of the Peirce-Russell theory. One does not have to establish a definite truth-value for a supposedly assertive saying before being safe to formalize it, since the conclusions one draws from one's formalizations are in any case to be regarded as conditional on the sentence's satisfying the axioms of one's logical system. A two-valued logic is in the same position here as a multi-valued one, as Euclidean geometry, and as any other deductive system. The theorems need not hold for anything except what satisfies the axioms, but one need not find out whether something satisfies the axioms before finding out what would be the case if it did.

Waismann's form of the argument does consider the adaptation of meanings to truth-values. But he concludes nevertheless that it can never be finally established whether this process of adaptation has succeeded. Because there are always directions in which a concept has not been defined and aspects of a particular that have not been completely described, the particular may yet turn out to be not subsumable under the concept after all. Even when the philatelist has revised his colour-chart and therewith his concept of redness, he may find that he has omitted to consider what the stamp looks like in moonlight, say, and that though it is now unmistakably red, by the new definition of redness, in bright sunshine, it is still much more like orange in moonlight. But this kind of argument is unfair to the philatelist. It assumes that his conception of the stamp always lags at least one step behind his concept of redness. It assumes that when he predicates redness of the stamp he delimits his concept of redness but not quite sufficiently for his conception of the stamp. Why should he not be assumed to delimit the subject of his assertion *pari passu* with its predicate? On this assumption if he says that the stamp is red he would be implying that if the object under examination is considered in those respects, and in those respects only, in which redness has been defined it turns out to be red. The meaning of his saying-sentence is to be construed in terms of factors in the situation to which he might reasonably be expected to pay attention and the sentence's truth-value is to be established in terms of the meaning so construed, not in terms of any meaning that new approaches to the description of postage-stamps might give the same culture-sentence.

The everyday distinction between complete and incomplete description testifies to this being the way in which the meaning of a saying-sentence is normally determined. A stamp's description would be said to be complete if, say, its provenance, paper, size, face-value, design and colour in midday sunlight had been detailed, and incomplete if one of those features had been disregarded. The description is judged by the relevant standards of completeness operative at the time, not by some metaphysical standard of absolute completeness that would make all finitely long descriptions incomplete and thus put complete descriptions beyond the reach of mortal beings. But if the stamp is completely described when just such-and-such features have been described then the colour-chart can be designed to cope with just those features. No doubt the relevant standards of completeness may alter, and therewith the concept of a postage-stamp, much as the relevant concept of redness may also alter. But at any one period the meaning of a saying-sentence 'The stamp is red' needs to be judged in terms of both concepts' current forms. It is not surprising that Waismann's argument produces the paradoxical conclusion that no statement is conclusively verifiable, since it relies on the false premiss that though the words to be used as predicates may be redefined in adapting meanings to truth-value the words to be used as subjects must remain for ever the same in meaning. The meanings of the former are temporal, precisifiable, relative to human purposes; those of the latter are timeless, unchangeable, absolute. Yet the same words function now in subject-phrases, now in predicate-phrases, and if we can change or limit their meaning in one role we can surely also do so in the other.

Perhaps one main source of temptation to suppose that subjects are somehow different from predicates in this respect is the feeling that when we refer to a postage-stamp or a hand (and especially when we use demonstrative pronouns) so as to ascribe it some characteristic, we direct attention right through the net of concepts to some concrete particular in unconceptualized reality. But when someone asks for a full description of what we are referring to, or includes it in a count, or denies that he sees it, we should have to admit that it had after all been caught in the net. It is not counted as one particular, but as one piece of paper rather than two heraldic emblems; and a man perhaps sees the envelope without seeing the stamp on it – he does not see or fail to see a particular. The core of truth in the feeling that the subjects of discourse are inexhaustibly concrete, that their descriptions can never be absolutely completed, derives from the truism that all culture-words are intrinsically vague. The inexhaustible concreteness of particulars is just as much part of the indefinite changeability of concepts, and the non-existence of any single norm-setting or ideal language, as is the open texture of descriptive terms. When people think up new determinables under which to classify members of a familiar universe of discourse they alter their conception of this universe and thereby the criteria for membership of it: when they think up additional criteria for subsumption under a familiar concept they extend their standards of completeness for the description of anything that might conceivably fall under it.

But though these meanings in a culture are essentially fluid the meanings of people's remarks are not. The meaning of a saying-sentence is fixed by the circumstances of its utterance, and there is no reason in principle why the philatelist cannot contrive to say something about his stamp's colour that is conclusively verifiable and therefore subject to the laws of non-contradiction and excluded middle. All he has to ensure is that requisite developments in his concept of a postage-stamp and requisite developments in his concept of redness are co-ordinated with one another, and that when he utters the culture-sentence 'The stamp is red' it is clear what form those developments have taken in his case and to which stamp he is referring. Of course, if culture-sentences with fixed references, instead of sayings, were taken to constitute the objects of verification and the domain of propositional logic, both forms of the argument for universal indeterminacy would succeed, because the meanings of culture-sentences are intrinsically fluid. Nothing would be conclusively verifiable and nothing would obey the laws of non-contradiction and excluded middle. But to see this is to see part of what is gained by insisting that verification and logical analysis are or ought to be concerned with sayings, not with culture-sentences, and constitute or should constitute a form of timeless, not temporal, discourse about meaning.

X

The Concept of Meaning in the Problem
of Natural Necessity

---

§37. Is there a satisfactory theory of natural necessity?

Most people believe, and believe correctly, that if a man throws a stone into the air it *must*, under normal circumstances, fall to the ground. What goes up, runs the adage, *must* come down. But what accounts for the use of the term 'must' in such generalizations or for the use of closely related terms like 'necessarily', 'causally impossible', 'prevents', 'produces', etc.? Answers to this question have often been proposed, but at least seven of the most familiar proposals are unsatisfactory for various reasons. A review of those reasons will show just how much a new approach to the problem is needed, and the distinctions drawn in earlier chapters of the present book will enable such an approach to be made.

Consider Hume's theory first. Insisting, as he put it, that 'all our simple ideas in their first appearance are deriv'd from simple impressions, which are correspondent to them, and which they exactly represent', Hume argued that in no single instance of the operation of body on body, or of mind on body, could we find any impression from which the idea of a necessary connection between events might derive. All we ever perceive in cases where we affirm one kind of event to cause another is just the one event constantly followed by the other. Accordingly Hume contended that our idea of necessity in such cases can only arise from a certain feeling or impression their repetition generates in the mind. There is no impression, he argued, 'that has any relation to the present business, but that propensity, which custom produces, to pass from an object to the idea of its usual attendant'. It is this origin of the idea of necessity that determines the 'true meaning' of statements about necessary connections between objects. When we say, for instance, that the vibration of this string is the cause of this particular sound, we 'either mean that this vibration is followed by this sound, and that all similar vibrations have been followed by similar sounds: or, that this vibration is followed by this sound, and that upon the appearance of one the mind anticipates the senses, and forms immediately an idea of the other'.[1]

But expressions like 'it is physically necessary that' are frequently used in ways to which Hume's account of their meaning is quite inapplicable. In the first place statements about necessary connections of a comparatively specific nature are often inferred from established laws or theories of much greater generality in circumstances other than those that Hume's account would lead one to expect. Such assertions are often inferred even when no one has yet had the opportunity to form the relevant association of ideas because no one has yet observed the particular conjunction of events that is being asserted. The inevitable course of a satellite in orbit may be known before ever a rocket powerful enough to project it has been constructed.

Perhaps Hume's doctrine could plausibly be modified to meet this objection. Statements about necessary connections can be said either to have the meaning Hume proposed or to be deducible from statements which have such a meaning. But there is another and more serious objection to Hume. If statements about necessary connections mean what he says they do, then the rules he proposes[2] for telling when one kind of event is in fact the cause of another are quite insufficient. In addition to checking over the relations between the events concerned in the various ways prescribed by these rules we must also check over the relations between the ideas of all those who perceive these events. We must make sure that upon the appearance of the one event their minds always anticipate the appearance of the other; for, if this is part of what a causal statement means, the truth of the statement will in part depend on its being so. But manifestly this kind of check is neither commonly practised nor readily practicable.

Perhaps someone may suggest that Hume has merely been careless in saying that statements about necessary connections 'mean that' the mind behaves in such-and-such ways. What he should have said, it may be urged, is that these statements merely 'express' certain mental propensities, and do not assert them: if the existence of those propensities

---

[1] *Treatise of Human Nature*, ed. L. A. Selby-Bigge (1888), pp. 4, 162, 165; *Enquiry concerning the Human Understanding*, ed. Selby-Bigge (1902), p. 77.

[2] *Treatise*, pp. 173 ff.

is said to be their meaning, then the word 'meaning' here is used in the sense of expressive rather than informative content. But even if we accept this distinction between 'expressive' and 'informative' meaning we cannot use it to save Hume's account of statements about necessary connections. The phrase 'it is physically necessary that' must be taken to function informatively in such statements rather than expressively. This is because its occurrence in a statement generates non-extensionality in the clause or clauses that fall within its scope, as has been illustrated with similar phrases like 'it is chemically certain that' or 'it is a causal law that' in §24, and all statements formed by non-extensionality-generating operators on sayings have been shown in §25 to be equivalent for logical purposes to statements about these sayings. To say 'The vibration of this string must be followed by this particular sound' is therefore tantamount to saying something informative about the statement 'The vibration of this string is followed by this particular sound' rather than just to repeating that statement in a form which expresses a certain attitude or propensity of mind. The problem of natural necessity narrows down to the problem of exactly what information about the statement is thus conveyed. But this information need not be of an immediately experienceable kind. We do not have to accept Hume's supposition that we have what he called an 'idea' of necessity and must therefore also have what he called an 'impression' of which this idea is a copy. For we should reject his belief, which he shared with Locke and Berkeley (see §7), that the meaning of a sentence about necessary connections, or about any other matter, is to be understood in terms of the 'ideas' commonly associated with that sentence. If we look for the use of expressions like 'it is physically necessary that' rather than for some associated idea – if we study their function in human discourse rather than the state of mind of those who utter them – we shall not be confined in our search for their meaning to the comparatively narrow field of Hume's enquiries. We shall not have to refute his argument that we have no 'impression' of necessity in any single operation of body on body or mind on body.

Admittedly some philosophers have argued that the word 'necessary', and the various other idioms that generate a similar kind of non-extensionality, are quite dispensable in such contexts. Hume was right, they claim, to say that causal statements assert uniform conjunctions of events: beyond that we need not go. In science we need only talk about what does happen, not about what could or must happen. Quine, for example, admits that people sometimes do talk about what could happen if certain initial conditions were present, even though they accept that it will never happen because the appropriate conditions will never be present. But where 'could' goes beyond 'will', Quine suggests, the 'vast supplementary force of "could" ... is perhaps a vestige of Indo-European myth, fossilized in the subjunctive mood. ... Our basis for saying what "could" be generally consists ... in what *is* plus *simplicity* of the laws whereby we describe and extrapolate what is.' Quine deals similarly with any other subjunctive conditionals that are scientifically acceptable, as in the articulation of dispositional properties. 'To say that an object *a* is (water-) *soluble* at time *t* is to say that if *a* were in water at *t*, *a* would dissolve at *t*.' Such a statement seems to suggest that events of one kind may be connected with events of another kind by a bond that cannot be reduced to the mere constant conjunction of which Hume wrote, since the connection is asserted even of hypothetical and non-actual cases. Quine admits that the ordinary conditional of truth-functional logic – the conditional of Russell, Frege and Philo of Megara – would not suffice for logical reconstruction here, for it loses its point when the truth-value of its antecedent is known. If the antecedent is known to be true we might just as well assert the conjunction of this statement with the statement forming the consequent, and if the antecedent is known to be false the conditional is therewith known to be true; and 'we want to speak of *a* as soluble ... at *t* though knowing that it is not immersed ... at *t*'. But in such cases, Quine points out, science supplies us with a theory of 'subvisible structure'. 'What we have seen dissolve in water had, according to the theory, a structure suited to dissolving; and when now we speak of some new dry sugar lump as soluble we may be considered merely to be saying that it, whether destined for water or not, is similarly structured.' True, men talked easily of solubility before this explanation was at hand, 'but only because they already believed there was a hidden trait of some sort, structural or otherwise, that inhered in the substance and accounted for its dissolving on immersion'. In short, we can legitimately simplify our logical reconstructions if we paraphrase 'x is soluble' by '$(\exists y)(Mxy$ and y dissolves)', where 'M' corresponds to the words 'alike in molecular structure' in some appropriate sense.[1]

---

[1] From a *Logical Point of View*, p. 54, and *Word and Object*, pp. 222 ff.

Quine points out that 'such paraphrases would be strictly for regimentation of theory, ... not epistemological reduction'. But it is not at all clear that a theory so regimented would include all it should. The statement that something which does actually dissolve at some time has the same molecular structure as x would only be a satisfactory paraphrase for 'x is soluble' within a theory in which molecular structure was said to determine the presence or absence of solubility. Otherwise the structural similarity of x to an actual dissolver might be as irrelevant as its external similarity of shape or colour. What is needed somewhere in the logically regimented theory, therefore, is a way of saying at least that for any y and any z, if y dissolves in water at some time, then, if z has the same molecular structure as y, z would dissolve if immersed in water. But obviously this statement contains a generalized conditional of just that subjunctival form which Quine sets out to eliminate. For, if its domain of discourse is confined to objects that at some time are in fact immersed, x is not one of the values for z, and the statement does not achieve the relevance required of it; and if its domain includes objects that are never immersed then for that section of its domain it is trivially true. Even if there were a level of scientific theory where structural properties alone were described and all conditionals were therefore truth-functional in character, we should still need subjunctive conditionals to trace the consequences of such theory in our day-to-day lives, where experiments are sometimes done and sometimes left undone and proposals to make use of theory are sometimes successful and sometimes unsuccessful. If these important purposes of uttering subjunctive conditional sentences can never be served by theories about structural traits, Quine's proposal fails to satisfy his own criterion for adequacy of paraphrase. Even if at a certain level of theory all dispositions could profitably be 'conceived as built-in, enduring structural traits' in Quine's words, yet our total body of knowledge would be very much the poorer if we allowed such a conception to drive out altogether the everyday concept of a visibly testable disposition. Indeed, Quine himself writes at times as if the fact that a certain structure is 'suited to dissolving' is something that our theory should tell us.

Apparently, therefore, we cannot altogether dispense with idioms like 'it is physically necessary that' and the subjunctive conditional. These idioms are useful for distinguishing cases of supposed causal connection or natural law, which a barely truth-functional conditional is inadequate to describe, from cases of supposed coincidence, which such a conditional would describe quite adequately. At the experimental and technological level our science cannot dispense with these idioms, even though they may not be needed in articulating the more fundamental theories that explain our experimental results or the successes of our technology. Accordingly it has sometimes been suggested that the non-truth-functional element in subjunctive conditionals about the dissolving of sugar-lumps, say, consists just in their deducibility from more general theories about molecular structure, etc. 'Suppose', writes Braithwaite, 'that a person who has never considered whether or not there are any A's has come to accept a scientific deductive system in which the proposition that nothing is both A and non-B is deducible from higher-level hypotheses in the system'; and suppose these higher-level hypotheses 'have been established by induction from evidence which does not include any instances of the generalization "Every A is B". If the person then makes this deduction in the scientific system he will have confirmed the proposition "Nothing is both A and non-B" indirectly; if he regards the higher-level hypotheses as established, he will also regard it as established that nothing is both A and non-B, and will add this proposition to his body of rational belief. Now suppose that he subsequently discovers that in fact there are no A's. Had he acquired reasonable belief that there are no A's before he had acquired his reasonable belief that nothing is both A and non-B, he could have deduced this latter proposition from the former, and would not have required to establish it by deducing it from higher-level hypotheses in the scientific deductive system. But he did not do this; he arrived at his reasonable belief in the generalization "Nothing is both A and non-B" quite independently of his subsequently acquired belief that this generalization was "vacuously" satisfied. The assertion of a subjunctive conditional may be regarded as a summary statement of this whole situation.'

In short Braithwaite's theory about what differentiates a subjunctive conditional from a barely truth-functional one is not psychological, like Hume's theory of statements about necessary connections, but epistemological. The subjunctive conditional may be general as in 'Although there are no gases whose molecules have zero extension and do not attract one another, yet if there were to be such gases, all of them would obey Boyle's law, $PV =$ a constant', or it may be particular as in

'Although the wire of this picture did not break at noon yesterday, yet, had it done so, the picture would have then fallen to the floor.' In either case to assert it is to assert not only the correspondingly truth-functional conditional but also the deduction or deducibility of this conditional from hypotheses in an established scientific deductive system – conjoined, in the latter case, with any appropriate statements of initial conditions. Moreover Braithwaite extends the principle of this theory to cover the concept of a natural law also. 'The condition', he writes, 'for an established hypothesis h being *lawlike* (i.e. being, if true, a natural law) will then be that the hypothesis either occurs in an established scientific deductive system as a higher level hypothesis containing theoretical concepts', i.e. concepts like those of an electron, a wavefunction, a field of force, etc., 'or that it occurs in an established scientific deductive system as a deduction from higher level hypotheses which are supported by empirical evidence which is not direct evidence for h itself. This condition . . . will not exclude a hypothesis which is supported partly directly by evidence of its instances and partly indirectly by evidence of instances of same-level hypotheses which, along with it, are subsumed under a higher-level hypothesis.' But the condition 'will exclude a hypothesis for which the only evidence is evidence of instances of it'.

Braithwaite is not worried by this exclusion because 'a hypothesis to be regarded as a natural law must be a general proposition which can be thought to *explain* its instances'; and 'if the reason for believing the general proposition is solely direct knowledge of the truth of its instances, it will be felt to be a poor sort of explanation of these instances'. He does 'not wish to emphasize unduly this relation between explanation and natural law'. He grants that 'the marginal uses of both these concepts are indefinite, and the boundaries of their uses will certainly not agree'. Generally speaking, however, he considers that 'a true scientific hypothesis will be regarded as a law of nature if it has an explanatory function with regard to lower-level hypotheses or its instances'; and 'to the extent that a scientific hypothesis provides an explanation, to that extent will there be an inclination to endow it with the honourable status of natural law'.[1]

But the trouble is that, even if we follow Braithwaite in reserving the honorific title of 'natural law' for generalizations which can be thought

[1] *Scientific Explanation* (1953), pp. 297 ff.

to explain their instances, we have still to account for the way in which certain other expressions tend to generate non-extensionality. Braithwaite's theory implies that if a statement is neither a higher-level hypothesis, containing theoretical concepts, in an established scientific deductive system, nor yet deducible within such a system, it is not lawlike, and it does not provide sufficient ground for the assertion of any subjunctive conditional. But this is unduly restrictive on our discourse. Suppose we have a well-tried drug in our pharmacopoeia that has never been known to fail in curing a certain malady under certain specifiable conditions. Suppose too that it has also been subjected to properly organized clinical trials, with properly matched control groups, over a very large number of patients, with widely varied backgrounds, histories, constitutions, diets, etc. Suppose also, as is often the case for long periods, that the reason for the drug's efficacy in the specified conditions has up to now baffled all investigators: the biochemistry of its action in curing the malady is completely unknown. No hypothesis about the drug's curative power is deducible within any established scientific deductive system. According to Braithwaite's theory a physician would apparently do wrong to say about a patient of the specified kind who refused to be prescribed this medicine 'Although he did not take the drug, yet, had he done so, he would not then have died when he did.' No assertion of such a subjunctive conditional is warranted, despite all the evidence in favour of the drug. The patient would not only have been right, on Braithwaite's theory, in denying the title of 'natural law' to generalizations about the drug's curative power. He would also have been right in seeing no difference of truth-value between the physician's statement 'If you take this drug you will be cured' and his own statement 'If I take this drug I will not be cured', since if he is a good logician he knows both statements to be purely truth-functional conditionals and so to be rendered trivially true by his own firm intention of refusing the drug. This situation seems repugnant alike to good medical practice and to everyday ways of thinking. It is both usual and useful for a patient to suppose that a physician's statement 'If you take this drug you will be cured', which does not purport to be derivable within an established deductive system, must have some other backing than the physician's belief that the patient will not take the drug. Yet on Braithwaite's theory its meaning is such that it need have no other backing than this.

Perhaps someone may seek to defend Braithwaite's theory on the ground that even a single hypothesis, such as a generalization about a drug's curative power, can be regarded as constituting a scientific deductive system, albeit a system of minimal size. 'The system will have only one postulate,' he may say, 'and only one rule "From A derive A", but it is none the less a deductive system. The non-extensional character of the hypothesis derives from the restricted number of concepts in terms of which the system is set up, however large or small the system may be.'

But the whole point of Braithwaite's theory is lost if the notion of a deductive system is thus reduced to its limiting case. We require a good reason for not letting the law of extensionality apply, not just an arbitrary fiat that it shall not do so, which is in effect all we get when a single statement is said to constitute a system. The reason implicit in Braithwaite's theory was respectable enough, so far as it was relevant. It was that if an assertion of the form 'Every *A* is *B*' is not purely truth-functional the generalization is either a higher-level hypothesis containing theoretical concepts or deducible from such hypotheses and does not have to be supported by the evidence of its own instances. The trouble is that though many a pharmacological generalization belongs to neither of these two categories, because it contains no theoretical concepts and yet has to be supported by the evidence of its own instances, its assertion may nevertheless be not purely truth-functional. Even if the title of 'natural law' is perhaps somewhat too grand for generalizations of the kind that normally occur in or are implied by the text of a pharmacopoeia, we still need some other distinguishing rubric for those of them that are sufficiently well established, such as Hume's 'statements about necessary connections'. What is being claimed is not that all those sufferers who take the drug in the specified conditions are people who, as it happens, recover from the malady, but that their recovery is ensured by their medication: the sequence of medication and recovery is not a fortuitous but a necessary one. Unless this were so, such a generalization could not constitute a premiss for the deduction of particular subjunctive conditionals. Nothing would have been said except that as things actually turn out the antecedent is never satisfied without the consequent's also being so. Nothing would have been said about what would have happened if the antecedent had been satisfied in cases where in fact it was not. If you say that all your dogs happen to be white, you say nothing whatever about what the colour of your neighbour's present dog would have been if instead it had belonged to you: it might equally well have been white, brown or black. The assertion of a generalization must not be purely truth-functional if it is to serve as a premiss for subjunctive conditionals, and Braithwaite's theory does not allow a sufficient variety of generalizations to be of this kind.

It might therefore seem plausible to ignore Braithwaite's injection of an epistemological element into the analysis of such assertions, while retaining his belief that deducibility from higher-level statements is closely relevant. It might be claimed that if a connection is said to be physically necessary what is implied is that the statement of the connection is deducible from some true statement of higher level, whether or not such a statement has yet been discovered. This claim would in effect amount to accepting Popper's theory[1] on the subject. Popper stipulates that a statement 'may be said to be naturally or physically necessary if, and only if, it is deducible from a statement function which is satisfied in all worlds that differ from our world, if at all, only with respect to initial conditions'. He admits that the phrase 'all worlds that differ from our world, if at all, only with respect to initial conditions' contains implicitly the idea of laws of nature. 'What we mean is,' he says, 'all worlds which have the same structure – or the same natural laws – as our own world.' But Popper claims that his definition is not viciously circular. 'Its *definiens* operates with a perfectly clear intuitive idea – that of varying the initial conditions of our world; for example, the distances of the planets, their masses, and the mass of the sun.' Hence what the definiens does in effect is to relate the concept of physical necessity to the distinction between variations of structure and variations of initial conditions. It serves to clarify in one's mind just which kinds of statement one would normally regard as physically necessary. But it does not explain how one comes to have this concept of physical necessity. To explain that fact Popper proposes a theory which resembles Braithwaite's in referring to deducibility from higher-level statements, but differs in not supposing actual knowledge of these statements to be implied.

Popper agrees with Hume that if two events are necessarily connected the necessity of this connection is not to be found in the events

[1] *The Logic of Scientific Discovery* (1959), pp. 62 ff., 420 ff.

themselves. But he locates the necessity in the fact that the corresponding truth-functional conditional 'follows *with logical necessity* from a law of nature – that it is necessary, relative to a law of nature'. Moreover 'it may be said', he thinks, 'that a law of nature is necessary in its turn because it is logically derivable from, or explicable by, a law of a still higher degree of universality, or of greater "depth"'. Hence, on Popper's view, 'one might suppose that it is this logically necessary dependence upon true statements of higher universality, conjectured to exist, which suggested in the first instance the idea of "neccessary connection" between cause and effect'.

It is no use attacking Popper's theory on the ground that true universal statements are conceivable which will necessarily imply, though not be implied by, even the most obviously accidental truths such as the generalization that all your dogs are white. The conceivability of a true, and more universal, statement like 'All your pets are white' is insufficient, on Popper's view, to render such a generalization physically necessary. For the generalization is 'numerically' universal, but not 'strictly' so, in Popper's terminology. It 'refers only to a finite class of specific elements within a finite individual (or particular) spatio-temporal region' and does not claim 'to be true for any place and any time'. It 'can, in principle, be replaced by a conjunction of singular statements; for given sufficient time, one can *enumerate* all the elements of the (finite) class concerned', whereas a strictly universal statement cannot be so replaced. Popper admits that strict universality is not a sufficient condition for a true statement to be a law of nature or other assertion of physical necessity, since there can be strictly universal statements that are only true by accident. Extinct species of animals provide an obvious subject for such generalizations, and Popper cites 'All moas die before reaching the age of fifty' as an example of a strictly universal statement that might be accidentally true if one could assume that unfavourable circumstances, rather than biological structure, were responsible for the early deaths of the moas. But though strict universality is not a sufficient condition for a statement to be one of physical necessity it is nevertheless on Popper's view a necessary one. His theory would not allow 'All your dogs are white' to be made into a statement of physical necessity by the mere fact that statements of higher universality can be conceived which afford premises for its deduction. Certainly, it might be argued that the requirement of strict universality is not a good way to exclude such statements, because it excludes too much. No subjunctive conditional about an individual can then be a statement of natural necessity, nor can a numerically universal statement that owes its truth to being a particularization of some strictly universal one. The physician has no right to say 'If these patients are given such-and-such a drug they are bound to recover.' Even Kepler's laws are excluded from being statements of natural necessity. But Popper could perhaps surmount this apparent paradox in his theory by allowing a statement that is not strictly universal to be regarded as a statement of natural necessity so long as it was of the right kind in other respects. To call it a statement of natural necessity would have to imply its deducibility from premisses that consisted of a natural-law conditional conjoined with an assertion to the effect that its subject satisfied the antecedent of this conditional.

Nevertheless it becomes clear from the way in which Popper would have to deal with these difficulties that it is not the mere logical necessity of their implication by more universal statements that makes certain statements physically necessary. In each case it is the nature of these other statements that really counts. The fact that the term 'necessary' may be used of the implication can hardly play any part at all in suggesting that the implicates may also be said to be necessary, though physically rather than logically so. Otherwise we should expect to find yet a third form of necessity, belonging to those accidentally true statements which follow with logical necessity from accidental truths of higher universality. 'All your dogs are white' would be describable as 'accidentally necessary', say, because it follows with logical necessity from 'All your pets are white.' But the expression 'accidental necessity' is obviously absurd in this context, since the whole point of calling certain statements accidentally true is to mark them off as a purely matter-of-fact, purely truth-functional form of discourse – to contrast statements about what is the case with statements about what must be the case.

Once we accept this it becomes clear that Popper's theory, like Braithwaite's, says nothing to tell us *why* those strictly universal truths that are deducible from others or higher universality should be called 'necessary'. The most it could tell us is just that calling a statement physically necessary ascribes it this deducibility by implication. Even there the theory would probably be wrong, and certainly would need reformulation. It would probably be wrong because it is most unlikely that all the causal and law-like platitudes of everyday life, like 'What goes up must come down', originated in places and periods in which the notion of deducibility from statements of higher universality was also a commonplace. To judge from the very gradual growth and relatively late systematizations of sciences like geometry, chemistry, physics, etc., it seems much more likely that the conception of certain truths as truths of natural law or natural necessity, as distinct from merely accidental truths, arose long before it ever occurred to anyone, implicitly or explicitly, that such law-like statements might be arranged in hierarchies of higher and lower universality. Of course, it might be claimed that, even if human cultures had not always drawn this close connection between the concept of natural necessity and the concept of deducibility from strictly universal truths of higher universality, nevertheless the connection is one that ought to be drawn: if the concepts are not already interlocked in our language, as well as coinciding in their application, nevertheless they ought to be. But to this kind of claim Popper's formulation of his theory is quite inappropriate. His definition of higher universality renders it trivially easy to produce a statement of higher universality than a given statement such that the given statement is deducible from it.

Popper's definition runs as follows.[1] 'A universal conditional statement ... may be written in the form: "$(x)(\varphi x \supset fx)$" or in words: "All values of x which satisfy the statement function φx also satisfy the statement function fx".' Now, 'let p and q be two statements written in this "normal" form; then we can say that p is of greater universality than q if the antecedent statement function of p (which may be denoted by "$\varphi_p x$") is tautologically implied by (or logically deducible from), but not equivalent to, the corresponding statement function of q (which may be denoted by "$\varphi_q x$"; or in other words, if "$(x)(\varphi_q x \supset \varphi_p x)$" is *tautological* (or logically true)'. By this criterion 'All orbits of heavenly bodies are ellipses' – to quote an example of Popper's – is of greater universality than 'All orbits of planets are ellipses.' But so too is 'All orbits of planets, or ellipses, are ellipses.' Given any true statement of the form '$(x)(\varphi_p x \supset fx)$' we can obtain a true statement of greater universality by the simple expedient of defining a statement-function '$\varphi_q x$' as equivalent to the function '$\varphi_p x \vee fx$', where the symbol '$\vee$'

represents the term 'or'. Popper's criterion of greater universality would make all true truth-functional conditionals deducible from true statements of greater universality simply in virtue of their logical form. To say of a truth-functional conditional that it was so deducible would add nothing to what was already implied in calling it a truth-functional conditional. Instead of mentioning this deducibility one might just as well say quite simply that all strictly universal truths are, or ought to be, regarded as physically necessary.

Nor is it easy to see how the notion of greater universality can be protected from cheapening in this way. Even if Popper required in addition that p should only be considered of greater universality than q if q does not logically or analytically imply q, yet assuming only some strictly universal truth with the same consequent statement-function as a given one, though not analytically equivalent to it, we can always construct a truth of higher universality than the given statement. If all moas and dodos die before reaching the age of fifty, then 'All moas or dodos die before reaching the age of fifty' is of greater universality than 'All moas die before the age of fifty.' So long as we can assume that there is more than one strictly universal truth with any given consequent statement-function we have again no need to mention the deducibility requirement: on Popper's theory all strictly universal truths, even accidental ones like 'All moas die before reaching the age of fifty', turn out to be physically necessary.

It seems correct to conclude, in view of these various difficulties in theories like Braithwaite's and Popper's, that the concept of natural necessity cannot be accounted for in terms of systematization. The construction of deductive systems is no doubt a vital facet in the progress of natural science, but it cannot explain why we suppose the truth of some conditional statements to be physically necessary. Perhaps therefore we should consider instead whether this necessity does not lie rather in the deducibilities that such statements establish than in their own deducibility from other statements – in the inferences they themselves license rather than in the systems by which their assertion is licensed. It is sometimes argued, as by Toulmin,[1] for instance, that 'it is because, and only because a physical theory involves techniques of inference-drawing that a "must" enters in'. 'The important thing', he says, 'is not to confuse the questions, what theory *has been found*

[1] *The Philosophy of Science* (1953), pp. 94 ff.

reliable in a given field, and what phenomena according to this theory *must* occur in any given circumstances. When one is talking *about* a theory – whether establishing it, or identifying a system as one to which it applies – one is concerned with what has been found to be the case, not with what must be; but when one is talking *in terms of* a theory – applying it to explain or foretell the phenomena occurring in such-and-such a situation – one is then concerned with what, according to that theory, must happen in that situation.' In short, what lies behind the Lockean view of laws of nature as statements of necessary facts is the use of such laws as principles of inference: 'the necessity to which they point is the necessity with which conclusions follow when one argues in accordance with these principles'.

Toulmin's kind of theory, however, cannot account for what is really important in the concept of natural necessity. On his view any statement that may be used or reformulated as a principle of inference licenses a conclusion about what *must* be the case under certain conditions. But the trouble is that this 'must' need not always be the 'must' of natural necessity. If it is true that all your dogs are white, then we are licensed to infer, when told that Fido is one of your dogs, that Fido must be white. Toulmin's theory would not account for the fact that generalizations like 'All your dogs are white' are commonly thought not to be naturally necessary. On the contrary, the theory would lead one to suppose that these generalizations, too, express principles of natural necessity, and so the whole point of the distinction between accidental truths and truths of natural necessity would be lost. Admittedly, the 'must' of our conclusion that Fido must be white is a very trivial 'must' indeed, and so far from its being the 'must' of natural necessity one may well doubt whether it is anything but the 'must' of logical necessity, transposed into its usual idiomatic position. If so the use or reformulation of some general statement as a principle of inference is irrelevant to the matter, and what is implied in this use of 'must' is merely that given such a statement as a major premiss, and an appropriate subsumption under its subject as a minor, we cannot – logically cannot – avoid concluding that so-and-so. Use of the word 'must' may well make some other point also, or instead, when the major premiss is a law of nature or causal generalization. But this specifically natural function of 'must' cannot be elucidated or explained in any way along the lines of Toulmin's theory.

It may be thought, however, that while the distinction between necessary and accidental truth must at all costs be maintained the distinction between analytic and natural necessity is without foundation. This seems to be the view of those so-called conventionalist philosophers like Le Roy who think of science 'as nothing but a well-made language'. Scientific theories, they tell us, 'are essentially definitions of symbols, setting up the fundamental terms of the scientific vocabulary and the great laws of grammar that control the combinations of these'.[1] If this kind of conventionalism is correct it is easy to account for the non-extensionality of passages within the scope of such operators as 'it is a law of nature that' or 'it is causally necessary that'. By prefixing such operators to a saying we imply, according to the conventionalists, not only that the saying is true by definition but also that it is worded in accordance with the lexical and grammatical rules of the language which our factual beliefs have led us to adopt.

But this merger of analytic and natural necessity seems plausible only on a *de jure* theory of meaning in a language. It presupposes rules of word-use, which determine what may and may not properly be said: to call a statement analytic or necessary is to assert that its denial is excluded by these rules. A language is assimilated to a deductive system, where the constitutive rules control which statements may be asserted as theorems. If however we reject such a *de jure* theory, for reasons already canvassed in previous chapters, the concepts of analyticity and natural necessity fall apart from one another. Statements about analyticity require factual studies of word-use to back them, while statements about physical necessity are backed by experimental data which for the most part are non-linguistic. Within any one natural language, like English or French, both the assertion and the denial of an analytic truth are grammatically significant (conform to customary patterns of sentence-construction), while within any one scientific theory the same sentence cannot both be asserted and denied. Linguistic innovation requires a change in the customs of a speech-community: it may be initiated by the idiosyncratic usage of one individual, but it cannot be constituted by this alone. Theoretical innovation, on the other hand, can be the work of a single scientist and does not require any change in the customs of the scientific community as a whole. It

---

[1] 'Science et Philosophie', *Revue de Métaphysique et de Morale*, vii (1899), pp. 375 ff. and 503 ff. (esp. pp. 511, 528), and viii (1900), pp. 37 ff.

does not entail any linguistic convention. A language is a social fact, a theory the construct of one or more individuals.

Nor will it do to say therefore that theories are proposed languages rather than actual ones; for the general adoption of a theory is not at all like the general adoption of a language. When a certain community, hitherto perhaps using a variety of tribal languages, has come to adopt English as its common language, it is not construed as changing its mind about this as the English language slowly changes throughout the world. But to adopt a theory and then change it, is to change one's mind about the form or contents of the theory that should be adopted. Only if a language is conceived as something that is constituted once and for all by a set of lexical and grammatical rules, all deviation from which is impropriety, does it become plausible to suppose that a scientific theory is a proposed language. No doubt much of our most familiar experience tends gradually to become entrenched, one way or another, in our customs of word-use. Our visual experience of colour, for instance, has led to its being analytic in our culture that nothing is both green and blue all over at the same time. But if a scientific theory once gets into our language like this our minds are thereby much more closed to the possibility of its revision than if the language itself, as distinct from some of those who speak it, remained uncommitted to the theory. Indeed a good case could be made out for saying that many beliefs about what is physically necessary should never be allowed to become entrenched in our language, for fear of making it too difficult to envisage their need for revision. The progress of science has too often been held up in the past by conceptual prejudices that scientists acquired in their childhood language-learning. We should hardly wish to add many more such prejudices to our language. Having laboriously emancipated ourselves from the notion that nature has only three dimensions, for instance, we would do well not to enslave ourselves to the notion that she has just four. But, if this is so, to think of scientific theories as proposed languages would be to think of them as proposals that ought often to be rejected, even when the theories themselves, so far as is known, are unobjectionable. The conventionalist's identification of theory with language-proposal has then collapsed, since a theory is sometimes to be accepted while the corresponding language-proposal is to be rejected.

It might therefore be thought that what distinguishes physical from analytic necessity is the need for empirical research into the subject-matter of the relevant statements. The word 'necessity' may be supposed to have the same sense in both cases: it is just that if a statement were said to be physically necessary its truth would be implied open to confirmation or disconfirmation by the evidence of observation or experiment, while if it were said to be analytically necessary its truth would be implied to be *a priori*. Kneale seems to take a view somewhat of this kind.[1] There are, he holds, principles of natural necessity, and the word 'necessity' has precisely the same sense here as elsewhere. 'A principle of necessitation is a boundary of possibility, and we know quite well how possibility is bounded from consideration of such cases as the incompatibility of redness and greenness.' Such an incompatibility is not the product of arbitrary linguistic convention. 'It is, no doubt, arbitrary that we should forbid ourselves to use the shapes "red" and "green" together in a certain way, but only because it is arbitrary that we should use these shapes to mean red and green, respectively. It is not arbitrary that we should forbid ourselves to use together in that way those shapes, whatever they may be, which are to mean red and green. . . . The rule is not something which has been introduced by an unmotivated convention and without regard to the use of the shapes in the statement of empirical facts, but rather a necessary condition of their signifying what they do signify.' For 'if a sound or shape is to be a word with meaning, rules must be established for its use', and these must be of the form 'Do not say so-and-so, unless such-and-such is the case.' Hence according to Kneale 'to understand the meaning of a word such as "red" I must be able to recognize occasions on which the restrictive condition for its use in a statement is *not* fulfilled, and this is as much as to say that I must know some principles of incompatibility'. The rules of language 'incorporate our knowledge' of such principles. The only difference between these principles, on Kneale's view, and principles of natural necessity seems to be that the latter are not 'knowable *a priori*'.

But unfortunately Kneale does not explain how we can have principles that are incorporated in our language and yet not knowable *a priori*. Certainly, the distinction he goes on to draw between objects of perception, like lightning or sugar, and objects of sensation, like red or green, is hardly sufficient to explain this. By no means all *a*

[1] *Probability and Induction* (1949), pp. 80 ff., cf. pp. 34 ff.

priori knowable principles are concerned with what he calls objects of sensation, and so, even if all naturally necessary statements were concerned with what he calls objects of perception there would still be the problem of explaining why some statements concerned with these objects are naturally necessary and some, like 'Brothers are male siblings', are analytic. Kneale seems, in fact, to be in a dilemma. Either a principle of natural necessity is never knowable *a priori*, in which case it cannot be entrenched in language, or if such a principle is to be conceived as a principle of incompatibility entrenched in language, then it must be knowable *a priori*.

§38. Natural necessity conceived as a form of *a priori* truth

Certain positive conclusions emerge from these criticisms of existing theories. The concept of natural necessity must be distinguished with equal sharpness from the concept of analytic truth on the one side and that of accidental truth on the other. It must be capable of fitting isolated and independent statements as well as it fits certain statements in actual or conceivable deductive systems. To predicate it of a saying is to state something about that saying which suffices to bestow non-extensionality on any occurrence of a saying within the scope of the corresponding operators, such as 'it is physically necessary that', 'it is a causal law that', and so on. But these few results are far too jejune to provide the basis for a more satisfactory theory than those considered. They merely serve to impose certain conditions on the fresh attempt to get at the roots of the problem which is so obviously needed.

Why is the problem so difficult to solve? Clearly because we seem to be presented with an antinomy. On the one hand we cannot deny the role of observation and experiment in establishing the statements to which physical necessity is ascribed, on the other we cannot deny that to ascribe this necessity is to claim that such statements transcend the mere description of observable regularities. On the one hand the statements seem thoroughly empirical in content, on the other they seem to be thought capable of applying to the future without having any need to wait on future experience. On the one hand they seem testable and *a posteriori*, on the other they seem to anticipate observation and their necessity seems a form of *a priori* truth.

Most modern theories on the subject tend to accept the thesis of this antinomy wholeheartedly, and reject the antithesis by trying to explain away the appearance of *a priori* truth. Perhaps they claim, like Quine, that any such appearance can safely be disregarded, or they connect it, like Hume, with some alleged quirk of human nature, or they suppose that the quality of necessity somehow rubs off on to a statement, whether from the *a priori* validity of the logical principles that govern its derivation in a system of scientific theory or merely from the fact that it is so derivable. But for reasons already given none of these empiricist theories of natural necessity is satisfactory. The antithesis of the antinomy, however, is more rarely embraced: few philosophers seem willing to assert the *a priori* character of any scientific law. Their education in the history of philosophy has taught most of them to associate this kind of assertion with Plato's belief in a science of pure essences, with Descartes's rash claim to deduce the laws of nature from self-evident first principles, with Spinoza's neglect of the difference between pure and applied mathematics, or with Kant's unfortunate attempt to read a passing phase of scientific progress into the permanent structure of the human mind. Conventionalists like Le Roy are among the few who have freed themselves from such associations. They have sought to reconcile a conception of scientific laws as *a priori* truths with a repudiation of any such old-fashioned theories about how *a priori* truths are established. In their view fundamental *a priori* truths are invented rather than discovered. Though these truths are rooted in this or that language, we are free to adopt one language rather than another and to invent new ones. The trouble with Le Roy's theory is, as was shown above, that it fails to achieve any distinction between the analytic and the physically necessary forms of *a priori* truth. Yet if a suitable distinction could be drawn here the problem might be solved. It will be convenient to sketch the rough outline of such a distinction first, and to fill in the details later by gradually expanding its implications.

To say of a statement that it is analytic is to say that the meanings of the culture-words occurring in it determine its truth-value *a priori*. Not only, therefore, is the question of its truth-value a closed one, which no amount of observation of, or experiment on, its subject-matter could serve to reopen. But also, as a consequence, the meaning of the corresponding culture-sentence is to be conceived of as quite settled so far as affects the sentence's capacity to make an analytic statement. When the truth-value is said to depend on meaning, and on meaning alone, then neither truth-value nor meaning is implied open to revision. Both are *a priori* relative to our knowledge of the relevant subject-matter, even though observation of linguistic behaviour may be required to show that they are so (cf. §20). Suppose, however, instead that we were to leave open the question of meaning and confine our anticipations to the question of truth-value. To treat a given statement thus would be to take for granted that any statement made by the utterance of the given statement's culture-sentence is true, say (or false), but to leave the question of the exact range of senses in which this sentence is true as a question to be answered by the evidence of research into its subject-matter. To call a statement physically necessary is tantamount to saying that it should be treated in this way.

The point is most evident with statements of a kind to which the title of 'law of nature' is normally given. Newton's law of gravity, Snell's law of refraction, Boyle's law about the pressure and volume of gases, are all equally good examples. In each case the word 'law' is commonly used of them without query. They are statements of a very general kind, purporting to cover an indefinitely wide variety of phenomena. The movements of the planets, the ebb and flow of the tides, and the falling of apples are just a few of the cases in which Newton's law may be observed to hold. But when a case is found in which such a law does not hold we do not normally say that the law as a whole has been falsified and is to be rejected. Just because there are so many kinds of phenomena in which the law does hold it is more fruitful to ask where it applies and where it does not, than to ascribe to it some absolute sense and ask whether it has yet been shown false. If Newton's law does not apply to sub-atomic particles, it has not thereby lost all right to the title of 'law'. Even if the original discoverer of a law thought it applied with complete and unrestricted universality, we do not have to surrender the law altogether when we find that his claims on its behalf were exaggerated in certain respects. By calling it a law we profess sufficient respect for it to believe that its truth is no longer at issue but only its scope of application. Or in other words, if we suppose that in formulating the law we enunciate a universally quantified conditional or biconditional, what is left open is not the truth of this statement but its exact universe of discourse. The statement itself is sufficiently vague for us to be able to ask, given that the corresponding culture-sentence is in any case to be uttered in a sense in which it makes a true statement, just what sense this culture-sentence should have for it to be as precise and determinate as our observations and experiments permit.

When the question of a law's scope is viewed thus as a question of meaning, it becomes clear how we may dissolve the *prima facie* antinomy that is generated by the concept of physical necessity. Physically necessary statements are *a posteriori* in respect of their meaning and *a priori* in respect of their truth. No question arises about the exact sense an analytic truth's culture-sentence should have, since its meaning is such that it is true for all universes of discourse whatever. We do not wait on the evidence of experiments or observation to tell us where an analytic truth applies and where it does not. If we asked whether the truism 'Brothers are male siblings' applied in all cultures, we should either be taken to be asking of a culture-sentence whether it made an analytic truth in all cultures or of a law-like statement whether it applied universally. In short, with regard to analytic statements themselves the application-problem does not arise. On the other hand, with a statement like 'All your dogs are white' the issue of meaning and the issue of truth-value might both be open. By calling it an accidental truth we imply that its truth waits on the full evidence: anyone who anticipated the evidence of observation in even a single case would have done so at his peril. The wise man only asserts it *after* all the reports have come in. It is an *a posteriori* truth. Equally, however, the statement as a whole might be given a certain vagueness and made open to qualification, in case it seems preferable to qualify it rather than to reject it outright. Perhaps it only applies to your house-dogs and not to your farm-dogs.

It is quite evident on this theory why statement-forming operators like 'it is physically necessary that' generate non-extensionality of the particular kind they do. If to predicate physical necessity of a saying is to say that though its meaning is *a posteriori* its truth is not, the culture-sentence which may thus vary its meaning when uttered must be supposed to have an element of continuity that preserves its identity throughout any such minor variations. Hence we must admit some restrictions on substitution within the scope of 'it is physically necessary that' if we are not to destroy the identity of the culture-sentence occurring in the range of statements to which, implicitly, physical necessity is being ascribed. Substitutions licensed by an analytically true biconditional are all right. These could never suffice to destroy the relevant identity of culture-sentence – the relevant grouping of sentence-tokens – because they would permit just the same variation in universe of discourse as before. We express Newton's law of gravity more clumsily if we replace the term 'mass' in it by 'product of the density and volume', but it is still recognizably Newton's law. Substitutions licensed by an accidentally true biconditional are quite different, however, since they would completely destroy the identity of the underlying culture-sentence. They would vary its meaning far beyond the relatively narrow limits involved in adjusting its scope of application: they would affect the content of what is said rather than just the universe of discourse. It would be a different law, or alleged law. Hence arises the special kind of non-extensionality generated by 'it is physically necessary that', and so on. Correspondingly the prefixing of these operators to ordinary biconditionals constitutes a stronger criterion of intersubstitutability (in the sense defined in §24) than does assertion of the biconditional by itself, and a weaker criterion than is constituted by prefixing 'it is analytic that', 'it is *a priori* that', or 'it is logically true that'.

Laws of nature are generally found embedded in more or less elaborate systems of scientific theory. Newton's law of gravity is deduced from the axioms of his *Principia Mathematica*. Indeed, when certain hypotheses come to corroborate one another by being systematized into a theory that is relatively economical in its postulates, this corroboration may be viewed as tantamount to a widening of each hypothesis-sentence's domain of discourse so as to coincide with the domain of the widely applicable principles which have come to function as postulates in the theory. A philosophical account of natural necessity, however, must do no less justice to unsystematized generalizations of relatively narrow scope than it does to laws of such splendid universality as Newton's. But questions of application hardly seem to arise in connection with comparatively specific generalizations like the statement that such-and-such a dosage of penicillin normally cures such-and-such a state of septicaemia. There does not seem to be a wide variety of different kinds of phenomena that are capable of being explained by such a generalization, as there is in the case of Newton's law, and if there seems therefore to be no application-problem about such statements it may seem doubtful whether we can suppose them *a posteriori* in respect of meaning and *a priori* in respect of their truth. It may seem as though the only question that arises is whether they are true or false accounts of their own restricted range of subject-matter.

These appearances are misleading. Just as a characteristic kind of non-extensionality is found at all levels, however great is the difference in other respects between a grand law of physics, at one extreme, and a humble hypothesis of pharmacology, say, at the other, so too it is convenient to construe all such statements as *a posteriori* in regard to their meaning and *a priori* in regard to their truth. The question of meaning may fruitfully be regarded as open, and the question of truth-value as closed, at even the humblest level of scientific generalization, so long as mere plurality of instances is considered an insufficient basis for argument.

Two theories are familiarly in contest here. Some philosophers claim, like J. S. Mill, that a special 'inductive' logic is required to show just which modes of argument tend to establish the truth of generalizations which extend beyond the limits of what has already been observed. Variation of possibly relevant circumstances is said to be all-important, so that one can tell whether the penicillin alone is producing the cure, say, or some other factor present along with it. On this view Mill's methods of agreement and difference, for all their well-known errors and crudities of formulation, indicate the essential principles of inductive argument. Another school, however, led by K. R. Popper, protests that there is no special 'inductive' logic, nor does scientific argument ever attempt to establish the truth of generalizations. Hypotheses are formed first and then put to the test: we do not proceed from consideration of the evidence to the formation of hypotheses about it. Falsification, not verification, is what scientists seek for their hypotheses, and to show the way in which a counter-instance falsifies a generalized conditional nothing but the standard principles of formal logic are required. But though hypotheses are never shown to be true, or even likely to be true, on this view, they can at least be corroborated by the severity of the various tests to which they are successfully subjected, and the severity of the tests varies, in the main, with the degree of universality and precision they attribute to the hypothesis.

These two theories are, of course, nowhere nearly as much in conflict with one another as their supporters sometimes proclaim. What one theory calls the canons of inductive logic the other refers to as criteria for the corroboration of hypotheses. What one calls evidence, the other calls tests. When one theory says that generalizations are to be examined in as wide a variety of circumstances as seems relevant, the other implies the same when it says that the generalizations tested should be as bold and exact as their subject-matter permits. When one theory talks about forming hypotheses to fit the facts, it is not necessarily committed to the sociologically false proposition that study of the evidence is always temporally, as well as logically, prior to scientific generalization. When the other theory talks about the priority of hypothesis-formation it can hardly be denied that hypotheses have to be suggested by something, and generally by what little we know already about the subject-matter. Finally, even if one theory speaks of seeking to establish the truth of generalizations which go beyond what is given in evidence, it need not assume that the truth of any such generalization is ever conclusively established. Even if the other theory prefers to place its emphasis on the falsification of hypotheses, it cannot deny that by the laws of formal logic a hypothesis is either true or false and that if a hypothesis is corroborated rather than falsified something has been done towards showing that the hypothesis is not false, i.e. is true.

In short there is little or no serious dispute about the essential structure of scientific argument, but various differences of emphasis and terminology in the description of this structure. Moreover, both accounts, by assuming that the truth-value of scientific hypotheses is an empirical question, make it impossible to solve the problem of natural necessity. What is needed is yet a third way of describing the same model of argument, which will carry with it a solution of the problem about necessity. We must view scientific argument as being designed, ideally, neither to verify nor to falsify hypotheses, but rather to precisify hypothesis-sentences. Hypotheses must be viewed neither as empirically verifiable in principle nor as empirically falsifiable, but as *a priori* truths that are empirically precisifiable. Hence the process of testing a hypothesis by experimental variation of circumstances is to be viewed as the process of discovering exactly what meanings we can assign a certain culture-sentence, viz. the sentence to the truth of which, in some meaning, we are committed so long as we maintain the hypothesis. The wider the meaning we can successfully assign this sentence (by standards of wideness to be discussed in §39), the better confirmed is the hypothesis. The narrower the meaning, the better we should do by turning our attention to the precisification of some quite different hypothesis. We never prove the original hypothesis false, since we can always account for any imaginable variety of unfavourable evidence by taking this evidence to narrow further and further the meaning of the culture-sentence to which we are committed. Indeed the phrase 'in normal circumstances', which is often prefixed to the statement of a generalization or hypothesis, may be viewed as an express acknowledgement of our right to take such statements to be inherently imprecise as to their proper universe of discourse. If penicillin does not cure septicaemia under certain conditions, then these conditions, it may be said, are not normal: our hypothesis about the curative powers of penicillin requires qualification but is not refuted. The situation is thus quite analogous to that with regard to those grander and more comprehensive generalizations that are commonly called laws of nature. There is, after all, an application-problem even for the most specific forms of hypothesis.

Of course, philosophers often had very creditable motives for insisting that scientific hypotheses should be in principle verifiable, or falsifiable, by empirical evidence. They wanted to set up criteria by which we could distinguish law-like hypotheses of a genuinely natural-scientific form – hypotheses that might be worth entertaining and investigating – both from pseudo-scientific claptrap of various kinds and also from statements belonging to a quite different form of discourse, such as pure mathematics. They often wanted to bring out some of the crucial differences, for example, between medieval and postmedieval theories of scientific explanation. The reason why the soporific power of opium is not explained by attributing it a dormitive virtue, they have claimed, is because a hypothesis connecting soporific power to dormitive virtue is not empirically falsifiable and if such a hypothesis is not exposed to falsification by our observations of nature then it cannot advance our knowledge of nature or afford any explanation of events in nature that puzzle us. Certainly, it is altogether admirable for philosophers to insist on the role of experiment and observation in advancing the science of nature. Only one does not have to view this role as being fulfilled in verifying or falsifying. The same purposes are achieved just as well if one views it as being fulfilled in precisifying: the distinction between analytic truth and pure mathematics on the one side, and natural necessity on the other, is just as safe. Empirical precisifiability is the *sine qua non* of hypotheses in natural science. In any case, the statement that such-and-such a statement is naturally necessary is not itself *a priori*, since its implication that such-and-such a culture-sentence is worth precisifying against experience is obviously exposed to refutation by experience, namely by those same experiences that would force one to narrow the culture-sentence's meaning rather than broaden it. One can never be finally certain that a given statement is naturally necessary, even if one has no hesitation in adopting it as a hypothesis, much as one may remain in some doubt whether a sentence is always analytic in one's culture even though one readily speaks as if it were. So that the open, *a posteriori* truth-value which the present theory denies to any statement rightly described as physically necessary is restored, at a higher level, as it were, by the admission that any such description is itself *a posteriori* and that so is any equivalent statement formed by the corresponding operator 'it is physically necessary that'. The element of paradox involved in declaring scientific hypotheses to be *a priori* truths is comparatively superficial.

A hypothesis, after all, is not just a statement but a statement 'assumed for argument, or to explain certain facts', as dictionaries put it.[1] Philosophers have been able to suppose that treating a statement as a hypothesis leaves its truth-value a quite open question, only by persistently ignoring this aspect of the ordinary meaning of the word 'hypothesis'. So far as a man adopts some statement as his hypothesis he treats it as an *a priori* truth. Perhaps it will be objected that this implies the *a priori* quality of a statement to be something which does not necessarily belong to the statement as such, but can be an accidental property of it in the discourse of one or more individuals. The distinction between empirical and *a priori*, it may be said, loses its point if it is not always rooted in the statements themselves or at least in their language. How can we make sense, it may be asked, of controversies whether mathematical statements are empirical, as J. S. Mill believed, or *a priori*, as Kant did, unless we suppose that how people treat statements is irrelevant to their real nature? But it could just as well be argued that such controversies are conducted with greater clarity if both sides are in a position to identify precisely the same statements as being the topic of dispute, and neither can do this if part of a statement's identification is, implicitly or explicitly, to declare whether it is

[1] E.g. *Webster's Collegiate Dictionary* (1932).

empirical or *a priori*, as is the case with analytic statements. Since difference of meaning entails difference of statement, we cannot unambiguously specify a statement that is analytic in our language without implying that it is *a priori* true. But we can specify statements of many other kinds without implying this. So perhaps one main source of temptation to suppose *a priori*-ness an inherent quality in those statements that have it is the old positivist dogma (criticized in §20) that all *a priori* truths are analytic.

There is also perhaps another source of this temptation in the widespread belief that the *a posteriori–a priori* distinction among our statements is exactly paralleled by a similar distinction among our items of knowledge. Every *a priori* truth we state, it is often believed, articulates an item of our *a priori* knowledge. But this parallelism only holds if we retain the old-fashioned view, which Descartes, Spinoza and Kant shared with Plato, that fundamental *a priori* truths are discovered rather than invented. If instead we are right to believe that the only element of *a priori* discovery is in ascertaining what may be proved or deduced from given premises – if fundamental *a priori* truths are postulated rather than discovered – then there is no *a priori* knowledge in the sense in which Plato and the others believed in it. There is no question of validation, whether by analyticity or intuition, for the *a priori* truths we take to be fundamental: we can only argue whether we are wise to accept these statements *a priori*. Hence we do not need to suppose that there is some special quality in *a priori* statements, some inherent source of self-evidence, perhaps, or intuitability, which qualifies their truth for *a priori* discovery. Any statement whatever can be taken as an *a priori* truth, and any non-analytic statement can be taken as an empirical one. Whether or not it is correct or profitable to do so depends in either case on considerations germane to the subject-matter of the statement and the context of its utterance. The same truth-functional conditional about moas, for instance, stating that if anything is a moa it dies before a certain age, might be regarded either as physically necessary, so far as some feature in the biological structure of moas is thought responsible, or as accidentally true, if the various unfavourable circumstances in which moas lived are under attention. Of any non-analytic statement, therefore, we may safely say what Quine wanted to say of all statements (see §21): there is no sharp line between those statements that have an *a priori* truth-value and those that have not – only a varying reluctance on our part to call them in question.

To put the same point another way, we might distinguish a strong sense of '*a priori*' from a weak one. In the strong sense a statement is correctly termed an *a priori* truth if its truth is only discoverable either by some special faculty of rational intuition, like an 'eye in the soul', as Plato described it,[1] or by deduction from truths so discovered. In the weak sense a statement is correctly so termed in a given context if it should be taken there as not exposed to any verification or falsification by the evidence of a person's senses or powers of introspection. Any truth that is strongly *a priori* is also weakly *a priori* in all contexts. But the converse does not hold, if we accept that, as in effect Hume and many others have argued, there are no strongly *a priori* truths at all, because the whole notion of a special faculty for their discovery is muddled and empty. So unless we are to jettison the *a priori*-empirical dichotomy altogether, except in writing the history of philosophy, we shall do well to confine ourselves to the weak sense of '*a priori*'. This is the contemporary sense in which the truths of logic and arithmetic, say, are commonly termed *a priori*, and it is also the sense in which it is here being argued that where a statement is being taken as a law of nature or a causal hypothesis it is being taken as *a priori*. This sense is all that is required for *a priori*-ness to carry with it necessity: to insist that the truth of a certain statement should be taken for granted is to insist that what it says *must* be the case. Perhaps, as already suggested, it was a tendency to suppose the expression '*a priori*' can only have its strong sense that has so often prevented philosophers from recognizing that natural necessity is a form of *a priori* truth. Despising all beliefs in a faculty of rational intuition they have let their legitimate distrust of the non-empirical, in one sense, blind them to the importance of the non-empirical in another sense. No wonder they have often found it so difficult[2] to achieve a definition of empirical statement that would embrace scientific hypotheses as effectively as it embraced reports, narratives and other paradigm cases of empirical assertion. There is a lot to be said in favour of reverting to the old sense of 'empirical statement' – the sense in which both Bacon and Mill condemned

---

[1] *Republic*, 533D.

[2] Cf. I. Scheffler, 'Prospects of a Modest Empiricism', *Review of Metaphysics*, x (1957), pp. 383 ff.

empiricism in science.[1] 'Empirical' in their sense is the contrary of '*a priori*' in my weak sense.

Hence it is no use objecting to the present theory of natural necessity that by calling natural laws, etc., *a priori* truths we should speak as if final and ultimate truths were knowable in natural science. The theory does not regress to a conviction like Descartes's that the work of scientists can in principle be completed beyond all possible need for revision in a finite period of time. What is being claimed is that culture-sentences believed to state natural laws are sentences which are treated as if they expressed *a priori* truths: it is not being claimed that these sentences are believed to report *a priori* discoveries. Moreover the wisdom of so treating them and the precise senses in which they should severally be so treated are issues that remain for ever more or less open.

In the light of all this it becomes much easier to understand the way in which people's discoveries of fact often become absorbed into their languages – a process about which something has already been said in §18. How is it that an observed property of phosphorus, say, such as its melting-point at 44° C., may come to be included in the commonly accepted definition of 'phosphorus'? If natural laws and other physically necessary generalizations are held to be empirical statements the passage of knowledge from laboratory to language may seem rather puzzling. We apparently have to suppose not only a transition from synthetic to analytic but also one from empirical to *a priori* – as if there were a change not only in our mode of speech but also in the way we validate the relevant belief. One moment, it seems, we look to experiments to tell us the melting-point of phosphorus: the next moment we survey the speech-habits of our fellows to get the very same information. But these appearances are illusory and generated by the mistaken view that natural laws and other physically necessary generalizations are empirical statements. In fact it is precisely the same experiments that justify the new definition of phosphorus as corroborate the old generalization. In both cases a statement that the melting-point is 44° C. is *a priori*, though the onus of maintaining such a statement's *a priori* status, the onus of ensuring that its truth be taken for granted, has passed from the individual speaker to the speech-habits of his community. The meaning in which the corresponding culture-sentence may be asserted as true is now believed to be so broad that attempts to precisify this meaning yet

[1] *System of Logic*, VI, i, 1 and x, 8, and *Novum Organum*, I, lxiv, respectively.

further would be unprofitable. Hence the sentence can now be safely asserted as an analytic truth with the unrestricted universe of discourse to which analytic statements are characteristically entitled.

Indeed, since among non-analytic statements there is no sharp line between those statements that have an *a priori* truth-value and those that have not, but only a varying reluctance on our part to call them in question, we could in principle place all our true statements, or at least those of them in which the non-logical terminology is purely descriptive and not evaluative, hortative, or in any way prescriptive, on a single scale in accordance with the degree to which we think they deserve entrenchment in our language. At the top of the scale, perhaps, would be the truth-functional tautologies of propositional logic, and at the bottom would be truths of an apparently quite accidental character, like 'All your dogs are white.' In between might come other logical and mathematical truths, the already analytic truisms of everyday life, and then statements believed physically necessary in descending order of the narrowness of the meanings in which they are so believed. If we imagine a corresponding series of statement-forming operators on statements, beginning at the bottom with 'it is true that', 'it is worthy of linguistic entrenchment that', 'it is very worthy . . .', 'it is very very worthy . . .', and so on, then the logical liaisons of these operators may be studied in the calculus O_4 or O_4^3 (developed in §30), by taking them to be represented by the symbols $\square^0$, $\square^1$, . . . $\square^n$, in that calculus.

But it should be noted that just as scientific theories are not the only form of truth which sometimes deserves or achieves entrenchment in human language, so too physically necessary statements are not the only common form of synthetic *a priori* truth. It was remarked in §18, for instance, that our changing moral sensitivity may come to affect the descriptive implications of words like 'justice' in ordinary usage; and no doubt this passage of moral values into analyticity is aided by the fact that the statement of a moral principle is commonly taken as an *a priori* truth. Suppose, for instance, we believe it morally unjust for a country's laws to discriminate among its citizens in accordance with the colour of their skins. We do not normally shed this belief when we learn of countries where all the men of one colour are primitive and illiterate and all those of another are civilized and well-educated. Perhaps in such a country other principles of justice require that laws regulating taxation, court procedure, political representation, etc., should vary somewhat for the different groups, if one group is not to be given an unfair advantage over the other. But even if we accept this we do not have to abandon our views on the injustice of discrimination in accordance with colour. We merely have to regard the latter belief as restricted to cases where discrimination is on grounds of colour alone rather than for reasons of justice and no attempt is concurrently being made to remove other differences such as those of literacy or civilization. In other words, instead of sticking to our moral generalization in some single absolute sense unless or until disgust at its consequences leads us to regard it as false, we suppose the truth of the generalization to be beyond recall but are prepared to modify its meaning. Nor need this modification always be such as to narrow the principle's application. Beginning with moral objections to violence which he applies solely to violence between individuals acting in their private capacities, a man may begin to broaden his principle so that at first it leads him to oppose infliction of corporal or capital punishment by any state on its citizens and later to oppose any use of force whatever by one state on another. No doubt such precisifications of principle are often isolated developments in the life-histories of particularly open-minded individuals. But sometimes, over a sufficiently long period, they occur almost throughout a community. The moral justice of universal adult self-government has been applied by some people first to entail the right of parliamentary suffrage for each male with a substantial economic stake in their own country, then to entail it for all their countrymen, then for all the adults of their own country, then for all the adults of their own culture – for the inhabitants of continental Europe, say, as well as for those of Great Britain – and finally for all adults everywhere, so that they can no longer deny self-government to colonial territories. When a commonly accepted principle has become so unqualified in its application, the onus of maintaining its *a priori* character can conveniently be laid on the languages of those who support it. Children can learn it as they learn to speak instead of imbibing it as a special piece of moral instruction. If it has become analytic, for instance, that democracy is the only just form of government, children will learn to use the words 'democratic' and 'undemocratic' as terms of moral approval and disapproval, respectively, like 'just' and 'unjust'. They will no more dispute whether democracy is a virtue in a country's system of government than whether justice is. The focus of live controversy will shift from the extent to which democratic principles of any kind should be applied, to the proper way in which universal parliamentary suffrage should be operated: should there be a plurality of political parties or is just one sufficient to represent the people's real interests?

In keeping with this *a priori* character of moral principles it is worth noting that expressions like 'one of my moral principles implies that' or 'justice is not done unless' generate their own kind of non-extensionality. This may be seen in at least two ways.

First, many moral subjunctive conditionals like 'If you had told a lie you would have done something very wrong' are clearly not truth-functional in their logic. They need to be distinguished from statements rendered trivially true by the falsity of their antecedents, just as do the subjunctive conditionals of experimental science. They are to be viewed as tantamount to statements formed by prefacing some such expression as 'one of my moral principles implies that' to the corresponding truth-functional conditional; and the latter would have a non-extensional occurrence in the statement thus formed because no merely truth-functional biconditional would license substitution in it.

Secondly, if we consider some presumably very rare vice, like necrophily perhaps, we can produce an example partly analogous to the case of the moas. It may well turn out as a matter of pure accident, so rare are the kinds of people concerned, that all and only hunchback albinos are necrophiles (though, so as not to give offence, I must add that I know of no evidence for this and can equally well imagine that all hunchback albinos are models of virtue). But this accidentally true identity-statement does not license substitution in 'It is a moral principle deserving universal respect that anyone who indulges in necrophily does something that he ought not to do.' Even if, with increasing psychological knowledge, we discovered that it was physically inevitable for all and only hunchback albinos to be necrophiles, the statement of that physical necessity would still not license substitution in a statement of moral principle about necrophily, since we might then come to think that necrophily should only be considered a vice in cases, apparently unlikely to arise, where it was not the inevitable result of physiological deformity. That is, though an analytic truth or another statement of moral principle might, if appropriately worded, license substitution in these contexts, a statement of physical necessity would not. The kind of non-extensionality that arises here is therefore

L

different from that generated by 'it is physically necessary that', though in some respects co-ordinate with it. Further kinds of some-what similar non-extensionality are generated by such expressions as 'it is a principle of English law that', 'aesthetic standards of town-planning require that', and so on.

It follows that we must be careful about what we try to include in a scale of statements like the one just suggested, in which truths are arranged in accordance with the degree to which we think they deserve entrenchment in our language and the corresponding series of state-ment-forming operators on statements ('it is true that', 'it is worthy of linguistic entrenchment that', etc.), are taken to be representable by the symbols $\square^1, \square^2, \ldots \square^n$ of O_4 or O_4^3. In such a scale we cannot include more than one at a time of the various different kinds of synthetic *a priori* statement – physical necessities, principles of moral argument, principles of law, and so on. Correspondingly we must be careful about what is implied by the expression '*a priori*' when we use it in its weak sense. There may be accidentally true moral statements, for instance, like 'All hunchback albinos are vicious and depraved' which are not *a priori* in the same sense as statements of moral principle are, and yet are not so fully confirmable by observation as 'All my dogs are white.' As Hume in effect pointed out,[1] we cannot see the viciousness of people's behaviour in the same way as we see what they actually do. But what is required for these statements to be *a posteriori* in the re-quired sense is not that their truth should be fully demonstrable from the evidence of our senses alone, without reference to any *a priori* standards or principles whatever, but that such evidence should be at least a part of what is required for their demonstration. Where we take a culture-sentence to be *a priori* true in utterance, the evidence of our senses has no bearing on its truth but only on its meaning. But with 'All hunchbacks are vicious and depraved', as with 'All my dogs are white', observable evidence has a direct bearing on truth-value. A man must be caught out in his vices for his critics to be reasonably sure that he is vicious. Even if we may wish to make a further distinction within the class of *a posteriori* truths, between those that, in principle, are fully demonstrable from sensory evidence and those that are only partly so, yet there is much to be gained by classing accidentally true moral statements along with accidentally true descriptive ones as *a posteriori*.

[1] *Treatise of Human Nature*, ed. Selby-Bigge, pp. 455 ff.

Even if we wish to make a further distinction within the class of *a priori* truths, between those that are precisifiable by reference to sensory evidence alone and those whose precisification requires also some appeal to *prima facie* conflicting principles, yet there is much to be gained by classing statements of moral principle along with physically necessary truths as *a priori*. The mode of classifying statements that is most helpful for understanding the origins of non-extensionality cuts across the mode of classification most helpful in understanding the difference between natural science on the one side, and ethics, aesthetics or jurisprudence on the other. To elucidate the naturalness of natural necessity we need the latter kind of distinction: to elucidate its necessity we need the former. No doubt the elusiveness of the concept derives in part from its position at the intersection of these two modes of classification.

§39. Inductive confirmation conceived as the precisification of hypotheses

Yet another qualification needs to be added to what has already been said about a scale of true statements arranged in accordance with the degree to which they deserve entrenchment in our language. It is not easy, unless all statements that anyone thinks physically necessary are put on the same level (in which case the operator 'it is physically necessary that' could be represented by $\Box^1$ in O_3), to see how such an arrangement could be at all comprehensive without being arbitrarily determined in at least some respects.

The difficulty here is essentially the same as one which has been much discussed by Popper, Carnap, Nagel and others[1] in the recent literature of the subject known variously as inductive logic, confirmation-theory, or the logic of scientific discovery. It has often been asked whether it is possible to set up reasonably based criteria defining the measure of confirmation enjoyed by a given hypothesis at a given time, or on a given body of evidence, as a function whose values are real numbers, or alternatively whether at least it is possible to set up

---

[1] Cf. K. R. Popper, *The Logic of Scientific Discovery* (1959), pp. 112 ff.; R. Carnap, *Logical Foundations of Probability* (1950), pp. 226 ff., 428 ff.; E. Nagel, *Principles of the Theory of Probability* (1939) in *International Encyclopaedia of Unified Science*, I, 6.

reasonably based criteria defining two relational concepts, 'better confirmed than' and 'equally well confirmed with', which would permit a non-metrical comparison of hypotheses. If even the latter were possible, then clearly there need be nothing arbitrary in the arrangement of true statements in the serial order of their supposed deserts at a given time with regard to linguistic entrenchment: of any two statements the better confirmed one would be the more deserving. But if no such criteria are available this arrangement would have to be determined in part by relatively arbitrary considerations, such as the supposed interest or importance of the statements concerned. That is, some arrangement would be psychologically possible for most people, and no doubt many people could state criteria sufficient to establish the order of arrangement they themselves would choose, but there would be insufficient grounds for saying that only one choice of order is correct at any one given time or on any one given body of evidence.

A comprehensive treatment of this complex issue would be out of place in a book devoted to the problem of meaning. But it would be equally unsatisfactory not to explore the general implications for inductive logic that are carried by the theory of natural necessity which has been proposed. What follows is an attempt to sketch those implications in a way that will help to show the content of the theory more fully than has already been done but will stop very far short of constituting a general treatment of inductive logic. Though such a treatment would be quite inappropriate here, enough will be said to show that the theory is not at a disadvantage *vis-à-vis* the main current theories of confirmation.

What then is involved in precisifying a hypothesis? That is the crux of the matter. In what sense is it true to say that confirmation or disconfirmation of a statement is tantamount, respectively, to widening or narrowing its culture-sentence's meaning? Let us confine our attention, for simplicity's sake, to statements that have the familiar form of a generalized conditional in which only monadic predicates occur, though the same basic principles apply to all kinds of generalization. The logical structure of such a statement, though not its *a priori* truth or physical necessity, can be represented by a wff of truth-functional logic $(\alpha)(\varphi\alpha \supset \chi\alpha)$, i.e. $\sim(\exists\alpha)(\varphi\alpha . \sim\chi\alpha)$. Now, it was shown in §33 that all our ordinary assertions of existence and non-existence require the implicit or explicit assumption of a domain of discourse: to assert the emptiness of a class is to assert its non-intersection with that domain. What is characteristically imprecise in a statement that is assigned the *a priori* truth of a hypothesis, is its domain of discourse. What is never fully specified, until the corresponding culture-sentence becomes an obvious candidate for analyticity, is the range of values for the quantified variables. Even if it seems a little strained to speak of determining a sentence's proper domain of discourse as a determination of its meaning, at least the assignment of values to quantifiable variables is commonly regarded as an essential part of the assignment of meaning to the formulas of a logical calculus.

Assuming therefore that any step in precisification, at the stage with which we are concerned, will still leave some element of imprecision remaining, we can distinguish four different kinds of step that might conceivably be made. First, the culture-sentence might be found to be assertable *a priori* with a meaning that definitely includes things or events of such-and-such a description in its domain of discourse, or, secondly, with a meaning that excludes them. But it would also be a step forward, though perhaps not so big a step, to know the contrary of one or other of these two assertabilities. Hence, thirdly, the culture-sentence might be found to be assertable *a priori* with a meaning that does not definitely include things or events of such-and-such a description, or, fourthly, with a meaning that does not definitely exclude them. To take a step of the first or fourth kinds is what is here connoted by the expression 'to widen a meaning', and to take a step of the second or third by 'to narrow a meaning'.

Consider, for example,

(1) Anyone who regularly breathes in the air of a swampy district develops bouts of malarial fever

which was for long taken to be necessarily true in normal circumstances. Exceptions were known, such as the relative immunity of people living in the upper stories of high buildings, but these circumstances were considered abnormal with respect to the supposed causal agent: the air higher up was in any case known to be purer than the air lower down. But Manson and Ross, the great investigators of malarial infection, showed in effect that (1) did not hold for certain other ranges of circumstances also, which could not thus be regarded as abnormal. It did not hold for anyone who wore gloves and a veil if he went out at

night, nor did it hold for anyone who stayed indoors at night and protected his windows with gauze netting; and these circumstances could
hardly be considered abnormal with respect to the air that such a person
breathed. The meaning in which (1) might safely be held true had therefore been narrowed to an important extent. On the other hand the
hypothesis

> (2) Anyone who is bitten by a parasite-infected anopheles mos-
> quito develops bouts of malarial fever

is not affected by any of these variations of circumstance, and appears
to hold equally well for swampy and non-swampy districts. The circumstances in which it does not hold, as when a man takes daily doses
of quinine, may reasonably be regarded as abnormal because of their
effect on the parasite. In other words it seems justifiable to assign to (2)
a much wider meaning than to (1).

But in such cases, strictly speaking, we cannot say that such-and-
such circumstances have been discovered to include individuals in, or
exclude them from, a hypothesis-sentence's domain of discourse. All
we can say is that the circumstances have been discovered not to exclude
them from, or not to include them in, this domain. Living in a non-
swampy district is not itself sufficient to include a man in the domain of
(2): it merely fails to exclude him from it, because one man is known
who both lived in a non-swampy district and was bitten by an infected
mosquito and developed malaria. After all, another man might live in
a non-swampy district and take quinine as well.

Schematically the position is, therefore, that if

> (3) $(x)(Fx \supset Gx)$

is the hypothesis to be precisified and something, a, is observed such
that 'Fa.Ga.Ha' (or '∼Fa.∼Ga.Ha') is found to be true, then we
have learnt that describing a thing as an H does not exclude it from the
hypothesis's domain. We have not learnt that all H things are included
in that domain, only that they are not all outside it, which enables us to
say that the property of being an H does not itself exclude a thing from
the scope of (3). In other words in precisifying (3) with respect to its
domain of discourse we are talking about the latter non-extensionally.
We are not listing the members of this domain, sub-class by sub-class,
but investigating what is, or should be, implied by assertions of mem-

bership in it, and when the implication of excluding the members of a certain class is learnt to be absent, it does not follow that the implication of including them is thereby learnt to be present. We may define an expression up to a certain point of precision, and not feel entitled to go beyond it. Even in ordinary usage, for instance, to call a man wise does not imply he is not well-educated, but it does not therefore imply that he is well-educated. Similarly if something else, b, is observed such that 'Fb. $\sim$Gb. Jb' is found to be true, then we have learnt that describing a thing as a J does not include it in that domain. But we have not learnt that all J things are excluded from it. In short, of the four conceivable steps in precisification that were mentioned above only the third and fourth can be taken, on the discovery of appropriate evidence, without any risk at all.

To what extent are these various widenings and narrowings comparable with one another? It is reasonable to suppose that, if neither '(x)(Hx$\supset$Kx)' nor '(x)(Hx$\supset$Gx)' nor '(x)(Kx$\supset$Gx)' nor '(x)(Fx$\supset$Hx)' nor '(x)(Fx$\supset$Kx)' is analytically true, then, when it is learnt that not only H things but also K things are not excluded from the domain of (3), the meaning justifiably assigned to (3) is wider than when it was known only that H things are not excluded. Correspondingly a hypothesis that has been seen not to suffer under two variations of circumstances would normally be said to be better confirmed than when it has only been seen not to suffer under the first of these two variations. The same could be said if we were comparing not two different stages in the history of the same hypothesis, but two quite different hypotheses. If there are no analytic connections of the kinds already mentioned, then, other things being equal, the hypothesis whose meaning is known not to exclude from its domain either H or K things has a wider meaning, i.e. is better confirmed than, the hypothesis whose meaning is known not to include either H or K things. Again, if two hypotheses have the same consequent, and the meaning of the first is known not to include the circumstances described by the contradictory of the second's antecedent, while the meaning of the second is known not to exclude the circumstances described by the contradictory of the first's antecedent, as is the case with (1) and (2), then the second has a wider meaning than the first.

But is there much more that can be said? If there are no analytic connections of the kind already mentioned and '(x)(Kx$\supset$Hx)' is not an analytic truth either, then it is not immediately clear whether the justifiable meaning of (3) should be said to be wider when it is only known not to exclude K than when it is only known not to exclude H, or narrower, or of just the same width. Nor is it clear, when the meaning is known neither to exclude nor to include H, whether it is wider or narrower than, or just as wide as, when neither of these facts were known, though it is certainly more precise.

In practice, however, we do often assert comparative degrees of confirmation in such cases. First, a pathological hypothesis like (2) would probably be thought better confirmed if it was merely shown to be unaffected by differences of climate than if it was merely shown to be unaffected by differences of eye-colour. This would be because differences of climate have often been found to affect the incidence of disease, and differences of eye-colour have seldom, if ever, been found to do so. Secondly, a hypothesis is not infrequently thought better confirmed if it has been shown to be unaffected by variations of a kind that it is important for our practical interests to make, or that occur very commonly in our own region of space-time, than if it has been shown to be unaffected by variations that hardly interest us at all. If (2) is shown to be unaffected by variations of climate, it is better confirmed from the ordinary human point of view than if it were shown to be unaffected by various kinds of inoculation a man might undergo in a laboratory. Thirdly, no doubt, a hypothesis like (2) is thought better confirmed if it has been shown to be unaffected by a major variation of climate, say, than if by a minute variation in height above sea-level. If (2) is believed to hold good for both tropical and temperate zones, it will appear better confirmed than it would do if believed to hold good both at an altitude of 300 feet and also at one of 310 feet. More information seems to have been discovered in the former case than in the latter, and a bolder hypothesis seems to be vindicated.

It is the third of these three kinds of comparison, rather than the first or second, that generally seems to have caught the attention of philosophers seeking to set up criteria for a comparative or quantitative concept of confirmation. They have concentrated on those methods of comparing degrees of confirmation that seem to depend wholly on the meaning of the hypothesis and its evidence-statements, as distinct from those that seem to depend at least in part either on collateral facts about its subject-matter or on the circumstances that determine its utility to us. Thus they have claimed to find the required criteria, like Popper, in some way of measuring the information conveyed by a hypothesis that has survived attempts to falsify it, or they have developed a logic of induction, like Carnap, based on methods of measuring the extent to which the range of one sentence – roughly, the circumstances in which it would be true – is included in that of another. But in order to do this they have to assume, for the purposes of making any one comparison at least, a fixed and static language within which certain sentences may be regarded as atomic, or elementary, in order to constitute the basic units on which all comparisons or measurements of confirmation are ultimately grounded. In Carnap's theory, for instance, the degree of confirmation afforded to a given hypothesis by a given set of evidence-statements sometimes depends on the number of primitive predicates in the language-system in question.[1] In Popper's theory a hypothesis's degree of confirmation sometimes depends on the number of supposedly atomic statements that need to be conjoined together in order to constitute a statement incompatible with the hypothesis.[2] Certainly, the way in which confirmation-criteria are constructed on such a basis varies very much from theory to theory, and it is often enormously complicated. But fortunately these details are irrelevant here. All that is important for present purposes is that degree of confirmation (or corroboration, as Popper calls it) becomes relative not only to a certain set of statements about the evidence for the hypothesis or the tests to which it has been successfully exposed, but also to a certain terminology. For if we could not assume any sentence to be atomic, i.e. if any sentence may make a statement that could be broken down into a truth-functional compound of statements other than itself, we could never know, for instance, whether variations of altitude measured by feet above sea-level were to count the same as variations of temperature measured by degrees centigrade, or whether perhaps 'feet-of-altitude-above-sea-level' is an umbrella term equivalent to a conjunction of two other terms which denote factors that may be varied independently of one another, each counting as much as a variation in degree of temperature.

Interesting as the construction of such theories may be, they can therefore never come very near to explicating the everyday concept of

[1] *Logical Foundations of Probability*, pp. 70 ff., 283 ff., esp. p. 284.
[2] *Logic of Scientific Discovery*, pp. 100 ff., 126 ff., esp. p. 129.

confirmation. The trouble is not just that the assumption of atomic sentences is incompatible with the post-Herder conception of language which in so many other respects has proved more profitable (see especially §§3, 4, 8 and 11) than the older belief in the existence of changeless atomic meanings. After all, perhaps here the older doctrine might have found some much needed support, if it was required to justify an otherwise satisfactory theory of confirmation. But, more seriously, people often do feel themselves entitled to compare degrees of confirmation in a way that will be unaffected by mere linguistic change. The comparisons they seek to establish are ones that will remain invariant under differences in the choice of language-system, or in the choice of which sentences, if any, are to be regarded as relatively atomic; and theories like those of Popper and Carnap do not provide any basis for such comparisons. The measure of confidence that a hypothesis deserves may reasonably be affected, people think, by the results of new experiments to test it, or the discovery of new collateral information about the kinds of variation of circumstance to which it has already been submitted, or even by changes in human concerns. But it seems very paradoxical to suppose that this measure of confidence can be affected merely by changes in human terminology. To suppose the degree of a hypothesis's confirmation to be relative to a certain state of language seems quite out of accord with the normal patterns of scientific discourse, and it is highly doubtful whether scientists would profit by adopting such a supposition.

Of course, in practice language does not change in a causal vacuum. If sentences hitherto accustomed to make atomic statements begin to have a more complex logical structure in human utterance, it is quite reasonable to search for an explanation of this. The explanation may well be that in fields collateral with that of the hypothesis immediately in question it has been found crucial to vary independently two factors that hitherto were only describable when they occurred in conjunction with one another. Or alternatively perhaps those concerned have come to value differently two factors that hitherto were always valued as a single indivisible whole. So that in practice it may not be so unwise after all to regard estimates of confirmation as liable to be affected by changes of language. But it is the facts that cause, or, more properly, the facts that justify the change which really determine whether or not a previous estimate of confirmation should now be revised. It is not language that justifies assigning such-or-such a degree of confirmation to a given hypothesis on given evidence: rather it is the choice of such-or-such statements to be atomic that is justified by the extent, say, to which certain hypotheses have been confirmed or disconfirmed. Justification runs in the opposite direction to that which Carnap and Popper suggest, analogously to the way in which it runs in the opposite direction to that which Strawson suggests in regard to the relation between language and formal logic (cf. §32). Language is not a fundamental source of norms for the evaluation of theories about non-linguistic matters: rather it is itself exposed to criticism by standards of extra-linguistic origin.

Moreover, it does not matter if such scientific discoveries have not yet achieved, or even never achieve, any impact on human language. They still afford ground for reconsidering the earlier estimate of confirmation. Hence philosophers like Popper and Carnap cannot defend the utility of their theories on the ground that in practice linguistic change may very well be relevant to degrees of confirmation, unless they are prepared to extend the foundations for their assessments of this degree so as to take into account the factors that make linguistic change relevant. Nor is it easy to see how any single theory could usefully embrace so diverse a body of considerations. How, to mention one of the most glaring difficulties, could we weigh the implications of collateral information against the implications of our practical concerns, without attaching some personal measure of value to these concerns which others may well dispute? Perhaps instead we should be content with a variety of different ways for estimating degree of confirmation, or at least distinguish estimates based in part on collateral information from those based in part on our practical concerns.

In short the main current theories about degree of confirmation only afford highly incomplete directions as to how we should estimate it in a given case. They base their criteria on the assumption of a chosen language-system, but they do not provide us with further criteria to govern our choice of language-system. It is as if we wanted to know how to estimate the size of a library, and we were merely told how to count instead of what to count – as if we were told to count in units according to the rules of elementary arithmetic but not told whether the units should be books, readers, linear feet of shelving, or what.

The unorthodox view of confirmation that is being advocated here is therefore at no great disadvantage *vis-à-vis* these current theories. Admittedly in its present form it leaves undetermined what is to be regarded as the degree of a hypothesis's confirmation in certain kinds of case, because it does not specify exactly what is to be regarded as a wider or a narrower meaning in those cases. What is required is a definition which would ensure that if a hypothesis's domain of discourse includes, or does not exclude, some circumstances that are theoretically or practically of greater importance than others, the hypothesis will be said to have a broader meaning than if its domain of discourse included, or did not exclude, only the circumstances of lesser importance. But in effect, as has been shown, the more orthodox theories are deficient in just the same respects. Utility and relevance are discussed by Carnap but not their effect on language.[1] No doubt it is a fruitful principle of philosophical method here to conceive the impact of all relevant factors as being crystallized into a language-system of some kind, so that the relation of the hypothesis to other statements in the system can then be gauged. But we need to know more about assessing the reliability of a language-system in terms of what has gone into it, before we can be sure how to assess the reliability of a hypothesis in terms of the language-system from which it comes. Hence for present purposes it suffices to conceive the process of confirming or disconfirming a hypothesis as a process of precisifying the meaning of the corresponding culture-sentence, so long as it is clear that the width of this meaning is determined not only by the detailed results of experimental variation in the circumstances of the hypothesis itself, but also by such factors as collateral information and practical interests. We cannot say just how much the experimental details should broaden the sentence's meaning except in the light of what we already know about those other factors. But to offer a complete account of how the experimental details affect meaning, so that we can both compare and measure widths of justified meaning in every kind of case, would be in effect to offer a complete theory of induction which no one – not even Popper or Carnap – has yet done.

Perhaps it should also be remarked that it is not altogether clear just how much should be included under the head of 'confirmation'. Are all criteria of choice between hypotheses to be regarded as measures of confirmation? Or is measure of confirmation just one such criterion

[1] *Logical Foundations of Probability*, pp. 252 ff. and 346 ff.

among several? Certainly the relative simplicity of a hypothesis, for instance, and its relative fertility in suggesting further lines of research are important criteria of choice about which I have not so far said anything, though they may well generate additional difficulties in regard to commensurability. But if they too are to be conceived of as measures of confirmation, then this concept of confirmation is somewhat wider than the mode of precisification so far considered. For they concern the content of a hypothesis-sentence, not its domain of discourse, and the variations in meaning that affect them are not necessarily variations in precision. A relatively vague hypothesis-sentence might even be more simple, or more fertile, than a relatively precise one. But it does not follow from this that the common use of simplicity and fertility as criteria of choice between hypotheses affords an argument against the conception of natural laws as *a priori* truths. Just the opposite: what differentiates simplicity and fertility from the measures of confirmation already considered is that their use as criteria of choice between hypotheses does not wait on observation or experiment at all. They are typical *a priori* considerations.

§40. Inductive inconclusiveness as a corollary of changeability of meaning

In all that he wrote about causal reasoning Hume paid very little attention to the way in which our confidence in a hypothesis tends to be strengthened by its success in surviving experiments where circumstances have been appropriately varied. Perhaps he makes some acknowledgement of this in his list of 'rules by which to judge of causes and effects'.[1] But when he talks about the origin of our beliefs in necessary connections between matters of fact, or when he proposes a definition of what it is for one event to cause another, it is only the constant repetition of a conjunction that counts. Hume's attitude here is still, in essence, the attitude of some writers on the subject. C. G. Hempel, for instance, construes a hypothesis as confirmed by a given observation-report if the hypothesis is satisfied in the finite class of those individuals which are mentioned in the report.[2] He does not require, for confirmation to be achieved, that the report should mention an

[1] *Treatise*, pp. 173 f.
[2] 'Studies in the Logic of Confirmation', *Mind*, liv (1945), pp. 109 f.

THE DIVERSITY OF MEANING

importantly different kind of individual from those mentioned in previous reports. Similarly Nelson Goodman assumes that if, say, a given piece of copper is known to conduct electricity, this alone increases the credibility of statements asserting that other pieces of copper conduct electricity.[1]

This way of thinking about confirmation, which Hempel and Goodman share with Hume, is not compatible with the theory of natural necessity that was advanced in §38. On that theory to confirm a hypothesis is tantamount to widening the meaning in which the hypothesis-sentence may justifiably be taken to assert an *a priori* truth. Such a widening can be achieved only if the confirmatory information implies that the sentence's domain of discourse should include, or at least should not exclude, certain circumstances about which this was previously unknown. The information must therefore go beyond a mere mention of one or more individuals that satisfy the hypothesis. It must also mention some relevant characteristic of such an individual or individuals. Schematically the position is that (3) is not confirmed by the truth of 'Fa.Ga' but only by the truth of some statement like 'Fa.Ga.Ha', where neither '$(x)(Fx \supset Hx)$' nor '$(x)(Hx \supset Gx)$' is an analytic truth. Once 'Fa.Ga.Ha' has been observed to be true, the only purpose served by observing that 'Fb.Gb.Hb' is also true, where b is a different individual from a, is to provide alternative grounds for the belief that there is at least one individual x such that 'Fx.Gx.Hx' is true. Mere multiplication of instances serves only to counteract mistakes and omissions in observation. If we accept the theory of precisification we must reject the reliance on induction by simple enumeration which is endorsed by philosophers in the Hume-Hempel-Goodman tradition.

But though the issue has been much discussed it is difficult to see that there is any defence at all for the Hume-Hempel-Goodman tradition here. Admittedly the constant repetition of a conjunction in apparently identical circumstances often suffices to make people believe the conjunction necessary. That is how so many people came to believe that malaria is caused by swampy air. But the origins of people's beliefs are a topic for psychological, not philosophical, theory. What is at stake here is not how people in fact come to their beliefs about what is physically necessary, but how such beliefs may be rationally justified. Indeed error in these beliefs is perhaps most commonly due to the fact

[1] *Fact, Fiction and Forecast* (1954), p. 73.

that multiplicity of instances exercises a much more persuasive force on untrained minds than does variation of circumstances. For, though only the latter has rational value, such variation requires much more effort to detect or control than does mere repetition.

Again, it is clear that a single experiment is more likely to decide a question about the application of some comparatively high-level generalization in physics than it is to decide anything about a comparatively low-level hypothesis in pharmacology, say, or physiology. There will often be much greater confidence felt in stating just what circumstances have been varied in the former kind of case than in the latter, because the variable factors in a piece of apparatus constructed in the laboratory are often felt to be better known than those present in some experimental animal.

Moreover, if the hypothesis in question does not affirm a uniform correlation like (1) but rather a proportional one like

    (4) 99·4 per cent of those bitten by an anopheles mosquito develop malaria

it is clear that under each variation of circumstance sufficient numbers of patients have to be studied to provide a fair sample for inferences to such a ratio. But multiplicity of instances serves a different purpose here from what it does according to the Hume-Hempel-Goodman tradition. We do not take each new case of malaria as it comes up to add a further mite of confirmation to the generalization as a whole. Rather we take each specifically circumstanced group of a thousand, or perhaps a hundred thousand, patients to constitute a single instance for the purpose of widening or narrowing the hypothesis's domain of discourse. Great multiplicity of instances is required by the specific content of the generalization even if only a very slight confirmation is to be achieved: it is not required only in order to achieve a very high degree of confirmation. Of course sometimes we seem to encounter hybrid cases where an apparently non-proportional hypothesis like

    (5) Anyone who smokes cigarettes very heavily is liable to develop lung-cancer in later life

is the subject of researches that are apparently designed to show the proportion of heavy cigarette-smokers to light ones, or non-smokers, among those who develop lung-cancer. It looks as though we have here a non-proportional hypothesis that nevertheless requires great multiplicity of instances for its confirmation. But in fact we should not let ourselves be forced to this conclusion. For we can either say that (5) is not a physically necessary truth at all but only a guiding principle for research, and that the physically necessary truth which is precisified by such researches is a proportional hypothesis, though we may not be able to enunciate this hypothesis until *after* our researches are completed. Or alternatively we can say that assertion (5) is tantamount to asserting the physical necessity of

> In normal circumstances anyone who smokes cigarettes very heavily will develop lung-cancer in later life

and that statistical researches into the incidence of lung-cancer among different kinds of smokers and non-smokers may be viewed merely as guides in any attempt to discover the precise circumstances in which heavy smoking is uniformly followed by lung-cancer.

Finally the whole doctrine of induction by simple enumeration rests on the presupposition that there really are uniform correlations in nature of a kind that can be described with absolute precision in our everyday vocabulary. Hume, for instance, defines a cause to be 'an object precedent and contiguous to another, and where all the objects resembling the former are plac'd in a like relation of priority and contiguity to those objects that resemble the latter'. Only on the assumption that a hypothesis already states a precise uniformity is it reasonable to suppose that its confirmation can proceed without any attempt's being made to render the hypothesis-sentence more precise. But it seems very doubtful whether any such uniformity is likely to exist, unless by chance. Thus the trouble lies deeper than Hume allows in his argument that we can never conclusively demonstrate any such uniformity. There is also reason to believe that no such uniformity exists.

In the first place, whenever any supposed uniformity of a familiar sort is mentioned, like Hume's example of how one billiard ball's impact on another makes the other move also, it seldom seems at all difficult to think of circumstances in which the supposed uniformity fails to hold. Perhaps the second billiard ball has been nailed or glued to the table, or contains a piece of iron and is held in position by a strong magnet. The theory of precisification can accommodate these facts, because that theory takes the hypothesis to be inherently vague as to its domain of discourse and therefore does not suppose it to describe an exact uniformity. The uniformity supposed is only of the more-or-less kind – a uniformity which at best holds good only in circumstances that may reasonably be described as normal. Of course, some philosophers in the Humean tradition are alive to the fact that commonly acknowledged causal connections only hold good in normal circumstances, and believe that a complete list of such normal circumstances is no more obtainable than a conclusive demonstration of the causal law itself. But then these normal circumstances, or relevant conditions, as Goodman describes them,[1] constitute a special problem for any supporter of induction by simple enumeration. They do not seem germane to the process of confirmation, as a Humean views that process, and their whole standing in the matter is obscure. It becomes immensely difficult for a philosopher like Goodman to see how the concept of normalcy or relevance should be defined. On the theory of precisification, however, the problem of confirmation and the problem of relevant conditions are one and the same problem: attempts to confirm or disconfirm a hypothesis are in effect attempts to determine relevant conditions.

Secondly, it is well worth asking why on earth one should suppose that a vocabulary developed over millennia for the purposes of narrative, classification and generalization within the relatively restricted limits of everyday experience should be adequate to the description of unrestricted uniformities, if there are any. Hume's supposition here seems just as unreasonable as the view criticized in §32 that the familiar, everyday concept of deducibility is readily suited to the purposes of formal-logical systematization. For it would surely be only by chance that, if there were such uniformities, our everyday vocabulary would be adequate to the task of picking out those features of reality which the uniformity relates. Only by chance, I say, because the deliberate attempt to devise a vocabulary in terms of which such uniformities can be described is by no means an everyday activity. Instead it has formed an essential part of the scientific enterprise, from Galileo's time to the present day. Only when Newton had abstracted from material objects their familiar features of being coloured, being hot or cold to touch, being an apple or a planet, and so on, so as to describe them only under a very few determinables, some of which, like mass, were quite unfamiliar to the

[1] *Fact, Fiction and Forecast*, pp. 16 ff.

ordinary man of his day – only then was he able to formulate his laws of motion which for so long seemed to have no exception, and to require no qualification, whatever. Our everyday patterns of thinking seem to disclose to us an indefinitely large variety of circumstances with respect to which a hypothesis-sentence's domain of discourse for ever requires further precisification, so that no unrestricted uniformity is ever asserted. But it is reasonable to try and devise an artificially abstract and limited vocabulary with the express purpose of penetrating through this confused welter of partial regularities to the description of any total regularities that may underlie them.

In short the theory of precisification requires us to reject not only Hume's account of natural necessity but also his endorsement of induction by simple enumeration and his belief that the familiar causal connections of everyday life are uniformities of unrestricted generality. It is worth asking, therefore, whether Hume's notorious scepticism with regard to the possibility of causal knowledge must also be rejected. If induction is not just a process of jumping from statements about some members of a class to statements about all members of it, is it more rationally justifiable than Hume allowed? Does the theory of precisification do anything to bridge the so-called inductive gap – the gap between the particularity of our observational knowledge and the universality of the conclusions we draw from it? The answer seems to be that the gap is completely bridged. The classical problem of induction disappears. But it disappears only to reappear in another form.

Consider first a statement like (2), put forward as a hypothesis to be confirmed or disconfirmed. If, as has been argued, its truth is thereby taken for granted, and only its meaning – or, more exactly, the meaning of its culture-sentence – is left open to determination by empirical evidence, no problem can arise about the justification of the statement. Its truth is *a priori*: what it says *must* hold.

It might however be objected that there clearly still arises the problem of how to justify putting forward the statement as a hypothesis. If there is no problem about justifying (2) in a given context, then at least there is a problem for the theory of precisification, as for conventionalist theories, about justifying the statement that (2) should be taken as *a priori* true in that context. But it turns out that very little is required to justify this. Even if a scientist had only observed one situation in which a person bitten by an anopheles mosquito developed malaria, he would have some ground for putting forward (2) as a hypothesis. Admittedly he could say nothing whatever about (2)'s domain of discourse except that it did not exclude this one kind of situation that he had observed, so that the meaning in which he could assert his hypothesis-sentence would be so vague as to deprive it of almost all informational content. What he could say would be of almost no use at all as a reliable premiss for prediction or explanation in the case of another person bitten by an anopheles mosquito, since he could give hardly any information as to whether persons of that nature and circumstances were included in the hypothesis's domain of discourse. Hence normally, if a hypothesis-sentence has to remain as vague as this, we simply do not bother with it for practical purposes. Other hypotheses attract our attention instead. Nevertheless, provided a man is careful not to assign his hypothesis-sentence more than this very minute element of precision he is theoretically quite justified in taking it *a priori*.

Nor is it at all surprising that the theory of precisification should short-circuit the problem of induction in any of its usual forms. According to the usual accounts we have on the one hand a perfectly precise generalization, and on the other a statement of how likely that generalization is to be true or necessarily true – a statement that must always fall short of ascribing certain truth to the generalization. According to the theory of precisification, however, there are not two statements but only one, not a precise generalization plus an account of its likelihood but just a relatively imprecise generalization. The state or degree of confirmation has been absorbed into the meaning of the hypothesis-sentence, and no Humean scruple remains to stand in the way of claiming *a priori* truth for the resultant statement.

Nevertheless the old problem reappears whenever a man wants to use the hypothesis as a warrant for his predictions or explanations of particular events. It seems that he can never be so justifiably certain, beyond all possibility of correction, that the individual person, object or event in which he is interested falls within the domain of his hypothesis-sentence. Schematically, the position is that if (3) is his sentence and he learns the truth of 'Fa' he can never be quite sure that 'a' is, or ought to be, one of the substitution-instances for the quantified variables of (3) so that he would be entitled to infer the truth of 'Ga'. He cannot ever be quite sure of this because he cannot ever achieve final precision in his hypothesis-sentence. If the sentence were to be conclusively precisified, its domain of discourse would need to be determined with respect to every observable characteristic whatever. With respect to every such characteristic and conjunction of characteristics that is physically possible he would need to know at least whether it served not to include its instances in, or not to exclude them from, the sentence's domain. He would then be in a position to check over the characteristics of the individual person, object or event in which he is interested in order to settle whether or not it is a member of this domain. For either it is a member or not; and if the conjunction of its characteristics does not serve to exclude it there is sufficient reason to suppose it included, since if this conjunction does not exclude it nothing else can, and similarly if the conjunction of its characteristics does not serve to include it there is sufficient reason to suppose it excluded. But to require that a sentence's domain should be determined with respect to every observable characteristic whatever is to require something that there are grounds for thinking impossible. Three arguments for this impossibility are worth mentioning, though only one is really strong.

First, among the observable characteristics of an object or event are its spatial and temporal relations to other objects or events, by reference to which its existence may be dated and located. Hence if spatiotemporal relations are included among the characteristics with respect to which any hypothesis-sentence is to be precisified, its complete precisification would require the study of all individual objects or events whatever, so far as these differ from one another in date or location. But if a man is exercised to discover a 100 per cent uniformity, and not a proportional one like (4), it is reasonable to assume that mere difference of date or location is not a variation of circumstance that he need take into account in any way in the process of precisifying his hypothesis-sentence. If two objects or events resemble each other in everything but date or location, it will be sufficient to study one of them alone. To suppose otherwise is to give up the search for laws that hold uniformly throughout nature. We may conclude, therefore, that the inevitable spatiotemporal differences between one individual and another do not provide a strong ground for thinking the complete precisification of a hypothesis-sentence to be impossible.

Secondly, it might well be argued that we have no reason to expect all observable characteristics, or even just all the non-spatiotemporal ones, to be exemplified or exemplifiable in any region of space-time that is sufficiently small to be studied by a single intercommunicating group of scientists. However many variations a man makes in the circumstances that are to determine the meaning of his hypothesis-sentence, how can he be sure, it may be asked, that no other variations are physically possible, if not in his part of the universe then at least in some other part? But, even if his limited view of things prevented him from ever achieving complete precision for his hypothesis-sentence, it would not itself suffice to prevent him from precisifying the sentence with respect to all the characteristics exemplified in the individual object or event about which he wished to infer some prediction or explanation. If he could be finally sure of the complete list of this individual's characteristics, then he could presumably at least discover whether his hypothesis-sentence would stand having its meaning widened so as not to exclude the conjunction of those characteristics from its domain of discourse. At any rate for such a presumption to be correct it is only required that those characteristics should be capable of conjunction in some other individual that is also within the scope of his observation. Hence, schematically, it seems that if only a man can be finally sure of all the observable characteristics possessed by a given object or event, a, he can test whether the hypothesis-sentence (3) can stand having its meaning widened so as not to exclude the conjunction of these characteristics, and if the test has a positive result he has an unquestionable license to infer the truth of 'Ga' from the truth of 'Fa'. In short, we first cut down the totality of variable characteristics that affect the precisification of a hypothesis to those that are not merely determinants of date or location, and we have now cut this totality down still further to those that are found in the familiar region of space-time with reference to which the hypothesis is to be employed as a license for our inferences. If a hypothesis could even be precisified thus far, the classical problem of induction would have disappeared without a trace.

But, thirdly, even this relatively meagre totality is not a possible object of study, unless we assume concepts and meanings to be timeless and unchanging in the pre-Herder manner, and such an assumption would hardly be compatible with a theory like the one being advocated here that construes all confirmation and disconfirmation as being tantamount to the discovery of justification for changes of meaning. The trouble is that we now come up against the inexhaustible concreteness of individuals, in the sense in which this was briefly discussed in §36. A man can never compile an absolutely complete list of all the characteristics exhibited by individuals in a given region of space-time, however small, because what we take to be a characteristic is determined by the variety of predicates available in our language. The progress of our empirical discoveries affects the growth and development of our vocabulary, and is in turn affected by it. Even an object of great familiarity can reveal hitherto unnoticed characteristics to us when our conception of it changes so as to prompt new questions. And we are forced so to change our conceptions each time an object does not behave as it should do according to a hypothesis which seems *prima facie* not to exclude the conjunction of the object's characteristics from its domain – i.e. a hypothesis for which the circumstances of the object are among the supposedly normal ones. In such a case we can only conclude that the object has some importantly relevant characteristic which we should now be prepared to look for in other such objects also. Thus if, and only if, we could be sure that we had a perfect language – a language that contained all and only the predicates any language ever should contain – could we in principle be sure of our correctness in using a hypothesis for prediction and explanation in any given case. The perfection of our language would both ensure and be ensured by the certainty of our predictions and explanations. It was no accident that philosophers like Descartes who envisaged the possibility of completing the edifice of scientific knowledge in some finite period of time were also concerned to project the construction of a perfect language (as was mentioned in §2) that would meet the needs of all men at all times. The modern view of science, as unlimitedly corrigible, turns out to be implicit in Herder's rejection of the old assumption that some particular language or culture was the classical, norm-setting, or ideal one. Moreover, while the theory of precisification acknowledges this unlimited corrigibility, it does so in a form that does less violence to the continuity of scientific knowledge than some other current theories. We do not have to suppose a staccato process by which hypotheses are for ever being put up and knocked down, whereupon they presumably disappear from respectable society, but rather a gradual increase in the number of hypotheses available for study and a gradual ebbing and flowing of the extent to which each hypothesis is held not inapplicable.

A seriously contrived hypothesis, that had some value in its day, should never be thought of as having finally and completely disappeared from the corpus of scientific knowledge. One day it may need reviving, as once the atomic theory of matter and the heliocentric theory of planetary motion were revived.

It would be folly to claim that the actual word-uses of all scientists and historians of science conform to the pattern commended by the theory of precisification, or indeed to any other consistent pattern. Sometimes, no doubt, people speak as if they suppose a hypothesis, which they use in some prediction or explanation, to have been held out to them as fully confirmed by its authors, so that whatever element of inductive risk there is in using it is the authors' rather than the users': it is the authors who have jumped from a particularity to a generality, and the users merely take this on trust. Sometimes people speak as if the authors have gone a long way towards confirming the hypothesis's universal validity as a perfectly precise statement, though it is up to a user to assure himself that they have gone far enough: the inductive risk is then shared between author and user. Sometimes people speak as if the authors of a hypothesis have done no more than report the evidence for it that they know, or adjust its meaning to that evidence: the whole risk is then to be borne by the user. Philosophical theories about induction tend to be preoccupied with the first and second of these three modes of speech at the expense of the third. The theory of precisification attempts to redress the balance by favouring a different selection from these three existing patterns of usage: it concentrates on the third pattern at the expense of the first and second. Similarly in the history of science unsuccessful hypotheses have sometimes been thought of as falsified beyond recall, and sometimes as having been qualified into insignificance in their range of application. Perhaps at lower levels of generality, as in pharmacology, the former alternative is more common: perhaps at higher levels, as in theoretical physics, the latter is. Again, while most philosophical theories of induction draw attention to the former mode of conception, the theory of precisification draws attention to the latter. Neither kind of theory has a monopoly of truth here so far as the description of actual usage goes. But it remain̲ can give as shown whether any other theory than the theory of preci good an account of natural necessity and the non-extensionality.

Some writers in the conventionalist tradition have come near to this theory at times. In particular William Whewell emphasized how in induction 'the question really is, how the Conception shall be understood and defined in order that the Proposition may be true'. But on the whole conventionalists, as their name implies, have been preoccupied with the entrenchment of scientific discoveries in scientific language. 'In an advanced science', wrote Whewell, 'the history of the Language of the Science is the history of the Science itself. . . . In learning the meaning of Scientific Terms, the history of science is our Dictionary: the steps of scientific induction are our Definitions.'[1] Hence the characteristic doctrine of conventionalists is normally taken to be that scientific generalizations are analytic.[2] But the theory advocated here is incompatible with this conventionalist doctrine, because the domain of an analytic truth is not open to empirical precisification.

[1] *Novum Organon Renovatum* (1858), pp. 36, 355, 368.
[2] Cf. G. H. von Wright, *The Logical Problem of Induction* (2nd ed., 1957), pp. 40 ff.

Index

Academy, French, 9, 35, 93
accidental truth, 285 ff., 309 f., 295,
    307
aesthetic statements, 310 f.
Algonquian, Central, 58, 77
Ambrose, A., 161
analysis, paradox of, 140
analytic statements, 153 ff., 172 ff.,
    223, 242 f., 245, 250, 272, 292, 295,
    298 f., 302, 306 f., 309, 313
Anscombe, G. E. M., 48, 119
anthropology, 67, 77, 90, 91, 101, 244
antinomy, semantical, 193 f., 197 f.,
    200, 205
a posteriori statements, see empirical
    statements
a priori knowledge, 130, 294, 304
a priori truth, 62, 153 ff., 175 f., 204,
    216, 226, 295 ff.
a priori valid argument, 135, 137, 144
argument, rules of, 137 f., 169, 262
Aristotle, 9, 20, 114 f., 119, 153, 156,
    161, 247, 250
arithmetic, 114, 153, 166, 175, 179,
    254
atomist theory of concepts, 84 ff.,
    104, 120, 160, 165, 270, 318
Austin, J. L., 53, 63, 76 ff., 89, 160
Ayer, A. J., 61, 154, 156, 172

Bacon, F., 6, 94, 119, 234, 305
Bacon, R., 19
Barcan, R. C., 179, 221, 224, 227 f.
behaviourism, 26, 47 f.
Bennet, J., 155, 252 f.
Berkeley, 52, 61, 83, 106, 109, 279
Berlin, I., 168

biology, 114
Black, M., 266
Bloomfield, L., 13, 30
Boas, G., 21
Bock, H., 17
Boethius, 7
Bohr, N., 250
botany, 114 ff.
Boyle, R., 282, 297
Bradley, F. H., 76
Braithwaite, R. B., 282 ff.
Braly, K., 90
Bréal, M., 13
Bridgman, P. W., 167
Bright, T., 6
Brouwer, L. E. J., 112
Brugmann, K., 105
Brunot, F., 8
Buridan, 17
Burtt, E. A., 18

calculus, assignment of meanings to
    a, 26 f., 32, 151, 157 f., 180, 186,
    193, 200, 202, 213, 219, 224, 226 f.,
    229 ff., 313
calculus, predicate, 201, 203 ff., 222,
    226 f., 243, 255 ff.
calculus, propositional, 143, 200 f.,
    205, 222, 226 f., 245, 272, 307
Candolle, A. de, 115 ff.
Cantor, G., 113
Carnap, R., 28 f., 60, 97, 156 ff., 178,
    188, 196, 200, 311, 317 ff.
Cassirer, E., 19 f., 67, 77, 90 f., 100
categories, theory of, 106
causal connections, statements of,
    177, 277 ff.

333